HISTORICAL AND DESCRIPTIVE ACCOUNT OF BRITISH INDIA

HISTORICAL AND DESCRIPTIVE ACCOUNT OF BRITISH INDIA

From

The Most Remote Period to the Present Time:

BY

HUGH MURRAY, ESQ. F.R.S.E.

JAMES WILSON, ESQ. F.R.S.E AND M.W.S.

R.K. GREVILLE, LL.D.

PROFESSOR JAMESON;

WHITELAW AINSLIE, M.D., M.R.A.S.,

Late of the Medical Staff of Southern India;

WILLIAM RHIND, ESQ., M.R.C.S.

PROFESSOR WALLACE;

AND CAPTAIN CLARENCE DALRYMPLE,

Hon. East India Company's Service

WITH A MAP, AND TWENTY-SIX ENGRAVINGS BY BRANSTON.

IN THREE VOLUMES.

VOL. III.

GYAN

Published by

GYAN

Gyan Publishing House
5, Ansari Road
Daryaganj, New Delhi-110002
Phone: 011-47034999, 9811692060
E-mail: books@gyanbooks.com

Distribution Network
gyanbooks.com
India, USA, Canada, UK, Australia, France

ISBN : 978-81-212-6067-1 (PB)
ISBN : 978-81-212-6070-1 (3 Vols. Set)
First Published, 1832

2nd Impression 2021

Printed at: Gyan Press, Delhi.

Historical and Descriptive Account
of
British India, Vol. III
Author: Hugh Murray

HISTORICAL AND DESCRIPTIVE ACCOUNT OF BRITISH INDIA,

FROM

THE MOST REMOTE PERIOD TO THE PRESENT TIME

BY

HUGH MURRAY, ESQ., F. R. S. E.

JAMES WILSON, ESQ., F. R. S. E. AND M. W. S.

R. K. GREVILLE, LL. D.

PROFESSOR JAMESON;

WHITELAW AINSLIE, M. D., M. R. A. S.,
Late of the Medical Staff of Southern India;

WILLIAM RHIND, ESQ., M. R. C. S.

PROFESSOR WALLACE;

AND CAPTAIN CLARENCE DALRYMPLE,
Hon. East India Company's Service.

WITH A MAP, AND TWENTY-SIX ENGRAVINGS BY BRANSTON.

IN THREE VOLUMES.

VOL. III.

CONTENTS OF VOL. III.

CHAPTER I.

CHAPTER II.

THE QUADRUPEDS OF INDIA.

CHAPTER III.

THE BIRDS OF INDIA.

CHAPTER IV.

THE REPTILES AND FISHES OF INDIA.

CHAPTER V.

THE SHELLS AND INSECTS OF INDIA.

CHAPTER VI.

PROGRESS OF INDIAN BOTANY—GENERAL DESCRIPTION OF THE VEGETATION.

CHAPTER VII.

SOME ACCOUNT OF A FEW OF THE MORE REMARKABLE INDIAN PLANTS, IN WHICH THE SPECIES ARE ARRANGED ACCORDING TO THE NATURAL FAMILIES TO WHICH THEY BELONG.

CHAPTER VIII.

CLIMATE.

CHAPTER IX.

HYDROGRAPHY.

CHAPTER X.

GEOLOGY AND MINERALOGY.

CHAPTER XI.

CONSTITUTIONS BEST SUITED TO INDIA—PRESERVATION OF HEALTH ON BOARD OF SHIP AND AFTER ARRIVAL—MANAGEMENT AFTER RETURN TO EUROPE.

CHAPTER XV.

COLONEL LAMBTON'S SURVEYS.

CHAPTER XVI.

PRESENT STATE OF NAVIGATION BETWEEN ENGLAND AND THE EAST INDIES, WITH INSTRUCTIONS FOR THE GUIDANCE OF PASSENGERS.

CHAPTER XVII.

PROPOSED STEAM COMMUNICATION BETWEEN ENGLAND AND THE EAST INDIES BY THE RED SEA.

ENGRAVINGS IN VOL. III.

HISTORICAL AND DESCRIPTIVE

ACCOUNT

OF

BRITISH INDIA.

ZOOLOGY.

CHAPTER I.

Introductory Observations.

THE great Asiatic division of our globe, when considered under its zoological relations, may be partitioned into several different departments. The Siberian or most northern portion, in consequence of the severity of its winter season, possesses even in its southern districts many attributes of the Arctic regions; but, at the same time, its inland valleys and the upper basins of its numerous and far-flowing rivers are enriched, during a brilliant though short-lived summer, with many of the more gorgeous features both of animal and vegetable life. Another vast and imperfectly-known region of Asia is bounded to the north by Siberia, and to the south by those highly-elevated table-lands which terminate among the Himmaleh mountains. This division still presents several features which prove its assimilation in some respects to the characters which distinguish animal life in Europe; for although it is undoubtedly characterized by numerous *peculiar* forms of existence, yet many of its genera and species are either the genuine types of groups which occur in countries with which we are familiar, or pertain to groups which are themselves well exemplified by European species. Among the Himmaleh mountains, however, and other southern portions of this division, we discover many of the genera which occur in the low lands of Indostan, and the peninsular projection of Malacca. The same circumstance indeed occurs,—we mean the like transition of species,—in all the great geographical sections of animal life. Each extensive division is characterized by several peculiar forms, and yet at the same time nourishes many species which are common alike to it and to other regions; and it is only under some peculiar circumstances of local situation, that either the zoological or botanical products undergo a sudden change in character and condition. As the adventurous and observant traveller advances on his journey, a few species are continually perceived to decrease in numbers, and then to disappear,—while their places are supplied by others, which, at first but thinly scattered, gradually acquire an accession of numbers, till they too have reached their full amount or centre of dominion; but the change being only partial from place to place, the difference is no more suddenly perceptible than that in the horizon by which the traveller is himself surrounded, and a portion of which in his onward progress becomes insensibly from the circumference the very centre of the field of vision.

Many species indeed can scarcely be said to have

any proper centre of dominion, but are rather repeated again in different and far-distant regions; thus showing that certain peculiar combinations in the physical character and constitution of countries, which we cannot always perceive or appreciate, lead to an analogous character among the tribes of living nature, almost independent of latitudinal or longitudinal position. These latter circumstances, however, —that is to say, the position of a place in relation to latitude and longitude, especially when combined with a knowledge of its height above and distance from the sea,—are on a general view highly influential in regulating the distribution of species, and form, if not an indispensable, at least a highly interesting element in our knowledge of the geography of natural groups. Although under similar climates the species may be singularly diversified, yet an identity, or close resemblance of specific forms, may no doubt be relied upon as indicating an analogy in the climate. It is now to be sure somewhat inaccurately said by botanists, that a mountain is high enough to enter "into the region of the rhododendrons," just as it was formerly said that such a mountain attained to the limits of perpetual snow,—an erroneous mode of expression, as admitted by Humboldt, if it be thereby meant to intimate, that under the influence of a certain temperature, or any other climatic influence, certain vegetable forms must of necessity be developed.

Heat and cold certainly produce very different effects upon different species of living creatures. A quadruped or bird, which has its centre of dominion or characteristic locality in a temperate region, will be so far influenced by an amelioration of climate as to extend its range somewhat further north, under a meridian where, from local causes, a greater warmth prevails than is customary in the same degree of latitude; but a truly northern species, which dwells by preference "in thrilling regions of thick-ribbed ice," would rather extend southward on a meridian line of more than usual coldness. The one would advance in the direction of the Pole, attracted rather than driven northwards by the increase of temperature;—the other would migrate in a southerly direction, not to avoid but to accompany the cold. Thus the musk-ox, one of the most remarkable of the North American animals, which affects a cold and barren district where grass is replaced by lichens, owing to the greater mildness of the climate, does not range so far to the southward on the Pacific coast as it does on the shores of Hudson's Bay;—for it is neither found in New Caledonia nor on the banks of the Columbia, nor does it occur on the Rocky Mountain-ridge at the customary crossing-places near the sources of the Peace, Elk, and Saskatchewan rivers.

In tracing each parallel throughout its whole extent we shall find, as we advance from the polar and temperate to the equatorial regions, that the species become restricted in their distribution, and that although they may occupy in reality as great an extent of actual space, they yet extend over a smaller portion of the earth's circumference. Thus in the northern hemisphere we find the wolf, the seal, the walrus, and the Polar bear, occupying a large portion of the entire circumference of the higher latitudes, from the vicinity of the Pole itself to the Arctic circle. But as we proceed southwards these and many more inhabitants of the colder climates disappear, and their places are occupied by others which, however extended may be in some instances their latitudinal distribution, are yet much more restricted in the amount of meridians through which they pass than are those to which we have just alluded. Thus, of the numerous feline animals which inhabit Asia, the lion alone extends the "reign of terror" to the corresponding parallels of the African continent, while the wolverene of the North prowls alike over the snows of Europe, Asia, and America.

It is probable, however, that most of those species which have their centre of dominion in temperate countries are capable of enduring the most widely-extended geographical distribution. This may be illustrated even by the different varieties of the human race. A native of Britain braves alike the most fiery breath of the torrid zone and the frozen climates of Greenland; but an Esquimaux would perish on the shores of the Congo; and a negro, although better supplied than were the Russian sailors under similar circumstances, would barely survive a winter amid the desolate snows of Spitzbergen. Most of those animals which we have domesticated, and carried along with us in our almost universal migrations, such as the horse, sheep, and goat, have their origin in the temperate countries of higher Asia, among the mountains and elevated plains of which their originals are still to be traced. It is no doubt owing to the physical conditions of clime and country, that these and certain other species have been enabled to follow their masters, and to breed and prosper under almost every variety of climate. On the other hand, had they been native to an equatorial region, they would have been comparatively of little service in the northern parts of Europe or America; or had they been naturally confined to the vicinity of the Arctic circle, their value would have suffered a corresponding diminution in relation to the inhabitants of intra-tropical climes. It is thus, by an admirable law of divine benevolence, that all those animals, from the domestication and culture of which the most widely-spread and essential advantage was capable of resulting to the human race, have been created and retained the natural inmates of the temperate regions of our globe; while those, again, the general distribution of which must have been regarded rather as a curse than a blessing, have been, with few exceptions, rendered the invariable inmates either of the hottest or the coldest climes. By way of illustration, let us take an example from each of the two extremes. Were a tiger conveyed from the jungles of tropical Asia to the northern steppes of Siberia, or the shores of the Arctic Sea, how soon would he lose his gigantic strength and ferocious vigour!—or, were a Polar bear transferred from his bleak eternity of floating icebergs to a sultry island of the Indian Archipelago, how speedily would the surly savage cease to create alarm! The spirit of the same observation might be applied to much more serviceable animals, which, however, not being natives of temperate countries, are for that very reason incapable of being rendered useful in the most universal and therefore highest degree. We may adduce as familiar examples the rein-deer and the dromedary, the former of which the wandering Bedouin of the desert would as vainly attempt to rear amid the shifting sands of Arabia, as the Nomadian of the North would the latter on the cold and lofty plains of Finmark or Norway.

But to proceed with the more immediate subjects of our present inquiry:—No sooner do we enter upon the zoology of India Proper, than the European forms of animal life almost entirely disappear, and are succeeded by others of a richer and more varied character of form and aspect, some of which, however, extend to the parallel latitudes of the African continent. The Asiatic Islands, again, present us with another picture, and this latter change may be said to commence at the southern extremity of the Isthmus of Malacca. Java and Sumatra will probably be found to be the metropolis or central region of this range, which still produces several of the forms of Northern India;* while in New Guinea and New Ireland, the Asiatic forms, properly so called, begin to disappear, and are replaced by many singular and interesting species, which exhibit the commencement of what may be named the *Australasian* kingdom. For example, the genus *Meliphaga* (including those honey-sucking birds which so strongly characterize the latter region) are also found in the above-named islands, as are likewise

---

* Among birds, for example, the singular genus *Enicurus* of Temminck, which that naturalist places between *Accentor* and *Motacilla*, which M. Reinwardt regards as pertaining to *Lanius*, and M. Lesson classes with the *Muscicapidæ*, has been recently received by Professor Jameson from the northern parts of India. It was formerly believed to belong exclusively to Java and Sumatra. In like manner, the genus *Myophonus*, regarded as peculiar to Java (*M. metallicus*, Tem., being a short time ago the only known species), is now known to contain two additional species (*M. Horsfieldii* and *Temminckii*, figured by Mr Gould), both of which occur among the Himmaleh mountains.

species belonging to *Dacelo, Barita,* and other groups, which were long believed to pertain exclusively to Australasia. In all those countries the larger quadrupeds of the Indian Islands entirely disappear, and the suctorial family of birds are displayed in all their brilliancy; while the New Guinea *Promerops* unites with the *Meliphagidæ,* and beautifully exhibits the finely-graduated transition in the forms of animal life from one region to another.* None of the perching-birds (*Insessores*) of these southern countries are generically the same as those of Europe, and an examination of the insects and shells leads us to the same general results.

For the present, however, we must confine our observations chiefly to the territories which lie to the south and west of the great mountain-chains of Himmaleh and Hindoo Cush,—to Cabul, Cashmere, and Indostan, properly so called. We shall also refer occasionally to the zoological productions of the great Island of Ceylon; so that our sketches will comprehend a space extending from the 6th to the 34th degrees of north latitude, and from about the 65th to the 90th degrees of east longitude. This division of the Asiatic territory is convenient, not only in a political, but also in a zoological point of view; for while it embraces all our great Indian

* The genus *Pomatorhinus,* Horsfield (*Linn. Trans.,* vol. xiii. p. 164), in relation to the preceding observations may be said to exhibit a more complicated distribution. It was established by its founder for the reception of a species from the wooded mountains of Java; but the *dusky bee-eater* of Latham (*Gen. Hist.,* vol. iv. p. 146, No 31) belongs to the same genus, and a new species has lately been added to it under the name of *P. superciliosus* (*Linn. Trans.,* vol. xv. p. 330). Both of these are native to New Holland, where, I believe, they were first observed by Mr Robert Brown. Lastly, the *P. erythrogenys,* a recently-discovered species, has been ascertained to inhabit the Himmaleh range.

possessions, it also marks out the line of demarcation between these and the adjacent countries, which, in regard to many important features of their natural history, present a considerable disresemblance.

Although these regions, or the greater portion of them, are situated beneath a tropical sun, they yet present many modifications of soil, temperature, and climate. Immense plains, either richly wooded and well watered, or exhibiting a more barren and uncultivated aspect;—a great extent of seacoast intersected by large and numerous rivers, the mouths of which are enriched by deltas of alluvial land;—sloping hills, and upraised terrace-lands, embowered amid the most gorgeous vegetation,

> "Shade above shade, a woody theatre,
> Of stateliest view;"—

lofty mountains, with their "crags prerup't," separated by dark ravines where the foot of man has never trod;—and, finally, the snow-covered summits of the loftiest Alps, piercing even above the regions of cloud and storm, and contrasting magnificently their stainless and star-like peaks with the deep blue ether of that crystalline sky,

> "Through which the sun walks burning without beams;"—

these, and other diversified localities, present, as may be supposed, the most apt abodes to a vast variety of species in the brute creation.*

---

* The following extract conveys a striking picture of the scenery of the Asiatic Alps:—"The dazzling brilliancy of the snow," says Captain Hodgson, "was rendered more striking by its contrast with the dark-blue colour of the sky, which is caused by the thinness of the air; and at night the stars shone with a lustre which they have not in a denser atmosphere; it was curious, too, to see them, when rising, appear like one sudden flash, as they emerged from behind the bright snowy summits close to us; and their disap-

pearance, when setting behind the peaks, was as sudden as we generally observed it to be in their occultation by the moon.

"We were surrounded by gigantic peaks, entirely cased in snow, and almost beyond the regions of animal and vegetable life, and an awful silence prevailed, except when broken by the thundering peals of falling avalanches; nothing met our eyes resembling the scenery in the haunts of men; by moonlight all appeared cold, wild, stupendous, and a Pagan might aptly imagine the place a fit abode for demons. We did not see even bears, or musk-deer, or eagles, or any living creature, except some small birds.

"To form an idea of the imposing appearance of a snowy peak, as seen here under an angle of elevation of nearly 33°, and when its distance is not quite three miles, and yet its height 8052 feet above the station, one should reflect, that if, even when viewed from the plains of Indostan, at angles of elevation of one and one-and-a-half degrees, these peaks, towering over many intermediate ranges of mountains, inspire the mind with ideas of their grandeur, even at so great a distance,—how much more must they do so when their whole bulk, cased in snow from the base to the summit, at once fills the eye. It falls to the lot of few to contemplate so magnificent an object as a snow-clad peak rising to the height of upwards of a mile and a half, at the short horizontal distance of only two and three quarter miles."—*Journal of a Survey to the Heads of the Rivers Ganges and Jumna.* By Captain T. A. Hodgson.

CHAPTER II.

The Quadrupeds of India.

The Gibbon—Entellus Monkey—Wanderoo—Bats—Bears—Jackal—Thibet Dog—Ichneumon—Lion—Tiger—Hunting-tiger—Squirrel—Gigantic Rat—Pangolin—Elephant—Rhinoceros—Camel—Musk-deer—Nepaul Stag—Rusa Deer—Spotted Axis—Hog-deer—Roebuck—White Oryx—Chiru—Four-horned Antelope—Nyl-ghau—Cashmere Goat—Jemlah Goat—Wild-sheep—Buffalo—Arnee—Grunting-ox—Gayall—Cetaceous Animals—Dugong—Gangetic Dolphin.

In our zoological sketches, we must of course confine ourselves to the history and attributes of but a small portion of the animal kingdom compared with the total species; but we shall at the same time endeavour to make such a selection as may illustrate most of the peculiar and more remarkable features of Indian zoology. We shall therefore proceed, conformably with the systematic arrangements of naturalists, to the *quadrumanous order* of the class Mammalia, which, containing the monkeys and other species, one of which even Linnæus regarded (under the name of *Homo nocturnus*) as nearly allied to the human race, may be considered as entitled to our earliest consideration.

Of the orang-outang, the most remarkable of the order, we cannot here speak, as it occurs only in Borneo and certain other districts which lie beyond the bounds of our present jurisdiction; but many of the smaller species are native to the Indian forests. Indeed nowhere in the known world are monkeys better provided for than in India, where in some districts the weak and idolatrous superstition of the natives has raised them even to the rank of gods. Temples of the most magnificent structure were erected in their honour; and when one of these was plundered by the Portuguese in Ceylon, they found in it the tooth of an ape enclosed in a casket of pure gold. In such veneration was this relic held by the natives, that they offered seven hundred thousand ducats as the price of its redemption,—but in vain; for it was burnt by the viceroy with a view to stop the progress of idolatry. There are hospitals for apes in Ahmedabad; and in many parts of India they are so familiarized by indulgence, as to breed in numbers among the bamboo-copses by the wayside.

The gibbon, or long-armed ape (*Hylobatis lar*), has been brought from Pondicherry. The name by which it is distinguished appears to be of ancient origin. According to Delachamp, the animal called cephos by Pliny is designated *keipon* by Strabo, and from the latter term gibon or gibbon may have been derived. Both terms probably originate from koph or kophin, which in Hebrew and Chaldee signifies ape; but the description of the cephos given by Pliny does certainly not coincide with the ascertained characters of the modern gibbon, which is chiefly distinguished by the enormous length of its arms. The eyes are large and deeply seated, the nose is flat, and the ears resemble those of the human race. A circle of gray hairs passes over the eyes, cheeks, and beneath the under-jaw, and, completely surrounding the visage, gives a singular aspect to the animal. The general colour of the hair is black, except on the backs of the hands and feet, which are gray. The disposition of the long-armed ape is mild and gentle. In a state of domestication it receives its food without any impatient greediness, and manifests a strong attachment to those with whom it becomes acquainted. This long-armed ape is native to the coast of Coromandel, and occurs also in the Peninsula of Malacca and the Molucca Islands. It was in one of the latter that Father de Compte had an opportunity of examining an individual of the species, which he says walked on two feet, used its hands like a man, and had a face like a Hottentot. The whole of its body was covered over with a dark-gray wool, and its voice, by which it expressed a variety of passions, exactly resembled that of an infant.

Intermediate between the gibbons and macaccas may be placed the genus *Semnopithecus,* of which the entellus monkey offers a characteristic example. Though the tribe to which this species belongs resemble the gibbons in the shape of their heads, and in their physiognomical expression, they are easily distinguished by their lengthened tails, of which the gibbons are entirely destitute. The entellus monkey, though extremely common in Bengal, appears to have been recorded in systematic works only at a comparatively recent period, by M. Dufresne. It differs from its congeners in its long and slender limbs, the slowness of its motions, and a certain unalterable apathy of expression. It is of a uniform ashy-gray in the upper parts, somewhat darker on the tail. The under-surface of the body is of a dingy yellowish-white; and the fore-arms, hands, and feet, are of a dusky black. The fingers of both extremities are very long, and the thumbs comparatively short. The face is black, tinged with violet, and is surmounted above the eyebrows by a line of long, stiff, black hairs projecting forwards, and slightly upwards. The sides of the cheeks and the under part of the chin are margined by a beard of grayish-white, which passes along the line of the jaws, and extends upwards in front of the ears, which are large, prominent, and of the same colour as the face. The height of the specimen in the Zoological Gardens exceeded two feet when in a sitting posture, and its tail, which was rarely unfurled, measured nearly thirty-six inches. This is one of the species worshipped in the religion of the Bramins. According to Mr Bennet, it is identical with the Ceylonese species described by Thunberg and Wolf. It frequently occurs in a domestic state in that island; and such is the respect in which (whether wild or tame) it is held by the natives, that, whatever ravages it may commit, the latter dare not venture to destroy it, but merely endeavour to frighten it away by cries more discordant than its own. "Emboldened by this impunity, the monkeys come down from the woods in large herds, and take possession of the produce of the husbandman's toil with as little ceremony as though it had been collected for their use; for, with a degree of taste which does them credit, they prefer the cultivated fruits of the orchard to the wild ones of their native forests. Figs, cocoa-nuts, apples, pears, and even cabbages and potatoes, form their favourite spoil. The numbers in which they assemble render it impossible for the sufferer to drive them away without some more efficient means than he is willing to employ; he is consequently compelled to remain a spectator of the devastation, and to submit without repining to his fate."* This species appears to be very susceptible of cold, and cannot stand a removal from its native regions. Thunberg's specimen died in the latitude of the Cape, and the individuals more recently transported both to London and Paris have since expired.

When the government of Dubhoy, after its surrender to General Goddard in 1780, was intrusted to Mr Forbes, the city contained about 40,000 inhabitants, and as many monkeys. The governor, on his first arrival, resided in a house, the back part of which was separated by a narrow court from that of a Hindoo; and, in consequence of the coolness afforded by its shaded situation, he usually retired with his book to a veranda there during the heat of the afternoon. Here small portions of mortar and tiles frequently fell upon him, to which at first he paid no attention, till one day a blow from a larger piece than usual made him turn round to discover the cause. To his surprise, he observed that the opposite roof was entirely covered with monkeys, which, having probably taken a dislike to his European complexion, had commenced a system of warfare which finally left him no other alternative than that of changing his lodgings.

The Wanderoo monkey (*Macacus silenus*) is

* The Gardens and Menagerie of the Zoological Society Delineated, vol. i. p. 86.

also indigenous to the East Indies. It appears to be figured in Knox's History of Ceylon, although that author erroneously applied the name to several different species, which he regarded as varieties of one and the same. The prevailing colour of this animal is a fine black, but the sides of the head and chin are surrounded by a broad beard or ruff of a dingy-white or pale-gray colour. The tail is about half as long as the body, and is terminated by a tuft of hair; on which account, probably, it has by some authors been named the lion-tailed monkey. "There are," says Father Vincent Marie, "four sorts of monkeys on the coast of Malabar. The first is perfectly black, covered with glossy hair, with a white beard surrounding his chin, and extending a span or more in length. To this monkey all the rest pay such profound respect, that they submit and humiliate themselves in his presence as though they were capable of appreciating his superiority and pre-eminence. The princes and great lords hold him in much estimation, because he is endowed above every other with gravity, capacity, and the appearance of wisdom. He is easily trained to the performance of a variety of ceremonies, grimaces, and affected courtesies; all which he accomplishes in so serious a manner and to such perfection, that it is a most wonderful thing to see them acted with so much exactness by an irrational animal." Of this species there is a fine example in the Edinburgh College Museum. It was kept alive in a domestic state for a couple of years; but the most remarkable instance of its courtesy during that period consisted in its biting off the calf of a negro's leg. It was accordingly slain.

The preceding examples must suffice to illustrate the history of the quadrumanous tribes of India. We come next to the *Cheiropterous* family, which includes and is constituted by the bats.

When the "knell of parting day" announces the approach of the long-continued twilight of our temperate regions, we see our own diminutive species flitting about on leathern wings, or dimpling the surface of the still waters in search of insects and other natural prey; but these give us but a feeble idea of the monstrous forms which inhabit equatorial countries. The Indian species belong chiefly to the genus *Pteropus*. The eatable roussette (*Pt. edulis*), called kalon by the natives, is abundant in the great Asiatic Islands. Its flesh is white, delicate, and remarkably tender. Its wings extend more than five feet from point to point, and its muzzle resembles that of a dog with the point of its nose cut in two. It is taken by means of a sack fastened to the extremity of a pole. Its flesh is rendered less pleasing to European palates on account of the strong odour of musk with which it is infected.

We now enter upon the history of the carnivorous tribes, of which the first family is the *Plantigrada*, including the extensively-distributed though not very numerous group of bears, as well as the racoons, coati-mundis, badgers, and other species, characterized, as the family-name implies, by their walking on the entire under-surface of the foot, and not merely on the points of the toes after the manner of dogs and cats. Among carnivorous quadrupeds there are many gradations of ferocity, from the blood-thirsty tiger, which so greatly rejoices over the palpitating flesh of a living victim, to the more omnivorous propensities which distinguish the subjects of our present paragraph. This versatility of instinctive habit is no doubt closely connected with, if it does not proceed from, a less determinate formation of the digestive and prehensile organs, such as the stomach, teeth, and claws. The unequalled strength and rapacity of the tiger,—his sharp retractile talons,—the great development of his canine teeth, and the compressed and cutting character of the molars, combined with the simplicity of the stomach and the shortness of the intestinal canal, render it as it were the type of carnivorous animals. It exhibits no tendency in any of its forms to the herbivorous structure, but is strictly and characteristically a flesh-eating animal,—" a most beautiful and cruel beast of prey." The contour and physiognomy of the bears are very different. Heavy and inactive in their forms, with unretractile claws, more elongated muzzles, and consequently weaker jaws, their teeth also, though sufficiently formidable, show a decided relation to the herbivorous structure in the breadth of the molars, and their bluntly tuberculated crowns. " One of those phenomena," observes the editor of the English translation of the *Règne Animal,* " which is most worthy the attention of the naturalist, and most calculated to lead us to appreciate the infinite power of the Creator, consists in the insensible and gradual changes which the same organ will pass, by which its nature will in some measure be transformed, and results produced entirely different from those which constituted the object of its original destination. The organs of sense and motion offer frequent examples of this phenomenon; and the teeth of certain animals present a remarkable instance of the same. The true *Carnivora,* the cats for instance, have in each jaw teeth evidently destined by their form and position to cut, like the two blades of a scissors, the fibres of the muscles of their prey. But in proportion as the destination of an animal is more decidedly carnivorous, the teeth lose their trenchant character, and grow thicker, and thus we at last arrive at a limit where they can no longer be distinguished from the tuberculous teeth, whose office simply consists in triturating the food. These teeth, when sharp and slender, are opposed face to face; but when thick, they are opposed crown to crown; so that they become truly transformed into molar teeth; and nature, in operating so considerable a transformation, has no need of making any essential change in those organs. It is sufficient for the purpose, that a very small tubercle, which is already found on the internal face of the slenderest teeth, should simply receive a more augmented development."* Even the bears of the Arctic circle, which, from the scarcity of vegetable food in those frost-bound regions, are probably the most carnivorous of their kind, have in a state of captivity been sustained for a length of time, and in vigorous condition, on bread alone.

The labiated bear (*Ursus labiatus*) inhabits the mountainous districts in the north of India. It dwells in holes and caverns, which it sometimes excavates with its long claws, and feeds chiefly on fruits, ants, and honey; but the structure of its

---

* Griffith's Animal Kingdom, vol. ii. p. 246.

teeth indicates strong carnivorous propensities, and its natural habits are in truth but little known. It seems more docile and intelligent than others of the species, and is frequently taught certain "fantastic tricks" by the jugglers in Bengal, where it is exhibited for the amusement of the people. It is not uncommon among the mountains of Sihlet, and in the environs of other inhabited places.

According to M. Duvaucel, three species of bear inhabit India and the neighbouring islands. The first is the one just noticed, which the reader may have seen exhibited in menageries under the inapplicable name of *ursine sloth;* the second species is the Malay bear (*U. Malayanus*); the third is the Thibet species described by M. Duvaucel, and observed by Dr Wallick among the Nepaul mountains. It is supposed to occur likewise in Sumatra. A fourth Asiatic form of this genus, the Bornean bear (*Helarctis eurypsilus* of Horsfield), inhabits the great island from which it derives its English specific name.

The ratel or honey-eater (*Viverra mellivora* of Sparmann), an animal of singular habits, long regarded as peculiar to the African continent, appears from the testimony of General Hardwicke to occur in India. Its manners, however, do not at all correspond with those assigned to the African individuals of the species. The Asiatic variety inhabits high banks on the borders of the Ganges and the Jumna, from which it rarely issues by day. At night it prowls around the Mohammedan habitations, and will sometimes even scratch up recently-interred human bodies, unless the graves are protected by a covering of thorny shrubs. So rapid are its subterranean exertions, that it will work its way beneath the surface in the course of ten minutes. Their favourite food consists of birds and small quadrupeds. The specimen in the Zoological Gardens is remarkable for its playfulness and good humour. It solicits attention by a variety of absurd postures, and tumbles head over heels with the greatest delight as soon as it has succeeded in attracting the notice of visiters.*

The rivers of India are so well stored with fish, that we naturally expect on inquiring into the history of the *Digitigrada,* which form the second tribe of carnivorous animals, or such as walk upon their toes, to find the insidious otter lurking along their shores. We must not, however, confound the Pondicherry otter (*Lutra nair,* F. Cuvier) with the corresponding, though not identical species of Europe or America. Its hair is of a deep chestnut colour above, paler on the sides, and of a reddish-white on the under parts of the body. The end of the muzzle is reddish, and there are two spots of a similar colour one above and the other beneath each eye. It measures about two feet and a half exclusive of the tail, which is a foot and a half in length. This species was sent from Pondicherry, where it is named *Nir-nayie* by M. Leschenhault; and other Asiatic otters have been described by Sir Stamford Raffles (*Linn. Trans.,* vol. xiii.), by Dr Horsfield, and by M. Diard.

We come next to the history of the canine tribes,

* Gardens and Menagerie, &c., vol. i. p. 20.

one or more of which are distributed over the East, as they are over almost all the other known countries of the earth. The real origin of our domestic breed of dogs, whether from a single or complex source, may be said to be entirely unknown as a subject either of history or tradition. It is lost in the usual obscurity of a remote ancestry, and can now be ascertained (if at all) only by the investigations of the naturalist. So infinitely varied is the external aspect of the domestic dog, and so much does it seem to depend, not only on the physical conditions of clime and country under which the animal exists, but on the moral and political state of the particular nation by which it is held in subjection, that in numerous instances all traces of resemblance to the original stock, or to any known species of wild animal, have disappeared; and after the lapse of ages, we are in fact at last presented with what may be called artificial creatures, incapable of subsisting without the aid of man, and of which accordingly no strictly natural type can be said to have ever existed in any age or country. They have arisen in some cases from the necessities, in others from the caprices of the human race, which, in this respect, may be said to have fulfilled the threat of Caliban, and "peopled the isle with monsters."*

The jackal or chacal (*Canis aureus*) is extensively spread over all the countries of the East. Its great voracity, gregarious habits, and dreadful nocturnal cries, are well known to Indian travellers; and poor Leyden has alluded to this animal in his

---

* See Quarterly Journal of Agriculture, No 5, p. 540.

address to a Indian gold coin,—written, it is said, when labouring under the fatal effects of a *coup de soleil*.

"Slave of the dark and dirty mine!
What vanity has brought thee here?
How can I love to see thee shine
So bright whom I have bought so dear?
The tent-ropes flapping lone I hear,
For twilight converse arm in arm;
The *Chacal's* shriek bursts on mine ear,
When mirth and music wont to charm.
By Cherical's dark wandering streams,
Where cane-tufts shadow all the wild,
Sweet visions haunt my waking dreams
Of Teviot, loved while yet a child;—
Of castled rocks stupendous piled,
By Esk or Eden's classic wave,
Where loves of youth and friendship smiled
Uncurst by thee, vile yellow slave!

The most remarkable of the canine animals of India is the Thibet-dog, a gigantic kind of mastiff, which inhabits certain portions of the table-land of the Himmaleh mountains. It is employed as a watch-dog by a tribe called the Bhoteas, and is said to have a strong aversion to Europeans, or, as Dr Wallick expresses it, "flies ferociously at a white face." "The mansion of the Rajah of Bootan," says Captain Turner, "stood upon the right; on the left was a row of wooden cages, containing a number of large dogs, tremendously fierce, strong, and noisy. They were natives of Thibet, and whether savage by nature, or soured by confinement, they were so impetuously furious, that it was unsafe, unless the keepers were near, even to approach their dens." The individuals transmitted to the Zoological Gardens came from the neighbourhood of Diggarchee, the capital of Thibet, and are supposed to be the only individuals which were ever domesticated by Europeans. Their colour was a deep black, slightly clouded on the sides; their feet, and a spot over each eye, being of a full tawny or bright brown. They had the broad, deep, truncated muzzle of the mastiff, and lips still more deeply pendulous. We regret to add that both these animals died soon after their arrival in England.

Another species of Indian dog (*Canis quoa*, Hardwicke) inhabits the mountains of Ramghur.

The group which is next to claim our attention is that of the mangoustes or ichneumons, the most celebrated of which is of Egyptian origin. Several species, however, inhabit the Asiatic continent and islands, and the mungos (*Viverra mungos*, Linn.) is characteristic of India. The last-named species, like its brother of the Nile, is celebrated for its destruction of reptiles and poisonous snakes, and is still more deservedly renowned for its discovery of the medicinal virtues of the plant called *ophiorhiza mongos*, as an antidote to the otherwise fatal effects of their envenomed fangs. Buffon appears to have confounded the Indian mangouste with the ichneumon of the Nile. It is scarcely half the size. Another Indian species is named the gray ichneumon (*Ichneumon griseus*). It is easily domesticated, and although it thrives well on bread and milk, its carnivorous propensities are unsubduable; and, as we know from experience, it forms, even in the most thoroughly-reclaimed condition, a dangerous neighbour in the vicinity of ornithological pets or poultry. It may be rendered useful in the destruction of rats and other vermin.

We have now to present a brief sketch of a few

of the feline animals which occur in the countries with the natural history of which we are at present engaged; and the first, "grand chat," as the French term him, which attracts our attention, is what we more poetically call the lion, or "king of beasts." We shall not here repeat what we have already stated regarding the geographical distribution and general attributes of this majestic creature,* but shall merely remark, that the lion (*Felis leo*) is easily distinguished by his large and flowing mane and tufted tail. His colour is uniform, of a tawny hue, approaching to whitish on the belly, and the mane is sometimes dark-brown or black. When full grown he has been known to measure from eight to nine feet in length, and four feet and a half in height. His general aspect is strikingly bold and majestic: his large and shaggy mane, which he can erect at pleasure, surrounding his awful front,—his huge overhanging eyebrows,—his bright commanding eyes, which upon the least irritation seem to glow with unearthly lustre,—together with his muscular paws, extensile talons, and formidable tusks,—all these, combined with the voice of thunder with which he springs upon his prey, render him an assailant of the most formidable kind. The elastic bound of the swift-footed antelope is then in vain; for, paralyzed by terror, and heart-struck even by the glare of those terrific eyes; it falls to the earth as powerless as a dead leaf from a blasted tree, and life is extinct almost before the "empurpled stream" has begun to flow. A horse also is

---

* See the former volume of our series (No 2 of Edinburgh Cabinet Library), entitled "Narrative of Discovery and Adventure in Africa," &c., p. 415.

"a vain thing for safety," for his quivering limbs and large dilated eyes exhibit the depth of uncontrollable dismay, and he, too, falls an unresistant victim to the "king of terrors." One blow upon the neck with that tremendous paw, and a single infliction on throat or shoulder of those all-piercing tusks, and the turmoil is for ever done. One short and interrupted cry or rather shriek responds to the lion's roar, and the blood of the beautiful courser bedews the shaggy mane of his relentless and insatiate foe.

The elephant is found to be the only efficient coadjutor in the pursuit of this noble game. "But of all the diversions of the field," says Bernier, "the hunting of the lion is not only the most perilous, but it is peculiarly royal; for, except by special permission, the king and the princes are the only persons who engage in the sport. As a preliminary step, an ass is tied near the spot where the gamekeepers have ascertained the lion retires. The wretched animal is soon devoured, and after so ample a meal the lion never seeks for other prey, but, without molesting either oxen, sheep, or shepherd, goes in quest of water, and after quenching his thirst, returns to his former place of retirement. He sleeps until the next morning, when he finds and devours another ass, which the gamekeepers have brought to the same spot. In this way they contrive, during several successive days, to allure the lion, and to attach him to one place; and when information is received of the king's approach, they fasten at the spot an ass where so many others have been sacrificed, down whose throat a large quantity of opium has been forced. This last meal is of course intended to produce a soporific effect upon the lion. The next operation is to spread, by means of the peasantry of the adjacent villages, large nets, made on purpose, which are gradually drawn closer in the manner practised in hunting nyl-ghaus. Every thing being in this state of preparation, the king appears on an elephant barbed with iron, and attended by the grand master of the hunt, some omrahs mounted on elephants, and a great number of gourse-berdars on horseback, and of gamekeepers on foot, armed with half-pikes. He immediately approaches the net on the outside, and fires at the lion with a large musketoon. The wounded animal makes a spring at the elephant, according to the invariable practice of lions, but is arrested by the net, and the king continues to discharge his musketoon until the lion is at length killed."*

The Asiatic lion, it has been observed, seldom attains the dimensions of the full-grown individuals from Southern Africa. Its colour is also more uniform and of a paler yellow, and its mane is in general fuller and more complete. He is also a much rarer animal in Asia than in Africa. "In the sandy deserts of Arabia, in some of the wilder districts of Persia, and in the vast jungles of Indostan, he still maintains a precarious footing; but from the classic soil of Greece, as well as from the whole of Asia Minor, both of which were once exposed to his ravages, he has been utterly dislodged and extirpated."† The fine Indian lion, which is at present an inhabitant of the Tower of London under the name of George, was procured by General Watson in the following manner, according to

* Travels, vol. ii. p. 115. † Tower Menagerie, p. 6.

the account published by Mr Bennet:—It was about the commencement of the year 1823, when the general was on service in Bengal, that, being out one morning on horseback, armed with a double-barrelled rifle, he was suddenly surprised by a large lion, which bounded out upon him from a thick jungle, at the distance of only a few yards. He instantly fired, and the shot taking complete effect, the animal fell dead almost at his feet; but no sooner was this formidable foe thus disposed of than a second, equally terrible, made her appearance in the person of the lioness, whom the general also shot at, and wounded so dangerously that she retreated into the thicket. As her following so immediately in the footsteps of her mate afforded strong grounds for suspecting that their den could not be far distant, he determined upon pursuing the adventure to the end, and traced her to her retreat, where he completed the work of her destruction by again discharging the contents of one of the barrels of his rifle, which he had loaded for the purpose. In the den were found a beautiful pair of cubs, male and female, supposed to be then not more than three days old. These General Watson brought away with him, and succeeded, by the assistance of a goat, who was prevailed upon to act in the capacity of foster-mother to the royal pair, in rearing them until they attained sufficient age and strength to enable them to bear the voyage to England. On their arrival in this country, in September, 1823, he presented them to his majesty, who commanded them to be placed in the Tower.*

* Tower Menagerie, p. 7.

The extreme youth of these lions at the time of their capture, and the constant control exercised over them, produced of course the expected results. They continued so tame and docile, that for twelve months after their arrival they were suffered to walk at large in an open yard, where they were played with and caressed by all and sundry. But no sooner had the female given birth to her first litter of cubs, than a total change was effected in her disposition. Absorbed by one idea, the support and preservation of her young, she no longer suffered the slightest familiarity, even on the part of her accustomed keepers, and, apparently haunted by the fear that every person who approached her den was about to deprive her of her cherished offspring, she gave full scope to the violence of her passion, and exhibited a beautiful but appalling picture of maternal tenderness and the most savage ferocity. The cubs, which were three in number, two males and a female, were whelped on the 20th October, 1827, the day of the battle of Navarino; and it was discovered by the curious in such coincidences, that they were the only lions born in the Tower since the year (1794) of the great naval victory gained by Lord Howe over the French fleet.

Inferior to the lion in the majesty of his deportment, but nearly equal in strength, and perhaps excelling him in activity, the tiger (*Felis tigris*), though his nature and aspect are known to all, forms too prominent a feature in the zoology of Indostan not to require from us a brief record. This savage and very powerful animal has a more slender body and a rounder head than his great congener. His motions are full of graceful ease, and the bright tawny-yellow of the prevailing portions of his coat, contrasted with the numerous sloping lines of black, and the pure white of the under portions of his body, constitute one of the most perfect pictures of savage beauty presented by the brute creation. The geographical distribution of the tiger is considerably more extended from north to south than that of the lion, as it not only advances far into those desert countries which separate China from Siberia, but is also found between the Irtysch and the Ischim, and even, though rarely, as far as the banks of the Obi. On the other hand, it is more restricted in a longitudinal direction, as it appears rarely to pass to the westward of a line drawn from about the mouths of the Indus in a northerly direction to the shores of the Caspian Sea. The tiger was therefore much less familiarly known to ancient writers than the lion, and even among the Romans it was long regarded as an extreme rarity. Megasthenes alone, among the Greeks, seems to have been acquainted with it from personal observation; for Nearchus had only an opportunity of seeing the skin, and Aristotle merely mentions it as an animal of which he had heard by name. Among the Romans, according to Pliny, the first tiger ever exhibited to the people was a tame one belonging to Augustus, which had been sent to that emperor in sign of homage by an Indian king. Claudius afterwards exhibited four at one time, and it has been conjectured that the beautiful mosaic picture of four tigers, discovered some years ago in Rome near the Arch of Gallienus, was executed at that period in commemoration of so striking and unprecedented a display.*

* See Ossemens fossiles, nouv. ed., t. 4, p. 415.

The pursuit of this animal is of course attended by considerable danger. In the following anecdote, however, as related by Mr Williamson, no damage appears to have resulted either to the huntsman or his elephant. "The tiger had satiated himself upon a bullock he had killed, and lay lurking in the grass, which was as high as the backs of the elephants, and very thick, not far from the remains of the bullock. He was extremely cunning, and crouched so close as to render it for a long time doubtful whether he was in the jungle or not. The symptoms displayed by the elephants, in approaching the place where he lay concealed, induced the party to persevere in their efforts to rouse him. One gentleman particularly urged his mahout to make his elephant beat the spot where the scent was strongest, which being done in spite of the tremendous tones of the agitated animal, the tiger finding himself compelled either to resist or to submit to being trodden upon, sprang upon the elephant's quarter, and so far succeeded as to fix his claws in the pad; his hind-legs were somewhat spread, and their claws were fixed into the fleshy membranes of the elephant's thigh. Actuated by the excess of fear, occasioned by so sudden and so painful an attack, the elephant dashed through the corn at a surprising rate, the tiger holding fast by its fore-paws, and supported by its hinder ones; unable, however, in consequence of the rapid and irregular motions of the elephant, either to raise himself any higher, or to quit the hold he had so firmly taken with his claws. The gentleman, who had much ado to keep his seat, was precluded firing at his grim companion, as well from his unprecedented situation, as from the great danger of wounding some of the numerous followers, who were exerting the utmost speed of their respective elephants to come up to his assistance. The constant desire felt to get rid of his unwelcome rider, which produced a waving and irregular pace, gave the opportunity for those who were mounted on light and speedy animals, to overtake the singular fugitives. Another gentleman of the party coming up close, was enabled to choose his position; when, taking safe aim, he shot the tiger, which fell to the ground and required no farther operation."*

The following anecdote illustrates the character both of the tiger and the sepoy. It is about twenty years ago since Major Hull, the commanding-officer of a battalion on the Bombay establishment, was proceeding along the banks of a ravine, with eight or ten men of his corps, in search of some lions which had been seen near the cantonment of Kaira in Guzerat, when a royal tiger suddenly sprang upon him. The ground gave way, and the tiger and Major Hull rolled together to the bottom of the ravine. Though this fall prevented the latter from being killed by the first assault, still his fate seemed certain; and those who know the terror which this ferocious beast is wont to inspire, can alone appreciate the character of that bravery which induced every sepoy who was with him to rush at once to his succour. The tiger fell under their bayonets, though not before it had desperately wounded two of the assailants, one of whom lost his leg, and the other was so severely lacerated as to be

* riental Field Sports, p. 72.

incapable of any future service. But they deemed their wounds trivial, when they saw that the officer whom they loved had escaped unhurt from his perilous encounter.*

The hunting-tiger or chittah (*Felis jubata*, Schreber) is one of the most picturesque and elegant of the genus. It is considerably less than the panther, and of a more slender form. Its legs are proportionally higher, its tail longer, its head somewhat smaller and shorter, than in any of its congeners. It may also be distinguished by a black line which passes from the anterior angle of the eye to the corner of the mouth, and by another shorter one which proceeds from the posterior angle of the eye towards the temple. The upper parts of the body are of a beautiful clear tawny-yellow, adorned by numerous small round black spots, which are simple,—that is, not eye-shaped, or *en forme de rose*, as in the most nearly-allied species. The under parts are white, marked by larger and more waving spots. The upper half of the tail is tawny-yellow above and white below, with black spots; the lower half is marked by twelve alternate rings of black and white. This animal measures rather more than three feet in length, and stands about two feet high. Its toes are lengthened like those of a dog, and the claws are blunter and less curved than in the other animals of the cat-kind.

In conformity with these characters the disposition of the chittah is more gentle, and its nature more readily admits of domestication and a certain degree of regulated culture than the rest. In eastern countries it is trained to the chase of antelopes and

* Quarterly Review, vol. xviii. p. 404.

other wild animals, being carried in a small waggon chained and hoodwinked till the game appears. It is then let loose, and generally makes its first advances by creeping insidiously like a serpent, with its belly close to the ground, till within a short distance, when it makes five or six tremendous bounds, and falls upon its prey with the velocity of an arrow. One, which died some years ago in the Royal Menagerie of Paris, had been so completely reclaimed from a state of nature that it was left in a park to the freedom of its own will, and where it yet obeyed in every thing the commands of its keeper, and showed a great attachment to the society of dogs.

The geographical history of this species appears to have been but little known till of late years. Its distribution is very extensive. It occurs, as we have already mentioned, in Indostan; it is known in Persia by the name of *youze,* and great quantities of skins, apparently identical, are transmitted to Europe from Senegal and other parts of Africa.

Several other species of the feline race are indigenous to that portion of Asia which it is our present endeavour to illustrate; but the three above described will probably suffice to represent the habits and history of the whole.

Passing over the great and eccentric order of marsupial or pouched animals, which, though not entirely unknown to the great Asiatic division of our globe, are yet strangers to Indostan and the other countries of our present inquiry, we proceed to the order *Rodentia* or *Glires,* which includes what are designated *gnawers,*—such as rats and mice, and many others too numerous to mention. Of this order the squirrel tribe (genus *Sciurus*) are among the most beautiful and most to be admired, and of these the Malabar species (*Sc. maximus*) is the largest known,—measuring fifteen or sixteen inches from the muzzle to the root of the tail, which is itself nearly a foot and a half long. The upper parts and outsides of the limbs are of a bright chocolate-brown, which changes suddenly on the under parts, fore-arms, and inner sides of the limbs, into a pale yellowish-brown. The back and shoulders are sometimes of a deep black. The ears are short and covered with tufted hair, the whiskers are long and black. The tail is broad and branching from the centre to the sides, and its colours are bright chocolate-brown at the base, black in the intermediate portion, and chestnut at the extremity. This beautiful species was observed and figured by Sonnerat. It is native to the coasts of Malabar.

Of the rat tribe we shall here mention only a single example of enormous size. It is the Malabar-rat of Dr Shaw, and the *Mus giganteus* of General Hardwicke.* The nose is rounded, the under jaw much shorter than the upper, the cutting-teeth broad, incurved, compressed, the lower ones measuring eight-tenths of an inch, and the upper four-tenths in length. The body is thick, and greatly arched; the upper part is most hairy and black, the lower inclines to gray. The legs and toes are black, and the tail is thinly covered with hair, and measures two and a half inches in circumference at the root. The specimen above described was a female, and weighed 2 pounds 11 ounces and a half. The male

---

* In Linn. Trans., vol. vii. p. 306.

weighs above three pounds, and measures, including the tail, which is above a foot long, nearly 30 inches in length. This gigantic rat is found in many places on the coast of Coromandel, in Mysore, and in several parts of Bengal, between Calcutta and Hurdwar. It is partial to dry situations, and scarcely ever occurs at a distance from human habitations. The lowest caste of Hindoos, according to General Hardwicke, eat the flesh of this rat in preference to that of any other species. It is extremely mischievous, and will burrow to a great depth, passing beneath the foundations of stores and granaries, if these are not deeply laid; and it perforates with ease the walls of such buildings as are formed with mud or unburnt brick. It is destructive in gardens, and roots up the seeds of all kinds of leguminous plants. Fruits also suffer from its depredations, and it will even attack poultry when it finds itself stinted in a vegetable diet. The bite of this animal is considered dangerous; and a European serving in the Honourable Company's artillery is known to have died in the Doab of confirmed hydrophobia, in consequence of having been bit by the species in question. We may here add, that the common rat (*Mus decumanus*), now the pest of most of the great cities of Europe, is supposed to have come originally from India.

The animal kingdom presents no species of a more singular form and aspect than the pangolins, or manis tribe, sometimes denominated scaly lizards. They occur both in Africa and the East, and belong to the order *Edentata*. The short-tailed manis (*M. pentadactyla*, Linn.) appears to have been described by Ælian under the name of *phattagen.* Its body is covered with thick scales disposed over the surface like tiles on the roof of a house. It is destitute of teeth, but has a long extensile tongue, with which it preys on ants and termites. The tail is shorter than the body, and the total length is from three to four feet. They kill lizards according to Erxleben. Their dispositions are gentle, their voices feeble, their progression slow. They seldom appear except during the night, and their flesh in some countries is sought after as a delicate article of food. The species alluded to is called *Alungu* on the coast of Coromandel. It inhabits several parts of India, and likewise occurs in the islands of Formosa and Ceylon.

We now enter on the order of *Pachydermatous,* or thick-skinned animals, which includes the largest land-species of the brute creation.

The elephant (*Elephas Indicus*), supposed by many to be the "wisest of brutes," is alleged by others to owe much of its apparent sagacity to that admirable instrument its proboscis, by which it is enabled to perform many actions, which the dog and the horse, though probably superior in wisdom, are incapable of achieving from their different if not more defective organization. Still we can entertain no doubt, either from the ancient records or the modern exhibitions of its docile disposition, that this animal is highly gifted for an irrational being; and it generally retains its finer natural instincts even in conjunction with those more artificial acquirements, which in several other species seem to deaden or counteract the influences of pure instinctive feeling. For example, it is mentioned by Mr Johnson, that an elephant, belonging to Mr Boddam of the Bengal civil service at Gyah, used every day to pass over a small bridge leading from his master's house to the town. He one day, however, refused to cross it; but was at length, by being cruelly gored about the head with an iron instrument, forced to make the attempt. When he was about half-way over, the bridge gave way, and the ponderous animal was precipitated with violence into the ditch and severely injured. The driver fortunately was killed.*

Elephants in this country are usually fed on hay and carrots, and the quantity of food which they are capable of consuming is enormous. Those of the Emperor Akbar had a daily allowance of 200 pounds in weight, with an additional supply of ten pounds of sugar, besides rice, milk, and pepper; and during the sugar-cane season each was provided daily with 300 canes. The Mogul princes are known to have kept up their stud of elephants at an enormous expense, and according to Pliny even the Romans, a people so addicted to extravagance, found the sustaining of the Carthaginian elephants captured by Metellus so costly, that they were afterwards slain in the circus. Yet, according to Ælian's account, less rigid economy prevailed in the days of Germanicus. His elephants were exhibited in the arena, reposing on splendid couches adorned with the richest tapestry. Tables of ivory and cedar-wood were placed before them, and on these their viands were presented to them in vessels of silver

* Indian Field Sports, p. 56.

and gold. They danced to the sound of "flutes and soft recorders," or moved in measured and harmonious steps around the theatre, scattering the freshest and the choicest flowers around them. Arrian mentions an elephant which played on cymbals, one being fastened to each knee, and another held in his proboscis, while his unwieldy companions danced in a circle, keeping time with the greatest exactness.

So many contradictory accounts have been given of the size of the adult elephant, that we find some difficulty in stating its true dimensions in a few words. The African are alleged to be superior in size to those of Asia. Major Denham, while journeying to the Tchad, saw individuals so enormous that he calculated their height to be sixteen feet. These, however, he had no opportunity of measuring; but another, which was killed in his presence, was found to be nine feet six inches from the foot to the hip-bone, and three feet from the hip-bone to the back,—or twelve feet six inches in all,—which is more than twice the height of the taller races of the human species. When we consider that, even in proportion to its height, the elephant is an animal of enormous bulk, and of the most massive proportions, we may conceive what a load of flesh and bone its rugous coat must have contained. Mr Scott of Sinton, whose authority is frequently quoted and deservedly valued on such points, states, in relation to the Asiatic species, that he never heard of more than a single instance of the elephant much exceeding the height of ten feet. The following are the proportions which he gives of a fine male belonging to the Vizier of Oude:—

	Ft.	In.
From foot to foot over the shoulder, .	22	10½
From the top of the shoulder, perpendicular height,	10	6
From the top of the head when set up, .	12	2
From the front of the face to the insertion of the tail,	15	11

Nothing is more deceptive than the dimensions of an animal, which, obviously exceeding in size any thing that we had been previously accustomed to, has yet been unsubjected to accurate measurement, for our astonishment magnifies its actual size. Thus a celebrated elephant belonging to the Nabob of Dacca, which was generally said to be fourteen feet high, and which even Mr Scott's practised eye estimated at twelve, was found by measurement not to exceed ten feet. Those from Pegu and Ava are, however, larger than the elephants of Indostan, and the Ceylonese variety is also of great dimensions. The skeleton of an individual in the Museum at Petersburgh, which was presented by the King of Persia to the Czar Peter, measures sixteen feet and a half in height; but we are uncertain how much of this prodigious stature may be owing to the mode in which the bones have been articulated, and the more or less natural curvature of the spine.

A large elephant weighs from six to seven thousand pounds, and we may easily conceive that when journeying through the forests, with any very special object in view, he must force his way through all intervening obstacles, more after the manner of a steam-engine, than of any mere animal force of which we have a clear and accustomed conception.

"Trampling his path through wood and brake,
And canes which crackling fall before his way,
And tassel-grass, whose silvery feathers play,
O'ertopping the young trees,
On comes the elephant, to slake
His thirst at noon in yon pellucid springs.

Lo! from his trunk upturn'd, aloft he flings
The grateful shower: and now,
Plucking the broad-leav'd bough
Of yonder plume, with waving motion slow,
Fanning the languid air,
He waves it to and fro."*

The new-born elephant measures about thirty-five inches high; he grows about eleven inches during the first year; eight in the second; five in the fifth; three and a half in the sixth; and two and a half in the seventh. He takes from twenty to thirty years to attain his full growth.

It has been said that the invention of gunpowder in the practice of war, and the application of steam to machinery, have superseded the uses of this great living engine. It is still, however, extensively used in the East for a variety of purposes, and Bernier in his travels has given a spirited description of a grand procession of Aurengzebe's retinue. The conveyance of the "lovely and distinguished females" seems chiefly to have attracted the observance of the lively Frenchman. "I cannot avoid," he observes, "dwelling on this pompous procession of the seraglio. It strongly arrested my attention during the late march, and I feel delight in recalling it to my memory. Stretch imagination to its utmost limits, and you can conceive no exhibition more grand and imposing than when Rochinara Begum (Aurengzebe's sister), mounted on a stupendous Pegu elephant, and seated in a mik-dember blazing with gold and azure, is followed by five or six other elephants with mik-dembers nearly as resplendent as her own, and filled with ladies attached to her household. Close to the princess are the chief eunuchs, richly adorned

* Curse of Kehama.

and finely mounted, each with a cane in his hand; and, surrounding her elephant, a troop of female servants from Tartary and Cashmere, fantastically attired, and riding handsome pad-horses. Besides these attendants are several eunuchs on horseback, accompanied by a multitude of pagys or lackeys on foot with large canes, who advance a great way before the princess both to the right and to the left, for the purpose of clearing the road and driving before them every intruder. Immediately behind Rochinara Begum's retinue appears a principal lady of the court, mounted and attended much in the same manner as the princess. This lady is followed by a third; she by a fourth; and so on, until fifteen or sixteen females of quality pass, with a grandeur of appearance, equipage, and retinue, more or less proportionate to their rank, pay, and office. There is something very impressive of state and royalty in the march of these sixty or more elephants, in their solemn and as it were measured steps; in the splendour of their mik-dembers, and the brilliant and innumerable followers in attendance: and, if I had not regarded this display of magnificence with a sort of philosophical indifference, I should have been apt to be carried away by the similar flights of imagination as inspire most of the Indian poets, when they represent the elephants as conveying as many goddesses concealed from vulgar gaze."

It appears, however, that these journeys are not always unattended by danger, for Bernier was himself an eye-witness of the following catastrophe:— "The king (Aurengzebe) was ascending the Peer-Punchal mountains, from which a distant view of the kingdom of Cashmere is first obtained. He was followed by a long line of elephants, upon which sat the ladies in mik-dembers and amaris (seats with canopies). The foremost, appalled, as is supposed, by the great length and acclivity of the path before him, stepped back upon the elephant that was moving in his track; who again pushed against the third elephant, the third against the fourth, and so on until fifteen of them, incapable of turning round or extricating themselves in a road so steep and narrow, fell down the precipice. Happily for the women, the place where they fell was of no great height; only three or four were killed; but there were no means of saving any of the elephants. Whenever these animals fall under the immense burden usually placed upon their backs, they never rise again, even on a good road. Two days afterwards we passed that way, and I observed that some of the poor elephants still moved their trunks."*

In regard to the pecuniary value of the elephant, Mr Forbes informs us that a common price is from 5000 to 6000 rupees, but that he has seen one valued at 20,000. The Hindoos become much attached to these animals when they have been long in their service, and a wealthy owner will not part with one of extraordinary qualifications for any consideration. A well-disciplined war-elephant will stand a volley of musketry. "I have seen one," says the last-named author, "with upwards of thirty bullets in the fleshy parts of his body, and perfectly recovered from his wounds."†

---

* Bernier's Travels, vol. ii. p. 149.

† The difficulty of destroying elephants by fire-arms, may be conceived on perusal of an anecdote in Captain Beaver's "African

Though much remains untold of the habits and history of this ponderous creature, we must now proceed to other subjects, having already devoted more space to the preceding notices than we can well afford.*

Inferior in size to the elephant and of a much more restricted capacity, the rhinoceros (*Rh. Indicus*, Cuv.) is yet of sufficient dimensions to form a very imposing feature in the zoology of the East. There are three species of this animal in Asiatic countries. The Indian and Javanese have each a single horn, while the Sumatran is "doubly armed" like the African species. It is to the first of these that our present observations may be understood to apply.

A young rhinoceros, preserved in the Garden of Plants, was habitually gentle, obedient to its keepers, and extremely sensible of kindness. At times, however, he exhibited paroxysms of violent rage, during which it was necessary to keep beyond his reach, as it would have been but a poor consolation to those whom he might have impaled, to be informed that for the most part his intentions were innocent. He was generally calmed by a liberal supply of bread and fruit, and as soon as he saw those who were in the habit of feeding him, he would stretch his muzzle towards them, open his mouth, and push out his tongue. His proportions were thicker, and

---

Memoranda." See also the painful narrative in the 3d volume of Mr Griffith's edition of the Animal Kingdom.

* We beg to refer the reader to the Library of Entertaining Knowledge, vol. ii., entitled The Menageries, where a complete and very ample account is given of the ancient and modern history of elephants. We have availed ourselves of several of the authorities brought forward in that amusing volume.

still more unwieldy than those of the elephant. His height was about 5 feet 6 inches, and his length nearly 8 feet, and his whole body was covered by a thick nearly naked tuberculous skin, disposed in irregular folds. Its natural colour appeared to be gray tinted with violet; but as it was apt to crack, it was kept lubricated, which altered the natural hue. His senses, with the exception of that of touch, appeared to be tolerably acute.

"The power of this species is frequently displayed to a surprising degree when hunting it. A few years ago, a party of Europeans, with their native attendants and elephants, when out on the dangerous sport of hunting these animals, met with a herd of seven of them, led, as it appeared, by one larger and stronger than the rest. When the large rhinoceros charged the hunters, the leading elephants, instead of using their tusks or weapons, which in ordinary cases they are ready enough to do, wheeled round, and received the blow of the rhinoceros' horn on the posteriors. The blow brought them immediately to the ground with their riders, and as soon as they had risen, the brute was again ready, and again brought them down, and in this manner did the combat continue until four out of the seven were killed, when the rest made good their retreat."*

Wild-boars are among the most ferocious of the animals of India. They chiefly inhabit the woods and jungles; but when the grain is nearly ripe, they occasion great damage in the corn-fields, and still

* Griffith's Animal Kingdom, vol. iii. p. 426.

more among the sugar-plantations, as they are extremely fond of canes. Their irascible nature is indeed remarkable for creatures of a herbivorous disposition, and their pursuit and capture is consequently not unattended by personal danger. They are spread over a vast tract of eastern territory, and exist in great abundance in the Archipelago of the Papuas, to the north of the Moluccas, and the westward of New Guinea. It would even appear that two wild species occur in the Celebes (independent of *Sus babyrussa*), and some writers maintain the opinion that there exists in the Indian and Chinese dominions a species of wild-boar distinct from that of Europe, and the more probable source from which the Siamese breed and that of China have been derived. Thus if the domestic races peculiar to, or characteristic of, the northern and temperate parts of Europe, have sprung (as we think cannot be doubted) from the wild-boar (*Sus aper*), we shall have three distinct sources from which to trace the rise and progress of domestic swine.*

The *Ruminating* order is the next in succession to that of which we have just treated, and contains many of the species from which man derives his most valuable supplies both of food and raiment. The order may be divided into two great divisions, those without horns, and such as are provided with those weapons.

The camel (*C. Bactrianus*), by which term the two-humped species is usually designated, is indigenous to the central deserts of Asia, and is used as a beast of burden in Turkestan and Thibet, and even as far north as the shores of Lake Baikal. The more abundant and better-known species, which is in fact the dromedary (*C. dromedarius*), is now spread over the whole of Arabia, Syria, and Persia. It is this species which in India precede the nabobs on state-occasions to fire salutes; and Major Hamilton Smith informs us that the East India Company maintains a corps of dromedaries, mounted by two men each, and armed with musketoons or swivels. These animals are very savage at particular seasons.

* See Forrest's Voyage to New Guinea; some observations by Antoine Desmoulins in the Diction. Class. d'Hist. Nat., t. iv. p. 271; and the Quarterly Journal of Agriculture, vol. iii. p. 50, Note.

An instance is related of a *must*-camel (an individual rendered furious by the excitement of the rutting-season) tearing off a young man's arm in India: the writhing body of his victim was with difficulty withdrawn from the enraged animal, who stood in terrific exultation over the torn limb, and for some time would suffer no one to approach it.

If we may judge from the close and efficient covering of fur with which, except towards the termination of the rutting-season, both the camel and dromedary are clothed, we should infer that these animals came originally from a temperate climate, where, as in the central parts of Asia, a considerable degree of cold was at times experienced. The coat appears to become scanty only in such individuals as reside in very hot regions, and this circumstance is regarded by Major Smith as a fair indication that their primitive *habitat* was in a region occasionally subjected to a pretty severe temperature. The southern base of the Caucasian mountains has been assigned to what is named the Arabian species or dromedary; and the arid plains beneath the northern confines of the Paropamisaden range, with the wildernesses of Jasnak and Chorasmia, east of the Caspian, may perhaps be regarded as among the native abodes of the camel or Bactrian species. Something to this effect may be inferred from scattered hints in the Zend, the poems of Schah, named Ferdusi, and in the Arabian epic, the romance of Antar.* The articles used in manufactures, and known under the names of mohair and camlets, are the produce of the fur of these animals.

* Griffith's Animal Kingdom, vol. iv. p. 46.

The musk-deer (genus *Moschus*) are the only other tribe which we include among the hornless ruminants of Asia. Of these the musk-deer, *par excellence* (*M. moschiferus*), is one of the most remarkable. Although the drug called musk has been known throughout Central Asia from time immemorial, it does not appear that the animal which produced it was known to the ancients, or indeed in any way identified till it was described by Abu-zeid Serassi, an Arabian author, who stated that it was a deer without horns. A knowledge of it was first introduced in Western Europe by Serapion, who flourished in the eighth century. It is nearly the size of a roebuck, with an exceedingly short tail, and covered by a very coarse coat. Its native regions are the Alpine tracts of Central Asia, where it dwells amid barren rocks and perpetual snows, descending occasionally to the region of the pines. It is a nocturnal animal of solitary disposition, and extremely timid. The province of Thibet is the most renowned for the superior quality of its musk. This prized perfume is obtained from a small bag situated in the lower region of the abdomen of the male. The flesh, though strongly impregnated with a musky odour, is also much esteemed.

Ceylon produces a small species of this genus called the *memina*. It is about 17 inches long, of a cinereous-olive ; the throat, breast, and belly white, and the flanks ornamented by long bars of that colour. It inhabits the jungles, and was first described by Knox.*

Such of the ruminating order as we have still to describe are furnished with horns. We shall speak

* Historical Relation of Ceylon.

in the first place of the *deer tribe*. These animals are remarkable for their elegant forms, their light but strong proportions, and the energy and activity of their general movements. As among the nobler subjects of the chase, they have long been objects of interest in various countries to the aristocracy of the human race. The genus is pretty widely distributed over all the greater divisions of the globe, with the exception of New Holland.*

We shall not enter into the history of the elk, because, although it is an Asiatic animal, it does not proceed so far to the southward as to enter within our present boundaries, and the same reason of exclusion will apply to the red-deer or stag.

There are, however, many magnificent examples of this tribe of animals to be found to the south of the Nepaul mountains. Of these we shall mention in the first place the Nepaul stag itself (*Cervus Wallickii*), which in several respects exhibits a resemblance to the red-deer of our own heath-clad hills. The only known individual of this species was brought by Dr Wallick to Calcutta from Nepaul. It was figured by a native artist from a live specimen in the menagerie of the governor-general at Barrackpore; the drawing was transmitted by Duvaucel to Paris, and has been published by M. F. Cuvier. The horns are rather short, with two small antlers at the base, pointing to the front; half-way up the beam a small snag turns forwards; the suborbital openings are large; the general colour is

* We have ourselves introduced deer into Jamaica, and those imported by the Portuguese thrive well in the Isle of France. It is to be hoped, that the vast pastures of New Holland will be ere long stocked with what would prove a valuable accession to those otherwise unpeopled wastes.

yellowish-brown-gray, with a large paler-coloured disk upon the croup. The tail is very short.

The *Rusa* group of stags is entirely Asiatic, and is distinguished by round horns, with a brow-antler, but without any median or bezantler; the beam terminates in a single perch, with a snag more or less elongated, placed midway or higher, on its anterior or posterior edge.

The great Rusa (*Cervus hippelaphus*) is nearly as large as a horse. It has trifurcated horns, very coarse hair, of a fulvous-brown in summer, changing during the winter season to a grayer hue; it has no disk, and the tail is rather long. This species is found in several of the Asiatic Islands, and in continental India it occurs chiefly in the Jungleterry district of Bengal. It corresponds to the great axis of Pennant.

The exact nature of the animal described by Aristotle under the name of ἱππελαφος has been a subject of considerable controversy. Linnæus and Erxleben applied the name to a species which occurs in the forests of Germany; but, according to M. Duvaucel, it is undoubtedly the *black deer* of Bengal.* Its horns are forked at the extremity, and bear only a single antler at the base, similar, as Aristotle expressed it, to those of a roebuck.†

The Gona Rusa (*Cervus unicolor*) inhabits Ceylon, and is the largest species of that island, surpassing in size the stag of Europe. The throat is load-

* Asiatic Researches, vol. xv. p. 157.

† In relation to this point, we should bear in mind Buffon's important observation regarding the Latin translation of Aristotle by Theodore Gaza. The word *capra* is there given as the interpretation of δοκος, instead of *caprea*; so that in the passage regarding the horns, we must substitute *capreæ* for *capræ*, or the horns of a roe for those of a goat.

ed with long bristly hair, the tail is short, and the general colour is a uniform dark-brown. This species is very bold and fierce, and dwells in the jungle and the deepest recesses of the forests.

The saumer, or black Rusa of Bengal (*Cervus Aristotelis*), inhabits the Prauss Jungles. The male is nearly as large as an elk, and is represented by British sportsmen in India as exceedingly vicious as well as strong. Some of these, while engaged in a shooting-expedition, had crossed an arm of the Jumna to a well-wooded island in search of game; they were mounted on an elephant, and, entering the jungle suddenly, they roused an old male of this species. "On seeing the elephant," says Major Smith, "he started up with a loud shrill pipe or whistle, which caused others to rise and dart into cover, while he stood at bay with his bristly mane on end in a most threatening attitude; but before the sportsmen could prepare proper shot, he wheeled round and dashed through the underwood with the facility of a rhinoceros." It is to this species that the name of elk is erroneously applied by many Anglo-Indians. Its head, shoulders, back, and buttock, are dark-brown in summer, and in winter nearly black. The belly, and a ring round the nostrils and mouth, are whitish. The insides of the legs are fawn-colour, and the breast is black. Captain Williamson describes it as attaining to the size of a Lincolnshire cart-horse (fifteen or sixteen hands high), of a shining black, with tanned points. He adds, that the females are of a mouse-colour. There are heads of this species in the British Museum.

Other species of Rusa inhabit the Indian Archipelago, the Island of Timor, the Peninsula of Malacca, and the Marian Islands,—but our restricted limits will not admit of our entering into any farther details in illustration of this very striking and peculiar group.

The spotted axis (*Cervus axis*) resembles the fallow-deer, but is easily distinguished from it by the roundness of its horns, and the want of a terminal palm. The female, however, is with difficulty discriminated from the doe of the fallow-deer. It was the opinion of Pennant, that the spotted-deer of our preserves came originally from Bengal, but in the fourth edition of Gwillim's Heraldry (1660, p. 171) the *spotted buck* is quoted as borne in ancient coats of arms at a period long anterior to any British intercourse with India. The fallow-deer itself appears from various historical and etymological considerations, into which we cannot at present enter, to have been indigenous to the southern and central districts of Europe. The axis, however, is the best and most anciently-known of all the Asiatic species. It is found throughout India and the islands of the Archipelago, but is most abundant in Bengal and on the banks of the Ganges. Being an inhabitant of a country where the revolutions of the season do not produce alternately the extremes of heat and cold, the stag of the Ganges, unlike the species of most other countries, is coloured in a similar manner throughout the year. The antlers attain to a considerable size as the animal increases in years; but they are always of a simple form, bearing only a single frontal branch or snag, and the main stem forming two terminal forks. This species has been frequently imported into England and France, in both of which countries it propagates freely. According to Peter Collinson, they have even bred with the fallow-deer. Their sense of smell, as observed by Pennant, is so singularly acute that, although remarkably fond of bread, they will not eat it if it has been previously blown upon; and M. F. Cuvier confirms this trait in their character, by stating that he has observed them refuse that favourite article after it had been much handled by the keepers. Their disposition in a state of captivity is remarkably mild and accommodating.

A large fulvous variety of the axis, with high shoulders and two rows of oval white spots upon the back, is found in the Rohilla country and the Dacca districts. These are the true *hog-deer* of Indian sportsmen on the Cossimbuzar Island, in the Jungleterry, and Bahar. The forests of Ceylon produce a large variety, with a straight back like a cow. The oval spots are wanting; the face is entirely of a buff-colour, with a rather prolonged nose. "In India," says Major Smith, "all the varieties are known by the general name of hog-deer, and are called in the Moorish language, used in the country, *parrah*. They are found most usually in the heavy grass-jungles in the lower provinces, and to the northward in the *Jow* and *Jurput* jungles along the banks of rivers; they feed in preference on the silky grass used for making twine, called *moonge*, if it be found near some heavy covers, where they breed, and from whence the female leads her fawns in twelve or fifteen days after birth. They are extremely indolent, feeding at night, and passing most of the day in sleep; and, perhaps, on that account they are averse to, and will not remain in the vicinity of wild pea-fowl. They are fleet for a short distance. The does are seldom seen in an advanced state of pregnancy, keeping at that time in the cover; and the bucks are then very vigilant and fierce in their defence."

Another section of horned ruminants is called the *capreoline* group, or roes. The common roebuck (*Cervus capreolus*), according to Captain Williamson, is not unknown in Bengal; but it is only found on the borders, particularly among the crags and ravines of the western frontier. It there frequents elevated situations, and prefers especially such covers as are divided into small patches. They are extremely shy, and their dimensions are said to be less than those of Scotland.

Passing over the muntjaks, which are numerous in India, the next group which presents itself is that of the swift and elegant antelopes. Of these, the greater proportion being of African origin, a brief notice will suffice for the Indian species.

The white oryx (*Antilope leucoryx*) measures about three feet seven inches in height at the shoulder. The body is rather bulky, the legs slender, and the horns of the male are horizontal, bent backwards, obliquely annulated, with smooth tips, and about three feet long. There is a black spot at the base of the horns passing down the face, and a second which passes through the eyes towards the mouth, widening upon the cheek; a dark band passes from the upper arm down the fore-legs; the lower parts of the thighs are rufous, darkening into black about the houghs and upon the hind-legs. This species has a dark short mane, and a black tuft at the end of the tail. The other parts of the body are white. It inhabits sandy and desert districts, and has been shot on the west side of the Indus, in the deserts of the Mekran.

We may here mention a remarkable species, called the chiru (*Antilope Kemas?* Smith), an inhabitant of the inaccessible and piny regions of Chandany, which verge on the eternal snows of the Himmaleh mountains. It is sometimes found with only a single horn, and in that accidental condition is supposed to have given rise to the belief in monocerotes or unicorns,—animals which all who are acquainted with the structure of the skull, and the position of the frontal sutures, must also know to be incapable of existing without a violation, we may almost term it, of the laws of nature. This species is remarkable for an abundant coating of wool, a provision which beautifully coincides with its position as a mountain-dweller in a cold and icy clime. The characters of the female are still unknown. The male is nearly six feet long, and measures about three feet in height at the shoulder; the croup is higher than the withers; the horns are black, slender, slightly lyre-shaped, annulated, with sharp points turned forwards. The hair is thick and coarse, but conceals beneath it a finer covering of downy wool. The face and legs are dark, the neck and back grayish slate-colour, passing to rufous, and the belly, insides of the limbs, and tip of the tail, are white.

The forests of Indostan produce the chickara, or four-horned antelope. According to General Hardwicke, this species inhabits the forests and hilly tracts along the western provinces of Bengal, Bahar, and Orissa. It is a wild and agile creature, incapable of being tamed unless when taken young. It is about twenty inches in height, and measures two feet nine inches from the nose to the root of the tail, which is about five inches long. The larger pair of horns are smooth, erect, slightly inclined forwards, and somewhat divergent,—their length about three inches. About an inch and a half in front of these horns, rise a very short stumpy pair, scarcely an inch in length, and about an inch and a half in circumference. The general colour of this animal is uniform bright bay on all the upper parts. The chin, under-line of the neck, abdomen, and insides of the thighs, incline to white, with a mixture of sand-colour. The female is of a lighter colour than the male, and is unprovided with horns.* It does not clearly appear whether the various contributions which have been made towards the elucidation of the history and structure of this animal by General Hardwicke, MM. F. Cuvier and Duvaucel, and Drs Leach and De Blainville, apply to one and the same species. Is the *Antilope quadricornis* distinct from the *Antilope chickara*? And if so, to which of the species does the *Tetracerus striaticornis* of Dr Leach belong?

We shall conclude our notices of this tribe by introducing the *nyl-ghau* to the attention of the reader; and we place it in its present position, rather in accordance with the customary practice than from any conviction of its natural alliance with the antelopes. Its name signifies blue-ox, and it is never classed with the above-named animals by the native observers in any of the countries where it occurs. The nyl-ghau was unknown to the ancients, and one of the first notices of it with which

* Linn. Trans., vol. xiv.

we are acquainted was published by Dr Parsons.* A pair were transmitted to England from Bombay by Lord Clive in the year 1767, and these bred regularly for several seasons. The species is not very widely distributed over the Peninsula of Indostan. They still occur in the districts of Kamaghur in Central India, and spread from thence to the foot of the Himmaleh mountains. They are also met with in the north-western provinces, and are not uncommon in many of the countries which are intermediate between these and the Persian dominions. Bernier describes it as one of the objects of the chase which delighted the Mogul emperor Aurengzebe, in his progress from Delhi to Cashmere. It is a treacherous animal, vicious and full of vigour, and a dangerous neighbour even in the domestic state.

The country last mentioned reminds us of a beautiful species of another genus, the coat of which is highly prized in commerce as the ingredient of a valuable manufacture. We allude to the Cashmere goat, commonly so called, which inhabits the countries of Thibet, and produces the long white silky substance, for we can scarcely call it wool, from which are made the famous shawls of Cashmere. The ears are large, of a brown or blackish colour, and turned downwards, and the limbs are slender. According to Mr Moorcroft, the Tartars of Zadouk had a monopoly of all the wool produced in the districts behind Himmaleh, and they were in use to send it, in exchange for other goods, to be manufactured into shawls by the Cashmerians.†

---

* Phil. Trans., vol. xliii.

† Journey to Lake Manasawara in Undés, a province in Little Thibet.

Another singular goat (which however cannot be referred, like the one just mentioned, to the *Capra ægagrus*) inhabits the Jemlah chain of the Himmaleh mountains to the east of the Brahmapoutra, the most elevated portion of the vast Asiatic range. The horns are placed high above the frontlets, come nearly in contact in front, are depressed, flattened, inclined outwards, and taper suddenly at the points, which are curved inwards. They are about nine inches long. This species has no beard, but the sides of the head and whole body are covered with an abundance of long buff-coloured hair. A darker-coloured streak prevails down the face and along the spine. It is the *Capra Jemlahica* of Hamilton Smith.*

The wild-sheep, or Asiatic argali (*Ovis Ammon*), scarcely falls within the limits of our present inquiry; but the high mountains of Bootan are inhabited by an animal of the genus, which is supposed to be nearly allied, if not identical. This is the wild-sheep of Bhoti, the colour of which resembles that of the chiru. They are known under the name of *nervati*; but little has transpired of their history, and the form of the horns has not been ascertained.

The last of the ruminating order which we shall notice are the *Bovidæ*. The buffalo (*Bos Bubalus*), so long introduced to the southern countries of Europe, is of Asiatic origin. It is an animal of almost amphibious habits, loving the long, coarse, rank pasture which springs up in moist and undrained lands. Hence its love of the Pontian marshes, where, according to Scaliger, it will lie for

* See the Figure in the 4th volume of Griffith's Animal Kingdom, p. 308.

hours submerged almost to the very muzzle,—an instinctive habit which it exhibits equally in Timor, where it was more recently observed to indulge its aquatic propensities in a precisely similar manner by Dr Quoy of the Uranie. Although by no means remarkable for any intellectual qualities, nor distinguished even in the domestic state by more than a dull docility, the following anecdote related by Mr Johnson seems to indicate both courage and attachment:—" Two biparies, or carriers of grain and merchandise on the backs of bullocks, were driving a loaded string of these animals from Palamow to Chittrah. When they were come within a few miles of the latter place, a tiger seized on the man in the rear, which was seen by a *guallah* (herdsman) as he was watching his buffaloes grazing. He boldly ran up to the man's assistance, and cut the tiger very severely with his sword; upon which he dropped the biparie, and seized the herdsman. The buffaloes observing it, attacked the tiger and rescued the herdsman; they tossed him about from one to the other, and, to the best of my recollection, killed him. Both the wounded men were brought to me: the biparie recovered, but the herdsman died."*

A still more gigantic inhabitant of India is called the Arnee (*Bos Arnee*). The male is said to measure seven feet high at the shoulder, and three feet across the breast, and the horns are each nearly six feet long. The hide itself is white, but covered by a black and abundant coating of hair. This species is domesticated in China, the Indian Archipelago, and the Peninsula of the Malays. In a wild state it inhabits the woody valleys of the Birman empire,

* Sketches of Indian Sports.

and the southern base of the Himmaleh mountains. It is a rare animal, although perhaps regarded as more common than it is in reality, owing to the wild-buffalo being very generally named Arnee or Arnaa in the central districts of Bengal.* A party of British cavalry-officers stationed in the north of Bengal, who spent three months employed on a hunting-expedition, during which they killed 42 tigers and numerous buffaloes, shot only a single Arnee. "When the head of this specimen," says Major Smith, "rested perpendicular on the ground, it required the outstretched arms of a man to hold the points of the horns." A good figure of this animal is given by Captain Williamson.†

Another Arnee, somewhat less in size than the one just mentioned, but possessed notwithstanding of very gigantic proportions, is also an inhabitant of India. It is somewhat difficult in this tribe of animals to trace the range of specific character, or to draw the precise line of demarcation between a species and variety. However, the individuals now alluded to are more abundant than the greater Arnee. Their habits are gregarious,—they live in wooded swamps, and are sometimes seen in droves floating down the Ganges, apparently asleep. "An animal of this kind drifted down to near Shaugur Island, in 1790, and was shot by the crew of the Hawkesbury Indiaman, towed alongside, and hoisted in. The meat weighed three hundred and sixty pounds per quarter, exclusive of the head, legs, hide, and entrails, and the whole could therefore be

---

* According to Mr Colebrooke, the *Bos Arnee* is nothing more than the wild-buffalo called *Arna*.

† Oriental Field Sports.

scarcely less than two thousand pounds, although the ship's butcher pronounced it not above two years old.*

The mountainous regions of Bootan and Thibet produce another remarkable bovine animal called the yak (*Bos poëphagus*). This is the grunting-ox of Shaw and Pennant, and the *soora goy* of the Hindostanese. It is domesticated over a vast tract of country, from the Altaic mountains to the central parts of India, and over a great portion of China. The *horse-tails*, as they are commonly called, used as standards by the Persians and Turks, are in fact made of hair (usually dyed of a fine crimson) from the tail of the grunting-ox; and the *chowries*, or fly-drivers, employed in India, are composed of the same material. This species has a downcast heavy look. It is sullen and suspicious, and usually exhibits considerable impatience, on the near approach of strangers.† The yak pastures on the coldest parts of Thibet, upon the short herbage peculiar to the tops of mountains and bleak plains. That lofty chain which is situated between latitudes 8° and 27° north, and which divides Thibet from Bootan, where the summits are commonly clothed with snow, constitutes its favourite haunt. The southern glens afford a sufficiency of food and shelter during the severity of the winter season; while during summer the northern aspect is more congenial to its nature, and admits of a wider range. This animal is of great value to the Tartar tribes. It is an excellent beast of burden, and its milk is abundant, and very productive both of butter and cheese.

---

* Animal Kingdom, vol. iv. p. 391.

† In Turner's Account of an Embassy to Thibet this species is figured under the name of the *bushy-tailed bull*.

The last species we shall mention is the gayall (*Bos frontalis*, Lambert—*Bos gavæus*, Smith), which in size and shape resembles an English bull, but in reality is almost equal in strength and activity to the wild-buffalo. It delights to dwell in the deepest jungles, feeding on the tender leaves and shoots of the brushwood. It occurs in the wild state among the mountains which form the eastern boundary of the province of Chittagong, and is reared as a domestic animal by the people called Kookiés, who inhabit those regions. It is easily tamed.* We shall say nothing of the zebus, and other domesticated breeds of Indian cattle, having exhausted our limits in the descriptions of the foregoing species.

The great aquatic mammalia which compose the cetaceous class occur in the Indian Seas as well as elsewhere; but as a knowledge of the habits of these monsters of the deep is of difficult attainment, and a mere enumeration of their names, or a dry detail of their technical characteristics, would probably afford but slight amusement to the reader, we shall select two of the most remarkable, to "stand by their order" and serve as its representatives. These are the Halicore or Indian dugong, and the Gangetic dolphin.

Our readers are probably already aware, or, if they are not, we take this opportunity to inform them, that the terminal division of the class Mammalia, commonly called *Cetæ*, contains the whole of those extraordinary beings which seem to connect land-animals, or quadrupeds, with fishes, properly so called. In their forms and general aspect they resemble the latter; but in the structure and functions of all their vital and most influential or-

* Linn. Trans., vol. vii. pp. 57 and 302.

gans, they are formed entirely after the model of the higher terrestrial animals. The order is divided into two great families; 1*st*, The herbivorous Cetacea, consisting of the lamantins, dugongs, and stellers; and, 2*dly*, Of the ordinary Cetacea, including the dolphins, narwals, and whales. With the exception of the lamantins, which occasionally repose on the banks of rivers, none of the genera of this order ever leave their native element. The members of the first family (excepting the stellers, which are northern animals) are only found in equatorial regions; those of the second occur in almost every quarter of the globe, although the greater whales prefer the vicinity of the Polar circles. We shall present an example of each.

The Halicore, or "daughter of the sea," is called *douyong* by the Malays, and has hence acquired the name of dugong in our books of natural history. There is only a single species as yet ascertained. It inhabits the Indian Seas, especially the Sumatran coasts, and has been confounded by several voyagers with the lamantins, which belong to the African and American shores. It measures seven or eight feet long, and is covered by a thick hide, of a pale-blue colour, with whitish marks on the abdomen. The head somewhat resembles that of a young elephant deprived of its proboscis. The body is fish-shaped; the anterior extremities are contained within an undivided membrane, in the form of a fin. The rudiments of a pelvis are observable, and the caudal extremity is horizontally sloped, or cut like the arch of a circle. The flesh of this animal is held in great estimation, and is usually reserved for the tables of the sultan and rajahs. Its own food is said to consist of algæ, fuci, and other marine productions of the vegetable kind.

The Gangetic dolphin (*Delphinus Gangeticus*) is about seven feet long. Its head is round, terminated by a slender elongated muzzle, the jaws of which are armed with numerous teeth. The tongue is thick, fleshy, heart-shaped. The eyes are small and black. The skin is rugose, shining, of a pearly lustre on the back, and of a whitish-gray on the abdomen. This species inhabits the waters of the Ganges, and ascends that river as far as it is navigable. It chiefly abounds, however, in those numerous divided streams which form the delta of Bengal. When in pursuit of fish, on which it feeds, it moves with great velocity; but at all other times its motions are described by Dr Roxburgh as slow and heavy. The blubber or fat of this species is highly valued by the Hindoos, as an external medicine of great efficacy in the removal of various pains. Its habits are gregarious, and it is known to the natives by the name of *sousou*.

CHAPTER III.

The Birds of India.

Vultures—Lammergeyer—Pondicherry Eagle—Finch Falcon of Bengal—Hawk-owl of Ceylon—Fork-tailed Shrike—Jocose Shrike or Bulbul—Mina-bird—Locust-eating Grakle—Honey-suckers—Kingfishers—Hornbills—Woodpeckers—Wryneck—Parrot Tribe—Common Peacock—Aldrovandine Peacock—Polyplectron—Domestic Poultry—Jungle Cock—Lophophorus—Horned Pheasant—Bustards—Golden Plover—Coromandel Courier—Gigantic Stork—Anastomus—Rhynchea—Gulls—Terns—Geese—Widgeon—Pink-headed Pochard.

THE birds of India must be admitted to be on the whole less splendid than those of South America; but the class itself being in general remarkable, both for splendour of colour and gracefulness of form, many gorgeous examples of feathered life occur in the tropical regions of the Asiatic continent. The shining creepers, the ring-necked parakeets, the lories, and many others, are indeed very signal instances of ornithological beauty. We shall, however, commence with the accipitrine tribes, those "lords of the lion heart and eagle eye," which are usually more remarkable for strength of body and power of wing, than for the adornment of a showy or fantastic plumage.*

The vulture tribe occupies the foremost place in our ornithological arrangements, and is represented

* Let us here note, that collections lately transmitted to this country indicate a stronger analogy between the ornithological pro-

in India by several species. Of these we shall mention only two. The Pondicherry vulture (*V. Ponticerianus*) equals the size of a large goose; its head and neck are naked and flesh-coloured; there is a white collar on the upper part of the breast, but the prevailing colour of the plumage is brown. The legs are yellow, and the bill nearly black. It occurs chiefly in the district from which it derives its specific name. Another species is

---

ductions of the north of India and those of Europe than has been previously supposed. Our present limits exclude those details into which we might otherwise be tempted to enter in illustration of this curious topic; but we consider ourselves as authorized to name the following species, from the Himmaleh range, as identical with those of Europe: viz. The lammergeyer (*Gypætus barbatus*), the cuckoo (*Cuculus canorus*), the rose-coloured ouzel (*Pastor roseus*), the hoopoe (*Upupa epops*), the stonechat (*Saxicola rubicola*), the whinchat (*S. rubetra*), the black redstart (*Sylvia tithys*), the common redstart (*Sylvia phœnicurus*), the missel-thrush (*Turdus viscivorus*), the starling (*Sturnus vulgaris*), the kingfisher (*Alcedo ispida*), the sandpiper (*Tringa hypoleucos*), the wryneck (*Yunx torquilla*), the red-legged crow (*Coracias graculus*), the common heron (*Ardea cinerea*), the francolin partridge (*Francolinus vulgaris*), the pin-tail duck (*Anas acuta*), the red-crested duck (*A. rufina*), the ferruginous duck (*A. rutila*), the common wild-duck (*A. boschas*), the teal (*A. crecca*), the gadwall (*A. strepera*), the tufted duck (*A. fuligula*), the garganey (*A. querquedula*), the castaneous duck (*A. nyroca*). Many of these I have verified by an attentive examination and comparison with European specimens, while others rest upon the authority of Mr Gould, who, as the author of the accurate and sumptuous "Century of Birds from the Himmalaya Mountains," has necessarily directed a strict attention to the ornithology of Northern India. The following enumeration contains the names of certain species, for the most part as yet neither figured nor described, which approach so closely to the European species, that we may regard them as their Asiatic representatives. Certain perceptible, though, in some instances, very feebly-defined characters of distinction, prevent our considering them as identically the same. In the mean time, however, we shall indicate them merely by their corresponding English names, viz. The kestrel, sparrow-hawk, turtle-dove, raven, green woodpecker, black and white woodpecker, nutcracker, red-legged partridge, jay, golden oriole, nuthatch, blackbird, bullfinch, greater titmouse, all our wagtails, creeper, redbreast, titlark, tree-lark, sparrow, tree-sparrow, and several others.

called the Indian vulture (*V. Indicus*). Its plumage is of a fulvous-brown, each feather being paler on the edges. Like most of its congeners, it is extremely voracious, and frequents alike the shores of the sea and the banks of rivers, preying on dead fish or any other putrid substance,—from the bloated corpses of the human species, which are not unfrequently seen floating down the sacred waters of the Ganges, to the more insignificant carcasses of the reptile race.

Among the numerous links, which serve to connect one tribe with another, may be mentioned that remarkable bird the lammergeyer, or bearded-vulture (*Gypætus barbatus* of Storr). The Greek term, which has been adopted as the generic appellation, literally signifies *vulture-eagle,* and appropriately expresses its intermediate position between the species which rank respectively under one or other branch of that compound designation. The beak is long, compressed, convex, rounded on its upper edge, and furnished with a thin cere, covered by thick rigid hairs directed forwards. But one of its most remarkable characters consists in a brush or tuft of bristly feathers, which depends from either side of the angle of the lower mandible. The legs are short, thick, and feathered to the toes.

Although the attitude of this bird is more upright than that of the preceding species, its half-expanded wings, and neck retracted when at rest, remind the spectator of the vulture tribe. It is, however, a comparatively rare and unsocial bird, and is esteemed a valuable capture by the naturalists even of those countries in which it most abounds. The geographical range seems very extensive. In Europe it haunts the steeps of the Pyrenean mountains, and the central Alps, from Piedmont to Dalmatia; as an African species it has been described by MM. Larrey and Savigny, as occurring in Egypt, and by Bruce (under the name of *niser*) as an inhabitant of Abyssinia; while in Asia it is known to spread its "sail-broad vans" over the vast steppes of the Siberian deserts. Professor Jameson has recently called our attention to the same species, transmitted to the Edinburgh Museum from the Himmaleh mountains. The lammergeyer is the largest, or at least the longest-winged, of all the European birds of prey.

Of the nobler and more active birds of the predacious order may be named the Pondicherry eagle (*Falco Ponticerianus*), a very elegant species, nearly equal in size to the jer-falcon. The head, neck, breast, and upper part of the abdomen, are white; the remainder of the plumage is reddish-chestnut colour; the wings are tipped with black; the bill and legs are yellow, and the cere is blue. This species inhabits many parts of India, and is esteemed sacred in Malabar. It is said to be extremely voracious, and feeds, like the kite, not on living prey alone, but on the remains of dead animals.

The finch-falcon of Bengal (*Falco cærulescens*) is the smallest of all the accipitrine birds. It was described and figured by Edwards, under the title of the "little black and orange-coloured Indian hawk." The upper parts of the plumage are of a fine bluish-black, with a few spots and bars of white. There is also an elongated spot of black on the side of the head or cheek beneath each eye. The under-plumage is white, more or less tinged with orange, especially in the female. This beautiful little bird, which scarcely exceeds the size of a sparrow, is a native of Bengal, Java, and the Isles of Sunda. Those from the continental parts of Asia are asserted to be larger than such as occur in the islands; and, like other species, they also vary in colour, according to age and sex. It is said by M. Temminck, to feed on insects; but, from the strongly-toothed bill and muscular limbs, there is reason to believe that it does not confine itself to such humble game, but also attacks and overpowers many species of the gentler tribes, equal or superior to itself in size, though inferior in strength and courage. Indeed, Dr Horsfield states, that it was described to him, in the eastern parts of Java, as displaying uncommon boldness in the pursuit of small birds.*

The alliance between the hawks and owls is extremely close both in structure and habits, although the same difference is observable between them as that which distinguishes butterflies from moths,—that the one tribe fly by day and the other by night. Hence the more solemn associations, which we connect with these inauspicious tribes:—

> "Perch'd on the roof, the bird of night complains
> In lengthen'd shrieks, and dire funereal strains."

One of the smallest and most beautiful of the Asiatic species, and the only one to which we shall here

* Zoological Researches.

allude, is the little hawk-owl of Ceylon (*Strix Indica* of Gmelin). The back is dusky; the wing-coverts are gray, with black lines; the breast is buff-coloured, with small arrow-shaped markings. It is not above seven inches long.

We shall now pass to the butcher-birds (genus *Lanius*), which, presenting as it were a connecting or intermediate link, have been arranged by some authors as the terminal group of the *accipitres*, by others as the commencement of the *passerine* order. Their bills are elongated and but slightly curved, and their feet and talons are comparatively feeble. Yet their dispositions are fierce and sanguinary, and their general habits exhibit a bold and contentious nature. The genus, as characterized by Linnæus, has undergone numerous divisions by later systematists; but, as most of these belong to Africa, New Holland, and the intra-tropical regions of the New World, they do not come within the scope of our present publication. India, however, also presents us with several species.

The fork-tailed shrike (*Lanius cœrulescens*, Linn.) is a native of Bengal, where it is called *fingah*. Its superior colour is glossy black, with reflections of purple and green. The tail-feathers are long and forked at the tips. The under-plumage is of a dull white, with a few dusky crescents on the thighs. This bird is named by the Indians the king of the crows, on account of its frequently pursuing these birds from place to place with a loud clamour, and pecking them on the back, till they take their departure from its accustomed haunts. The Malabar shrike (*L. Malabaricus*, Lath.) is another singular species described by M. Sonnerat. Its size is about that of the missel-thrush, and its general colour is deep-black glossed with blue. On the head rises a large tuft, consisting of many plumes of various length. The exterior feather on each side of the tail is greatly extended, and ends in an elongated oval web. This bird is said to occur particularly in the hilly regions of the kingdom of Arracan. Both these species belong to the division called *drongos* (genus *Edolius* of Cuvier). The jocose-shrike (*L. jocosus*, Linn.) resembles a lark in size. Its colours are brown above and dull-white below, with some crimson or rose-coloured plumes beneath the tail. The crown of the head is black, with a finely-fibred crest in the centre. From the corners of the bill on either side runs a black stripe; and there is a bright crimson spot beneath each eye. This bird is of a very lively disposition, and its manners are extremely amusing. It has been very generally considered as the celebrated *bulbul*, or Persian nightingale, so often commemorated in the writings of Hafiz and Sadi, and known in Persia under the name of *hazardasitaun*, or the "bird of a hundred songs." But it would seem that the term bulbul is applied to different species in different countries of the East; at least it is only in this way that we can explain the discrepancies observable in the accounts of travellers. It appears however certain, that the present species is taught to combat with its kind by the natives of Bengal. It is also trained up by the young Indians to execute commissions of gallantry; and, at a signal given by the lover, will seize and carry off in the most dexterous manner, and convey to its expectant master, the small gold ornament usually worn on the forehead by the Indian females. So quick is its eye, and so rapid are its evolutionary movements, that it will follow the descent of a ring down a deep draw-well, and catch it in its fall before it has reached the surface of the water. The Persian poets have represented the bulbul as enamoured of the rose, and as grieved by its destruction or decay.

Among the more noted of the Indian species we must not omit to mention the mina-bird or grakle (*Gracula religiosa*, Linn.). The great Swedish na turalist appears to have confounded two species under a single name, and considerable uncertainty still pervades their history. The Indian species is somewhat larger than a blackbird. Its plumage is of a rich silky black, with a white spot about the central edge of the wing. The bill and feet are yellow, and a peculiar fleshy appendage or caruncle stretches from the side of the face, and behind each eye to the back of the head. This bird is easily tamed, and of very familiar manners in the domestic state. It is perhaps the most accomplished linguist of all the feathered tribes, and may be taught to pronounce long sentences in the most clear and articulate manner. It is consequently held in the highest esteem by the natives, and is not unfrequently brought alive to European countries, although the moral purity of the English tongue is not always exhibited by the result of its maritime education. "It imitates," says Willoughby, "man's voice much more accurately than a parrot, so that oftentimes it is troublesome with its prattle." The food of the mina in a state of nature is said to consist both of fruits and insects. In this country it is very fond of grapes and cherries.

The genus *Gracula,* as restricted by the Baron Cuvier, contains some interesting species, the general aspect of which will be more clearly comprehended by our readers when we mention as a close ally that rare and beautiful British bird the rose-coloured ousel. The *Paradisea tristis* of Linnæus, or the paradise-grakle of Latham, pertains to this genus. It is correctly named *Gracula gryllivora* by Daudin, and is remarkable, as its name implies, for its destruction of locusts. In illustration of its history we abridge the following curious particulars from Buffon:—The Island of Bourbon, where this species was formerly unknown, was at one time overrun to an alarming extent by locusts, which had been introduced from Madagascar. The governor-general and the intendant of the island, alarmed at the desolation which was taking place, deliberated on the means of extirpating the nuisance, and with that view they introduced several pairs of the paradise-grakle from India. The plan promised to be successful; but unfortunately some of the colonists observing the birds eagerly thrusting their bills into the soil of the newly-sown fields, imagined they were in quest of grain, and spread a report that the grakles, so far from proving beneficial, were likely to be highly detrimental to the country. The case was argued in due form. It was stated on the part of the birds that they ransacked the new-ploughed grounds not for grain but insects;—but the opposite view prevailed, and two hours after the edict of proscription had been pronounced against them, not a living individual was to be found in the island. But a speedy repentance followed this hasty execution; the locusts regained their ascendency, and becoming ere long more injurious than ever, the grakles were again introduced, and after an absence of nearly eight years, were received by the inhabitants with transports of joy. Their preservation and extension now became an affair of state, laws were enacted in their favour, the physicians, either in truth or policy, declared their flesh unwholesome, and the locusts quickly disappeared. But an opposite inconvenience is said to have since arisen. The birds, having prodigiously increased in numbers, and being no longer adequately sustained by insect food, have had recourse to grapes, dates, and mulberries, and have even proceeded to scratch up rice, maize, wheat, beans, and other useful produce; they enter the pigeon-houses and attack the eggs and young;—and thus, after destroying the destroyer, they have themselves become a greater pestilence than that which they extirpated. There is probably, however, some exaggeration in this account; because M. Duplessin, who resided several years on the island, has given it as his opinion that the paradise-grakle might be advantageously introduced into Spain, which, from its proximity to Africa, is not unfrequently ravaged by the locust hordes. He adds, that so far from having become a nuisance in the Isle of Bourbon the laws for its preservation are still in force.* We may mention that this species is of the same lively and imitative disposition as the mina-bird, and is easily taught to speak. When kept near a farm-yard, or other assemblage of domesticated creatures, it spontaneously acquires

* Shaw's General Zoology, vol. vii. p. 457.

the various cries of dogs, ducks, geese, sheep, pigs, and poultry.

The manners of this genus in general resemble those of the starling. They fly in troops, searching for insect prey; their habits are familiar, their docility remarkable, and their powers of imitation almost unparalleled. The only other species which we shall mention is the pagoda-thrush, so called from its frequent occurrence among the pagodas of Malabar and Coromandel. It is frequently kept caged for the sake of its song.*

That division of the great Linnæan genus *Certhia*, which includes the soui-mangoes, or honey-eaters (genus *Cinnyris*, Cuvier), is widely dispersed over all the southern regions of the old continent, and seems in those countries to represent the beautiful humming-birds of the Western World. Indeed these tribes greatly resemble each other both in form and habits. The soui-mangoes are subject to a double moult, which occasions a considerable diversity in the plumage, even of the same species, according to the season of the year; and hence our knowledge of this sumptuous family, though voluminous, is probably not as yet remarkable for its accuracy. Several splendid works, however, have been devoted, either in whole or in part, to their illustration.† The nuptial plumage is remarkable for its golden lustre, and the richness and variety of its innumerable hues; but after the termination of the breeding-

* Sonnerat, Voyage aux Indes.

† Le Vaillant, Hist. Nat. des Oiseaux d'Afrique, five vols. in 4to, Paris, 1799, and subsequent years. Audubert, Oiseaux dorés où à reflets métalliques, two vols. in folio, Paris, 1802. A continuation of this work has been published by M. Vieillot.

season, a much more humble garb is assumed, and many a *bizarre* appearance is presented by the intermediate links of that changeable costume which connects the holiday-suit of spring with the more quaker-like attire of autumn. Hence the difficulty of distinguishing between a specific difference and an individual variation, especially where foreign species are concerned; for in such instances we have seldom a prolonged opportunity of verifying our observations on external characters by an examination of natural habits and instinctive modes of life. Yet it is only by ascertaining the conformity presented by all these circumstances in a variety of individuals, that we are enabled to trace out the exact limits of specific identity. We shall not here enter into further details.

The next tribe which deserves our notice is that of the kingfishers. These are also distributed over a great portion of the earth's surface, though they are of rarer occurrence in America than in the ancient continents. In Europe, indeed, we have only a single species (unless the *Alcedo Smyrnensis* occasionally visits the Grecian shores and those of the Mediterranean Islands), but the umbrageous rivers of India are beautified more abundantly by their azure hues. The Asiatic kingfisher (*Alcedo Asiatica* of Swainson)* bears a strong resemblance to the European species, but may be distinguished on closer inspection and comparison by its smaller size, and the somewhat crested form of the occipital plumes. It inhabits the hottest parts of Continental

* Zoological Illustrations, first series, plate 50.

India, as well as the great Asiatic Islands; thus differing from the European species, which is known to brave the cold even of a Siberian winter, and, although not unfrequent along the banks of the comparatively tranquil streams of England, likewise haunts the snow-descended waters of the Alpine regions. Hence its appropriate introduction to a fine apostrophe by a modern poet,—

> "Not to thee,
> O wild and desert stream! belongs this tale.
> Gloomy and dark art thou,—the crowded firs
> Tower from thy shores, and stretch across thy bed,
> Making thee doleful as a cavern-well:—
> Save where the shy kingfishers build their nest
> On thy steep banks, no loves hast thou, wild stream!"

The last genus of the great passerine order is that called *Buceros,* which includes the calaos or hornbills. These birds are remarkable for their enormous dentated beaks, frequently surmounted by an additional horny structure, which bestows on them a very striking and peculiar physiognomy. They resemble the toucans in their heads; their port and general habits assimilate to those of crows, while their feet are somewhat analogous to those of the kingfishers. The hornbills exhibit an awkward and uncommon aspect while in the act of flying, in consequence of the great size of their beaks and lengthened tails, and altogether their appearance is extremely uncouth. Perhaps one of the most singular features in their economy, is the fact of their feeding greedily and without injury on the seeds of *nux vomica.*

A large and remarkable species of this genus has been recently described by Mr Hodgson. It measures four feet five inches from tip to tip of the wings, and is three feet six inches long, from bill to tail inclusive. The bill is eight inches long, and the tail one foot five inches. Its body exceeds that of the largest raven, but is very lank and incompact. The general colour is black, with a white pointed tail, and a patch of the same colour on the wings. It is often difficult to ascertain the natural habits of a shy and rare species; but it is believed that the bird in question feeds chiefly on fruits, although when pressed by hunger it will also seize upon reptiles. The bill is far less formidable than it would appear to be, and the claws are extremely blunt, from which it may be inferred that its habits are not raptorial, even in the meanest sense; and its freedom from any offensive odour, as well as the excellence of its flesh, which is much esteemed by the mountaineers as an article of food, go far to prove that its habits are almost entirely frugivorous. Mr Hodgson, however, observes, that in the domestic state it will eat meat either dressed or raw, and with apparent relish. The specimen in question was fed principally on boiled rice mixed with ghee, and made up into large balls. It was never observed to take any water. The throat is very wide, and the swallowing powers consequently great. Whatever is offered to it is first worked about between the huge mandibles, and then gulped entire. Should the morsel swallowed be so large as to produce any feeling of discomfort, it is immediately disgorged, and re-swallowed after having undergone a little additional mastication in the bill.*

* Transactions of the Physical Class of the Asiatic Society of Bengal, part i. p. 178.

Adopting, as we have hitherto done, the leading divisions of the system expounded by Baron Cuvier, the next order is that of the *Scansorial* birds or climbers, of which one of the most characteristic external marks consists in the structure and position of the toes, which are usually placed two before and two behind. From this result considerable strength and tenacity of grasp, which enable the species so constituted to adhere to the bark of trees, however vertical their direction, and even in some cases to run along the lower surface of horizontal branches with as much ease and safety as others execute such ordinary movements as seem less opposed to the laws of gravitation. It is no doubt true, that many species, such as the cuckoo, in which the toes are in pairs, or yoke-footed as M. Temminck has termed it, do not climb; while it is equally true, that several other species (such as the creeper, *C. familiaris*), which are constant and accomplished climbers, are yet excluded from this order on account of the structure of their feet; and that, consequently, the denomination cannot be applied in its most rigorous sense, as alike characteristic and inclusive. The ordinal characters, considered in their generality, are in fact seldom so precise and natural as to admit of no exceptions; and it is questionable whether a title should be immediately changed upon the discovery of every species which may not coincide with its most rigorous interpretation. It is not very easy, indeed, to understand how this alteration can in every case be effected, merely upon the consideration of a single character, without producing greater inconveniences than those which it is intended to obviate. In the zygodactylous genus *Galbula*, for example, we have a three-toed species; and a similar anomaly occurs among the woodpeckers. In like manner, the order *Alcyones* of Temminck, which is characterized by its founder as having three toes before, united at their bases after a certain fashion, and one behind, contains a species which possesses only three toes in all, and which would therefore find some difficulty in complying with the regulation of the ordinal character. In short, what we mean to express is, that it may reasonably be doubted whether a mere change in the title of an order, which certainly so far tends to diminish that clearness of mutual intelligence which it is so desirable to establish and maintain in the scientific intercourse of different peoples, is productive of any decided advantage to the subject in hand, especially when it can easily be demonstrated that the characters of that order, by whatever name it may be known, are left not less vague than heretofore.

We may remark, that the bill of the scansorial tribe varies so greatly in the different genera, from the straight, lengthened, angular mandibles of the woodpeckers, to the deep, curved, compressed organ of the parrots, that we must omit all consideration of it in the ordinal characters. Its form may, however, be studied with great advantage in relation to the sections and other minor divisions. The species are, with few exceptions, inhabitants of the forests, and usually build their nests in the hollows of old trees. Their powers of flight are not remarkable. The European genera are almost entirely insectivorous: the parrot family feed on fruits; the toucans exhibit a tendency to the carnivorous habits of the accipitrine tribes; while other genera of the order enjoy a mingled or miscellaneous diet.

If our present space in any measure corresponded with the rich abundance of our materials, we could dilate with pleasure on many magnificent examples of the scansorial order peculiar to, or chiefly characteristic of, the Indian regions. But, in order to admit of our embracing a greater extent of the science in general, we must necessarily curtail our more detailed observations in relation to the history and attributes of particular tribes.

The woodpeckers (genus *Picus*, Linn.), of which we have six or seven well-known examples in Europe, seem distributed over the surface of the whole earth, with the exception of New Holland. In whatever countries they occur, they are characterized by strong affinities of form and colour, and constitute one of the most natural and well-defined groups with which we are acquainted. Buffon has drawn a melting picture of the miseries of a woodpecker's life. According to the views of the eloquent, but eccentric, and sometimes inconsistent Frenchman, no bird which earns its subsistence by spoil leads a life of such painful labour. Nature appears to have condemned it to incessant toil. While others freely employ their courage or address, and either glide along on fearless and rapid wing, or lurk insidiously in closer ambush, the woodpecker is constrained to drag on a miserable existence, in boring through the scaly bark and the unyielding fibres of the hardest trees. Necessity suffers no intermission of its labours, nor any interval of sound repose. Even the darkness of the night brings no solace to its sufferings, for the nocturnal hours are spent in the same painful posture as those of day. It never shares in the joyous sports of the other inhabitants of the forests, and so far from joining in their glad responses, it rather deepens the sadness of the woodland glades by its wild and melancholy cries. Its movements are quick, its gestures full of inquietude, and it seems to shun the society even of its own kind.

Such is a sketch of Buffon's more lengthened picture. Let us console ourselves by an inspection of another and more pleasing portrait. "No sooner," says Mr Audubon, "has spring called them (the golden-winged woodpeckers) to the pleasant duty of making love, as it is called, than their voice, which by the way is not at all disagreeable to the ear of man, is heard from the tops of high decayed trees, proclaiming with delight the opening of the welcome season. Their note at this period is merriment itself, as it imitates a prolonged and jovial laugh, heard at a considerable distance. Several males pursue a female, reach her, and to prove the force and truth of their love bow their heads, spread their tails, and move sideways, backwards and forwards, performing such antics as might induce any one witnessing them, if not of a most morose temper, to join his laugh to theirs. The female flies to another tree, where she is closely followed by one, two, or even half-a-dozen of these gay suitors, and where again the same ceremonies are gone through. No fightings occur, no jealousies exist among these beaux, until a marked preference is shown to some individual, when the rejected proceed in search of another female. In this manner all the golden-winged woodpeckers are soon happily mated. Each pair immediately proceed to excavate the trunk of a tree, and finish a hole in it sufficient to contain themselves and their young. They both work with great industry, and apparent pleasure. Should the male, for instance, be employed, the female is close to him, and congratulates him on the removal of every chip which his bill sends through the air. While he rests he appears to be speaking to her on the most tender subjects, and when fatigued is at once assisted by her. In this manner, by the alternate exertions of each, the hole is dug and finished. They caress each other on the branches, climb about and around the tree with apparent delight, rattle with their bill against the tops of the dead branches, chase all their cousins the red-heads, defy the purple-grakles to enter their nest, feed plentifully on ants, beetles, and larvæ, cackling at intervals, and ere two weeks have elapsed, the female lays either four or six eggs, the whiteness or transparency of which are doubtless the delight of her heart. If to raise a numerous progeny may contribute to happiness, these woodpeckers may be happy enough, for they have two broods each season. Even in confinement the golden-winged woodpecker never suffers its naturally lively spirit to droop. It feeds well, and by way of amusement will continue to destroy as much furniture in a day as can well be mended by a different kind of workman in two. Therefore, kind reader, do not any longer believe that woodpeckers, I mean those of America, are such stupid, forlorn, dejected, and unprovided-for beings, as they have hitherto been represented."*

* Ornithological Biography, or an Account of the Habits of the Birds of the United States of America. By John James Audubon, F.R.S.L. and E., &c., vol. i. p. 191.

In regard to the Indian woodpeckers, we shall merely mention that they inhabit a great extent of country, from the southern point of the Peninsula to the sombre forests of the Himmaleh mountains. From the latter locality, that fine species, the *Picus squamatus*, has been lately transmitted to the Edinburgh Museum. It is figured by Mr Gould.*

The limited genus *Yunx*, which contains the European wryneck, is remarkable for its wide distribution. Though the species are few in number, one or other of them occurs in Europe, Asia, Africa, and America, and the one above named (*Yunx torquilla*), a rare bird in Britain, is well known in the northern parts of India.

The magnificent family of the parrots is the last of the scansorial order to which we shall here allude. Abundant in almost every region of the torrid zone, and in the New World extending from the shores of the Ohio to the Straits of Magellan, this tribe, though presenting considerable differences of structure, is yet strongly marked by many characters common to all the species. The strong, hard, curved, solid bills, surrounded at the base by a membrane in which the nostrils are perforated,—the thick, rounded, fleshy tongue,—the inferior larynx of a complicated structure, and provided on each side with peculiar muscles,—the splendid plumage, exhibiting every imaginable hue,—and the extremely imitative and very garrulous habits of these birds, distinguish them from every other tribe. The genus *Psittacus* of Linnæus forms a vast assemblage of

* A Century of Birds from the Himmalaya Mountains, part 1.

species from every country of the world, excepting the comparatively cold and cloudy clime of Europe, and has been partitioned into numerous sections or sub-genera by modern observers.*

The most anciently known of the parrot race belong to the genus *Palæornis* of Mr Vigors. To this section pertain the Alexandrine parrakeet, and others of the long-tailed species, distinguished by their elegance of form, their ruby-coloured beaks, their semicircled necks, and the rich *verdure* of their plumage. The one above named is native to India and Ceylon, and derives its designation from the fact, real or supposed, of its having been first transported from Asiatic countries by Alexander the Great. The most distinguishing characters of the species consist in the broad black patch which, occupying the fore-part of the throat, extends laterally in two narrow processes on each side of the neck; a black line extends from the base of the beak to the eyes; and there is a deep purplish-red patch at the base of the wings. Its bill is larger than that of the rose-coloured parrakeet (*Palæornis torquatus*), which, however, in general it greatly resembles. It is of rarer occurrence than the last-named species, and is not so easily domesticated. It may, however, be taught to speak with tolerable distinctness. The

* For representations of these gorgeous birds, see Vaillant's Histoire Naturelle des Perroquets, Swainson's Zoological Illustrations, Temminck's Planches Coloriées, and Illustrations of the Family of the Psittacidæ by E. Lear. Consult also, for a knowledge of the subdivisions, Kuhl's Monagraph of the Genus in the tenth volume of the Nova Act. Acad. Nat. Cur., Observations on the Psittacidæ by Mr Vigors in the second volume of the Zoological Journal, a paper by that accomplished ornithologist, in conjunction with Dr Horsfield, in the fifteenth volume of the Linnæan Transactions, and volume fourteenth, part first, of Shaw's General Zoology, as continued by Mr Stevens.

P. torquatus is widely spread over India, and as far to the eastward as Manilla. It appears indeed to be identical with another species extremely abundant on the African coasts, and well known in France under the title of *Perruche de Senegal.* In as far as any conclusion can be drawn from the vague and brief descriptions handed down by ancient writers, it would appear that the present species was, as it still continues to be, more frequent in the days of antiquity than any of its congeners. No allusion is made to those specific marks by which the Alexandrine parrakeet is so clearly distinguished, and the general sketch applies very closely to the rose-necked kind. "That the species before us," says Mr Bennet, "was extensively known, and held in high estimation on account of the brilliancy of its plumage, the docility of its manners, and its imitative powers of voice, is proved by innumerable passages in the classical writers of Rome, more especially from the earliest times of the empire, to a very late period of its annals."*

The singular poem of "Speake-parrot," written by John Skelton, an English poet who flourished in the time of Henry VIII., no doubt alluded to the *P. torquatus.*

"My name is parrot, a bird of paradise,
By nature deuised of a wondrous kynd,
Dienteli dieted with diuers delicate spice,
Tyl Euphrates that floud driueth me into Inde,
Where men of that countrey bi fortune me find,
And send me to great Ladyes of estate,
Then parrot must haue an almon or a date.

"A cage curiously caruen, with siluer pin,
Properly painted, to be my couertowre,

* Zoological Gardens, vol. ii. p. 96.

A myrror of glasse, that I may lok therin;
There maidens ful mekely with many a diuers flour
Freshly they dresse, and make swete my bowre,
With, speak parrot, I prai you, ful courteously thei say,
Parrot is a goodly bird, a pretty popagey.

"With my beeke bent, my little wanton eye,
My feders freshe, as is the emeraude grene,
About my necke a circulet, like the ryche rubye,
My lyttle legges, my fete both nete and cleane,
I am a minion to waite upon the quene;
My proper parrot, my lyttle pretty foole,
With ladies I learne, and go with them to scole."

Among the more remarkable kinds are those furnished with cylindrical, elongated, tubular tongues.* Their cheeks are naked, and their upper mandible greatly developed. The two species best known are the *Psittacus gigas* of Shaw, sometimes called the giant-cockatoo, and the *Psittacus goliath* of Kuhl. These now form the genus *Microglossum*. The giant-cockatoo was first described and figured by Edwards, from a drawing taken from the living bird in the Island of Ceylon. Both species, however, are now said to be derived from the Papuan Islands, which lie beyond the bounds of our domain.

We have next to present a brief sketch of the *gallinaceous* order, which is represented in India by several species of importance.

The common peacock (*Pavo cristatus*, Linn.), so much admired for the surpassing splendour of its plumage, and now so familiarly known as a domestic bird, though it has been reduced to servitude for some thousand years, still occurs in the wild state in the forests of Indostan, as well as in Japan and

* The structure of the tongue in this limited section is probably not accurately known. If not elongated and tubular, it is at least cup-shaped at the extremity, and supported on a cylindrical stalk.

other parts of Southern Asia. Its earliest record is contained in the sacred writings :—" For the king's ships went to Tarshish with the servants of Huram: every three years once came the ships of Tarshish, bringing gold, and silver, ivory, and apes, and peacocks."* The introduction of this bird to the western and northern quarters of Europe has never been clearly traced ; but every step of its progress has no doubt been owing rather to the art of man than the instinct of nature. Its *natural* tendency would in fact have been to return to the countries from whence it came,—to seek again the perpetual sunshine and ever-verdant forests of Asia, the banks

" Of Ganges or Hydaspes, Indian streams."

It appears to have been unknown even in Greece during the early manhood of Alexander the Great, by whom it is said to have been first observed with no less wonder than delight in the course of his southern expedition, and to have been immediately transmitted to his native country. It must, however, have multiplied rapidly after its arrival, as Aristotle, who died within a year or two after " the great Emathian conqueror," mentions the peacock as a well-known bird. The Greeks were satisfied with the delight afforded to the eye, while contemplating its brilliant colours, and most graceful form, —" being so majestical, they would not offer it even the show of violence ;" and it was left to the more luxurious Romans, not only to serve it entire on the table of Hortensius, but to pamper the diseased appetite, or minister to the inordinate extravagance of Heliogabalus, by presenting enormous dishes of the

* 2 Chronicles, ix. 21.

brains alone. In more modern times, and during the progress of nautical discovery and commercial intercourse by which these were distinguished, the peacock has been transported to both the Americas, to many points along the African shores, and to numerous islands of the West Indies. A white variety has also sprung up in Europe, more frequent in northern than in southern kingdoms, which is not alluded to by ancient writers, and has probably resulted from the influence of a colder temperature, by which a natural tendency to albinism appears to be produced in many species of the feathered race.

There are only two species of this genus,—the one above alluded to, which is too well known to require description, and the Javanese peacock (*Pavo Javanicus* of Horsfield), of which we have figured both the adult and young, under the name of Aldrovandine-peacock, from the specimens in the Edinburgh Museum.*

It occurs in Japan, Java, and other eastern and southern regions of Asia. It is chiefly to be distinguished from the common kind by the form and structure of the feathers which compose the crest, and which are well barbed throughout their whole extent, or somewhat lance-shaped, instead of presenting little more than terminal expansions.

Another singular bird of the gallinaceous order, which by some authors has been classed with the peacocks, is the polyplectron, so called from the circumstance of its tarsi being armed with several spurs. It is the peacock-pheasant of Edwards' Gleanings and the Iris and Thibet pheasants of Latham's Ge-

* Wilson's Illustrations of Zoology, vol. i. plates 14 and 15.

neral Synopsis. This bird is extremely beautiful, a great proportion of its plumage being ornamented by very brilliant spots of greenish-blue, changing with the light to gold and purple; these spots are surrounded by a circle of black, and then by another of yellowish-white, and a spot of the latter colour terminates the tip of every plume. The male is about the size of the golden-pheasant. The plumage of the female is less brilliant, and her tail is shorter. The young birds are entirely of an earthy-gray, with large spots, and small lines of a brown colour. After the first moult the plumage becomes less irregular, and the position of the spots on the wings and tail becomes visible; the second moult produces a more determinate distribution of the colours, and the feathers begin to be distinguished by a fine golden-blue tint, with green reflections. It is not, however, till after the third change, which occurs about the completion of the second year, that the colours are manifested in their full perfection. The species is native to the mountains of Thibet. It is said to occur also in China. It is of easy domestication, and is not remarkable for shyness even in a state of nature.

The common cock and hen (*Gallus domesticus*) next demand a brief record. Of the numerous benefits which the goodness of Providence has enabled us to derive from the feathered race, there is probably none which surpasses in extent and utility the domestication of these most familiar birds. So ancient, however, has been the subservience of the species to the human race, that no authentic traditionary traces now remain of its original introduction to any of the more ancient kingdoms of the earth, and its existence under the guardianship of man seems indeed coeval with the most antique records. It may be regarded as one of those particular and providential gifts which, like the faithful and accommodating dog, may be said to have joined its fortunes at an early period of the world with those of the first families of the human race,—to have followed man in his wonderful and far-spread migrations,—and, adapting its constitution with facility to the diversified circumstances of clime and country which these migrations produced, to have finally lost, in consequence of such plastic nature, almost all resemblance to the source from which it sprung. For some thousand years the observers of nature were ignorant of any wild species, which, even in a remote degree, resembled any variety of the domestic breed; and from the era of Herodotus to that of Sonnerat, the domestic cock and hen might have been regarded as birds, the living analogues of which were no longer known to exist in a natural and unsubdued condition.

In consequence of the remote obscurity in which the subject is thus involved, few points in natural history have occasioned more inconclusive speculation, or are even now more difficult to determine with precision, than the source from which we primarily derived the different races of our domestic poultry. That they came originally from Persia has been inferred from this among other circumstances, that Aristophanes calls the cock "the Persian bird." Such an origin is, however, improbable, when we consider that the researches of modern travellers, and of all who have visited that country since the revival of learning, have failed to discover there any species of wild poultry; and although its ornithology is not yet known in detail, especially as regards the smaller species, that so conspicuous a feature in its natural history as the existence of the bird in question should have escaped the notice of recent inquirers is by no means likely. In fact no gallinaceous bird exists in Persia more nearly allied to the genus *Gallus* than a species of Lophophorus.* If, however, it is merely meant that the Greeks, during the intercourse, hostile or otherwise, which existed between them and the Persian nation, may have obtained a breed, previously domesticated, from that country, the appellation is less objectionable,—for it is known, that in a domestic state poultry have existed in Persia from a very remote antiquity.

It may be mentioned, as a curious fact illustrating the extensive distribution of these "household birds," that when the South Sea Islands were first visited by Captain Cook, they were found well-stocked with poultry; and the more recent, as well as more ample narratives of the missionaries, have confirmed the statements of the great navigator regarding the practice of cock-fighting in Otaheite and other islands of Polynesia.†

In regard, however, to the origin of our domestic poultry, the first approximation to the truth (and it can be regarded as nothing more) resulted from the discovery by Sonnerat, of a species of *wild* poultry, native to the mountains of the Ghauts in

---

* Macneill's Lophophorus (*Loph. Nigelli* of Jardine and Selby, Illust. of Orn. pl. 76), so called in honour of Dr Macneill, lately physician to the English embassy at the Persian court, and now our resident at Bushire. The species, of which the male is not yet known, was first transmitted to Europe by that gentleman.

† See more particularly Mr Ellis' Polynesian Researches.

India. This is the *Gallus Sonneratii* of systematic naturalists, better known to the British residents under the now familiar name of jungle-cock. But our knowledge of gallinaceous birds has so greatly increased during recent years, and so many additional species have been discovered, that we are able to proceed upon much more secure grounds in our present reasoning than were the naturalists of the preceding century. The jungle-cock is not only no longer the only claimant to the honour of having so greatly benefited the human race, but other species have become known which bear a resemblance so much closer to certain standard varieties among the domestic breeds, that his claims may fairly be considered as altogether set aside. In fact, several characters of the jungle-cock have never been traced in any of the domestic varieties, and many of these latter present features which, if not incompatible with, at least bear no resemblance to, any of the attributes of the supposed original.*

As the species which we consider as more justly entitled than the jungle-cock to be regarded as the natural stock of our domestic breeds occur chiefly in the great eastern islands, or at least have not been as yet ascertained to exist within our prescribed boundaries, we shall not enter into any details of their history or habits.† But as the jungle-cock, from its Indian locality, is a legitimate subject of

* For a more ample exposition of this subject, consult a paper "On the Origin of Domestic Poultry," in the 6th volume of the Memoirs of the Wernerian Society, p. 402.

† We allude more particularly to the Jago-cock of Sumatra (*Gallus giganteus*), and to another species discovered some years ago by M. Leschenault in the Island of Java, and which is called by the natives *ayam bankiva.*—See M. Temminck's *Histoire des Gallinacès.*

disquisition, we may add another circumstance which we consider as very decisive against its alleged claims. The native tribes of Indians, inhabiting the districts where the jungle-cock abounds, rear a breed of poultry which differs as much from the supposed original as our own, and which never intermingles with the forest-brood. Perhaps nothing points out the distinction of species more strongly than this fact, of their not seeking each other's society, when we know that even the pheasant, a bird now regarded as pertaining to a different genus, is frequently known to breed with the domestic hen.

The most remarkable character of the jungle-cock consists in the horny expansions of the central portion of the feathers of the neck and wing-coverts. Its best-known localities are among the mountains of the Ghauts in Indostan.

The genus *Lophophorus* contains several splendid species, of which the bird named the Impeyan-pheasant by Latham (*Loph. refulgens* of Temminck) is one of the most remarkable. The head is ornamented by a fine crest. The feathers of the neck are long and loose, like the hackles of a cock. The colours of the plumage are so exceedingly brilliant from their metallic lustre, and so variable according to the direction of the light or the position of the spectator, that they cannot be expressed by words; and even the skill of the most accomplished painter would in vain attempt to equal the bright original. Purple, and green, and gold, are the prevailing hues. The female is smaller than the male, and her plumage is destitute of metallic splendour. These birds inhabit the mountains in the northern parts of Indostan. Though naturally wild, they are said to submit to confinement with a tolerable degree of subservience. Lady Impey endeavoured to transport them alive to England, but they died on the passage. Were the attempt repeated, it would probably ere long succeed; for they endure cold well, although impatient of extreme heat. The male was never observed to crow, but uttered a strong hoarse cackle, resembling that of a pheasant. This fine species is named by the natives *monaul,* a term which we understand to signify the *bird of gold.* Another species, native to the hills of Almorah, has been more recently described by General Hardwicke.*

A singular genus of the gallinaceous order is that constituted by the horned-pheasant (*Phasianus satyra* of Vieillot). It is now named *Tragopan* by Baron Cuvier; and contains, in addition to the species just mentioned, another nearly-allied and equally gorgeous bird (figured by Mr Gould under the title of *Tragopan Hastingsii*), of which some beautiful specimens, including the adult male, not previously known to naturalists, were lately received at the Edinburgh Museum by Professor Jameson. Both species come from the Nepaul country.

Several species of the quail and partridge tribes inhabit India; but as there is nothing very marked or peculiar in their history or habits, we shall merely mention the fact of their occurrence.

The bustard tribe (genus *Otis,* Linn.) forms in some respects a connecting link between the gallinaceous birds and those called *Grallæ* or waders,

* Linn. Trans., vol. xv.

and they have accordingly been located in either division according to the peculiar views of different authors. Of the Indian species we shall notice only the Passarage bustard (*Otis aurita* of Latham), which is figured in Mr Forbes' Oriental Memoirs under the erroneous name of ruffed-bustard, or *Otis houbara*. It is of comparatively rare occurrence, and like its congeners is of a wild disposition, inhabiting plains and open districts. It is highly esteemed on account of the delicacy and fine flavour of its flesh, and consequently bears a high price in the Indian markets. In some districts it is called the black florikan.*

The golden plover (*Charadrius pluvialis*) has been supposed to exist in India. But the species most frequently found there, though very closely allied, does not seem entirely identical with the European kind. It is the yellow-lipped plover (*Charadrius xanthocheilus*) of Wagler.

Of the couriers (genus *Cursorius*) at least two species inhabit Asia, viz. the Coromandel courier (*C. Asiaticus*), figured on the 22d plate of our "Illustrations of Zoology," and the so-called European species (*C. isabellinus* of Meyer) which Professor Jameson lately received from the north of India.†

The gigantic stork (*Ardea dubia* of Gmelin, *Ci-*

---

* Both sexes of the eared-bustard are correctly figured by Sir Wm. Jardine and Mr Selby in their Illustrations of Ornithology. —See plates 40 and 92 of that work. Two other species (*Otis Himalayanus* and *Otis nigriceps*) are figured by Mr Gould.

† This species also occurs over a considerable extent of the African continent, and sometimes makes its way as far north as the temperate parts of Europe. It was once shot near St Albans in Kent. The specimen alluded to is now, we believe, in the British Museum, and is said to have been purchased by Mr Donovan, at the time of the Leverian sale, for eighty-three guineas.

conia argala, Vigors) is a species well known in India, where it performs the services of a scavenger, and is consequently protected even in the streets of populous cities. Its habits appear to be somewhat migratory. It arrives in Bengal about the commencement of the rainy season, and is useful in clearing the country of snakes and other reptiles, as well as of offal. It is a most voracious creature, and will devour as much at a single meal as would satisfy four hungry men. The bill is of enormous size, and the bird itself measures from five to seven feet in length, including the legs.*

The genus *Anastomus*, of which the Pondicherry and Coromandel herons of Latham may serve as examples, is peculiar to the East Indies. These birds present a remarkable peculiarity in the structure of their bills. The mandibles touch each other only at their points and bases, thus leaving an open gaping space in the centre. The last-named species is common on the banks of the Ganges and other Indian rivers, and frequents the Coromandel coast during the months of September, October, and November, feeding on fish and reptiles.

Of Indian birds allied to the snipe and woodcock kind we shall mention no more than the Bengal rynchæa, of which the synonymes seem very vaguely applied in books of natural history, probably in consequence of the strong resemblance which subsists between it, the Cape snipe (*Scolopax Capensis*, Gmelin), and other species by which the genus is at present constituted.

We have now arrived at the last great division

* For a lucid account of the differences between the species above named and the African *Marabou*, see Zool. Gar., vol. ii. p. 273.

of the class of birds, viz. the *Palmipedes*, or web-footed order. We formerly observed in our sketches of African Zoology,* that these tribes are of wandering habits, and that being possessed, in addition to great power of wing, of the faculty of resting on the water, we can scarcely place any limits to the extent of their migratory movements. They thus become more cosmopolite than many of the other groups, and are therefore less entitled to our attention during an exposition of the peculiar and more characteristic features of a particular country. For this reason a briefer notice will suffice. In truth, we have been already induced, by the overflowing riches of Indian ornithology, to extend and multiply our notices of many genera beyond such limits as are consistent with a due and proportional consideration of the remaining classes of the animal kingdom. We must therefore present our future observations with greater brevity.

The pearly-plumaged gulls and buoyant terns are found along the Indian shores, as elsewhere. Of the latter tribe we shall specify only a single example, that of the black-bellied tern (*Sterna melanogaster*, Temminck,†) of which the head, abdomen, and inferior coverts of the wings, are black, while the cheeks, throat, wings, and tail, are of a delicate ash-colour. It inhabits Ceylon and Continental India.

Among the Indian *Anatidæ* may be mentioned the black-backed goose (*Anser melanotos*,‡) which measures nearly three feet in length. The head and half of the neck are white, spotted and streaked with black; the rest of the neck and the under parts

* Edinburgh Cabinet Library, No 2, p. 466.

† Planches Col., 434.

‡ Zool. Ind., xxi. pl. 11.

of the plumage are white, with a tinge of gray upon the sides; the back, wings, and tail, are black, glossed with green and purplish reflections, for which reason it was named *l'oie bronzée* by Buffon. It is common in Ceylon, and also occurs both along the Coromandel coast and on the shores of the Ganges. The barred-headed goose (*Anser Indica*) occurs in the southern and central parts of Indostan during what may be called the winter-months. It is very destructive to corn; and is supposed to migrate from Thibet or other northern quarters, to which it again departs as the summer approaches. Of the duck tribe the spotted-billed wigeon (*Anas pæcilorhyncha,* Gmel.) may serve as an example. The beak is long and black, and is distinguished by a red spot on each side at the base. This species inhabits Ceylon. The pink-headed pochard (*Anas caryophyllacea,* Lath.) inhabits various parts of India. The bill, head, and upper portion of the neck, are of a fine pink colour. This bird is seldom seen in flocks. The female scarcely differs from the male. They are frequently tamed.

CHAPTER IV.

The Reptiles and Fishes of India.

Great Indian Tortoise—Gangetic Crocodile—Flying Dragon—Serpent Tribe—Viperine Boa—Russelian Snake—Whip Snake—Cobra de Capello—Water Snakes—Pomfret—Scir Fish—Gymnetrus—Indian Remora—Dolphin—Scorpæna—Insidious Dory—Zebra Sole—Chætodon—Unicorn Acanthurus—Climbing Sparus—Sóher—Wrahl—Leopard Mackerel—Indian Surmullet—Flying Gurnard—Exocætus—Mango Fish—Ostracion.

The principal characteristic of reptiles in general consists in this, that only a portion of the blood is transmitted through the lungs, the remainder being projected by the heart directly to the other parts of the body, without being specially subjected to the influence of the respiratory organs; whereas in the higher classes, such as man, the rest of the mammalia, and birds, the whole of the blood must pass by the lungs before it is transmitted to the more distant parts of the circulating system. The amphibious habits of such reptiles as are unprovided with gills, result in a great measure from the power which they thus enjoy of carrying on a partial circulation of the blood independent of respiration. The respiration of animals, or the process by which the blood is oxygenated, becomes weaker and less frequent in proportion to the diminution which takes place in the quantity of blood transmitted to the lungs, compared with that which passes directly from the heart; and as it is respiration which warms the blood, and produces in the fibres their susceptibility of nervous irritation, it follows, as observed by Cuvier,* that the blood of reptiles is cold, and their muscular strength much less than that of birds or quadrupeds. The seat of their sensations is also much less centralized than in the last-named classes; and hence many of them exhibit life and motion long after their heads have been severed from their bodies.

Of the first division, called *Chelonian* reptiles, India produces several species. A very large terrestrial kind is named the Great Indian Tortoise (*Testudo Indica* of Vosmaer). It was first described by Perrault in the History of Animals published by the Royal Academy of France. A specimen caught on the Coromandel coast measured four feet and a half from the tip of the nose to the tail, and its height or convexity was fourteen inches; the shell itself was three feet long and two feet broad, and was of a dull-brown colour.

The second order is named *Saurian* reptiles, and includes the crocodiles and lizards. Of the former, the gavial or Gangetic crocodile is one of the most noted. It is characterized by a cartilaginous prominence which surrounds the nostrils. It attains to an enormous size, and is well distinguished from the Nilotic species and alligator of America by its very projecting eyes and its narrow elongated muzzle. The teeth are extremely numerous.

The remarkable genus *Draco* is of easy discri-

---

* Règne Animal, vol. ii. p. 1.

mination from all others on account of its very peculiar structure. The first six false-ribs, instead of surrounding the abdomen, project on a straight line with the back, and support a membranous and wing-like expansion. Hence the species are known under the name of *flying dragons*; and although such appellation may convey to the mass of mankind the idea of formidable if not fabulous monsters, it in truth designates nothing more than a few harmless lizards. Several species, first clearly distinguished by Daudin, inhabit the East Indies.*

The third order of reptiles is named *Ophidian*, and includes the serpents. It was well observed by Linnæus, that if Nature has thrown these repulsive creatures naked upon the earth, destitute of limbs, and exposed to every injury, she has, in return, supplied them with a deadly poison, the most ter-

* About the middle of last century, a Hamburgh merchant greatly prided himself on the possession of a famous dragon, which he considered as worth 10,000 florins. It was, however, discovered by the penetrating eye of Linnæus to be a gross deception, formed by a combination of the skins of snakes, the teeth of weasels, and other heterogeneous elements. It is said that the great Swedish naturalist was obliged to flee the city to avoid the wrath of the enraged proprietor. A similar scientific fraud appears to have been practised in our own country towards the close of the seventeenth century. It is thus related by Dr Grainger, from a note of Dr Zachary Grey, in his edition of Hudibras, vol. i. p. 125:—"Mr Smith of Bedford observes to me on the word *dragon* as follows:—Mr Jacob Bobart, botany professor of Oxford, did, about forty years ago, find a dead rat in the Physic Garden, which he made to resemble the common picture of dragons, by altering its head and tail, and thrusting in taper sharp sticks, which distended the skin on each side till it mimicked wings. He let it dry as hard as possible. The learned immediately pronounced it a dragon; and one of them sent an accurate description of it to Dr Magliabechi, librarian to the Grand Duke of Tuscany: several fine copies of verses were wrote on so rare a subject; but at last Mr Bobart owned the cheat; however, it was looked upon as a masterpiece of art, and, as such, deposited in the Museum, or Anatomy School, where I saw it some years after." The curious in dragons may consult the works of Gesner and Aldrovandus.

rible of all weapons. From the earliest ages they have been regarded either as objects of unmingled horror, or of superstitious and fearful veneration, by the human race.

The poison of these subtle reptiles seems to produce death under a variety of aspects. A universal torpor and lethargy, without pain, was said to follow the bite of the asp. Hence its preference by Cleopatra. This fact, though doubted by medical observers, seems, in some measure, confirmed by the examples adduced by Captain Gowdie, in Dr Russel's splendid publication.* Lucan distinguishes the poisonous serpents that infested the march of the Roman army over the deserts of Libya by the various symptoms which they produced; but his dreadful catalogue should, perhaps, be regarded rather as a piece of poetical embellishment than as an historical relation. At all events it seems now decided that, however the symptoms may vary, the nature and action of the poison is the same in all, and is to be counteracted, in most cases, by the same means. The virulence of the bite of individuals of the same species varies according to the season of the year, just as their manners and external aspect also vary, according to the beautiful description in the Georgics :—

> " Postquam exhausta palus, terræque ardore dehiscunt;
> Exilit in siccum, et flammantia lumina torquens
> Sævit agris, asperque siti, atque exterritus æstu.
> Ne mihi tum molles sub dio carpere somnos,
> Neu dorso nemoris libeat jacuisse per herbas :
> Cùm positis novus exuviis, nitidusque juventâ,
> Volvitur, aut catulos tectis aut ova relinquens,
> Arduus ad Solem, et linguis micat ore trisulcis."
>
> *Lib. iii. l.* 432.

* Account of Indian Serpents.

The extreme rapidity with which death was sometimes produced by the bite of poisonous snakes, led Dr Mead to infer that its fatal influence affected the nervous rather than the circulating system. But the experiments of Fontana go far to demonstrate, that the venom of the viper is perfectly innocent when applied to the nerves only, but that it acts immediately upon the blood, and through the medium of this fluid destroys the irritability of the muscular fibre, and thus produces death. A more recent idea has been proposed,—that the poison of serpents acts upon the blood by attracting the oxygen which it contains, and which is essential to its vitality. The human heart, and in general the heart of all animals with warm blood, has two cavities or ventricles, and the blood, before it is returned to the right ventricle of the heart, has to perform two circles, a lesser between the heart and the lungs, and a greater between the heart and the rest of the body. While the blood passes through the lungs it undergoes a very remarkable change of colour, and of other properties; a certain portion of the atmospheric air is attracted and absorbed, while the remainder carries off, by expiration, that matter in the blood which is either useless or injurious to the system. The atmosphere we respire is a compound fluid, one portion of which is oxygen, or pure air, and another, and much larger portion, is noxious, or azotic air; and it is the former ingredient only which is attracted by the blood in its passage through the lungs, and contributes to the maintenance of animal life. It is from this combination that the heat of animals, and the red colour of the blood, are supposed to be derived.

These observations will enable the reader to judge more clearly of Mr Boag's theory of the action of animal poisons. He adduces the following arguments in its support:—1. Man, and other warm-blooded animals, exposed to an atmosphere deprived of oxygen, quickly expire. The poison of a serpent, when introduced into the blood, also causes death; but carried into circulation by a wound, and in very small quantity, its operation is comparatively slow and gradual. 2. The appearances, on dissection, in both cases, are very similar. The blood becomes of a darker hue, and coagulates about the heart and larger vessels. The irritability of the fibres is nearly, in either case, destroyed to the same degree, and, in both circumstances, the body exhibits a strong tendency to rapid putrefaction. 3. Although Dr Mead mingled the venom of a viper with healthy blood *out* of the body, without perceiving it to produce any change in its appearance, this arose from his mixing a very small portion of poison with a large portion of blood; but if two or three drops of venom be mixed with forty or fifty drops of blood, it immediately loses its vermilion colour, becomes black, and is incapable of coagulation. 4. It is, moreover, a remarkable circumstance, that the poison of serpents has most power over those animals whose blood is the warmest, and the action of whose heart is the most lively; whereas, on the contrary, it is but a feeble poison to the serpent itself, and a very tardy instrument of death to most cold-blooded animals. The reason of this, according to Mr Boag, appears to be, that cold-blooded animals do not require a large quantity of oxygen to preserve their lives; and this is indeed evident from the conformation of their heart and respiratory organs.

Fontana's experiments, with a view to the prevention of the fatal effects of poisons, may be stated in a few words. He applied lunar caustic, which is a preparation of silver in nitric acid, and found, on so doing, that not only was the venom thereby rendered innocuous, but that the corroding power of the caustic was greatly diminished. He next wounded a variety of animals, by means of envenomed teeth, and scarifying the wounds, he washed them in a solution of lunar caustic and water: by this means the lives of the greater number of the animals were saved, though they belonged to species which he knew, in general, to be most easily killed, and the death of the others was greatly retarded. These experiments, we may add, neither proceeded upon, nor conducted to, any theory.

Now, the application of the following admitted facts is supposed, by Mr Boag, to explain the efficacy of Fontana's treatment, and illustrates the accuracy of his own views:—1. Oxygen enters into the composition of all acids, and is the principle, as its name imports, upon which their acidity depends. 2. Metals are united with oxygen under various circumstances, but chiefly in two ways; the first is by burning them in an open fire, or, to speak more philosophically, by the contact of heat and air, when they are converted into metallic oxides; the second is by the decomposition of acids, when they form compound salts. 3. Oxygen is attracted by different metals, with different degrees of force; those which attract it with the least force are the more perfect metals, such as platina, gold, and silver, which cannot be converted into oxides, except at very high temperatures; whereas arsenic, and many other substances, attract it strongly, and are usually found in combination with it even in the bowels of the earth. If, therefore, the mortal effects arising from the bite of a serpent result, as stated by Mr Boag, from the subtraction of oxygen from the blood, it is natural to suppose that the most efficient cure must consist in the renewal of that vital ingredient, and the most obvious and easy mode of accomplishing this will be, to employ such substances as are known to contain oxygen in the greatest abundance, and to part with it with the greatest facility. This is precisely the character of the lunar caustic, which is made by dissolving silver in the nitric acid, and afterwards evaporating and crystallizing the solution.*

We may observe, that the strength of the poison varies greatly in the different kinds of serpents. Thus, the use of the lunar caustic, which, in the hands of the Abbé Fontana, proved so efficacious when applied as remedial to the bite of the viper, was found of little or no avail in India as a counteraction to the venom of the cobra de capello.

If it were not inconsistent with our necessarily narrow limits, we might here exhibit a very formidable list of species indigenous to India. But, referring the student of herpetology to the splendid work of Dr Russel on the serpents of the coast of Coromandel, and to the writings of Daudin,†

---

* See a paper, On the Poison of Serpents, by W. Boag, Esq., Asiatic Researches, vol. vi. p. 103.

† Histoire Naturelle des Reptiles, 8 vols. 8vo.

Schneider,* Wagler,† and other systematic authors, we shall confine our present attention to a very few species.

The viperine-boa (*Paduin Cootoo* of Russel) is not above a foot and a half long. It is said to produce, by its bite, a slow wasting of the fingers and toes, analogous to what has been observed to occur in some leprous cases. A living specimen, however, which was in excellent order, and bit some chickens ferociously, produced no more material consequences than might have followed from any ordinary wound.

The Russelian snake (*Coluber Russelii*) measures about four feet in length. It is an elegant species, of a pale yellowish-brown, marked throughout its whole length by a continued chain or series of large oval spots, of a deep-brown colour, paler in the centre, and encircled by a narrow white edging. A chicken, bitten in the pinion by this snake, was seized with convulsions, and died in 38 seconds. On the death of the chicken he bit a stout dog, which was seized with paralysis and stupor, and died in 26 minutes.

The whip snake is common in the Concan, where it conceals itself among the foliage of trees, and darts at the cattle grazing below, generally aiming at the eye. A bull, which was thus wounded at Dazagon, tore up the ground with extreme fury, and died in half an hour, foaming at the

---

* Historiæ Amphibiorum Naturales et Litterariæ, fascic. I. et II. in 8vo.

† Hist. Nat. des Esp. Nouv. des Serpents, décrite d'après les Notes du Voyageur (M. Spix), par Jean Wagler. Lat. et Fr., 4to, Munich, 1824.

mouth. This habit of the reptile is truly singular, —for it seems to proceed neither from resentment nor from fear, nor yet from the impulse of appetite; but seems, "more than any other known fact in natural history, to partake of that frightful and mysterious principle of evil, which tempts our species so often to tyrannize for mere wantonness of power."*

The hooded-snake (*Coluber naja*), or cobra de capello, so called in the Portuguese language from the appearance of a hood, which, when irritated, it produces by means of the expanded skin about the neck, is one of the most noxious of the Indian reptiles. Its general length is from three to four feet, and the diameter of its body about an inch and a quarter. The head is small, and is covered on the fore-part with large smooth scales, resembling in that respect the majority of the innocuous kinds. At a short distance below the head is a lateral swelling, or dilatation of the skin, which is continued for about four inches downwards, after which it gradually sinks into the cylindrical form of the rest of the body. This portion is capable of being raised and expanded at the pleasure of the animal. It is marked above by a large and conspicuous patch, closely resembling the figure of a pair of spectacles. The usual colour of the body is pale ferruginous-brown above; the under parts being of a bluish white, occasionally tinged with pale-brown or yellow. The terminal portion tapers gradually, and terminates in a slender sharp-pointed extremity.

In India this dreaded species is more universally

* Quarterly Review, vol. xii. p. 183.

known than any other. It is frequently exhibited as a public show, and being carried about in a covered basket, is made to assume a kind of dancing motion, for the amusement of the public. It raises itself up on its lower extremity, and moving its head and body alternately from side to side, it appears to keep time with the measured melody of "flutes and soft recorders." It is probable that the love of music, on the part of the serpent tribe, was anciently known in Palestine, as the inspired Psalmist compares the ungodly to the deaf adder, which stoppeth her ears, and refuseth to hear the voice of the charmer, charm he never so wisely. The individuals so exhibited are, in the first place, deprived of their poisonous fangs, although this customary extraction does not seem universal. "When the music ceases," says Mr Forbes, "the snakes appear motionless; but, if not immediately covered up in the basket, the spectators are liable to fatal accidents. Among my drawings is that of a cobra de capello, which danced for an hour on the table while I painted it; during which I frequently handled it to observe the beauty of the spots, and especially the spectacles on the hood, not doubting but that its venomous fangs had been previously extracted. But the next morning my upper servant, who was a zealous Mussulman, came to me in great haste, and desired I would instantly retire and praise the Almighty for my good fortune: not understanding his meaning, I told him that I had already performed my devotions, and had not so many stated prayers as the followers of his prophet. Mohammed then informed me that, while purchasing some fruit in the bazar, he observed the man who had been with me on the preceding evening entertaining the country-people with his dancing snakes; they, according to their usual custom, sat on the ground around him; when, either from the music stopping too suddenly, or from some other cause irritating the vicious reptile which I had so often handled, it darted at the throat of a young woman, and inflicted a wound of which she died in half an hour."* The rattlesnake has been known to kill a dog in two minutes; but Dr Russel informs us, that he never knew the bite of the hooded-snake prove mortal to a dog in much less than half an hour. It can kill chickens, however, in less than half a minute. There are several varieties of this species.

Snakes are numerous in Guzerat, and occasioned considerable annoyance to Mr Forbes during his residence near Baroach. Harrabhy, his head-gardener, may be said to have paid them religious veneration, and his assistants called them by the most endearing names. It happened, however, that on one occasion a young lady, more alarmed than Eve, though in the same condition, was obliged to make a precipitate retreat through the garden from her bath, in consequence of the appearance of a cobra de capello. War was thereafter denounced against them.

The garden occupied by Sir James Macintosh, while he resided at Torala near the town of Bombay, is also described by an eye-witness as a little paradise, but for its reptile inhabitants. "Snakes, from the enormous rock-snake, who first breaks the

* Oriental Memoirs, vol. i. p. 44.

bones of his prey by coiling around it, and then swallows it whole, to the smallest of the venomous tribe, glide about in every direction. There the cobra capello, whose bite is in almost every instance mortal, lifts his graceful folds, and spreads his large many-coloured crests; here, too, lurks the small bright-speckled cobra manilla, whose fangs convey instant death."*

We shall here give a short account of some remarkable water-snakes, belonging to the genus *Hydrus*. Soon after the opening of the bar in the month of October 1815, reports prevailed at Madras that a great shoal of sea-snakes had entered the river, and that many natives while crossing had been bitten, and had in consequence died. A reward was offered for each of these animals caught, on the condition of its being carried to the superintendent of police. Pandauls were erected opposite to the two principal fords, and skilful natives, under the superintendence of Dr M'Kenzie (to whom we are indebted for the information), were provided with eau-de-luce and other remedies, and directed to afford immediate aid to those persons who might be unfortunately bitten. Many were bitten accordingly, and all of them exhibited the symptoms usually consequent upon the action of a powerful animal poison; but none of them died. We shall briefly state a couple of cases:—A native woman, in crossing near the land-customhouse, was seen, while stepping out of the water, to shake something off which had grasped her foot, and which to several spectators appeared to be a

* Journal of a Residence in India, by Maria Graham.

water-snake. The woman, after advancing a few paces from the river, fell down, and was carried to the pandaul in a state of apparent insensibility. On examining her feet, two small but distinct wounds were perceived on the ankle of her right leg; her skin was cold, her face livid, her breathing laborious, and her pulse scarcely perceptible. A ligature was immediately applied above the wound, which had been previously enlarged with a lancet, and a piece of the carbonate of ammonia, well moistened with pure nitric acid, applied, and 30 drops of the eau-de-luce were administered nearly at the same time in a glass of water. In five minutes more a similar dose was poured down her throat, which seemed rather to increase the spasm at the chest, but the pulse became distinct at the wrist, though feeble. A third dose was repeated in three minutes more, on which she uttered a scream, and began to breathe more freely. About ten minutes had now elapsed since she had been carried to the pandaul, and in about three minutes more a tea-spoonful of the eau-de-luce was given, which almost immediately produced violent nausea, and profuse perspiration. When a little salt was put into her mouth, she declared it was not salt but sugar; and this the natives deemed an infallible sign of still-continued danger. She was soon, however, entirely relieved, and merely complained for three or four days of a numbness in the limb above the wound.

Another case was that of a lascar, who was bitten by a snake when about the middle of the river. He advanced a few paces after quitting the bank, and then fell down in violent convulsions. When brought in, his breathing was laborious, his skin cold and clammy, his countenance livid, and his pulse feeble at the wrist, but distinct at the temples. A quantity of froth and foam was ejected from between his closed teeth. He too recovered after a similar treatment; but he complained for many days that he had no left leg.

A large healthy chicken was exposed to the bite of a hydrus major four feet long. It was bit in the foot, and in about ten minutes began to droop, and to show a slight convulsive flutter in both wings. In three minutes more it was convulsed; and at the end of seventeen minutes from the infliction of the wound, it suddenly dropped down dead.*

While on the subject of poisonous snakes, it may not be uninteresting to the reader to peruse the recorded experience of a medical gentleman, who had himself nearly fallen a victim to the bite of one of these insidious reptiles. On the night of the 12th of May 1809, Mr John Macrae, civil surgeon at Chittagong, while stepping into the southern veranda of his house, observed a small dark-coloured snake running along the terrace. After several unsuccessful attempts, he succeeded in killing it with a small cane; but in doing so the creature struck against one of his ankles, which it touched with the point of its fangs, but so slightly as to draw no blood. A few minutes afterwards, while undressing to go to bed, he felt a peculiar glow over his whole body, with a strong palpitation at the heart; but this he at first attributed merely to his exertions in killing the snake. He soon, however, became very restless, and experienced a singular sensation as if a warm

---

* Asiatic Researches, vol. xiii. p. 329.

fluid were circulating through his veins to the extremities of his fingers. He was then attacked by violent sickness, the heat of his body abated, and was succeeded by a deadly coldness of the skin, and profuse perspiration. He took repeated doses of the *spiritus ammoniæ compositus ;* after which the sickness subsided, and his breathing became easier. So entirely was the nervous sensibility of the palate affected, that on swallowing the first doses he was insensible to the nauseous taste of the alkali. In the course of three hours he was out of danger.

From the foregoing statement it appears, as observed by Mr Macrae, that the first effect of the poison, on being received into the body, is to excite the action of the heart and arteries, and to produce a great heat over the whole body; and as a similarity of effect proves a similarity of cause, and the effect of all stimuli is to excite, it follows, in his opinion, that the poison of the serpent is a stimulus of the most powerful nature, which destroys life by its excess.

Dr Russel has figured and described 43 of the most common serpents of Indostan; and he informs us that a quantity of warm Madeira taken internally, with an outward application of eau-de-luce on the punctures, was generally successful in curing the bite of the most venomous species. He also states that the medicine called the Tanjore-pill is equally efficacious. Of the 43 serpents examined by Dr Russel, he found only seven that were provided with poisonous organs; and, on comparing the effects of the poison of five of the oriental species on brute animals with those produced by the poison of the rattlesnake and the European viper, he remarked that they all produced morbid symptoms nearly similar, though they might differ in the degree of their deleterious power, and the rapidity of its operation.

We shall devote the remainder of this chapter to a short indication of a few of the fishes of India.

Bombay is supplied by the surrounding sea with a variety of excellent fish. The *pomfret* is not unlike a small turbot, but possesses a more delicate flavour; and the kind called the black pomfret is still more highly esteemed. The *robal,* the *scir-fish,* and several others, are also excellent; but the *bumbalo,* a small species of an exceedingly nutritious nature, is the favourite food of the natives, who capture it in immense numbers. In a dried state it furnishes an important article of commerce, and forms a principal article of food among the lascars, or Indian sailors.

The Indian eel described by Willoughby (*Ichth. appen.* t. 3, p. 3), belongs to the genus *Trichiurus.* The colour is pale-brown, varied with spots of a somewhat deeper hue. It is said to possess a certain degree of electrical power, from which it derives its name of *Trichiurus electricus.*

The extraordinary genus *Gymnetrus,* of which the fish popularly called the king of the herrings, which is ten feet long and not more than six inches in diameter, is a northern example, also occurs in the Indian Seas. The Russelian gymnetrus, described by Dr Shaw from a drawing in possession of the gentleman after whom it was named, was taken near Vizagapatan.

The Indian remora (*Echeneis neucrates*) appears

to occur in many different quarters of the world. According to Commerson, it is common about the coasts of Mozambique, where it is used for the catching of turtles. A ring is fastened to the tail of the fish, and a long cord inserted through the ring. It is then carried to sea in a vessel of salt water; and as soon as the boatmen perceive a turtle asleep upon the surface, they endeavour to approach as close to it as possible, and then throwing the remora into the sea, they give it the proper length of cord. If it perceives the turtle, it immediately attaches itself to its breast, where it adheres so firmly as to enable the fishermen to draw the turtle within their reach. This species, according to Bloch, sometimes attains to the length of seven feet.

The Coryphene, or dolphin (*C. Hippurus*), distinguished by the splendour of its varying hues, occurs occasionally in the Indian Seas. The gradual disappearance of its gorgeous colouring when about to die, is regarded by the rude sailors with as much delight as were the changes of the expiring mullet by the luxurious Romans. The dolphin is a strong and vigorous fish, a voracious eater, and extremely rapid in its movements. Flying-fish constitute its favourite food. Its flesh is excellent.

The genus *Scorpæna* presents some singular and uncouth forms of animal life. The truncation of the head, its enormous size, and the remarkable processes with which it is furnished, bestow on several of the species a peculiar aspect. The horrid scorpæna (*S. horrida*) may be presumed from its name to present a somewhat unamiable appearance. It resembles, in truth, rather some imaginary or fictitious monster, than the legitimate production of Nature. We shall not venture to describe it at present.

The insidious dory (*Zeus insidiator*) inhabits the rivers and other fresh waters of India. Its colour is bright silvery, with a bluish-green tint above, speckled with black spots. The body is apparently without scales. The mouth is of a much more lengthened shape than in the others of the genus, and is so constituted as to form at pleasure a kind of tubular snout, by means of which this fish possesses the singular faculty of ejecting a drop of water against such insects as happen to alight near the surface, or to hover over the foliage of aquatic plants.

We may mention, as an example of the flat-fish of the warmer regions of the world, the zebra sole (*Pleuronectes zebra*), a very elegant species, easily recognised by its contrasted colouring, the upper parts being white, with a tinge of brown towards the back, and marked from head to tail by numerous double deep-brown transverse bands, which pass also across the fins; the body is rather longer in proportion than that of the common sole (*P. solea*), and the dorsal and anal fins are continued onwards in a line with the tail. This inhabitant of the Indian Seas is highly esteemed as an article of food.

Many species of *Chætodon* inhabit the Indian Seas. The only example of the genus which we shall here adduce is a fresh-water species,—the rostrated chætodon (*Ch. rostratus*). The length of this curious fish is about six inches. The colour of the body is whitish, with a dusky tinge upon the back. It is marked by five transverse and nearly equidistant brown bands, with milk-white edges: the first band, which is narrower than the rest, passes across the head, through the eyes; the three next across the body; and the last across the base of the tail. The dorsal and anal fins are very broad behind, and the former is marked by a large black spot, bordered with white. This extraordinary little creature is famed for the method by which it captures its prey. When it perceives a flying insect, either hovering over the water or quietly sunning its gauzy wings on the leaf of some aquatic plant, it shoots out a drop of water from its tubular mouth, so suddenly and with such unerring aim, as to tumble the insect in a state of stupefaction on the surface of the stream. "In shooting at a sitting insect," says Dr Shaw, "it is commonly observed to approach within the distance of from six to four feet before it explodes the water. When kept in a state of confinement in a large vessel of water, it is said to afford high entertainment by its dexterity in this exercise, since, if a fly or other insect be fastened to the edge of the vessel, the fish immediately perceives it, and continues to shoot at it with such admirable skill as very rarely to miss the mark."*

The unicorn acanthurus (the *Monoceros minor* of Willoughby) is said to occur both in the Indian and Arabian Seas. It was in the latter locality that, according to Forskal, a fisherman observed an eagle descend among a shoal of this species, and which, happening to transfix one with each foot, was instantly killed and nearly torn asunder by their sudden and violent separation in opposite directions.

The genus *Sparus* produces many interesting

* General Zoology, vol. iv. p. 338. See also Naturalist's Miscellany, ii. pl. 67, and the Phil. Trans. for 1765.

species along the shores of Indostan. The climbing-sparus (*Sp. scandens*) is not unworthy of special record. It measures about a span in length. The skin is covered by a blackish mucus, and the dorsal-fin is occasionally sunk in a longitudinal fossule. The most remarkable peculiarity of this fish is the power of climbing, from which it derives its specific name. It performs this action by means of the spiny processes of the gill-covers, and moves at pleasure up the trunks of trees which grow by the water-side. It was observed by Lieutenant Daldorff, at Tranquebar, ascending by a fissure in the stem of the palm called *Borassus flabellifer*, and was also found to be so tenacious of life as to move about upon the dry sand for some hours after it was captured on the tree. The natives regard the spines of the gill-covers as poisonous.

The Alacananda, or that branch of the Ganges which has its source among the inferior hills on the southern side of the snowy mountains, produces, according to Messrs Raper and Webb, a beautiful fish called *sóher*, which attains to the length of six or seven feet. The scales on the back and sides are of an exquisite green, encircled by a bright golden border; the belly is white, slightly tinged with gold; the tail and fins are of a dark bronze; and its flavour is equal to its external beauty.*

A fish called *wrahl* in India inhabits the lakes, and is so highly esteemed as a nutritious and healthy food, as to be recommended for the diet of convalescents. It is the *Ophicephalus striatus* of Bloch.

Of the scomber tribe, the leopard-mackerel (*Sc.*

* Narrative of a Survey for the Purpose of Discovering the Sources of the Ganges.

leopardus) is nearly three feet long. Its colour is dusky-blue above, and silvery on the sides and abdomen. The sides are also marked by numerous oval black spots. This species is much esteemed by the European residents as an article of food. It is described by Dr Russel under the name of *wingeram.* The *rahtu goolivinda* of that author (pl. 157) is the Indian surmullet (*Mullus Indicus*). The aspect of the living fish is singularly beautiful, but speedily fades after death. The upper parts of the head, neck, and back, are of a dark changeable purple, fainter on the sides, which are marked by a few longitudinal lines of azure and gold. There are two oblong spots on each side; the first, situated near the centre of the body, is smallish, and of an opaline colour, or changeable from bluish-white to gold; the second is nearer the tail, of a larger size, and of a dark-purple hue. The abdomen is white; the dorsal-fin purple, streaked with light-blue; the pectoral and anal fins are pink. This beautiful creature was observed by Dr Russel near Vizagapatan. As an article of food it is not greatly esteemed.

We may here mention the flying-gurnard (*Trigla volitans*), which swims in shoals, and ever and anon darts into the air, and makes its way to a considerable distance. It is familiar to the Indian voyager. Several other species of flying-fish (belonging, however, to the genus *Exocœtus*) are likewise common to the Indian Seas. According to Bloch (who quotes from Plumier), the spawn of one of them is so highly acrimonious, that the smallest portion cannot be applied to the tongue or palate without producing immediate excoriation.

The mango-fish (*Polynemus paradiseus*), so called probably on account of its yellow colour, which resembles that of a ripe mango, is said by Dr Russel to be regarded as by much the most delicate food of any of the Calcutta species. It is called *tupsee mutchey* by the natives. Another species of the same genus (*P. plebeius* of Broussonet) is also an excellent fish for the table, and is much esteemed by the inhabitants of the Malabar coast. It is dressed in various ways, and is sometimes dried and salted for sale. It occasionally measures upwards of four feet in length.

Many cartilaginous fishes belonging to the ray and shark tribes are found along the Indian shores, and the file-fish (genus *Balistes*) are very numerous. The Ostracions or trunk-fish are distinguished by a bony crust or covering. The triquetral trunk-fish (*O. triqueter*) is about a foot long. It feeds on the smaller crustacea, shell-fish, and marine worms, and is itself much esteemed by East Indians as an excellent fish for the table. Species belonging to the genera *Diodon, Tetradon, Pegasus*, and others, inhabit the fresh and saline waters of Indostan.

CHAPTER V.

The Shells and Insects of India.

Sepia—Conus—Oliva—Cypræa—Ovula—Marginella—Voluta—Mitræ—Terebra—Eburna—Buccinum, &c.—Bivalves—Spondyli—Pectens, &c.—Fresh-water Shells—Pearl-fisheries—Insects—Coleopterous Insects—Orthopterous Insects—Hemipterous Insects—Kermes—Gez or Manna—Hymenopterous, Neuropterous, and Dipterous Tribes—Silk-worm.

If, while engaged with the vertebrated or higher classes of the animal creation, we found ourselves embarrassed by the multitude of our materials, and, equally delighted with the beautiful forms and exquisite adaptation of structure which characterize so many species, were occasionally at a loss in our selection, how much more must that same difficulty press upon us when we enter on the examination of the lower tribes! When we consider that the ascertained insects of Great Britain alone are more than ten times as numerous as the known quadrupeds of the entire surface of the whole earth, we may conceive how vast a field the science of Indian entomology would lay before us were we to venture upon any thing approaching to a detailed exposition of its wonders. But it is not to be expected that a general work like the present should achieve what even systematic treatises, exclusively devoted to the subject, have as yet in vain endeavoured to accomplish; and all that we shall therefore here attempt is a cursory notice of a few of the more remarkable phenomena of insect life. In the first place, however, we shall devote a page or two to the testaceous productions of India, for there

> "the gorgeous East
> Showers on her sons barbaric *pearls* and gold;"

and shells are in themselves objects of too interesting and ornamental a nature to be left entirely unregarded.

It is thought by competent observers, that the organization and habits of the testaceous mollusca fit them more than those of any other class to illustrate the laws of geographical distribution. Slow of movement, and consequently neither able nor inclined to wander far from the places of their birth, they are less liable than most other living creatures to extend their sphere of action, or to become intermingled with the species of foreign climes; and they are consequently supposed, in the location of their various groups, still to represent with tolerable accuracy the positions in which they were originally placed. It is thus that they are qualified to throw light on the much disputed, and probably never to be resolved point, viz. whether animals, immediately subsequent to their original creation, were left to distribute themselves universally from a single centre, or whether each natural climate was at once supplied by other means than those depending on the wandering propensities of species, with such forms of animal life as were fitted to breed and prosper under the peculiar influences by which that climate was characterized.

Without a greater degree of precision than consists with the present state of our knowledge, it will, however, be a vain attempt to deduce any general laws in relation to this important subject; for in truth, notwithstanding the splendid collections which exist in several of the British and Continental cabinets, our knowledge of the distribution of species is extremely vague and imperfect, in regard to all other countries except those of Europe and North America. In respect to Asia, especially, we are in almost total darkness; for the collectors of Eastern shells have never paid the slightest attention to localities, and seem indeed not to have been aware that any importance could attach to the subject. However, the voyages of Leschenault de Latour, and of Messrs Diard and Duvaucel, have thrown some light on certain species of India and Ceylon. The testaceous productions of the Indian Archipelago are somewhat better known since the days of Rumphius and Seba, in consequence of numerous observations made by MM. Peron and Lesueur, during the expedition of Captain Baudin, and by the investigations of MM. Quoy, Gaymard, and Gaudichaud, in that of Freycinet. The shells of Java have also been well illustrated by Kulk and Van Hasselt.

The same general fact applies to most molluscous animals as to almost every other department of zoology, that the genera and species increase as we advance from polar and temperate to equatorial regions. Africa is probably too dry and sandy, but the more varied soils of Asia and America, combining nearly equal heat with greater moisture, produce in their torrid portions a more abundant store.

As the countries to the description of which this volume is devoted have long been known to Europeans, the beautiful shells of India and its islands are common in the cabinets of naturalists. The Dutch, at the period of their maritime glory, were the principal importers of Asiatic shells, in collecting which they seem to have found as much pleasure as in cultivating tulips and other gaudy productions of the vegetable kingdom; and of late years the English have abundantly supplied their own cabinets, as well as those of the Continent, with the more common or beautiful species, although little zeal has been displayed by them in attempting to elucidate, in a philosophical manner, the conchology of India. Although the shells of all warm climates possess the general character of brilliancy of colouring, those which inhabit the Indian Seas are so peculiarly remarkable in this respect, as to form indeed the principal ornaments of our collections. Notwithstanding this, however, they are not in general so keenly sought after as those of countries less generally or more recently known.

Of the cephalopodous mollusca which occur in the Indian Seas, we may mention the *Sepia officinalis* and *tuberculata*, from the black fluid contained in the abdomen of which, or of some other species of this family, China ink is said to be manufactured. The argonaut and the common and umbilicated nautili,—the two former common in collections,—also occur in these seas.

In the brief account which we have here to give of these productions, it is unnecessary to arrange our remarks in conformance with the order of systematic writers, more especially as we shall mention only a few of the most splendid. The genus *Conus*, celebrated for the beauty of its species, has numerous representatives in the Indian Seas. *Conus marmoreus*, with black and white spots, resembling brecciated marble, *C. cedo-nulli*, of which all the varieties are highly prized on account of their great beauty, *C. ammiralis*, *millepunctatus*, *literatus*, *generalis*, *princeps*, *aurantius*, and many others, the mere enumeration of which would be unprofitable, are well known as productions of India. Some of these are considered as of great value. A variety of *C. cedo-nulli*, according to Dillwyn, has been valued at three hundred guineas. Of the beautiful genus *Oliva* we need mention only *O. erythrostoma*, *maura*, *textilis*, *irisans*, and *fulminans*. Many rare and beautiful species of *Cypræa* from India adorn our cabinets, such as *C. Argus*, so named from its eyelike spots; *C. mappa*, the markings of which bear some resemblance to the sinuous coast-lines of a map; *C. tigris*, the most common, but at the same time one of the most beautiful species; *C. testudianaria*, which resembles tortoise-shell; and *C. moneta* and *helvola*, used as money. The *Ovula oviformis*, resembling a large white egg, and various species of *Marginella*, from India, are well known. Of the fine genus *Voluta* may be mentioned *V. melo*, *imperialis*, *pellis-serpentis*, *nautica*, *musica*, and *vexillum*, the latter, striped with white and orange, greatly prized by collectors. The *Mitræ* are almost peculiarly Indian, and the finest species have received distinctive names from a fancied resemblance to the headgear of the ecclesiastical dignitaries, such as *papalis*, *pontificalis*, *cardinalis*, and *episcopalis*. *Terebra maculata* and *flammea*, *Eburna Zeylanica*, *areolata* and *spirata*, may be mentioned as examples of these genera, and the like might be done with others; but, where technical terms alone could be employed, it would be useless to adduce a long list of the many beautiful species of *Buccina, Dolia, Purpuræ, Harpæ, Cassides, Tritons, Murices, Pyrulæ, Fusi, Turbinellæ,* and other tribes which inhabit the Indian Seas. Of the land and fresh-water shells belonging to the trachelipodous family, little is known; and we may conclude our remarks on the univalve shells by mentioning the *Umbrella Indica,* which resembles an expanded parasol, and *Patella granatina* and *testudinaria,* species of a similar form.

The conchifera or bivalve shells are usually less numerous in collections than the univalve; but a large proportion of those known to naturalists is from India. The beautiful and singular *Spondyli,* various *Pectens, Peda, Aviculæ, Mallei,* and others of the family of Malleaceæ, of which the most remarkable is the *Meleagrina margaritifera,* which furnishes the mother-of-pearl of commerce, are natives of the Indian Seas. *Ostrea folium* grows on the roots of the mangrove and other littoral trees. *Tridacna gigas,* the largest shell known, of which individuals have been found to weigh from 400 to 500 pounds, occurs in the Indian and Chinese Seas. A large valve of this shell, presented by the Venetians to Francis I. of France, is used as a baptismal font in the church of St Sulpice in Paris. The fresh-water shells of India are as yet little known; but although the genera *Unio* and *Anodon* have their finest representatives in the rivers and lakes of America, the species of these genera that have been brought from the East give promise of an ample store to reward the labours of scientific inquirers. There are many beautiful species of *Cardita, Cardium, Tellina, Mactra, Mya, Solen,* and *Pholas;* but we are unable to communicate any information regarding their history which would interest the general reader. The allied genera *Venus* and *Cytherea,* named after the goddess of beauty, whom the poets inaptly feigned to have emerged from the sea, are plentiful in all countries; but many of the Indian species, such as *V. literata, puerpera, Malabarica,* and *C. tigerina* and *erycina,* are peculiarly beautiful. With the *Aspergillum Javanum,* a tubular shell, having a disk surrounded by fimbriated rays, so as to resemble the pipe of a watering-pail with the water issuing from it, we shall conclude our necessarily brief enumeration. A few words, however, will not be misbestowed on the pearl-fishery.

The pearl-fisheries of Ceylon are among the most noted. The most skilful divers come from Collesh on the coast of Malabar, and some of these are alleged to have occasionally remained under water during the lapse of seven minutes. According to the testimony of Mr Le Beck, this feat was also performed by a Caffre boy at Carical. The following is the usual mode of diving for pearls:—By means of two cords, a diving-stone and a net are connected with the boat. The diver, putting the toes of his right foot on the cair rope of the diving-stone, and those of his left on the net, seizes the two cords with one hand, and shutting his nostrils with the other, plunges into the water. On gaining the bottom he hangs the net around his neck, and throws into it as many pearl-shells as he can collect while he is able to remain beneath the surface, which is generally about two minutes. He then resumes his former posture, and, making a signal by pulling the cords, he is instantly hauled up into the boat. On emerging from the sea, he discharges a quantity of water from his mouth and nose. There are generally ten divers to each boat, and while five are respiring, the other five descend with the same stones. Each brings up about one hundred oysters in his net at a time, and if not interrupted by any accident, will make fifty trips in the course of a forenoon.* The most frequent and fatal of the catastrophes to which they are subjected arise from sharks, which, by biting the diver in two, prevent his reascending to the surface.

The natives entertain opinions regarding the formation of pearls similar to those of the ancients. They deem that they are formed from dewdrops, in connexion with sunbeams. It is recorded in one of the Sanscrit books, that pearls are formed in the month of May, at the approach of the Sooatee star (one of their twenty-seven constellations), at which time the oysters come up to the surface of the water to catch the drops of rain! We find the same idea expressed in the following quaint yet beautiful passage from the 12th chapter of the *Cosmographe and Discription of Albion,* prefixed to Bellenden's translation of Hector Boece's History and Chronicles of Scotland:—" Now we will schaw the nature of mussillis and coclis, of quhilkis many kindis ar amang us. Sum ar small, with the meit thairof richt delicius to the mouth; utheris ar mair, nocht unlike, in forme and quantite, to the samin mussillis

* Account of the Pearl-fishery in the Gulf of Manaar, in March and April 1797. By H. J. Le Beck, Esq.

that hes the purpure; and howbeit thay have na thing thairof, thay ar yit richt delicius to the mouth; utheris ar lang and greter, callit hors mussillis, and are gotten in sindry reveris, specialie in De and Done; and in thir mussillis ar generit the perlis. *Thir mussillis airlie in the morning, quhen the lift is cleir and temperat, opnis thair mouthis a litill abone the watter, and maist gredelie swellis the dew of the hevin; and, aftir the mesure and quantite of the dew that they swellie, thay consave and bredis the perle.* Thir mussillis ar sa doyn gleg of twiche and hering, that howbeit the voce be never so small that is maid on the bra beside thaim, or the stain be never sa small that is cassin in the watter, thay douk haistelie at ains, and gangis to the ground, knawing weill in quhat estimation and price the frute of thair wambe is to al peple."*

We shall now devote the remainder of our space to a few brief notices of the insects of India. It has been observed that real insect climates, or those in which certain groups or species appear rather than others, may be regarded as by no means certainly regulated by any *isothermal* lines. Humboldt remarked in reference to the *simulia* and *culices* of South America, that their geographical position did not appear to depend solely on the *heat* of the climate, the excess of humidity, or the thickness of the forests,—but on local and unappreciable circumstances.† Under certain limitations, however, it may

* Tait's Reprint, Edin. 1821, p. 44.
† Personal Narrative, vol. v. p. 88.

be safely admitted that temperature is extremely influential on the distribution of insect life. An increase of caloric seldom fails to produce a corresponding increase in the number and variety of entomological forms; and if, reversing the journey from "Indus to the Pole," we travel from the hyperborean regions towards the sunny south, we shall find that the tiny multitudes accumulate in the warmer portions of the temperate zone till they swarm between the tropics.* A similar relation obtains between the base and the summit of mountains. Such species as inhabit the plains of northern countries are found to occur on the mountains in more southern ones. Thus the beautiful Apollo-butterfly (*Parnassius Apollo*) is a mountainous species in France, while it inhabits the valleys of Sweden.

Of coleopterous insects the genera *Mimela, Euchlora, Colliuris, Catascopus, Apogonia,* &c., seem peculiar to Asia. The genus *Mylabris* is widely spread over the old world, and in addition to the *M. Cichorii,* of which the vesicatorial powers were well known to the ancients,† General Hardwicke has described another species extremely plentiful in all parts of Bengal, Bahar, and Oude, and which as a blister insect is said to be equally efficacious as the Spanish fly.‡

Of the genus *Buprestis* many splendid species, such as *B. ocellata,* &c., occur in India; and throughout that vast and varied country innumerable examples may be found of many other coleopterous

* Introduction to Entomology, by Kirby and Spence, vol. iv. p. 484.

† Amœnitates Academicæ, t. vi. p. 138.

‡ Asiatic Researches, vol. v. p. 213.

tribes.* At night the fire-flies glitter by thousands among the dark recesses of the banian-tree; and these same insects are observed to dance in perpetual motion around the outmost branches of the spreading tamarind, producing a brilliant and singularly beautiful effect.

The *Orthopterous* order, which contains, among others, the locust and grasshopper groups, is the next in succession. The plague of locusts is known to India in like manner as to most of the warmer countries of the globe:

> "Onward they come, a dark continuous cloud
> Of congregated myriads numberless,
> The rushing of whose wings is as the sound
> Of a broad river headlong in its course
> Plunged from a mountain summit, or the roar
> Of a wild ocean in the autumn storm,
> Shattering its billows on a shore of rocks."†

We are told, indeed, that during the rainy season in India insects of all kinds are sometimes so numerous, and so active in their operations, that it becomes necessary to remove the lights from the supper-table. In regard to the Indian locusts, a correspondent of Messrs Kirby and Spence informed these authors, that he was eyewitness to an immense army of locusts which ravaged the Mahratta country, and was supposed to come from Arabia. This column extended five hundred miles, and was so compact when on the wing that it darkened the sun like an eclipse; so that no shadow was cast upon the ground, and some lofty tombs, distant not more than two hundred yards from the observer, were rendered

---

* See Histoire Naturelle des Insectes (*Coléoptères*) par A. S. Olivier, five vols. in 4to., avec planches enluminées, and Species Général des Coléoptères, par M. le Baron Dejean.

† Thalaba, vol. i. p. 169.

invisible. This was not the *Gryllus migratorius* of Linnæus, but a red species, and its peculiar colour added to the horror of the scene; for, after having stript the trees of their foliage, it congregated around the bare and desolate branches, producing a hue like blood. "And the sound of their wings was as the sound of chariots, and of many horses running to battle." Another orthopterous species, now sufficiently common in our kitchens and pantries, we mean the cockroach (*Blatta orientalis*), was originally and no doubt unintentionally imported into Europe from the countries of our present disquisition.

Among the lantern-flies, which form part of the *Hemipterous* order, the *Fulgora diadema* may be mentioned as an Indian species, remarkable for its long spiny muricated front, with a triple division at the crown. It is of a brownish colour, variegated with red and yellow.

The insects called *kermes* likewise belong to the hemipterous order, and were highly valued in commerce and manufacture before the introduction of the still more famous cochineal (*Coccus cacti*), which is a South American species. The *Coccus ilicis* is common in the south of Europe on the evergreen oak, and appears to be widely distributed over many of the south-eastern countries of the ancient world. Though supplanted over the greater portion of Europe by the American product, it is still extensively used in India and the Persian dominions.* It has been employed from time immemorial to impart a blood-red or crimson dye to cloth, and was known to the Phœnicians by the name of thola. It was called coccus (Κοκκος) by the Greeks, and kermes

* Introduction to Entomology, and Bochart's Hierozoic.

or alkermes by the Arabians. According to Beckman, the epithet *vermiculatum* was applied to it during the middle ages when its insect origin came to be generally understood; and hence our word *vermilion* is derived. The French term *cramoisi* is evidently from the Arabic. It is supposed to have been by means of this substance that the curtains of the tabernacle (Exodus, xxvi. &c.) were dyed of a deep red (which the word scarlet then implied, rather than the colour so named in more modern days, which was unknown in the reign of James I. when our Bible was translated), and from the same source have been derived the imperishable reds of the Flemish tapestries. The scarlet afforded by cochineal was unknown in its highest perfection till the year 1630, when the singular power of the oxide of tin in exalting its colours was discovered in Holland; it was soon after communicated to one of the celebrated MM. Gobelins of Paris, and may have contributed to the perfection of their tapestries.* Since the manufacture or preparation of morocco-leather has been established in this country, cochineal has been employed to produce the beautiful colour of what is called red morocco; but in Persia, Armenia, Barbary, and the Greek Islands, a similar colour was originally produced by the use of either kermes or lac.† The colouring matter of kermes is considered by Dr Bancroft as identical with that of cochineal, but combined with some astringent matter derived from the tree on which the insects feed.

Lac is also the produce of an insect of the coccus

* Quarterly Review, vol. ix. p. 210.

† Experimental Researches concerning the Philosophy of Permanent Colours, &c. By Edward Bancroft, M. D., vol. ii. p. 167.

kind, which is collected from various trees in India, where it is used in the fabrication of beads, rings, and other ornaments of female attire. When mixed with sand it forms grindstones; and added to lamp or ivory black, and previously dissolved in water with a little borax, it composes an ink, which, when dry, is said to be capable of resisting a considerable degree of damp or moisture. In this country, according to the different conditions in which it is imported, it is called stick-lac, seed-lac, lump-lac, or shell-lac. It is chiefly used in the formation of varnishes, japanned ware, and sealing-wax, although in later years it has been applied to a still more important purpose, as originally suggested by Dr Roxburgh,—that of a substitute for cochineal in dyeing scarlet. The first preparations from it with this view were made in consequence of a hint from Dr Bancroft, and large quantities of a substance termed *lac-lake*, consisting of the colouring matter of stick-lac, precipitated from an alkaline lixivium by alum, were manufactured at Calcutta, and sent to this country, where at first the consumption was so considerable, that in the three years previous to 1810, the sales at the India-House equalled in point of colouring matter half a million of pounds weight of cochineal.* "More recently, however, a new preparation of lac-colour, under the name of *lac-dye*, has been imported from India, which has been substituted for the lac-lake, and with such advantage that the East India Company are said to have saved in a few months £14,000 in the purchase of scarlet cloths dyed with this colour and cochineal conjointly, and without any inferiority in the colour obtained."†

* Bancroft, *ubi supra*. † Introd. to Entom., vol. i. p. 318.

The only mordant formerly used with kermes was alum, and the colour communicated was blood-red; but Dr Bancroft ascertained, that with the solution of tin used with cochineal it was capable of imparting as brilliant a scarlet as that dye, and one perhaps more permanent.*

Several other curious and valuable products are obtained from Asiatic insects. The *pe-la*, or white wax of the Chinese, is derived from an insect, probably of the coccus tribe, described by the Abbé Grozier; and a nondescript Indian species produces a wax analogous to pe-la, first noticed by Dr Anderson under the name of white lac. It may be obtained in any quantity in the vicinity of Madras, and at a much cheaper rate than bees-wax; but the results of Dr Pearson's experiments do not countenance the idea that it can be advantageously used for domestic purposes, or at least for the making of candles.† Geoffroy had long since attributed to a species of kermes the property of producing a sugary substance of a white colour, resembling manna; and Captain Frederick described an article called gez or manna, found in Persia and Armenia;‡ but he seemed doubtful whether to attribute to it an animal or a vegetable origin. More recently, General Hardwicke has described an Indian insect, under the name of *Chermis mannifer*, of the size of the domestic bug, and of a flattened oval form, with a rounded tail. From its abdomen a quantity of saccharine substance is exuded, and assumes the form

* It may be mentioned, however, that as ten or twelve pounds of kermes contain no more colouring matter than a single pound of cochineal, the latter at its ordinary price is after all the cheapest.

† Philosophical Transactions, 1794.

‡ Transactions of the Bombay Literary Society, vol. i.

of a bunch of feathers, with a consistence like that of snow. The insects are found on the branches and leaves of trees in millions, and they there generate this feather-like secretion, till it becomes elongated, and, dropping on the leaves, hardens upon them into a substance resembling the most beautiful wax.*

India abounds in hymenopterous insects, such as wasps and bees. The latter build their nests in hollow trees and rocky caverns, and produce great quantities of wax and honey. At times they prove troublesome and even dangerous, and often annoyed Mr Forbes in his visits to the caves at Salsette and the Elephanta, where they make their combs in the fissures of the rocks and the recesses among the figures, and hang in immense clusters. "I have known a whole party put to the rout in the caverns of Salsette, and obliged to return with their curiosity unsatisfied, from having imprudently fired a gun to disperse the bees, who in their rage pursued them to the bottom of the mountains."†

As we are not aware of any remarkable peculiarities in the history of either the *Neuropterous* or the *Dipterous* orders of Indian entomology, we shall leave these extensive divisions without any special comment, and conclude our present summary with a short historical notice of another insect-product of the East, of the highest value as a branch of manufacturing industry, and now so universally known under the name of *silk*. Though to ourselves "familiar as household words," its nature and origin were but obscurely, if at all, known in ancient times;

---

* Description of Gez or Manna, Asiatic Researches, vol. xiv. p. 182.

† Oriental Memoirs, vol. i. p. 46.

and in the days of Aurelian it was valued at its weight in gold. This was probably owing to the mode in which the material was procured by the merchants of Alexandria, who had no direct intercourse with China, the only country in which the silk-worm was then reared. Though the manufactures of silk were lauded in terms of the highest admiration both by Greek and Roman authors, they were in frequent use for several centuries before any certain knowledge was obtained either of the countries from which the material was derived, or of the means by which it was produced. By some it was supposed to be a fine down adhering to the leaves of trees or flowers; by others it was regarded as a delicate kind of wool or cotton;* and even those who had some idea of its insect-origin were incorrectly informed of the mode of its formation. The court of the Greek emperors, which surpassed even that of the Asiatic sovereigns in splendour and magnificence, became profuse in its display of this costly luxury; but as the Persians, from the advantages which their local situation gave them over the merchants from the Arabian Gulf, were enabled to supplant them in all those marts of India to which silk was brought by sea from the East, and as they had it in their power to cut off the caravans which travelled by land to China through their own northern provinces, Constantinople thus became dependent on a rival power for an article which its sumptuous nobles deemed essential to the enjoyment of refined life. Of course the Persians, with the accustomed and long-continued rapacity of monopolists, raised the price to an exorbitant height, and

* Robertson's Historical Disquisition concerning Ancient India.

many attempts were made by Justinian to free his subjects from such exaction. An accidental circumstance is said to have accomplished what the wisdom of the great legislator was unable to achieve. Two Persian monks, who had been employed as missionaries in one of the Christian churches established in India, had penetrated into the country of the Seres, that is, to China, where they observed the natural operations of the silk-worm, and acquired a knowledge of the arts of man in working up its produce into so many rich and costly fabrics. The love of lucre, mingled perhaps with a feeling of indignation that so valuable a branch of commerce should be enjoyed by unbelieving nations, induced them to repair to Constantinople, where they explained to the emperor the true origin of silk, and the various modes by which it was prepared and manufactured. Encouraged by the most liberal promises, they undertook to transport a sufficient supply of these extraordinary worms to Constantinople, which they effected by conveying the eggs in the interior of a hollow cane. They were hatched, it is said, by the heat of a dunghill, and the larvæ were fed with the leaves of wild mulberry.* They worked, underwent their accustomed metamorphosis, and multiplied according to use and wont; and, in the course of time, have become extensively cultivated throughout all the southern countries of our continent,—thus effecting an important change in the commercial relations which had so long existed between Europe and the East.†

It is curious to consider how the breeding of a

* Procopius, De Bello Gothico.

† See Gibbon's Decline and Fall, &c. (reign of Justinian) vol. iv.

few millions of caterpillars should occasion such a disparity in the circumstances of different tribes of the human race. When the wife and empress of Aurelian was refused a garment of silk on account of its extreme costliness, the most ordinary classes of the Chinese were clad in that material from top to toe; and although among ourselves week-day and holiday are now alike profaned by uncouth forms, whose vast circumference is clothed "in silk attire," yet our own James the Sixth was forced to borrow a pair of silken hose from the Earl of Mar, that his state and bearing might be more effective in the presence of the ambassador of England; "for ye would not, sure, that your king should appear as a scrub before strangers." King Henry the Eighth was the first of the English sovereigns who wore silk stockings.

The silk-worm cultivated in Europe is the same as that which produces the greater proportion of the Chinese manufacture. It is the larva of the *Bombyx mori*. But in Bengal and other parts of India, valuable silk is procured from the cocoons of other species of moth. The first of these, described by Dr Roxburgh under the name of *Phalæna paphia*, is found in such abundance over many parts of Bengal and the adjoining provinces, as to have afforded to the natives from time immemorial an abundant supply of a very durable, coarse, dark-coloured silk, called *tusseh*, much used by the Bramins and other sects of Hindoos. This species cannot be domesticated; but the hill-people go into the jungles, and when they perceive the dung of the caterpillars under a tree, they immediately search for them among the branches, and carry off whatever they require. These they distribute on the asseen trees (*Terminalia alata glabra* of Roxb.), and as long as they continue in the caterpillar state, the Pariahs guard them from bats by night and from birds by day. The natural food of this species is the *Byer* tree of the Hindoos, called *Rhamnus jujuba* by botanists. The Jaroo cocoons are produced from a mere variety of the kind just mentioned.*

The Arrindy silk-worm belongs, however, to an entirely different species (the *Phalæna cynthia*, Drury, vol. ii. tab. 6.), and appears peculiar to two districts in the interior of Bengal, viz. Rungpore and Dinagepore, where it is reared in a domestic state. The food of this caterpillar consists entirely of the leaves of the common *Ricinus* or Palma Christi, which the natives call Arrindy, and hence the name by which the insect is itself distinguished. The cocoons are in general about two inches long, and three inches in circumference, pointed at either end; they are of a white or yellowish colour, and their texture is extremely soft and delicate. The filament, indeed, is so exceedingly fine, that this silk cannot be wound off, but is spun like cotton. The yarn is wove into a kind of coarse white cloth, of a seemingly loose texture, but of such extreme durability, that the life of one person is seldom sufficient to wear out a garment of it; so that the same piece frequently descends from parent to child. It must always be washed in cold water.†

* The tusseh silk-worm moth appears to be synonymous with the *Bombyx mylitta* of Fabricius. It is figured by Drury in his Illustrations of Natural History, vol. ii. tab. 5.

† See Account of the Tusseh and Arrindy Silk-worms of Bengal. By William Roxburgh, M.D., F.R.S.E. Linn. Trans., vol. vii. p. 33.

The only other species of silk-worm to which we shall refer is alluded to in an extract of a letter published in the Annals of Agriculture by Mr Arthur Young. It has been introduced into India for a good many years. "We have obtained," says the writer alluded to, "a monthly silk-worm from China, which I have reared with my own hands, and in twenty-five days have had the cocoons in my basins, and by the twenty-ninth or thirty-first day a new progeny feeding in my trays. This makes it a mine to whoever would undertake the cultivation of it." We here close our sketch of the zoology of India.

"These are thy glorious works, Parent of good!
Almighty! thine this universal frame,
Thus wondrous fair; thyself how wondrous then!
Unspeakable; who sit'st above these Heavens,
To us invisible, or dimly seen
In these thy lower works; yet these declare
Thy goodness beyond thought, and power divine."

BOTANY.

CHAPTER VI.

Progress of Indian Botany—General Description of the Vegetation.

Climate—Investigators of Indian Botany—Foundation of the Calcutta Botanic Garden—Liberality of the East India Company—Dr Wallich's Exertions—His Return to Europe with large Collections—Generous Conduct of the Court of Directors—Some Results of Dr Wallich's Discoveries—Private Exertions of Dr Wight—Extent of the Indian Flora—General Features of Indian Vegetation on the Plains and on the Mountains.

Our knowledge of Indian vegetation, although extending itself with a rapidity almost unexampled in the botanical history of any country, is yet extremely limited. Nor can this be a matter for surprise when we call to mind the prodigious extent of our Asiatic possessions, reaching as they do from within six degrees of the equinoctial line to the thirty-fifth degree of northern latitude, with a range of temperature from that of the torrid zone to regions of perpetual snow. While, therefore, it is quite impossible, from deficiency of materials, to give any thing like a complete view of the Indian flora, whether we look to systematic details or the geographical distribution of its species, there is much interesting information, concerning the useful, singular, and beautiful plants of this fine country, that may be transferred to these pages.

What we do know of the vegetable productions of our Indian territories is to be ascribed almost exclusively to the munificence of the East India Company, as well as their rational desire to become acquainted with the economical resources of the country they govern, and to the unwearied exertions of the gifted individuals in their service. Before we proceed to the more immediate details of this sketch, it will not be uninteresting to trace an outline of the progress of Indian botany.

Of the earlier labours illustrative of our subject, the most eminent is the *Hortus Malabaricus* of Henry Van Rheede Van Drakenstein, governor of the Dutch settlements in the East Indies. This valuable work, consisting of twelve folio volumes with excellent plates, was published in the latter part of the seventeenth century, and made us acquainted with about 800 plants from Malabar. Subsequently appeared a catalogue of the plants of Ceylon by Paul Hermann, the *Thesaurus Zeylanicus* by Burmann, and in 1747 the *Flora Zeylanica* by Linnæus. Little seems to have been done between the date of the last work and the formation of the Botanic Garden at Calcutta, which took place in the year 1788; this was at first managed by its founder, the late Colonel Kydd, but soon came under the superintendence of the celebrated Dr Roxburgh, whose zeal and energy both enriched the institution and established his own fame. A *Hortus Bengalensis*, or "Catalogue of the Plants growing in the Honourable East India Company's Botanic Garden at Calcutta," was printed by Dr Carey in 1812, the year in which Dr Roxburgh was obliged to leave India on account of his declining health. The manuscripts of this excellent man contain descriptions of above 2500 plants, illustrated by nearly 2000 drawings executed by native artists, copies of which exist in the Company's Museum. From this source was compiled that magnificent work, Roxburgh's Plants of the Coast of Coromandel, in three volumes folio; and it has also served as a foundation for a *Flora Indica,* of which Dr Carey has published the two first volumes in octavo, extending as far as the first order of the Linnæan class *Pentandria.*

In 1814, when the Garden was for a short period under the direction of Dr Hamilton, well known by his Travels, his Account of the Fishes of the Ganges, and his Commentary on the *Hortus Malabaricus* and *Herbarium Amboynense,* the number of species amounted to 3500.*

Of Dr Wallich, the present superintendent, we must not in this place speak as the feelings of private friendship might otherwise dictate. He entered upon his arduous office in 1815, and his indefatigable energy and scientific perception have only been equalled by the devotedness with which he gave himself up to the duties of his situation. His exertions, it has been observed, have rarely been exceeded in any country, and certainly have never been paralleled in a tropical climate. "At his suggestion, the Directors of the East India Company placed the garden-establishment upon a footing far

---

* Hook. Bot. Misc., vol. ii.

surpassing any thing of the kind known in Europe. The spot of ground is no less than five miles in circumference, and upwards of three hundred gardeners and labourers are employed in the charge of it. Gardens in connexion with it have been formed in other remote parts of the Indian possessions; collectors have been sent out to discover new, and especially useful plants, and the residents and other gentlemen attached to science were invited to send the vegetable productions of their respective districts to Calcutta, both in a living and dried state; and among these, the Honourable Colonel Gardner, for a long time the Company's resident at Sylhet, furnished most extensive and valuable collections."*

The result of this enthusiasm has been a most noble and extensive collection, not only of living plants, which have been freely distributed, but of preserved specimens, which were transmitted from time to time to the Company's Museum. The herbaria, in fact, communicated by various individuals from all parts of India, and amassed by Dr Wallich himself in his excursions to Nepaul, to Singapore and Penang, to the kingdom of Oude, the province of Rohilcund, the Valley of Deyra, &c., and, lastly, to the court of Ava, the coasts of Martaban and Tenesserim, became so extensive as to contain nearly nine thousand species, and an almost incalculable number of duplicates.

A voyage to Europe having been pronounced indispensably necessary for the recovery of Dr Wallich's health, which had become greatly enfeebled by repeated attacks of fever, he arrived in England

* Hook. Bot. Misc., vol. ii.

in 1828, bringing with him the greater part of his enormous collections, in order that he might deliver them in person to the Court of Directors. Two great objects immediately occupied his attention: The first was the arrangement of the collection; for, with a princely liberality and due appreciation of the value and importance of natural science, the directors empowered him to proceed to the distribution of the duplicates among the principal public and private museums in Europe and America; and this laborious, yet pleasing task, he proceeded at once to effect. It is, however, yet more delightful to reflect, that the generosity of the Company has been every where met with an equally generous sentiment of gratitude, upwards of thirty of the most eminent botanists in Europe having come forward to undertake the publication of monographs of the more extensive and interesting families.* Thus will a splendid series of Asiatic plants, brought together at great labour and expense, be rendered available to the progress of science in the shortest possible period of time. The second object of Dr Wallich's attention, immediately after his arrival in this country, was the preparation of a magnificent work upon Indian plants, of which two volumes in large folio have already appeared under the patronage of the East India Company; and which, for scientific details and exquisitely-coloured plates, are worthy of appearing under such auspices, and of perpetuating the name of their most estimable author.†

---

* Wall. *Pl. Asiat. Rar.*, Preface.

† The work alluded to is the *Plantæ Asiaticæ Rariores*, or Descriptions and Figures of a select Number of East Indian Plants, by N. Wallich, M. et. Ph. D.

We cannot terminate this brief notice without mentioning another excellent friend, Dr Richard Wight, whose name will ever be associated with the cause of Indian botany. Besides contributing very largely to the herbarium brought home by Dr Wallich, he has for a considerable time employed two collectors and a draftsman at his own personal cost, and has returned to his native country with a finely-preserved collection of nearly 4000 species, and 100,000 specimens, all gathered in the presidency of Madras. It is Dr Wight's intention to publish his discoveries, and in the distribution of his duplicates to follow the example of the East India Company.

It is extremely difficult to form an estimate of the probable extent of the Indian flora, the vegetation of many parts of the country being entirely unknown, and almost every where very imperfectly explored. In fact, in the remote districts, little more has been done than to follow the courses of rivers. The herbarium in the Museum of the East India Company contains about 9000 species, including those known and described by Roxburgh in his manuscript catalogue, most of which were at that time new. To this amount remain to be added a considerable number of new species in the collection of Dr Wight. It is the opinion of the latter gentleman, that when he returns to India he shall be able to collect as many species in the presidency of Madras alone, as we possess at present from the whole of our possessions there. Dr Wallich obtained, from his own personal exertions in the Valley of Nepaul, and within an area of about sixty miles in circumference, upwards of 2500 species. Twelve months was the space of time devoted to this labour, and it cannot be supposed that he succeeded in discovering all the vegetable productions of that district. From these and other data, it has been calculated by Dr Wallich that we are not acquainted, at the present moment, with more than the eighth part of the flora of India; an estimate by no means improbable, but which gives to India itself as many species of plants as we find described in botanical works.

By the discoveries of Dr Wallich and his zealous coadjutors, a great accession of knowledge has been gained respecting the geographical distribution of many natural families of plants; and although this will be developed in a more perfect and useful manner when his collections shall have been described, yet even a list of those families which have been ascertained to belong (as far as we know) exclusively to India, or to abound, or to have their maximum in that country, will not, we hope, be without interest to the botanical reader.

The following families are exclusively Indian:— Chlenaceæ (confined to the Island of Madagascar), Dipterocarpeæ, Memecyleæ, Alangieæ, Aquilarineæ, Stilagineæ, Brexiaceæ (confined to Madagascar), Hydrocereæ (confined to the Island of Java), Nepentheæ (India and China).

The following families either abound in species or have their maximum in India:—

Araliaceæ, Nelumboneæ, Capparideæ, Flacourtiaceæ, Anonaceæ, Myristiceæ, Dilleneaceæ, Laurineæ, Menispermeæ, the true Sterculiaceæ and the section Dombeyaceæ of the same family, Moringeæ, Elæocarpeæ, Salicariæ, Myrtaceæ, Combretaceæ, Santalaceæ, Olacineæ, Leguminosæ, Urticeæ, Artocarpeæ, Euphorbiaceæ, Celastrineæ, Rhamneæ, Sapindaceæ, Vites, Meliaceæ, Cedreleæ, Aurantiaceæ, Connaraceæ, Amyrideæ, Burseraceæ, Anacardiaceæ, Ochnaceæ, Balsamineæ, Begoniaceæ, Piperaceæ, Cucurbitaceæ, Cinchonaceæ, Loranthеæ, Loganiaceæ, Asclepiadeæ, Apocineæ, Convolvulaceæ, Ebenaceæ, Jasmineæ, Myrsineæ, Cyrtandraceæ, Bignoniaceæ, Cycadeæ, Commelineæ, Scitamineæ, Smilaceæ, Pandaneæ, Aroideæ.

We are precluded, by the limits of this article, from entering into any details relative to the proportion which the number of species in the different families bears to that found in other parts of the world. Such calculations, besides, could we even introduce them, would be far from satisfactory, if drawn from such partial data. The number of species in some families is, however, already known to be very large. In the herbarium brought together by Dr Wallich, there are about 750 *Leguminosæ,* 500 *Cinchonaceæ,* nearly the same number of *Filices,* about 300 *Euphorbiaceæ,* 300 *Orchideæ,* and 300 *Gramineæ;* while, if we select a few of the genera, we shall find him to possess 114 species of *Conyza,* 105 kinds of *Ficus* (fig), 86 of *Convolvulus,* 88 of *Ruellia,* 78 of *Justicia,* 72 of *Cyperus,* 46 of *Urtica* (nettle), 43 of *Loranthus,* 40 of *Laurus,* 39 of *Tetranthera,* 27 of *Rubus* (bramble), 26 of *Quercus* (oak), 11 of *Viscum* (mistletoe), &c.

The vegetation which characterizes an Indian landscape depends upon so many circumstances, and varies so much according to situation and elevation, that it is not easy to convey more than a general impression by means of words. The warmer parts partake more or less of the features of a tropical,—the colder ones of those of an Alpine flora. In the low grounds bordering the seashore, especially of the peninsula and islands, the cocoa-palm, with its lofty, straight, and naked stems and feathery tuft of arching leaves, forms large groves, and, often lining the coast for many miles in succession, is a striking and conspicuous object. Sandy tracts of country on the seaside also produce various species of *Acacia,* whose finely-divided foliage is one of the first attractions to the eye of the stranger. In such places the *Euphorbia antiquorum* is common—an odd-looking, three-cornered, and thorny kind of spurge, the juice of which is supposed to furnish the Burmese with poison for their spears and arrows. One of the most frequent and pleasing features in the landscape throughout Indostan is the luxuriant and umbrageous mango-tope, yielding alike shade and subsistence to the inhabitants. The mango (*Mangifera Indica*) is a large tree with foliage somewhat resembling that of the Spanish chestnut, and producing a fruit which is said to vary in shape, colour, and flavour, as much as apples do in Europe. The fruit is brought to Europe in an unripe state, as a well-known pickle; but in India it is esteemed a delicacy by the rich, and a nutritious diet by the poor. According to Forbes, mango and tamarind trees are usually planted when a village is built. "Some of the plantations or topes are of such an extent, that ten or twelve thousand men may encamp under shelter. It is a general practice, when a plantation of mango-trees is made, to dig a well on one side of it. The well and the tope are married—a ceremony at which all the village attends, and large sums are often expended. The well is considered as the husband, as its waters, which are copiously furnished to the young trees during the first hot season, are supposed to cherish and impregnate them."*

No country in the world produces so large a number of forest-trees as India; many of them of the highest value for timber, and, unlike our European trees, often distinguished for ample leaves and large and fragrant flowers. Nothing can be more glorious than the appearance of an Indian scene during the period, or soon after the rainy season, when the whole country is replete with fragrance and verdure; when many of the more delicate herbaceous plants which had vanished, or languished under the intolerable heat, put forth their blossoms of every hue with astonishing rapidity, and seem by their wild luxuriance to express their joy and gratitude to the great Author of Nature. An endless variety of shrubs adorn the hedges, which are often formed of some kind of *Euphorbia* or the odoriferous *Pandanus*, while cucurbitaceous plants, and a vast number of bindweeds and other climbers, interlace their flexible branches, overtop the hedges, and decorate even lofty trees with festoons of living drapery. A species of *Trichozanthes* ascends to the tops of the highest trees, and produces a beautiful white flower with a fringed border, but which, expanding only in the night, is rarely seen; while the abundant fruit, nearly as large as a small orange and of a vivid scarlet-colour, is very ornamental. So numerous

---

* Forbes' Oriental Memoirs.

are climbers of this description, that trees and shrubs are lashed as it were together, and the Indian forests or jungles often rendered impenetrable except to birds and wild animals. Where the silk cotton-tree (*Bombax Ceiba*) and the Decannee-bean (*Butea superba*) abound, the effect which is produced, by the crimson blossoms of the one and the scarlet blossoms of the other, has been described as inconceivably splendid. These contrasted by their black stalks, observes Forbes in one of his poetic descriptions, give a brilliant effect to the western woods, which appear at sunset like immense forests in a glow of fire. The cocoa-palm has been already mentioned as forming a remarkable spectacle on the coasts of some parts of the country; other palms must not, however, be omitted in this picture, particularly the palmyra-tree (*Borassus flabelliformis*), one of the largest of the Indian palms, growing to fifty or even a hundred feet high, and surmounted by a circle of enormous fan-shaped leaves. The *Caryota urens*, nearly as lofty as the cocoa-tree, has a trunk sometimes nearly three feet in diameter, and a twice-feathered crown of leaves. All these, however, yield in grace to the betel-nut-tree (*Areca catechu*), the *po-ka-tshittoo* of the Hindoos,—a palm cultivated all over India for the sake of the fruit, the celebrated betel-nut. The trunk of this beautiful palm is perfectly straight, forty or fifty feet high and about twenty inches in circumference, smooth and of nearly equal thickness throughout its whole length. "There is a peculiar delicacy in the proportion and foliage of this tree," says Forbes, "which makes it generally admired; the Indians compare it to an elegantly-formed and beautiful woman." It will be at once felt how strikingly these princes of the vegetable kingdom must characterize the aspect of those districts where they most abound. Nor must we forget to particularly admire in the scenery of this country the several kinds of *Bambusa*, all passing under the popular name of bamboo. The bamboo is a native of tropical regions, and though a gramineous plant, attains almost an arborescent character: it is from thirty to a hundred feet in height; and, when bending gracefully before the wind, is affirmed by Humboldt to be one of the most remarkable objects in a tropical landscape.

The tanks and streams in India present a variety of beautiful flowers, mostly belonging to the genera *Nelumbo, Nymphæa,* and *Villarsia,* but going under the general denomination of water-lilies. These delight in a warm atmosphere, but the shade afforded by the surrounding groves is at the same time congenial to their nature; and their broad blossoms of various hues, as they float on the surface of the quiet water, are the admiration of natives as well as of foreigners.

As we leave the plains and ascend the hilly country, the vegetable forms are observed to change, and when we attain an elevation of about 5000 feet we begin to find a flora characteristic of a temperate region. "On arriving at what may be called the mountains, though they are not separated from the low hills by any distinct boundary, we have a very elevated region, consisting of one mountain heaped on another, and rising to a great height; so that when any fall happens in winter their tops are for a short time covered with snow. The inhabited valleys between these are in general very narrow, and are of various degrees of elevation, probably from 3000 to 6000 feet of perpendicular height above the plains of Puraniya. Of course they differ very much in their temperature; so that some of them abound in the ratan and bamboo, both of enormous dimension, while others produce only oaks and pines. Some ripen the pine-apple and sugar-cane, while others produce only barley, millet, and other grains. The timber-trees consist of various oaks, pines, firs, walnut, chestnut, hornbeam, yew, laurels, hollies, birches, *Gordonias*, *Michelias*, &c., most of them species hitherto unnoticed by botanists."*

Captain Raper, in his Survey of the Ganges, when speaking of the vegetation at a great elevation, mentions similar productions,—especially a species of oak, bearing acorns as large as pigeons' eggs and of the same form,—and abundance of hazel and walnut-trees.

Of many other European genera we find representatives in these regions, exhibiting a physiognomy derived from their elevated situation, which strikingly corresponds with that of species exposed to a similar temperature in other parts of the world. Roses are found in the tropical, but more plentifully in the temperate and frigid regions; while brambles delight in the two latter. The genus *Primula* occurs at an altitude of 5000 feet; *Androsace*, which is always more truly Alpine, at 10,000 feet. On the Himmaleh range we find *Geum*, and several species of *Ribes* (currants). Rhododendrons, Andromedas, and Gualtherias, have a range from the temperate

---

* Hamilton's Account of Nepaul.

to the frigid regions. *Rhododendron arboreum*, the most beautiful species of a beautiful genus, rises among the mountains to the height of a tree, with a trunk of above twenty feet, bearing large clusters of vermilion-coloured flowers at the ends of the smaller branches. Rose-coloured and white varieties were found by Dr Wallich on the very summit of the mountain Sheopur, in Nepaul, at an elevation of 10,000 feet. Even the strawberry flourishes, and the nearly-allied genus *Potentilla* furnishes among others two most remarkable species, *P. formosa* and *atrosanguinea*, which, for the sake of their fine red flowers, have been transported from the lofty summits of Nepaul to the flower-gardens of Europe. Among these mountains we also observe a species of *Cypripedium*, nearly allied to the European and American ones. *C. venustum* and *insigne*, which differ so much from their congeners, do not belong to Nepaul, as has been commonly believed, but were discovered, as Dr Wallich informs us, on the mountains of Sylhet. At about 1000 feet above the Valley of Nepaul, the genus *Pinus*, of which eight species are known to inhabit these regions, becomes conspicuous. Some of them are worthy of particular notice,—especially the *Pinus Deodar*, closely resembling the true cedar, and confined to great elevations; the *P. excelsa* of the *Plantæ Asiaticæ Rariores*, a gigantic tree with cones nine or ten inches in length; and *P. Webbiana* of Wallich, also an immense cedar-like tree with purple cones, from which the Tartars prepare a kind of indigo.

The discovery of a beautiful species of palm in the Valley of Nepaul must be regarded as an extraordinary phenomenon, and an exception to the general character of the vegetation of a mountain region. This palm was found by Dr Wallich in one circumscribed spot, at an elevation of 5000 feet above the lével of the sea, and has been named by him *Chamærops Martiana*,* after the celebrated Brazilian traveller and naturalist Von Martius, whose magnificent work on the Palms of Brazil fully entitles him to any distinction that one man of science can confer on another.

It is at an elevation similar to that of the Valley of Nepaul that the beautiful and graceful family of ferns begin to develop themselves in prodigious luxuriance and variety; nor do they cease to flourish under an elevation of 10,000 feet. Mosses, of which many very curious kinds have been forwarded to this country by Dr Wallich, prevail for the most part in similar situations. Lichens are more sparingly scattered than in Europe, and constitute, as in every other part of the globe, the limits of mountain vegetation.

---

* Since this notice was sent to press, we have received the ninth fasciculus of the *Plantæ Asiaticæ Rariores*, in which this palm is exquisitely figured from a drawing executed under the immediate inspection of Von Martius.

CHAPTER VII.

Some Account of a few of the more Remarkable Indian Plants, in which the Species are arranged according to the Natural Families to which they belong.

Plants deserving of particular Notice in the Families, Ranunculaceæ — Magnoliaceæ — Malvaceæ — Dipterocarpeæ — Combretaceæ — Thymeleæ — Santalaceæ — Rosaceæ — Leguminosæ — Urticeæ — Artocarpeæ — Betulineæ — Euphorbiaceæ — Cedreleæ — Aurantiaceæ — Anacardiaceæ — Piperaceæ — Sapoteæ — Valerianeæ — Cinchonaceæ — Loranthеæ — Apocyneæ — Verbenaceæ — Asphodeleæ — Palmæ — Gramineæ — Ferns and Acotyledonous Plants — Mosses — Algæ — Fungi.

RANUNCULACEÆ.

In this family are four species of aconite, natives of the mountain ranges of Northern India. All are said to be virulent poisons; but one of them in particular, the *Aconitum ferox*, of which a beautiful figure is given in the *Plantæ Asiaticæ Rariores*, is celebrated, and would appear from various experiments to contain a principle nearly, if not quite as powerful, as strychnine, the *upas*, and *woorara* poisons. According to Dr Wallich, it is probably the most deleterious vegetable poison of Continental India. The Sanscrit name is *visha* (poison), and Dr Wallich has satisfactorily ascertained that a poisonous plant, alluded to by Dr Hamilton in the following passage, and called *bish* or *bikh* by the natives, is really to be referred to the present species. "This dreadful root, of which large quantities are annually imported, is equally fatal when taken into the stomach or applied to wounds, and is in universal use for poisoning arrows; and, there is too much reason to suspect, for the worst of purposes. Its importation would indeed seem to require the attention of the magistrates. The Gorkhalese pretend that it is one of their principal securities against invasion from the low countries, and that they could so infect all the waters on the route by which an enemy was advancing, as to occasion his certain destruction."* Upon this account it has been remarked by Wallich, "his statement of the belief of the Gorkhas, that the bikh would protect them from foreign invasion, and his opinion that such a kind of defence might be easily frustrated, have been fully verified during the late war with Nepaul. In the Turraye, or low forest-lands which skirt the approach to that country, and among the lower range of hills, especially at a place called Hetounra, quantities of the bruised root were thrown into wells and reservoirs, for the purpose of poisoning our men and cattle; the attempt, however, was very soon discovered."†

It is added by the same author, that the *bikh* is employed in the northern parts of Indostan for destroying tigers. Arrows poisoned with that drug are shot from bows fixed near the tracks leading to their watering-places; and it generally happens that the animal is found dead at the latter. The tuberous roots are imported into the plains, and sold at the rate of a shilling a-pound.

* Hamilton's Account of Nepaul.
† Wallich's Plantæ Asiaticæ Rariores.

MAGNOLIACEÆ.

There are few genera in which the species are all so beautiful as in *Magnolia*. The family is a small one, and though its focus, as Professor Lindley has observed, is undoubtedly North America, where the woods, the swamps, and the sides of the hills abound with them, individuals straggle on the one hand into the West India Islands, and on the other into India, through China and Japan. A charming species, named by Wallich *Magnolia insignis*, was found by him at Sankoo, in the great Valley of Nepaul, and on the mountain Sheopur, towards its summit, a spot which appears to be singularly rich in a splendid vegetation,—for it was here where also grew the white and rose-coloured varieties of the tree rhododendron, and the *Quercus semecarpifolia*, a tree eighty to a hundred feet high, and with a trunk between twenty and thirty feet in circumference. Even *Magnolia insignis* is a tree of vast size, the trunk being frequently four or five feet in diameter. When in full blossom, it is affirmed by its estimable discoverer to be one of the most magnificent objects ever beheld; the large, fragrant, and beautiful yellowish-white flowers are produced in vast numbers amidst the dark-green foliage, and are succeeded by oblong cones of purple capsules, from which the scarlet seeds are suspended by delicate white threads. This noble tree will bear, there is little doubt, the climate of Great Britain; and to try the experiment, at least, is one of the many laudable objects to which Dr Wallich looks forward on his return to India.

The flower of the *champac*, which is either a species of *Magnolia* or *Michelia*, is frequently praised by Sanscrit poets for its elegant appearance in the black hair of the Indian women. A blue-flowering *champac* is said to exist; but the Bramins insist that it flowers only in Paradise.

MALVACEÆ.

Malvaceous plants abound in the tropics, forming, according to Humboldt, one-fiftieth of the flowering-plants. In India they are very numerous, and many species are put to economical uses. In China the well-known *Hibiscus Rosa Sinensis* is used by the people to blacken their eyebrows and the leather of their shoes. The different species of *Gossypium,* which furnish the cotton of commerce, and some of which are cultivated in India, belong to this place. *Hibiscus cannabinus,* the *gong-kura* of the Telingas, is much cultivated by the natives. According to Roxburgh, its leaves are used as an esculent vegetable, tasting like sorrel; and the bark is converted into a substitute for hemp, to which, however, it is in every respect greatly inferior. It is an herbaceous plant, from three to seven feet in height, with handsome flowers.

DIPTEROCARPEÆ.

The saul-tree (*Shorea robusta*) is a magnificent and much-esteemed forest-tree; it is indeed regarded as a staple timber of Indostan, and produces the best resin in the continent of India for naval and other purposes. The natives also prefer it to burn as incense in their temples. Lord Teignmouth and Sir William Jones collected evidence of this tree being employed in some of the superstitious practices of the country, which are too interesting not to transcribe: "To ascertain with a degree of certainty the persons guilty of practising witchcraft, the three following modes are adopted:—1. Branches of the saul-tree, marked with the names of all the females in the village, whether married or unmarried, who have attained the age of twelve years, are planted in the water in the morning for the space of four hours and a half; and the withering of any of these branches is proof of witchcraft against the person whose name is annexed to it. 2. Small portions of rice enveloped in cloths, marked as above, are placed in a nest of white ants; the consumption of the rice in any of the bags establishes sorcery against the woman whose name it bears. 3. Lamps are lighted at night; water is placed in cups made of leaves, and mustard-seed-oil is poured drop by drop into the water, whilst the name of each woman in the village is pronounced. The appearance of the shadow of any woman on the water during the ceremony proves her a witch."* Grains of rice are frequently resorted to by the deluded natives in other superstitious rites. When desirous of obtaining an answer to their prayers from any of their deities, they apply several grains of moistened rice to each side of the idol's body; then, after relating all the particulars of their case, they entreat him to signify his gracious pleasure by allowing some of the grains to fall on one side or the other. If the grains fall from the wrong side, the image is unfavourably disposed, and the petitioner begins the ceremony anew. The grains are again wetted and applied; and as they are just as likely to fall from one side as the other he never eventually fails of success.

* Asiatic Researches, vol. iv.

To *Dipterocarpeæ* belong some of the most splendid trees of India. The genus *Dipterocarpus* itself, the type of the family, is famous for affording the *carjan*, or wood-oil of the English; that obtained from one species in particular is, according to information kindly communicated by Dr Wallich, equal to linseed-oil as a drying oil for painting, and superior to it in conservative properties. Six *Dipterocarpi* are enumerated by Dr Wallich, and several are represented in Blume's *Flora Javæ*, of which *D. trinervis* and *retusus* are from one hundred and fifty to two hundred feet in height; *D. spanoghei*, one hundred feet in height and above ten feet in diameter; *D. gracilis*, equally thick, and one hundred and fifty feet in height. These trees must therefore rank among the most noble ornaments of an Indian forest, and deserve the appellation, "*arbores vastissimæ.*" *Dryobalanops camphora*, or the Sumatra camphor-tree, supposed by some botanists to be a species of *Dipterocarpus*, also rises to an elevation of one hundred feet, and is remarkable for yielding a kind of camphor, which is found lodged in cavities, a few inches wide, in the heart of the trunk. The trunk of one tree yields from ten to twenty pounds of camphor, called *se tantong*. It is said to be more pure than the common camphor of commerce, which is obtained from a kind of laurel, the *Laurus Camphora*.

The Indian genera, *Hopea* and *Vateria*, are likewise referred to this place; the former, containing some magnificent trees, was named in honour of Dr Hope, Professor of Botany in the University of Edinburgh; the latter is known for the resin it produces, which is said to resemble copal, and to be called by that name in India. The best specimens have the appearance of amber, and are manufactured into ornaments. In its recent and fluid state it forms a good varnish.

COMBRETACEÆ.

In this family are several plants extensively used in economy and the arts, some of which are produced in our Indian possessions. The most valuable is *Terminalia Chebula*, the *cadukay* of the Telingas, native of the mountainous parts of the Circars. It is a large tree, with a wide-spreading, shady, evergreen head, producing an oval yellow fruit about the size of a pigeon's egg. The timber is of considerable size, hard and durable; but the greatest use is made of the outer coat of the fruit, which is extremely astringent, by chintz-printers and dyers. A kind of gall found on the leaves, and which is sold in every market, is also extensively employed to produce one of the best and most durable yellows obtained in India. Ink made with the assistance of the fruit is said to stand the climate better than that imported from Europe. *Terminalia vernix* is believed to furnish the celebrated Chinese varnish.

THYMELEÆ.

From the bark of two or three species of *Daphne* the natives manufacture a very good paper, an account of which was published by Dr Wallich in the Asiatic Researches. As the information which he there gives is curious and interesting, and probably new to most of our readers, we shall lay it before them. The principal species made use of in the making of paper is the *Daphne cannabina*. It is a very branching shrub, six or eight feet high, with lanceolate shining leaves, and grows in the mountainous parts of Indostan, from Nepaul to the province of Kemaoon. The flowers are exquisitely fragrant, resembling those of the *D. odora* of our hot-houses. The paper manufactured from the bark is of various dimensions and texture. The finest kind measures ten feet in length by four feet in breadth, and is manufactured chiefly in Dotee, a province to the eastward of Kemaoon. It approaches in softness and size to that which is made in China, and Dr Wallich thinks it is not improbable that some of the latter may be produced from the same material. The following particulars are extracted by Dr Wallich from the MSS. of Lieutenant H. R. Murray, forming a part of that gentleman's official correspondence with the Military Board at Calcutta:—"The *Set-Burooa*, or paper-shrub, is found on the most exposed parts of the mountains, and those the most elevated and covered with snow, throughout the province of Kemaoon. In traversing the oak-forests between Bheemtah and Ramghur, and again from Almora to Chumpawat and down towards the river, it has come under the immediate observation of the writer of these communications, that the *Set-Burooa*, or paper-plant, only thrives luxuriantly where the oak grows; so that it is not likely that it will succeed in the plains. It is hardy, and attains a height of five or six feet; blossoming in January and February, and ripening its acrid red fruit about the end of April. The paper prepared from its bark is particularly calculated for cartridges, being strong, tough, not liable to crack or break, however much bent or folded, proof against being moth-eaten, and not in the least subject to dampness from any change in the weather; besides, if drenched or kept in water for any considerable time, it will not rot. It is invariably used all over Kemaoon, and in great request in many parts of the plains, for the purpose of writing *nusubnamees* or genealogical records, deeds, &c., from its extraordinary durability. It is generally made about one yard square, and of three different qualities. The best sort is retailed at the rate of forty sheets for a current rupee, and wholesale at eighty sheets. The worst sort, however, is of a much smaller size, and retailed at a hundred and forty sheets, and wholesale at a hundred and sixty or seventy for the rupee. The following is the very simple process of manufacturing this paper:—After scraping off the outer surface of the bark, what remains is boiled in fair water with a small quantity of the ashes of the oak,—a most necessary part of the ingredients,—which has the effect of cleaning and whitening the stuff. After the boiling it is washed, and immediately beat to a pulp with small mallets on a stone; so that, when mixed up in a vat with the fairest water, it has the appearance of flour and water. It is then spread on moulds or frames made of common bamboo-mats."*

Daphne Gardneri, another new species with fragrant flowers, described by Dr Wallich, and native of the mountains of Nepaul, also furnishes materials for making a very superior kind of paper.

SANTALACEÆ.

Few Indian productions are better known than the sandal-wood of commerce, the product of a small

* Asiatic Researches, vol. xiii.

tree, the *Santalum album* of Linnæus. Highly prized, however, as this fragrant wood is in Europe for various kinds of cabinet-work and ornamental articles, it is equally esteemed by the natives themselves. The best kind is brought from the western coasts of India. When the tree becomes old, the centre of the trunk acquires a yellow colour, great fragrance, and hardness, while the exterior part is less firm, white, and without fragrance. Among the Hindoos it is called *chandana,* and is frequently mentioned in their most ancient books. An elegant Sanscrit stanza, says Sir William Jones, of which the following version is literally exact, alludes to the popular belief that *vénus* (*veaugsa* according to others), or *bamboos* as they are vulgarly called, often take fire by the violence of their collision, and is addressed, under the allegory of a sandal-tree, to a virtuous man dwelling in a town inhabited by contending factions :—" Delight of the world, beloved *chandana,* stay no longer in this forest, which is overspread with rigid, pernicious *van-s'as,* whose hearts are unsound, and who, being themselves confounded in the scorching stream of flames kindled by their mutual attrition, will consume not their own families merely, but this whole wood."

ROSACEÆ.

Most of the plants belonging to this beautiful family are found in the temperate and cold climates of the northern hemisphere. In the West Indies only one solitary representative occurs, the *Rubus Jamaicensis.* In the East Indies, however, we find a richer flora,—the high lands of even the tropical part producing, according to Lindley, twelve species of *Rubus*. Dr Wallich's catalogue contains an enumeration of sixteen different kinds of *Rosa;* twenty-seven *Rubi;* two species of *Neillia;* ten of *Spiræa;* three of *Geum;* twenty-two of *Potentilla*, one only of which belongs to tropical India, &c. Were we to include in this family the POMACEÆ, considered by Lindley as distinct from the true ROSACEÆ,* we should be able to reckon in the Indian flora seven species of *Pyrus* (pear); eight of *Cotoneaster;* two of *Eriobotrys;* five of *Photinia*, &c. And among the AMYGDALEÆ, also a distinct family, according to the same author,† ten species of *Cerasus* (cherry); one of *Amygdalus*, &c. From the petals of *Rosa Damascena* is obtained that exquisite Indian perfume, attar of roses. This it is not unusual to adulterate, by adding raspings of sandal-wood during the process of distillation, or (as in Cashmere) the leaves of a sweet-scented grass. It is worthy of remark that genuine attar is of no peculiar colour. The same roses gathered on different days, but growing on the same piece of ground and treated in the same way, yielding attar of an emerald-green, a bright yellow, and of a reddish hue.

LEGUMINOSÆ.

We have already had occasion to notice how large a number of these plants are produced in British India. We have now to add, that there are few families which furnish more useful vegetables for the service of mankind. Here we find many gums and resins, many plants whose pods or seeds constitute

* Linnæan Transactions, vol. xiii. p. 93.

† Introduction to the Natural System of Botany, p. 84.

a nourishing diet, or, from their astringency, are sought after by the tanner and the dyer. The indigo, one of the most useful of all dyes, is yielded by *Indigofera Indica*. Some of our best timber is obtained from trees belonging to this family; and, where no striking property has been discovered, the exquisite beauty of many others entitles them to our attention and admiration. Some of the finest leguminose timber-trees are perhaps to be found in the genus *Dalbergia*. Roxburgh describes *D. latifolia* as one of the largest mountain-trees of the peninsula. The wood is known by the name of *blackwood*, and is of a grayish black with light-coloured veins, so heavy as to sink in water, close-grained, and admitting of the highest polish, which renders it highly esteemed for furniture. Dr Roxburgh mentions having seen planks of it from the Malabar coast full three feet and a half broad; and allowing nine inches of white wood to have been on the outside the circumference must have been fifteen feet exclusive of the bark. Equally useful, and possessing the advantage of being one of the quickest-growing timber-trees in the world, is *Dalbergia Cissu*. This wood, we are informed by Dr Wallich, has no rival for purposes where toughness and elasticity are required to be combined. It does not splinter when penetrated or perforated by a cannon-ball. Throughout Indostan the naves, felloes, and spokes of gun-carriage-wheels are made of it in preference to any other. In the navy it is chiefly excellent for what are called crooked-timbers. For all these purposes it attains a sufficient size in thirty-five or forty years: this is proved by several trees which were planted in the Botanic Garden at Calcutta in the year 1796, and which have now an elevation of eighty to a hundred feet, and a circumference of fourteen feet. *D. Cissu* is found only in the north of Indostan, and in point of geographical extension, we are assured by Dr Wallich, is one of the most limited species we know of. At the same time it is abundantly prolific in throwing up saplings; but though a forest produced in this way looks more promising than any other, the wood produced by sapling-timber is much inferior, and the greatest caution is therefore required. This propensity to throw up saplings is so striking, that no seedling is ever found within the confines of a *Cissu* forest, owing to the excessive luxuriance of the ground-shoots and the thin and perishable nature of the seed.

Butea frondosa, a rather large tree with a crooked trunk, is one of those considered holy by the Hindoos, who call it *Palása.* The leaves are twelve or sixteen inches long, composed of three oval leaflets; the flowers large and pendulous, and forming rich racemes,—their ground-colour a beautiful deep-red shaded with orange and silver-coloured down, which gives them a most elegant appearance. We are informed by Sir William Jones, that the *Palása* is named with honour in the Védas, in the laws of Menu, and in Sanscrit poems, both sacred and popular: it gave its name to the memorable plain called Plassey by the vulgar, but properly Palási. A grove of *palásas* was formerly the principal ornament of Chrishna-nagar, where we still see the trunk of an aged tree near six feet in circumference. From natural fissures, and wounds made in the bark during the hot season, there issues a most beautiful red juice, which soon hardens into a ruby-coloured brittle astringent gum, which may at some future time be applied to useful purposes.* A beautiful yellow dye is obtained from the flowers; and Dr Roxburgh mentions, that from the expressed juice of the fresh flowers, which, after diluting with alum-water, he evaporated by the heat of the sun into a soft extract, he procured a brighter water-colour than any gamboge he ever met with; nor did it fade during a period of twelve months. Another species of *Butea*, *B. superba*, is a very large climber, with a stem thicker than a man's arm, and bearing the most splendid flowers in such profusion as to render it one of the most gaudy vegetables known. They also yield a similar dye.

The next plant that we shall notice in our selection of leguminose species is perhaps one of the most interesting. This is the rice-paper-plant (*Æschynomene paludosa*), the *Shola* of the Bengalese. Much uncertainty has prevailed in regard to the real nature of the substance called rice-paper; and many people actually believe that rice enters in some way or other into its composition. This, however, is an erroneous impression. Rice-paper is prepared, or rather simply cut out of the stem of an herbaceous plant, to which Roxburgh gave the name above mentioned. The portions of the stem which we have seen are several inches in length, and from half an inch to above one inch in diameter, and entirely composed, to the very centre, of a fine white cellular tissue, marked in a transverse section with two or three delicate concentric circles, resembling those in the woody structure of dicoty-

* Roxburgh's Plants of Coromandel.

ledonous plants. In order, therefore, to procure a sheet of this substance, it is necessary to cut it in a circular manner, unrolling it, as it were, like a scroll. We learn from an account published by Dr Hooker,* that rice-paper was first brought to this country from China, about twenty-five years ago, by Dr Livingstone. The Chinese dye it of various colours, and employ it chiefly in the manufacture of their artificial flowers. Formerly, the size of each piece was about four inches square, but they may now be had upwards of a foot in length and five inches in breadth. This curious vegetable is not, however, confined to China. "It grows," says General Hardwicke, in a communication to Dr Hooker, "abundantly in the marshy plains of Bengal, and on the borders of jeéls or extensive lakes, in every province between Calcutta and Hurdwar. The plant is perennial, of straggling low growth, and seldom exceeds a diameter of two inches and a half in the stem. It is brought to the Calcutta bazars in great quantities in a green state; and the thickest stems are cut into laminæ, from which the natives form artificial flowers and various fancy-ornaments to decorate their shrines at Hindoo festivals. The Indians make hats of rice-paper, by cementing together as many leaves as will produce the requisite thickness; in this way any kind of shape may be formed; and when covered with silk or cloth the hats are strong and inconceivably light. It is an article of great use to fishermen; it forms floats of the best description to their extensive nets. The slender stems of the plant are bundled into fascines about three feet long; and with one of these

* Botanical Miscellany, vol. i.

under his arm does every fisherman go out to his daily occupation. With his net on his shoulders he proceeds to work without a boat, and stretches it in the deepest and most extensive lakes, supported with this buoyant fagot."

In a plant of the leguminose family, and one of the extensive genus *Crotallaria*, we have a very general substitute for hemp throughout the warmer parts of India, and even of Asia. This is the *Crotallaria juncea*, or *Sunn* as it is commonly called by the natives. Threads called *pavitraca*, from their supposed purity, have been made from it from time immemorial, and are mentioned in the laws of Menu. Many experiments were made upon the fibres of this and other Indian plants used as substitutes for hemp by the late Dr Roxburgh; and it was his opinion that *sunn*, when properly prepared, was very nearly as strong as hemp, and for various reasons preferable to it in India. The plant grows to about eight or ten feet high. An acre yields, of the half-cleaned substance (the state in which the natives carry it to market), about 600 pounds weight, and sells for about a rupee and a quarter per *maud* of 80 pounds.* This is the only plant cultivated by the natives of the Coromandel coast as food for their milch-cows during the dry season. Roxburgh also says, that he found it by experience to be very nourishing, and to produce more milk than most other fodder. It perishes after bearing two or three cuttings.

---

* For much interesting information on this subject, see "Observations of the late Dr Roxburgh on the various Specimens of Fibrous Vegetables, the Produce of India, which may prove valuable Substitutes for Hemp and Flax."

The last genus we shall notice is *Acacia*, well known for its airy and elegant foliage. Several species are highly prized on account of their useful properties, particularly *A. Arabica*, a pretty large tree, and abundant in most parts of India. Besides yielding the greater part of the gum-arabic of commerce, the wood is valued for its strong, tough, and durable qualities; it is excellent for knees and crooked-timbers in ship-building, for the wheels of carriages, and other purposes. The inner bark is a most powerful simple astringent, and is not only employed in tanning, but to dye various shades of brown; while the unripe seed-pods are used by the ink-makers. The gum is in great request by dyers and chintz-printers. *Acacia leucophlœa*, as large and as handsome a tree as the preceding, furnishes an astringent bark from which the natives distil an ardent spirit. The fresh bark, after having been cut in pieces, is fermented with water, palm-juice, and a little coarse sugar. When the fermentation is at its proper height, the liquor is distilled and the spirit drawn off. From a third species, whose wood is of uncommon hardness, the Bramins are accustomed to kindle their sacred fire by rubbing two pieces of it together.

URTICEÆ.

India is singularly rich in plants of this family. Dr Wallich's catalogue contains 47 species of *Urtica* (nettle), while in Sprengel's edition of the *Systema Vegetabilium*, the total number amounts only to 111 species. Fourteen species of *Procris* are also enumerated in the same catalogue. Several of the Indian nettles have been substituted for hemp by the natives, and experiments have been made upon the fibre, with a view of ascertaining its real value, but without much success. The *Urtica tenacissima* of Roxburgh is the most useful species for this purpose, and indeed is cultivated by the inhabitants of Rungpoor for the sake of the fibres of its bark, of which they make their fishing-nets. It is the *kankhura* of that district, and the *ramy* of the Malays. The plant grows from cuttings, and the fibres are certainly very fine and strong, but the cleaning is a tedious process. Every body is acquainted with the effects of the sting of the common European nettles, but they can hardly form an idea of the consequences which arise from handling some of the Indian species. Professor Lindley mentions a striking example in the case of M. Leschenault, who describes the effect of gathering *Urtica crenulata* in the Botanic Garden at Calcutta. The account is contained in the sixth volume of the *Mémoires du Muséum,* but as we have not that work at hand we shall quote Professor Lindley's own words. "One of the leaves (says M. Leschenault) slightly touched the first three fingers of my left hand: at the time I only perceived a slight pricking, to which I paid no attention. This was at seven in the morning. The pain continued to increase; in an hour it had become intolerable: it seemed as if some one was rubbing my fingers with a hot iron. Nevertheless there was no remarkable appearance; neither swelling, nor pustule, nor inflammation. The pain rapidly spread along the arm as far as the armpit. I was then seized with frequent sneezing, and with a copious running at the nose, as if I had caught a violent cold in the head. About noon I experienced a painful contraction of the back of the jaws, which made me fear an attack of tetanus. I then went to bed, hoping that repose would alleviate my suffering; but it did not abate: on the contrary, it continued during nearly the whole of the following night; but I lost the contraction in the jaws about seven in the evening. The next morning the pain began to leave me, and I fell asleep. I continued to suffer for two days, and the pain returned in full force when I put my hand into water. I did not finally lose it for nine days."* These effects did not arise from any peculiarity of constitution in M. Leschenault, for a workman in the garden was affected in the same way. There is, however, a nettle in Timor, called *daoun setan*, or devil's leaf, the effects of which are said by the natives to last for a year, or even to cause death itself.†

Cannabis sativa, or the common hemp, another plant of this family, is less known out of Europe for its useful fibre than the intoxicating and stupifying qualities of its leaves. The Hottentots resort to it for the purpose of inebriation, and call it *dacha*. By the Turks it is named *malach*; by the Persians *beng*. In some parts of India, among Europeans at least, it is known by the name of *bhang*, and is consumed very generally by the natives, especially in the northern parts of Indostan. It was formerly put to the vilest purposes. "State-prisoners in Mysore," says Dr Fryer, a writer in the latter part of the last century, "are sent by the king's order to a place of punishment, where the keeper, being informed of the heinousness of the crime, mingles for them a drink made of *bhang*,

* Introduction to the Natural System, p. 93. † Lindley.

the juice of an intoxicating sort of hemp. This at first they refuse; but on receiving the addition of some *dutry*, made from the deadly *solanum*, called *poss*, it makes them so foolishly mad, that, after a week's taking, they crave it more than ever they nauseated."*

ARTOCARPEÆ.

To the genus from which the name of the family has been borrowed belongs the well-known bread-fruit (*Artocarpus incisa*),† and the *jack* or *jaca* (*Artocarpus integrifolia*). The former, as well as the latter, is said to be found in India, besides eight other species, as appears from Dr Wallich's catalogue. The bread-fruit-tree is about forty feet in height, having a trunk commonly from one to two feet in diameter, and a large umbrageous head. The dark-green and glossy leaves grow to a great size, even two or three feet in length by fourteen to eighteen inches in breadth. According to Mr Ellis, the trunk is sometimes two or three feet in diameter, and rises from twelve to twenty feet without a branch. Speaking of this vegetable, the same author says, "A fine stately tree, clothed with dark shining leaves, and loaded with many hundreds of large light-green or yellowish-coloured fruit, is one of the most splendid and beautiful objects to be met with among the rich and diversified scenery of a Tahitian landscape. Two or three of these trees are often seen growing around the rustic native cottage, and embowering it with their interwoven and prolific branches. The tree is propagated by shoots from the root: it bears in about

* Dr Fryer's Account of East India and Persia.
† Botanical Magazine, tab. 2869, 2870, and 2871.

five years, and will probably continue bearing for fifty."* The fruit, which, in the South Sea Islands at least, is produced two or three, or even four times a-year, is something like a roundish or oval melon, with hexagonal marks, and six or eight inches in diameter. The seedless variety is most esteemed, and its substance, when roasted, resembles the crumb of wheaten-bread. The bread-fruit was called by Solander the most useful vegetable in the world; and Ellis, the excellent missionary, considers it the staff of life to the South Sea Islanders. Its praise has been sung by a noble poet, who has "married to immortal verse" less interesting and less innocent subjects.

> "The bread-tree, which, without the ploughshare, yields
> The unreap'd harvest of unfurrow'd fields,
> And bakes its unadulterated loaves
> Without a furnace in unpurchased groves,
> And flings off famine from its fertile breast;
> A priceless market for the gathering guest."

The wood of the tree is useful, and equally so the gum that exudes from it.

The *jaca*† is a larger tree than the preceding, the trunk being, according to Roxburgh, from eight to twelve feet in circumference. The fruit is oblong and very large, sixty or seventy pounds in weight, and containing several hundred seeds three or four times as large as almonds. As an article of diet it is not much esteemed, though the natives of Ceylon eat it freely. The milk-like juice which the plant gives out when wounded, in common with many others of its tribe, is so tenacious as to form good birdlime. The whole aspect of the *jaca* is extraor-

* Ellis' Polynesian Researches, vol. i. p. 353.
† Botanical Magazine, tab. 2833 and 2834.

dinary when seen for the first time, bearing, as it does, its "ponderous fruit, of the weight of sixty or seventy pounds, on the trunk and arms,—huge deformities for the lap of Flora."*

To the present family belong also the fig (*Ficus*), and the mulberry (*Morus*); of the former of which we have in Dr Wallich's catalogue 105 species, of the latter eight species. Of the Indian figs, very few indeed, we believe, are edible. *Ficus glomerata*, we are however told by Roxburgh, produces fruit in clusters nearly as large as the common fig, which is eaten by the natives, but not found palatable by Europeans. The most interesting species of this genus is unquestionably the banian-tree (*Ficus religiosa*), regarded with religious veneration by the Hindoos, because they believe their god Vishnu to have been born under it, and because they consider its long duration, and outstretching arms, and overshadowing beneficence, as emblems of the deity. Temples are often, from the same cause, erected near it, and images often planted under its shade. The most peculiar and striking feature of this remarkable tree is the property which it possesses of throwing out supports from the horizontal branches, which take root as soon as they reach the ground, enlarge into trunks, and, extending branches in their turn, soon cover a prodigious extent of ground. No tree can accommodate itself better to the situation where it happens to vegetate. According to Forbes, it frequently shoots from old walls, and runs along them. "On the inside of a large brick-wall one of these trees lined the whole circumference of the in-

* Guilding's Account of the Botanic Garden in the Island of St Vincent.

ternal space, and thus actually became a tree turned inside out." It has sometimes been known to enclose the trunks of palms or other trees, and has then received the name of the wedded-banian. A curious fact was communicated to us by Dr Wallich, which still farther illustrates its singular propensity to propel a shoot into every accessible quarter: A banian-tree in the Botanic Garden at Calcutta had extended a branch across one of the walks, and in due time a support thrown out by the branch took root and grew into a trunk on the opposite side of the walk. The original branch, now the connecting medium between the two trunks, happening to decay, an order was given for its removal; but it was ascertained that the offspring, finding the link between itself and its parent about to give way, had actually begun to send forth a healthy shoot along the centre of the decayed and yielding substance. It is hardly necessary to add, that the order was rescinded, and the two trunks are again united by what in this case may be metaphorically termed reciprocal affection. On the banks of the Nerbudda is a celebrated banian-tree; and though much of it has been swept away by high floods, what still remains is near two thousand feet in circumference, measured round the principal stems; the overhanging branches which have not yet thrown out supports cover a much larger space. The large trunks of this single tree amount to three hundred and fifty, and the smaller ones exceed three thousand. Each of these is constantly sending forth branches and hanging roots, to form other trunks, and become the parents of a future progeny. This tree is called *cubbeer-burr* by the Hindoos, in memory of a favourite saint, and has been known, in the march of an army, to shelter seven thousand men beneath its shade.* The leaves of this species are broadly ovate with a very long point, and, independent of the foot-stalk, not more than five or six inches in length; the fruit very small, of a bright scarlet-colour when ripe, and said to afford sustenance to monkeys, squirrels, and birds. Milton has admirably described the banian-tree in its principal phenomenon; but if it was indeed, as he makes it, the fig-tree of the book of Genesis, the leaves with which he invests it must have been larger in those days, to have served the purpose of our first parents, than the degenerate foliage which we now see.

"So counsell'd he, and both together went
Into the thickest wood; there soon they chose
The fig-tree; not that kind for fruit renown'd,
But such as at this day, to Indians known,
In Malabar or Deccan spreads her arms,
Branching so broad and long, that in the ground
The bended twigs take root, and daughters grow
About the mother-tree, a pillar'd shade,
High overarch'd, and echoing walks between:
There oft the Indian herdsman, shunning heat,
Shelters in cool, and tends his pasturing herds
At loopholes cut through thickest shade: those leaves
They gather'd, broad as Amazonian targe."

BETULINEÆ.

The northern parts of Indostan have furnished Dr Wallich with four new species of birch (*Betula*), and one of the allied genus alder (*Alnus*). The bark of *Betula acuminata*,† like that of *B. papyracea*, or the canoe-birch of America, is applied to economical purposes by the natives. The epidermis,

* Forbes' Oriental Memoirs.
† Plantæ Asiaticæ Rariores, vol. ii. tab. 109.

according to Dr Wallich, is employed by the mountaineers for writing upon instead of paper. Large quantities are brought down into the plains for covering the inside of the long flexible tubes of the apparatus used for smoking tobacco, called *hooka*. The Sanscrit name for birch is *bhoorja;* and Mr Graves Haughton, Oriental Examiner to the Honourable East India Company, observes Dr Wallich, " is of opinion that the word *bhoorja* is the etymon of birch, and that it is one of the many proofs of the descent of the Saxon part of the English language from the Sanscrita."

EUPHORBIACEÆ.

We have already mentioned that about three hundred species belonging to this family have been brought from India by Dr Wallich, among which are very many belonging to that difficult genus *Phyllanthus*. Various species of *Cluytia* are esteemed for their hard and durable wood of a red or pink colour. *Rottlera tinctoria* of Roxburgh yields a valuable dye. It is a middle-sized tree, growing in the mountainous parts of the Circars, having an erect trunk, and producing racemes of capsules about the size of a cherry, each of which is covered with a quantity of red powder. This powder is carefully brushed off the ripe capsules, and constitutes a considerable branch of commerce from those parts of the Circars, being purchased by the merchants trading to Hydrabad and other interior parts of the peninsula. It is said to dye silk of a very beautiful, bright, and durable orange or flame colour. The botanical reader will be aware that the genus *Rottlera* of Roxburgh is not the *Rottlera* of Vahl. The former is supposed by some botanists not to be distinct from *Trewia* of Linnæus.

CEDRELEÆ.

Swietenia febrifuga and *chloroxylon* furnish excellent timber. The former is the redwood-tree of Coromandel, a very large tree with a lofty, thick, and straight trunk. The wood is of a dull-red colour, remarkably hard and heavy, and used by the natives as the most durable kind they know for all the wood-work in their temples. *S. chloroxylon* is a native of the mountainous parts of the Circars, and is reported by Roxburgh to be of a deep-yellow colour, exceedingly close-grained, heavy, and durable, and to come nearer to boxwood than any other wood he had met with.

AURANTIACEÆ.

The orange tribe, so peculiarly Indian, is now, in regard to the orange, the lemon, the lime, and the shaddock, dispersed over the rest of the tropics; and although these plants are the most interesting ones that belong to the family, they are too familiar to our readers to require that we should devote to them any portion of this limited article. We shall therefore, after saying a very few words respecting the orange-tree, proceed to notice two or three less-known plants. We can form no idea of the size and luxuriance which the orange-tree is capable of attaining by the specimens cultivated with so much attention in this northern climate. It is said that in Spain there are old orange-trees forming large timber. "In the convent of St Sabina, at Rome, there is an orange-tree thirty-one feet high, which is said to be six hundred years old; and at Nice, in 1789, there was a tree which generally bore five or six thousand oranges, which was more than fifty feet high, with a trunk that required two men to embrace it."* Lindley mentions, when speaking of the productiveness of the orange-tree, that a single tree at St Michael's has been known to produce 20,000 oranges fit for packing, exclusively of the damaged fruit and the waste, which may be calculated at one-third more. "The duty upon oranges is £68,000 per annum, at the rate of two and sixpence for a package not exceeding five thousand cubic inches. Assuming the cubical contents of an orange as ten inches, there are five hundred in each package; and thus we see that 272,000,000 of this fruit are annually imported, allowing about a dozen per annum to every individual of the population."†

Ægle Marmelos is a pretty large tree in the mountainous parts of the Coromandel coast, producing a sort of berry of the size of a large apple, which is a wholesome, fragrant, and delicious fruit. Within this fruit are from 10 to 15 cells, containing, besides a few seeds, a great quantity of a very tenacious transparent gluten, which may be drawn out in threads of one or two yards in length, and so fine as to be scarcely perceptible to the naked eye; when dry it is hard and transparent. In the Island of Ceylon a perfume is prepared from the rind. The wood-apple (*Feronia elephantum*) is another fruit, the pulp of which is universally eaten on the Coromandel coast, according to Roxburgh, though Forbes

* Library of Entertaining Knowledge, on the authority of Risso, vol. ii. p. 330.

† Ibid.

says it is acid, full of seeds, and only eaten by the poorer natives. Externally it is circular, hard, and woody, and about the size of an orange, with the smell of a mellow apple. The tree is a large beautiful evergreen, bearing at the same time blossoms and fruit, the latter of which hang at the extremity of long slender branches, that bend with their weight. The last plant of the orange family which we shall notice is *Bergera Kœnigii,* a small tree growing in the mountainous parts of the Circars, but cultivated in gardens for the sake of the leaves. These are used both in a fresh and dried state for mixing with the curries of the natives, of which they form a principal ingredient, and are to be found in every bazar.

ANACARDIACEÆ.

One of the most interesting individuals in this family is the *Melanorrhœa usitata,* of which an excellent plate and ample account is given by our friend Dr Wallich in the *Plantæ Asiaticæ Rariores.* It is an enormous tree, with fine massy foliage, and splendid clusters of dark rose-coloured involucres, which at first sight look like the blossoms. Its known geographical range is from Munipur, in lat. 25° north, long. 94° east, to Tavoy, in lat. 14°, long. 97°. Every part of it abounds in a thick and viscid grayish-brown fluid, which turns black on exposure to the air. This fluid is collected in large quantities, and forms an admirable varnish, supposed to be the same made use of by the Chinese in their eastern and north-eastern provinces. There is also no doubt that it is the *theet-tsee,* or varnish-tree of the Burmese. This, as well as some other Indian varnishes, is dangerous to many constitutions, and produces painful and alarming effects.*

Another large tree producing varnish is the *Semecarpus Anacardium*, or marking-nut-tree of commerce, a native of the mountainous parts of India. The seed of this tree is a nut resting on a fleshy receptacle, and furnished with two coats, between which is the black, corrosive, resinous juice, from which the varnish is manufactured. The fruit, while green, is sometimes pounded into a pulp for bird-lime; and the acrid juice used externally to remove rheumatic pains, but it often produces inflammation. The fleshy receptacle of the seed is roasted in the ashes and eaten by the natives; the taste is exceedingly like that of roasted apples.

PIPERACEÆ.

The betel-leaf, familiar by name at least to the general reader, is a species of pepper, the *Piper betel* of Linnæus. It is highly esteemed by the natives of India, and cultivated in most of the provinces, but especially in Guzerat. It is a beautiful climber, and yields, after its fourth season, an abundant supply of leaves for six or seven years.

SAPOTEÆ.

In several trees of this family we find a singular substitute for an animal product. The máhwah-tree or Indian butter-tree (*Bassia butyracea*), the oil or illeepei-tree (*Bassia longifolia*), and the shea-tree or butter-tree of Africa, probably also a species

* Plantæ Asiaticæ Rariores, vol. i. p. 9.—See also, for an account of the poisonous qualities of vegetable varnishes, Brewster's Journal of Science, vol. viii. pp. 96 and 100.

of *Bassia*, are among the number. The máhwah-tree is the most remarkable one in India; it is about the size of an English oak, according to Forbes, but with a beautiful, large, shining foliage. The flowers are produced in full clusters at the ends of the smaller branches, and look exactly like berries; the true fruit, however, resembles a walnut, the olive-shaped seeds of which are replete with a thick oil, which is used as a substitute for ghee. To obtain the oil, the kernels are bruised to the consistence of thick cream, and then submitted to pressure. The oil or fat becomes immediately of the consistence of hog's lard, and is of a delicate white colour. The flowers are equally prized, for, when dried in the sun, they have been compared to Malaga raisins, both in flavour and appearance. They are eaten, in fact, in various ways,—as a preserved fruit, as an ingredient in curries and other dishes, or even in their fresh state. A good tree will produce in one season nearly three hundred-weight of flowers. Their greatest consumption, however, is in the distillation of a kind of spirit, which goes by the name of máhwah-arrack, and is so cheap that an English pint may be had for one *pice*, about the value of a halfpenny.

The oil expressed from the fruit of *Bassia longifolia* is constantly used by the common people instead of ghee and cocoa-nut-oil. The flowers are also collected for food, as in the preceding species, and almost every part of the plant put to some use. It is said that owls, squirrels, lizards, dogs, and jackals, eat the flowers, and that the latter sometimes become mad by partaking too freely of them.* Both

* Asiatic Researches, vol. viii. p. 480.

these plants must yield to the butter-tree of Africa. "The kernel," says Park, "is enveloped in a sweet pulp, under a thin green rind; and the butter produced from it, besides the advantage of its keeping the whole year without salt, is whiter, firmer, and to my palate of a richer flavour than the best butter I ever tasted made from cow's milk. The growth and preparation of this commodity seem to be among the first objects of African industry in this and the neighbouring states."* It is called *shea toulou*, or tree-butter.

VALERIANEÆ.

The spikenard of the ancients, about which there has been much learned controversy, has been at length satisfactorily referred by Sir William Jones to a species of valerian, named by the Hindoos *jatámánsì*, and which he therefore calls *Valeriana Jatamansi* (*Nardostachys Jatamansi*, D. C.) It abounds in the most remote and hilly parts of India, such as Nepaul, Morang, &c., near which Ptolemy fixes its native soil. The part of the plant known more particularly under the name of spikenard, or Indian nard of commerce, is a mass or series of numerous sheaths arising from the top of the root, and enveloping the lower part of the stem for the space of five or six inches; the outer ones, fibrous,—the inner ones, membranaceous,—and the whole bearing considerable resemblance to an ermine's tail. It is carried over the Desert to Aleppo, where it is used in substance mixed with other perfumes, and worn in small bags or in the form of essence, and kept in little boxes or phials like attar of roses.

* Park's Travels in Africa, p. 202.

As a perfume its use is of very remote antiquity, being alluded to several times in the Holy Scriptures, particularly in the Song of Solomon, iv. 13, 14.

"Thy plants are an orchard of pomegranates, with pleasant fruits; camphire, with spikenard.

"Spikenard and saffron; calamus and cinnamon, with all trees of frankincense; myrrh and aloes, with all the chief spices."

Considerable quantities of *jatámánsí* are brought in caravans from Bootan; but living plants cannot be exported without a license from the sovereign.*

CINCHONACEÆ.

A very numerous order, in which at least five hundred species are now known to be Indian. The beautiful gardenias are found here, so much prized for their delightful fragrance; *Gardenia dumetorum* produces a fruit like a small yellow apple, which, when bruised and thrown into tanks, intoxicates the fish, and in the hot season destroys them;—but in the cold season they are said to recover.

One of the most elegant among Indian trees is *Nauclea orientalis.* The flowers are capitate, and deck the charmingly-verdant foliage with, as it were, thousands of little globes of golden flowers. They have an odour very agreeable in the open air, which Sir William Jones says the ancient Indians compared to the scent of new wine; and hence they call the plant *Halipriya,* or beloved by Halim, that is, by the third Rama, who was evidently the Bacchus of India.† The leaves of *Canthium parviflorum,* a common scraggy thorny bush, are universally eaten in curries.

* Asiatic Researches, vol. ii. and vol. iv. p. 433, with a plate.

† Asiatic Researches, vol. iv.

LORANTHEÆ.

Eleven species of that most remarkable genus mistletoe (*Viscum*) are in the East India Company's collection; and it is a circumstance deserving of notice, that, according to Sir William Jones, the *Viscum* of the oak (he does not specify any species) is named *vandà*, the *vandáca* or oak being held sacred.* It has always been our opinion that the British mistletoe was not held sacred by the Druids, except when it was found growing upon the oak; and hence the association between the mistletoe and the oak. Perhaps the fact that it was hardly ever discovered in this situation gave rise to the superstition; for it is certain that it is an exceedingly rare event in this country to find it growing upon the oak, even in districts where it is a nuisance upon apple, thorn, and other trees.

APOCYNEÆ.

Strychnos potatorum will be known to some of our readers as the clearing-nut of India. It is rather a scarce, moderate-sized tree, growing mostly in mountainous districts, and producing a shining black berry about the size of a black currant. The peculiar purpose to which they are applied is thus described by Dr Roxburgh :—" The ripe seeds are dried, and sold in every market to clear muddy water. The natives never drink clear well-water if they can get pond or river water, which is always more or less impure according to circumstances. One of the seeds or nuts, as they are generally called, is rubbed very hard for a minute or two round the inside of the vessel containing the water, which

* Asiatic Researches, vol. iv.

is generally an unglazed earthen one, and the water left to settle; in a very short time the impurities fall to the bottom, leaving the water clear, and, so far as I have been able to learn, perfectly wholesome."* The fruit of another Apocyneous plant (*Carissa carandas*), resembling a black middle-sized plum, is said to make a pickle superior even to that of the mango. *Urceola elastica*, or the elastic-gum-vine, is a plant of this order, which yields a viscid milky juice possessing the properties of caoutchouc. It is an extensive climber, two hundred yards or more in length, winding among the branches of the loftiest trees, and rising above them into the open air. The milk, when exposed to the atmosphere, becomes solid; and by means of it Mr Howison succeeded in rendering cloth waterproof, and suggested that it might be applied to the making of hats, great-coats, tents, coverings for carriages, &c. The plant grows in Sumatra also, and Dr Roxburgh believes that the Chinese make their elastic rings from its juice.

VERBENACEÆ.

One of the largest Indian trees and one of the most valuable for its excellent timber is referred to this family,—the teak (*Tectona grandis*). The trunk is erect, lofty, and of an enormous size, the leaves above twenty inches long and a foot or more in width, the flowers small, white, and fragrant, and collected into very large panicles. It is a native of various parts of India, and was introduced into Bengal by Lord Cornwallis and Colonel Kydd.

Long experience has proved the wood of this tree

* Plants of Coromandel.

to be the most useful timber in Asia. It is light, easily worked, and at the same time strong and durable. For shipbuilding it is considered equal to oak, and many of the vessels trading between this country and India are constructed of it. That which grows near the banks of the Godavery is beautifully veined, closer in the grain, and heavier.

ASPHODELEÆ.

Very few examples of this family occur in India, and of those we shall only speak of the bowstring-hemp (*Sanseviera Zeylanica*), which Dr Roxburgh thought might be cultivated to great advantage for the sake of its fibre. It is a plant with one to four radical semi-cylindrical leaves, one to four feet long, with the flowers produced on a scape about two feet in height. The leaves contain a number of very strong white fibres, from which the natives manufacture their best bowstrings. Roxburgh obtained, from eighty pounds of the fresh leaves, one pound of clean dry fibres, and from half the quantity of better leaves, in a second experiment, the same weight of fibre; and this quantity might be produced on three square yards of ground. "I am inclined to think," says the same naturalist, "that the fine line called china-grass, which is employed for fishinglines, fiddlestrings, and other purposes, is made from these fibres."

PALMÆ.

On some of the Indian species of this magnificent tribe we have already made some observations; but they form too important a feature in the vegetation of the country, and are too extensively useful to mankind not to demand a more particular notice. The fruit of the *Areca catechu* is the celebrated betel-nut, esteemed, both for its narcotic qualities and as a fine preservative of the teeth and gums, by the inhabitants of the East. It resembles a large nutmeg enclosed in a thick membranaceous covering: when used it is cut into small pieces, and eaten with the pungent leaf of *Piper betel,* spread over with *chunam* or delicate shell-lime. The palmyra-tree (*Borassus flabelliformis*), formerly alluded to as one of the largest Indian palms, is not only a splendid but a most useful plant. The fruit forms an article of food in various states of preparation, and abundance of *toddy* or palm-wine is obtained by dividing the young spadix or branched receptacle of the fructification, and collecting the juice which flows from the wounded part. In old trees the wood, or that part which constitutes the shell or circumference of the trunk, is of singular hardness and durability, and is much employed for the making of rafters for roofs, &c. The centre is composed only of a coarse spongy farinaceous sort of pith. With the leaves the natives thatch their houses and construct baskets, and they are commonly used as a substitute for paper, being written on, or rather engraved, with an iron-pointed instrument.

In the Peninsula occurs a dwarf species of date-palm, named *Phœnix farinifera* by Roxburgh, but little known to botanists in general. It appears to be found chiefly on sandy lands at a small distance from the sea. The trunk is only one, or at most two feet high, and so entirely enveloped in the leaves, which are a good deal like those of the common date-palm (*Phœnix dactylifera*), that the whole appears like a large round bush. Baskets are constructed of the leaflets, and a great quantity of farinaceous substance is obtained from the centre of the stem, which in times of scarcity has frequently supplied the poor people with food. It is, however, less nutritious and palatable than common sago.

The cocoa-nut (*Cocos nucifera*) is of all palms most deservedly valued as one of the greatest of the many blessings showered down by a bountiful Providence upon the inhabitants of a tropical climate. It is a common saying that the cocoa-nut-tree has ninety-nine uses, and that the hundredth cannot be discovered. The limits prescribed to this article will only permit us to describe its general appearance, and give a brief outline of the purposes to which the various parts are applied. This palm is from sixty to a hundred feet in height, and one to two feet in diameter: at the top it is crowned with a magnificent tuft of leaves, each about fourteen feet in length, and resembling an enormous feather. It rejoices to grow in the moist low grounds that border the seacoast, or that form the neighbouring islands. Nothing can be more beautiful than these cocoa-groves. The bare trunks rise like columns to a vast height, and the regular foliage arching their summits carries the eye along the vistas, as it were, of a boundless Gothic edifice. It is a very prolific tree; flowers are put forth every four or five weeks, and thus flowers and fruit are generally to be seen at the same time. Of the roots are constructed baskets; of the hollowed trunk drums, pipes for aqueducts, &c. The reticulated substance at the base of each leaf, besides serving for infants' cradles, is manufactured into coarse sackcloth. The terminal bud is accounted a delicacy for the table. The leaves are employed for thatching buildings, for making baskets, fences, and torches, besides furnishing the chief diet in Ceylon of the tame elephants: in a young state they are transparent, and are made into lanterns by the Ceylonese. The woody ribs of the leaflets are formed into a kind of basket-work for catching fish, and into the brushes and brooms used for domestic purposes. Good potash is yielded by the ashes, and the latter is used instead of soap by the native washermen of Ceylon. From the unexpanded flower is procured the sweet juice, which is converted into a pleasant wine celebrated by one of our poets.

> "Stretch'd amid these orchards of the sun,
> Where high palmettos lift their grateful shade,
> Give me to drain the cocoa's milky bowl,
> And from the palm to draw its freshening wine;
> More bounteous far than all the frantic juice
> Which Bacchus pours."

The same fluid is unfortunately distilled into arrack; and frantic indeed and melancholy are the effects which spring from the intoxicating draught, from whatever source it be obtained! Even the juice of this fertile tree the wayward ingenuity of man has converted from a blessing into a curse. The spirit is manufactured in such large quantities in Ceylon, that it is sold for a trifle, and is productive of all the unhappy consequences which invariably follow its use as a common beverage. From palm-juice is likewise prepared in great abundance a coarse kind of sugar called *jaggery*. The value of the fruit of this tree, the well-known cocoa-nut, can only be fully appreciated in the countries that produce it. As an article of food it is inestimable.

The fibrous covering is an admirable substitute for hemp, and is largely manufactured into *coir*,—a substance peculiarly well adapted for the cordage of vessels. When the Dutch were in possession of Ceylon, they made annually, according to Mr Marshall, 3,000,000 lbs. weight of coir. A vast quantity of oil is expressed from the kernel, the excellent quality and commercial value of which are known to every one.

GRAMINEÆ.

It is in tropical countries that the tribe of grasses attains its utmost development in regard to size. Accustomed to behold them in cold and temperate regions, forming the verdant carpet that stretches far and wide over our hilly pastures and fertile meadows, or at most contemplating our fields of waving corn, or the reeds which fringe the borders of our streams, we can hardly imagine individuals of the same family emulating the stature of the trees of the forest, and constituting an equally imposing feature in the panorama of a living landscape. Such however is the bamboo (*Bambusa*), whose name is derived, as we are informed by Dr Wallich, from the Hindoo word *veangsa*, pronounced *bungsa*, signifying a family or tribe,—for the bamboo grows many together or in an associated manner. The bamboo is applied to a great variety of purposes, and no plant is more useful where a union of strength and lightness is required. In building it is so generally employed, that the houses of the inferior classes in India are almost exclusively constructed of it. It is adapted to the formation of bridges, masts for boats, and almost every article of domestic furniture. Bedding and sacking, and even cordage, are manufactured from it. It is the common fence for gardens and fields, and palanquins and light carriages are principally composed of it. The hollow stems serve for water-pipes, and in military operations it has often been resorted to for the construction of screens. Finally, according to Barrow, the Chinese find the bamboo invaluable for keeping the whole empire in due subordination, through the medium of incessant bastinading. We shall now proceed to notice briefly the different kinds of bamboo that are most valued for their useful properties. The most common one is the *Bambusa arundinacea:* this produces from ten to one hundred stems from the same root, and after continuing straight for fifteen or twenty feet begins to bend gently to one side. It bears innumerable branches, the joints of which are furnished with double or triple thorns. It is in the cavities of the joints of this species in particular that the curious substance called *tabasheer* is found, though it is not improbable that it may exist in most of the others likewise. This substance is named *vedroo paloo* (milk of bamboo) by the Telingas, and *mungil upoo* (salt of bamboo) by the Tamuls. Medicinal virtues are attributed to it, and it is mentioned in the Sanscrit works on medicine, such as the *Bhava Prakas* and *Raja Nighant.** Dr Turner has shown it to consist of "silica, containing a minute quantity of lime and vegetable matter." In Malabar this kind of bamboo is formed into an arch, by training it, while growing, over an iron frame, to the shape required for supporting the canopies of palanquins. Finely-arched speci-

* Dr Wilson, in Brewster's Journal of Science, vol. viii. p. 268.

mens have been known to bring five or six hundred rupees. *Bambusa stricta* is a smaller species, considerably more straight in the stem, and with a smaller cavity; on which accounts it is better adapted to some purposes, and the natives always select it for making shafts to their spears. *Bambusa spinosa* is in request for scaffolding and wicker-work. *Bambusa baccifera*,* a tall and very curious species, having for fructification a large pendulous one-seeded berry, is a native of the Chittagong mountains, and used in that country for all building purposes. It is said to be a foot in diameter at the base, from fifty to seventy feet in height, bare of branches except near the extremity, and so beautifully straight as to be without the least flexure or inequality of surface. According to M. Pierard's account, in Roxburgh's Plants of Coromandel, it yields more or less *tabasheer*; "sometimes, it is said, the cavity between the joints is nearly filled with this substance, which the people call *choonah* (lime)." There is another species which grows on the Martaban coast, having the stem about twelve inches in diameter, and a hundred feet in height: this appears to be undescribed.

All the species of bamboo are at first tender and succulent; they grow with amazing rapidity, but they are often many years before they produce flower and seed. This primary object being once accomplished, they die and are succeeded by a new generation.

The sugar-cane (*Saccharum officinarum*) was known in the East at a very early period; but it is cultivated to a very small extent with a view to the making of sugar. The cane is still in request, be-

* Roxburgh's Plants of Coromandel, vol. iii. p. 38, t. 243.

ing cut into small pieces, and sold like fruit in the bazars.

Several plants of this family are cultivated in India, in the same manner as corn is with us; of these the principal are *Oryza sativa* (common rice), *Sorghum vulgare, Pennisetum typhoideum, Eleusine corscana, Paspalum scrobiculatum, Panicum miliaceum.*

Poa cynosuroides, another species of grass, called *cut'ha* and *darbha* by the natives, is held in peculiar favour by them,—so much so, that, according to Sir William Jones, "every law-book, and almost every poem in Sanscrit contains frequent allusions to the holiness of this plant; and in the fourth *Véda* we have the following address to it at the close of a terrible incantation:—'Thee, O Darbha, the learned proclaim a divinity, not subject to age or death; thee they call the armour of India, the preserver of regions, the destroyer of enemies; a gem that gives increase to the field. At the time when the ocean resounded, when the clouds murmured, and lightnings flashed, then was *Darbha* produced, pure as a drop of fine gold!' Some of the leaves taper to a most acute evanescent point; whence the Pundits often say of a very sharp-minded man, that his intellects are acute as the point of *cus'a* leaf."*

In regard to the *Filices* and families of the acotyledonous class, little has hitherto been done to elucidate the Indian flora. We are, however, in possession of materials, which will, to a certain extent, supply this desideratum. It has already been stated that the collection in the East India Company's

* Asiatic Researches, vol. iv. p. 253.

Museum contains between four and five hundred species of Fern. Some of these have been represented and described in the *Icones Filicum*, by Hooker and Greville, and the publication of the remainder will be undertaken by the same gentlemen at no distant period. We have received from Dr Wallich many interesting mosses and *hepaticæ*, some of which have already been given to the world in Dr Hooker's *Musci Exotici;* and by Dr Wight we have already been put in possession of about one hundred species of *Algæ*. Of the Indian *Fungi* very little is known, and but few species have reached us. The natives hold them "in such detestation, that *Yama*, a legislator, supposed now to be the judge of departed spirits, declares, that 'those who eat mushrooms, whether springing from the ground or growing on a tree, are fully equal in guilt to the slayers of Bramins, and the most despicable of all deadly sinners.' "*

---

* Asiatic Researches, vol. iv. p. 311.

CLIMATE,

GEOLOGY, AND MINERALOGY.

CHAPTER VIII.

Climate.

Himmaleh Region—Middle India—Peninsular India—Height of the Land in the Peninsula—Meteorology—1. Changes in the Pressure of the Atmosphere; 2. Composition of the Atmosphere; 3. Effects of Mountain-air; 4. Temperature of the Atmosphere; 5. Making of Ice in India; 6. Snow-line; 7. Height of the Snow-line in the Himmalehs; 8. Evaporation; 9. Humidity of the Atmosphere; 10. Dew; 11. Rain; 12. Monsoons; 13. Hail; 14. Falling Stars and Meteoric Stones; 15. Mirage; 16. Black Colour of the Sky over the Himmalehs; 17. Zodiacal Light; 18. Miasmata; 19. Climate; 20. Sanitary Depôts—Table of Comparative Temperatures.

In the view we are now about to take of it, India may be considered as formed of three grand divisions, viz. 1. The Himmaleh. 2. The belt of flat country extending from the Indus to the Brahmapoutra, which may be distinguished by the name of *Middle India*. 3. The region which constitutes *Peninsular India*.

1. *Himmaleh or Alpine Region.*—The central and interior region of Asia, which forms neither an immense cluster of mountain-chains nor a continued table-land, is crossed from east to west by four grand systems of mountains, which have manifestly influenced the movements of the population;—these are, the Altai, which is terminated on the west by the mountains of Kirghiz, the Teen-shan, the Kwan-lun, and the Himmaleh chain. Between

the Altai and the Teen-shan, are placed Zungaria and the basin of the Ele; between Teen-shan and the Kwan-lun, Little or rather Upper Bucharia, or Cashgar, Yarkand, Khoten, the great desert Cobi (or Cha-mo), Toorfan, Khamil (Hami), and Tangout, that is, the Northern Tangout of the Chinese, which must not be confounded with Thibet or Sefan; lastly, between the Kwan-lun and the Himmaleh, Eastern and Western Thibet, where Lassa and Ladak are situated. The Himmaleh system, the only one which at prèsent particularly interests us, separates the valleys of Cashmere, Nepaul, and Bootan, from Thibet. To the west it stretches by Javaher to 26,420 feet; to the east by Dhwalagiri to 27,000 feet above the level of the sea. It ranges generally from north-west to south-east, and consequently is not parallel with the Kwan-lun; it approaches it so nearly in the meridian of Attok and Jellalabad, that between Cabul, Cashmere, Ladak, and Badakshan, the Himmaleh seems to form a single group of mountain-chains with the Hindookho and Tsung-ling.

In those parts of the Himmaleh that form the northern boundary of India are situated some of the highest mountains in the world. Of these the most elevated summit at present known is Dhwalagiri, or White Mountain, already mentioned. The following are other heights, as determined by Webb:—

	Feet.
Jumnotree,	25,500
Setghur, or the White Tower, north of Nepaul,	25,261
A mountain, supposed to be Dhaibun, above Catmandoo, in the direction of Cala Bhairava, 20,000 feet above the Valley of Nepaul, and above the sea,	24,625
Another mountain near it, 18,662 feet above the Valley of Nepaul, above the sea,	23,262
A third, in its vicinity, 18,452 feet, above the sea,	23,052
A peak, named St George, was estimated by Hodgson at	22,240

Mountain Region.—Interposed between the *Alpine* and *Pestilential Regions* of India is the richest mountain land in the world, the beautiful girdle of Assam, Bootan, Nepaul, Serinagur, Cashmere, and Peshawer. These delightful regions range in altitude upwards of 7000 feet above the level of the sea, rising with a steep ascent from the plains of the low country. According to Rennel, the southernmost of the Bootan mountains attain nearly a mile and a half of almost perpendicular height, in a horizontal distance of fifteen miles; and from the summit the traveller looks back with wonder on the extensive prospect of the plains beneath. When the great range changes to a westerly direction, near the upper part of the Ganges and Indus, the lower mountains are separated from it by a wide interval occupied by the lofty valley of Cashmere; and to the south and south-west is a mountainous country, which on the north bounds the Punjaub or country of the five rivers. When in December Turner returned from Thibet, then covered with ice and snow, in Bootan every thing was green, and the trees were loaded with apples and oranges,—so great is the difference of climate. Notwithstanding this, the summer temperature of Tassisudon in Bootan resembles that of the winter of Bengal, and the Bootan winter is too severe for the rajahs, who descend and spend that season in the warmer Chickacotta. The Bengalese clothe themselves in silk and muslin; the Bootanese in wool; the Thibetians in wool and fur; and not less characteristic is the contrast between the feeble Hindoo in Bengal and the Herculean Bootanese, or the active, abstemious Thibetian. The Hindoo, accustomed to the moist and sultry atmosphere of Bengal, cannot exist in the cold and dry Alpine air of Thibet, and conversely the Thibetian cannot live in the sultry India.

Pestilential Region.—A zone of unequal breadth, of a peculiar nature, lies between the northern mountainous and hilly boundary of India and the low country. It extends from the frontiers of Assam almost uninterruptedly to the banks of the Ganges and Jumna, at Hurdwar and Serinagur. It is thirty miles broad on the Bootan frontier, and here, as elsewhere, is filled with swamps, and covered with a dense and luxuriant vegetation. It forms the natural boundary between Bengal and Assam, Bootan and Nepaul. None of the neighbouring nations have been able to obtain an ascendency in this melancholy region; for man flies its marshes, which are inhabited principally by amphibious and other offensive creatures; and, where the woods penetrate among the lower hills, numerous herds of elephants range from Assam to Hurdwar. The exhalations arising from the multitude of springs, which the vicinity of the mountains produces, are collected and confined by those almost impervious woods, and generate an atmosphere through which no traveller ever passed with impunity. Its effects were fatal to Captain Jones, and to a great part of his troops in 1772.

Goître Region.—The pestilential region is not without inhabitants, though its influence has wholly debased in them the form, the size, and the strength of human creatures. Here the disease named *goître* prevails. From Rungpoor towards Bootan it is estimated that every sixth man has a crop or swelling. It occurs also in Lower Bootan; but Turner saw nothing of the kind in Thibet. The inhabitants of Assam are visited with great goîtres, and also the people of the valleys of Serinagur and those that dwell near the open land of Kemaoon. This disease, conjoined with cretinism, prevails throughout the whole zone, from the borders of Assam, in 27° north lat. and 110° east long., to Hurdwar on the Ganges, in Rohilcund, in 30° north lat. and 78° east long., in those districts bounded on the south by Bijnee, Cooch-bahar, Rungpoor, Dinagepoor, Purnea, Tirhoot, Bettiah, and the northern boundary of Oude through Gooracpore, Baraitsch, Pillibeat, and on the frontier of Rohilcund, through Hurdwar. It extends farther to the westward: Forster met with it on his mountain journey from the Jamboo pass towards Cashmere. Appearances of the same kind occur on the southern border of the Cobi above Pekin, in the Kolla and Magaza in Africa, in the marshy woods of Simbani, in the land of the Mandingoes, in the southern acclivity of the Alps, &c., as well in those places where snow-water is wanting as where it is met with,—a fact in opposition to that opinion which ascribes the goître disease to the bad qualities of the snow-water.

2. *Middle India.*—This great comparatively flat region, the richest and most productive part of our eastern empire, comprehends—1. The great tract watered by the Ganges. 2. The tract watered by the Indus. 3. The intermediate desert.

As this division of India is noticed in a preceding volume of this work, we need not enter into farther details, but merely remark that the alluvial tract from Hurdwar to the mouth of the Ganges, may, according to Hindoo speculators, formerly have been occupied by the sea,—thus giving to the peninsular part of India an insular form; and that the Desert, which in many of its characters resembles strongly the African and Arabian sandy plains, is the eastern portion of the vast series of deserts which stretch from the western boundary of the great Sahara in Africa across the whole of that continent, Arabia, part of Persia, to the west side of the Indus.

3. *Peninsular India.*—The Peninsula of India, which is totally unconnected with the Himmaleh range, is bounded by the waters of the ocean and the plains of Central or Middle India, and forms as it were a world for itself. It is bounded on the north by a mountainous, hilly, and table-shaped country, which includes the mountains extending from the Gulf of Cutch on the west to the Bay of Bengal on the east, viz. those of Guzerat, Malwah, Candeish, and Gundwana. We also, in a geological view, include in this region the mountainous and hilly ranges stretching around the great Western Desert as far as the neighbourhood of Oodipoor, Ajmere, Jyepore, to Delhi. On the south-west and south-east it is bounded by the Indian Ocean and the Bay of Bengal.

The Ghauts enclose the main body of the Peninsula, which consists of table-lands and mountains and hills, elevated from 2000 to 4000 feet above the sea. The ranges of the Ghauts join on the north side of the great pass or *gap* of Coimbetoor, first made known during the military excursion of Colonel Fullerton. This striking pass is about sixteen miles wide. It is well known that ships navigating the Malabar coast during the north-east monsoon commonly experience a stronger gale in the neighbourhood of Paniani than elsewhere; and this opening in the Ghauts appears to be the cause of this effect. It is also said that the lower part of the Coimbetoor country partakes of the rainy or south-west monsoon of the Malabar coast, which may be referred to the same cause. We regret we have not been able to find any statements in regard to the height of this pass above the Coromandel and Malabar countries.

From the south side of the gap the Ghaut range continues onwards in a southerly direction to Cape Comorin, where it terminates. The land at its extremity is low and flat, covered with trees, and not visible from the deck more than four or five leagues; but about half a mile inland is the mountain of Komari, the termination of the Ghauts, rising to a height of nearly 4000 feet. From this mountain the southern extremity of India takes its name; its position is lat. 8° 4′ north, long. 77° 45′ east. Daniel says it is quite smooth and verdant to the very summit. Near the base bursts forth a magnificent cataract.

Country below the Ghauts.—On both sides of the Peninsula, interposed between the foot of the mountains and the coast, there is a tract named Payeen-ghaut, or below the Ghauts; that above these ranges being named Balaghaut, or above the Ghauts. The country below the Ghauts is composed of hilly and low and flat country, varying in breadth from a few miles to eighty or ninety.

Height of the Land in the Peninsula.—The following determinations of heights we owe to Captain Cullen of the Madras Artillery:*—

* In Mr Babington's paper in the 5th volume of the Geological Society's Transactions, the height of one peak, Bónasson hill, is

Without taking into account those habitable but confined tracts in the Nhilgerry hills, which are from 5000 to 7000 feet, and those on the Shervaroy or Salem hills, from 4000 to 5000 feet above the level of the sea, the table-land of Mysore presents the most elevated surface of the Peninsula. The highest part of this table-land includes the stations of Bangalore, Nundidroog, Colar, and Oossoor, forming an area of sixty miles by fifty, and presenting a mean altitude of about 3000 feet. There is a rapid fall thence on every side; and the mean height of this belt may be stated at about 2400 feet. The valley of Seringapatam, including the town of Mysore, is also about the same height.

Trichinopoly, the capital of the southern division, is only about 250 feet above the sea; but the ground rises to the southward, attaining at one point the height of 800 feet; so that, if a line be drawn by Madura and Palamcotta to Cape Comorin, it would give a mean altitude of between 400 and 500 feet. The country in this quarter has a gradual rise from the eastern shore to the westward, where it is bounded by the great Travancore chain of mountains.

There is indeed a very remarkable ascent observable throughout almost the whole of the Peninsula south of Berar, from the eastern shore to the great Western Ghauts; and one need only cast his eye on the map to perceive this by the course of the rivers,

---

said to be 7000 feet above the sea; and in a description of the Nhilgerry region by Dr Smith Young, the peak of Dodapet, situated between 11° and 12° north lat. and 76° east long., is said to rise to an elevation of 8700 feet. It is much to be regretted that we have so few published reports of heights by actual geometrical or barometrical measurements, of the principal summits in the Peninsula.

which uniformly take an easterly direction, and fall into the Bay of Bengal. The country, from Madras by Arcot towards the bottom of the Pedanaigdroog pass, rises gradually to between 800 and 900 feet above the sea; and a similar slope may be considered to obtain for sixty or seventy miles southward of Madras, and for 130 or 140 miles north of it. The western coast is however more hilly, and is covered with jungles or forests, from the sea to the Western Ghauts. The mean height of the provinces of Malabar and Canara may be estimated at about 200 feet above the sea.

The Ceded Districts adjoining the Mysore territories on the north partake of the general slope which has been noticed. Bellary the capital, lying nearly in the centre of the province, is about 1600 feet above the sea, and the rise continues westward till it attains the elevation of 2500 feet. Belgaum in the Doab, situated at this height, is nearly the highest part of that province.

The average height of the province of Hydrabad, including an area of nearly the same magnitude as the Mysore table-land, is about 1900 feet above the sea; the city of Hydrabad lies low, near the northern edge of this area. The slope to the east and the north-west from this elevated tract is rapid; that to the north is much more gradual; the space to the south, between it and the Ceded Districts, comprehending the bed of the Kistna, is from 1100 to 1300 feet above the sea.

The elevation of Bangalore and Hydrabad thus interrupts the general slope of the Peninsula. The country round Jaulna is from 1600 to 1800 feet above the sea, and the general ascent from east to west is here very distinctly marked. Poonah, situated very near the Western Ghauts, is believed to be 2500 feet, or nearly so, above the sea.

The flat open plains of Nagpore seem to indicate their approach to the alluvial districts of the Ganges; for at the very base of the Peninsula, and at a distance of 400 miles from either the eastern or western sea, they attain only an elevation of 800 or 900 feet. Hinginghaut, fifty miles south of Nagpore, is only 700 feet above the sea.

The northern division, including Guntoor, is a series of level plains, elevated nowhere more than 50 feet above the sea. The Ghauts approach the coast near Vizagapatan, without causing any material alteration in the level of the intermediate valleys.

The following table contains some barometric measurements by Mr Babington across the Peninsula from Madras to Tellicherry:—

	Feet.
Arcot above Madras,	$624\frac{1}{2}$
Chittore above Arcot,	$432\frac{1}{2}$
Mooglee above Chittore,	$578\frac{1}{2}$
Pullamaurey above Mooglee,	579
Nungily above Pullamaurey,	116
Moolwagul above Nungily,	$437\frac{1}{2}$
Colar above Moolwagul,	$3\frac{1}{2}$
Mysore above Seringapatam,	283
Top of Ghaut above Peria,	251
Midway Hut below top of Ghaut,	$973\frac{1}{2}$
Bottom of Ghaut below Midway Hut,	$1320\frac{1}{2}$
Mr Dyer's house, Tellicherry, below bottom of Ghaut,	$329\frac{1}{2}$
The Sea below Mr Dyer's house,	119
Malabar Sea below Bangalore,	2698
——— Differs from Lambton's measurement,	210

METEOROLOGY.

The atmosphere of India is chiefly tropical, a small extent only being situated in the southern part of the northern temperate zone. In some districts, however, the atmosphere, owing to the form, elevation, and nature of the surface of the land, exhibits characters almost identical with those of the northern temperate, and even of the polar regions. To place in full array before our readers a complete view of a subject so vast and complicated as the meteorology of India, would very far exceed the limits of the present work. We must therefore rest satisfied with the following details and views, which will illustrate, in a popular view, the meteorology of Indostan:—

1. *Changes in the Pressure of the Atmosphere.*—The changes in the pressure of the atmosphere, as ascertained by means of the barometer, have not in India been traced out with that care and accuracy which the importance of the subject demands. Of the barometric phenomena, the most curious are those that point out the daily atmospheric tides, the horary motions, or the double rise and fall of the barometer within twenty-four hours. In India, as in the temperate and arctic regions, there are daily or hourly variations, in which the mercury in the barometer is always higher at 9 A.M. and 9 P.M., than at 3 P. M. and 3 A. M. These motions are much more distinct in India, and in tropical regions in general, than in temperate regions. From the observations of Humboldt we learn, that in tropical America these atmospheric tides are independent of changes in the weather and seasons. Thus, if the mercury is falling from nine in the morning until three or four in the afternoon, or if it be rising from four in the afternoon until nine or eleven at night, a storm, an earthquake, or violent tempest of wind, does not affect

or alter its course. It appears to be affected only by true time, or the position of the sun. In the tropical regions, he adds, the moment when the mercury begins to fall is so marked, that the barometer indicates true time within a quarter of an hour. Whatever truth may be in the latter observation of Humboldt, there can be no doubt as to the motions themselves. The only observations made in India with which we are acquainted, are the very interesting ones of Dr Russel at Burhanpoor, in 24° north lat., and of Mr Prinsep at Benares, in 25½° north lat., continued for three years, and which harmonize in general with those made in other tropical countries. At present we are not in possession of a range of observations sufficiently extensive to enable us to explain these horary motions. The speculations of Humboldt, Leslie, and others on this subject, are unsatisfactory. It is indeed evident, that these motions are connected not only with the atmospheric temperature, but also with its associated moisture. Until, however, we have a series of hourly-connected observations of the barometer and hygrometer we cannot attempt any explanation likely to be plausible.

The connexion of the mean monthly heights of the barometer with the south-west and north-east monsoons is also a subject of considerable interest, and is well illustrated in barometrical observations made at Seringapatam, Bangalore, Calcutta, Benares, Catmandoo, and Madras, for the particulars of which we refer to the original tables and observations of the observers.

2. *Composition of the Atmosphere.*—It would appear from experiments made in different countries and at different heights, that the proportions of

oxygen and azote, the principal constituents of the atmosphere, do not vary. Carbonic acid, another but minute constituent of the earth's atmosphere, is said to vary in quantity; for at one and the same place the carbonic acid suffers continued changes as to quantity, according to the temperature, wind, rain, and atmospherical pressure. Thus, near Geneva, according to Saussure, the mean quantity of this gas in 1000 parts by volume of air is at mid-day 5., or more accurately 4.9; the maximum is 6.2; minimum, 3.7. The same excellent observer finds, that in Switzerland carbonic acid *increases* in *summer*, but *diminishes* in *autumn*; farther, that the quantity of carbonic acid at *mid-day*, in December, January, and February, is to that in June, July, and August, as 77 to 100. He also found, that over a *wet soil* the atmosphere contains less carbonic acid than over a *dry* one; that more exists in the atmosphere during the *night* than during the day; that the *superior* strata of the atmosphere contain more than the *inferior*; and, lastly, that a *violent wind* generally augments the quantity in the lower atmospheric strata during the day, by the intermixture of the lower and upper aërial strata, and sometimes by the wind blowing from a dry quarter. Besides azote, oxygen, carbonic acid, and water, the atmosphere occasionally contains, probably in some measure as *accidental* mixed parts, a particular vegeto-animal matter, and salts of various descriptions. The preceding details show what is expected from those who may undertake to make us acquainted with the chemical nature of the atmosphere of India,—a subject of great importance, but hitherto neglected.

3. *Effects of highly-attenuated Mountain Air.*—It is well known that on ascending high mountains, owing to the diminished pressure of the atmosphere, the animal, and indeed also the vegetable, functions are more or less affected. Some individuals of the human species feel these changes very intensely, while others experience comparatively little inconvenience. This latter circumstance has led some philosophers to imagine, that these enervating effects are solely owing to fatigue, and not to the attenuated state of the air,—an opinion, however, which is disproved by a fact stated by Gay Lussac, who, during his ærostatic voyage, while calmly seated in his balloon, experienced all those distressing symptoms mentioned as occurring to travellers on their ascent of Alpine lands. Our enterprising countrymen, while exploring the Himmalehs, suffered from this cause. Thus Captain Gerrard, in the account of one of his journeys, says, "Our elevation was now upwards of 15,000 feet, although we had but ascended in company with the river against its current. Here only began our toils, and we scaled the slope of the mountain slowly; *respiration was laborious, and we felt exhausted at every step.* The crest of the pass was not visible, and we saw no limit to our exertions. The road inclined at an angle of 30°, and passed under vast ledges of limestone. The projections frowned above us in new and horrid forms, and our situation was different from any thing we had yet experienced. *Long before we got up, we were troubled with severe headachs, and our respiration became so hurried and oppressive, that we were compelled to sit down every few yards, and even then we*

*could scarcely inhale a sufficient supply of air. The least motion was accompanied with extreme debility and a depression of spirits; and thus we laboured for two miles."** Even the lower animals are observed to experience similar inconvenience from attenuated air. Thus the yak and the horse are mentioned by Moorcroft and others, as suffering considerably when driven into high mountainous situations.

The effects of the attenuated air on sound is also a curious subject for observation and experiment. Saussure found sounds very feeble on the summit of Mount Blanc; Dr Schultes experienced the same on the Glockner and Stiria; and other travellers notice the comparatively small extent to which the voice can be heard at an altitude of 13,000 feet on Mount Rosa. Observations have never, as far as we know, been made on this point among the Himmalehs, although such would prove interesting. They might be made by the explosions of a small detonating pistol loaded with a constant charge, and the distances should be measured; for the voice loses much of its force from the diminution of muscular energy in rarefied air, and distances are much underrated by estimation in such situations.

4. *Temperature of the Atmosphere.*—The problem of the distribution of heat over the globe is a very complicated one, the solution of which requires a vast series of data, founded on observations continued for a long period of years by experienced meteorologists, provided with a full complement of the best instruments. In this investiga-

* For other details on this subject, see that valuable periodical the Asiatic Journal.

tion, independent of other inquiries, we have to determine with accuracy the inflection of certain lines of equal annual temperature, the *isothermal lines;* also those of equal summer temperature, the *isotheral lines;* and of equal winter temperature, the *isochemenal lines:* we have to fix the relative positions of these lines in regard to each other, and to the meridians and parallels of latitude.* Such inquiries, although most interesting to the professed meteorologist, cannot be indulged in a work of this description with any prospect of advantage; and besides, the known data are by no means so satisfactory as to allow us to enter on the subject with that confidence which would be inspired by the conviction of our having to work with numerous good observations made with accurate instruments. Such being the case, we shall here simply notice the general range of Indian temperature, referring for the temperature of particular provinces to the observations under the head of each.

The range of temperature is very great, extending from the freezing-point of water, and even below it, to 130° of Fahrenheit's scale. The highest temperatures are met with in the great Western Desert and other sandy districts at the level of the sea, or nearly so, as the Circars and the Lower Carnatic. Elphinstone observed the thermometer at 112° in the Western Desert; but he remarks that, even where these high temperatures prevail, the evening air is cool to such a degree that the English gentlemen of the embassy used to suffer from cold during the night-marches, and were happy to kindle a large fire

* It is even of importance, in reference to climate, to determine by means of springs the *isogeothermal* lines.

as soon as they reached their ground; yet the sun became so powerful, early in the morning, that they always woke with a feverish heat which lasted till sunset. Humaioon, the father of the great emperor Akbar, lost most of his followers in the march over this dreadful desert; beneath a vertical sun, on burning sands and without water, tortured with violent thirst, they were seized with frenzies, burst out into piercing screams and lamentations; they rolled themselves in agonies on the parched soil, their tongues hung out of their mouths, and they expired in most exquisite tortures.* Speaking of the Circars, Heyne says, nothing can be more distressing than the failure of the sea-breeze for several successive days, when the land-wind blows all night, and heats every thing so much as to become distressing to the touch. This was the case in the year 1799, in the Northern Circars, for about a fortnight. The thermometer at *midnight* stood at 108° F., and at eight o'clock A. M. at 112°. Neither wood nor glass is capable of bearing the heat for any length of time; the latter, as shades, globe-lanterns, &c., crack and fly in pieces; the former warps and shrinks, and the nails fall out of the doors and tables. Heyne never saw the thermometer higher than 115° F. in the coolest part of the house. Some persons affirm, that in such cases they have seen it as high as 130° F. The climate in the lower part of the Carnatic is one of the hottest in India. Frost never occurs in the Deccan, or to the south of it; but sometimes the temperature of Hydrabad is only 6° or 8° above freez-

* Dow's Ferishta, 8vo edition, ii. 159.

ing. In Malwah, during the hot season, the parching winds from the northward and westward, that prevail in most parts of India to an intense degree, are comparatively mild and of short duration. The thermometer, however, during the day rises sometimes as high as 98°; but the nights are invariably cool and refreshing. During the cold season the thermometer sinks as low as 28°. In the higher parts of India, as at Delhi, in north lat. 28° 37′, for example, the winter's cold is sometimes 3° or 4° below the freezing-point of water, and the tanks are frozen entirely over. In a Persian work called Mutaghevin, or Modern Times, there is mention made of a frost at Delhi which continued three nights, in consequence of which brazen vessels filled with water burst.

5. *Making of Ice in India.*—Ice is considered a great luxury, and hence is made in many parts of the country. All over Upper India it is procured in a very simple manner. A number of broad shallow earthen pans are placed on a layer of dry straw, and filled with water. In the night even the slight frost felt is sufficient to cover these with a thin crust of ice which is carefully collected and packed up. An intelligent gentleman, David Scott, Esq., says, the subject of artificial congelation is not so well understood by scientific men in Europe as it might be. The old story of *evaporation* being at the bottom of the process, and *porous* pans being necessary for its success, is repeated by one author after another, although nothing can be more erroneous. In respect to the first, it seems sufficient to observe that, when ice is produced in temperatures above the freezing-point, a plentiful deposition of

dew is always going on, which seems to be altogether inconsistent with the idea of air being in a state capable of receiving fresh accessions of moisture. Mr Scott found, by repeated experiments, that ice may be produced although a thin film of oil be spread over the surface of the water,—the latter being contained in *glazed* plates, which indeed answer much better than the *porous* pans of the country, the ice in them being invariably thicker, and the water, when it does not actually freeze, somewhat colder than the similar contents of porous pans placed in exactly the same situation. The fact is, that the natives use *porous* pans from necessity, there being no other description of earthenware manufactured in the country; but so well are they aware that the *porosity* of the vessels is of no advantage, that they usually rub them with grease for the purpose of more easily taking out the ice, and also facilitating the process, by keeping the straw upon which they are placed in a perfectly dry and non-conducting state. Mr Scott repeated some of Dr Well's experiments, and obtained interesting results. On one occasion, a turban being suspended across the pit three feet above the pans, it, as it always does, prevented the formation of ice in those immediately under it; and in several which it only partially covered ice was formed on the half of the water out of this perpendicular line, while that under the turban was fluid. Two strings crossing each other, and placed at a less height above a pan, will also divide the ice into four quarters; but it is obvious that these results will not always be obtained; for, if the temperature be rather lower than would be necessary to freeze the water, supposing no impediment to exist, the whole may be frozen, although partially covered; and, on the other hand, if just sufficient to freeze the water under the most favourable circumstances, the contents of a vessel not fully exposed to the influence of the sky may remain fluid throughout. Mr Scott could never make ice (operating, however, on a small scale) when the temperature exceeded 41° F. on the level of the pits; but on such occasions the temperature is much higher at some distance from the ground, and a series of bottles filled with water, suspended from a mast of about seventy feet high, exhibited an increase of 1° for every ten feet of elevation. Mr Scott adds, that, therefore, Sir H. Davy is right in saying ice may be made when the thermometer is above 50°, if he allude to the upper regions of the air, or hills of moderate height; but, as has been already said, it cannot be made when the thermometer, suspended at three feet from the ground on the plain, stands at about 41°. Mr Scott's experiments extend to the height of 3400 feet, at which elevation, on a *detached* mountain, the temperature of the air at sunrise is several degrees *higher* than in the Plain of Bengal.

6. *Snow-line.*—Although, as already remarked, the thermometer sometimes stands as low as 28° F. in Malwah, yet, as far as we know, snow has not been observed in India to the south of the grand Himmaleh mountain-barrier. On several ranges of this vast Alpine land snow lies all the year. The lower boundary of this snowy covering is named the *snow-line,* which varies in height according to the season of the year, being highest during summer and lowest during winter. Of late years the height

of this line in different parts of the world has engaged the particular attention of meteorologists, and the investigation has led to interesting results. The subject has been pursued with energy among the Himmalehs by several active British officers,—of whom Webb, Gerrard, and Herbert, are the most distinguished. In November 1817, Captain Webb published a memoir on the heights of the Himmalehs, in which, by tracing the Gauri river upwards, he found that it bursts from the snow at the elevation of 11,543 feet,—a striking coincidence between actual observation and the calculated formula of authors, which assigns 11,400 feet. Mr Colebrooke, in a paper published in Brande's Journal from the observations of Captain Webb, for the first time remarked that the inferior limit of perpetual snow does not every where descend so low as theory would lead us to conclude.

According to theory, the height of the snow-line between latitudes 27° and 35°, about the range of latitude of the Himmalehs, is as follows :—

Latitude.	Height of the Snow-line. Feet.
27°	12,145
28°	11,930
29°	11,710
30°	11,484
31°	11,253
32°	11,018
33°	10,778
34°	10,534
35°	10,287

The following facts show not only the difference between the line of theory and that of actual observation, but also that the snow-line is higher on the northern than the southern side of the Himmalehs :—

7. *General great Height of the Snow-line on the Himmalehs.*—The village and temple of Milem were found by Captain Webb at the respective elevations of 11,405 and 11,682 feet above Calcutta; extensive fields of buck-wheat and Tartaric barley occupying the space between the two. A year after these observations were made, viz. on the 21st June 1818, Captain Webb proceeded southward from Joshi-mat-h, and from the Dauli river observed barometrically the altitude of a station on the ridge of mountains to the south. He found it to be 11,680 feet above the level of Calcutta; yet the place was surrounded by flourishing woods of oak, long-leaved pine, and arborescent rhododendrons, and the whole surface covered with a rich vegetation as high as the knee, extensive beds of strawberries in full flower, and plenty of currant-bushes in blossom all around, in clear spots of rich black mould. On the following day, Captain Webb reached the summit of the pass Pilgointi Churhai, and found its elevation to be 12,642 feet above the same level, or more than 12,700 feet above the sea. A dense fog confined the prospect; but no snow was to be seen contiguous to the spot. The surface exhibited a black soil, unless where the bare rock appeared, covered with strawberry plants, buttercups, dandelions, and a profusion of other flowers. The goatherds of the country are accustomed to lead their flocks to pasture during July and August upon a yet loftier ridge, estimated to be as much above the pass of Pilgointi as this was above the preceding day's encampment,—that is, nearly 1000 feet; and which therefore removes the snow-line to a still higher elevation.

The temple of Kedar-nath, according to a mean of five barometrical measurements, is 11,897 feet above Calcutta, or 12,000 feet above the level of the sea; but no snow remained in the vicinity of the temple later than the beginning of July; so that under the latitude of 30° 40′, at the last-mentioned elevation, the snows were not perpetual on the *southern side* of the Himmaleh mountains.

Captain Webb's observations on the summit of the Nitee Ghaut afford another example of this interesting fact. At the elevation of 16,814 feet, not a vestige of snow was to be seen on the Ghaut, nor upon the projecting shoulder of the mountain-ridge, rising about 300 feet on the western side of the pass; and we may hence conclude that the height of the snow-line on the *northern side* of the Himmaleh range cannot be less than 17,000 feet. The great elevation of the table-land of Tartary is, from its connexion with the distribution of the snowy boundary in these regions, deserving of particular notice. By observations made on the ridge of the Nitee pass, Captain Webb found the Sutledge to flow in a plain 14,924 feet above the sea; yet so far are the *undes,* or great plains, from being buried in eternal snow, as our common estimates would lead us to suppose, that the banks of the river afford the finest pasture for thousands of quadrupeds throughout the year. The town of Daba appears to be inhabited all the year, and not a temporary residence. In the neighbourhood of this place, and near Doompoo, both considerably higher than the bed of the Sutledge, Captain Webb was informed that the finest crops of the grain called *ora* were gathered, from which the natives make their bread.

Captain Gerrard, when proceeding by the Chárang pass, 17,348 feet high, to the valley of Nangalti, says many beds of snow were crossed, and that at the height of about 16,300 feet the "*continuous snow-beds commenced.*" In another place, however, he remarks, that the mountains in the neighbourhood of Chárang are all of blue slate, naked to their tops, and exhibiting decay and barrenness in their most frightful forms. They tower in sharp detached groups to about 18,000 feet, no vegetation approaching their bases, nor do their summits offer any rest to snow. Upon the left bank of the Tagla, mountains 16,000 feet high appear, on which no snow was observed. The summits on the right bank seem to be 18,000 feet, and with but little snow in streaks. The mountains also which enclose the dell of the Tagla are between 19,000 and 20,000 feet high, and just tipped with snow.

The difference of height of the perpetual snows on the northern and southern sides of the Himmaleh mountains is farther shown by the following remarks of Captain Gerrard. Zamsiri, a halting-place for travellers on the banks of the Shelti, is 15,600 feet above the sea,—a height equal to that of the passes through the outer range of the Snowy Mountains; and yet, he says, there is nothing to remind the traveller of the Himmalehs. Gently sloping hills and tranquil rivulets, with banks of turf and pebbly beds, flocks of pigeons and herds of deer, present the idea of a much lower elevation. But Nature has adapted the vegetation to the country; for did it extend no higher than on the southern face of the Himmalehs, Tartary would be uninhabitable either by man or beast. On ascending the *southern* acclivity of the snowy range, the extreme height of cultivation is found 10,000 feet; and even there the crops are frequently cut green. The highest habitation is 9500 feet; 11,800 feet may be reckoned the upper limit of forests, and 12,000 that of bushes, although, in a few sheltered situations, dwarf-birches and small bushes are found almost at 13,000 feet. But if we go to the Baspă river, the highest village will be found at an elevation of 11,400 feet, cultivation reaching to the same altitude, and forests extending to 13,000 feet at least. Advancing farther, we find villages at the last-mentioned elevation, cultivation 600 feet higher, fine birches at 14,000 feet, and *tama* bushes, which furnish excellent firewood, at 17,000 feet. Eastward, towards Manasawara, according to the accounts of the Tartars, crops and bushes thrive at a still greater height.

These facts, then, show not only that the snow-line generally is higher than was anticipated, but also that we must ascend several thousand feet more on the northern than the southern acclivity of this Alpine land before we reach the perpetual snow. Many explanations have been given of this striking fact which we cannot discuss here. It is sufficient to remark, that the radiation from the surface of the table-land of Thibet, the dryness of the air throughout Central and Northern Asia, the small quantity of snow which falls during winter when the temperature sinks to 10°4 F. or + 5° F.; lastly, the serenity and transparency of the atmosphere which reigns along the northern declivity of the Himmalehs, and which augments, at the same time, the irradiation of the table-land, and the transmission of the radiant heat which the table-land emits, may be considered as the principal causes of the great difference of the height of the snow-line on the north and south sides of the central mountain-ranges of India.

8. *Evaporation.*—Evaporation is that process by which the atmosphere is furnished with the moisture it contains. Water assumes the vaporic form at all temperatures, however low. Thus vapour rises not only from the plains of Bengal, but also from the icy and snowy mantles on the highest ridges and summits of the Himmalehs. Hitherto, owing to the want of observations, naturalists have not been able to trace out, in a satisfactory manner, the phenomena of evaporation in different climates; although we know, from its general relations to heat, that it is most powerful in the equatorial regions of the globe, and gradually diminishes towards the poles. The instruments necessary for ascertaining the power of evaporation have never, as far as we know, been used in India; but the time is not distant, we hope, when these will find a place in Indian meteorological observatories.

9. *Humidity of the Atmosphere.*—The earth, as is well known, is surrounded by an atmosphere of air and aqueous vapour. These two matters are mechanically mixed, and each is governed by its own peculiar laws. In order to supply the atmosphere with aqueous vapour, the process of evaporation is almost in constant activity; and Nature has set limits beyond which this vapour cannot pass, so as to prevent excessive moisture and long-continued

dryness. This dependence of moisture on temperature enables us to trace some of the phenomena of its distribution. There is, as is well known, a gradation of heat from the equator to the poles, and also from the surface of the earth upwards into the higher regions of the air. Generally speaking, the lowest stratum of the atmosphere, in whatever latitude it is found, must contain the greatest quantity of aqueous vapour, on account of its being nearest the source whence that moisture is supplied. If an equality of temperature existed, therefore, at the surface, the same quantity of air, in whatever latitude it was taken, would contain, when completely saturated, the same quantity of moisture. But since the temperature diminishes with the latitude, a given volume of air, in a perfect state of saturation, must contain less and less moisture as we approach the poles. From a similar cause the moisture of the atmosphere must diminish as we ascend above the earth. Local circumstances also affect the moisture of the atmosphere: thus over coasts it is much moister than in the interior of continents, as is well exemplified in the moist atmosphere of Western Europe, when contrasted with the very dry atmosphere of Asia. The atmosphere over wooded districts is moister than over those sparingly covered with vegetation; and the driest reposes upon arid sandy tropical plains. In India, for the most part, between December and June, while the general motion of the air is southward to the sea, the atmosphere is comparatively dry. It attains its maximum of humidity during the blowing of the south-west monsoon. After the rains cease, *fogs* in the mornings continue for some time, and reappear before the commencement of the rainy season. Such fogs are useful, Heyne remarks, to the growth of plants, as they clear them from dust, open their pores, and supply them with nourishment, which they could not obtain from the earth in this season. Without these irrigations very little saltpetre could be made, as the earth which contains it can be recognised only after it has attracted this moisture.

The only accurate mode of ascertaining the quantity of moisture in the air is by means of the *hygrometer*, an instrument which has hitherto been but sparingly used in India. We regret this, as the extensive employment of this instrument would throw much light on the climate of our eastern empire. Hygrometers ought, along with other meteorological instruments, to be distributed by government throughout India.

10. *Dew.*—Dews, in many parts of India, are heaviest in December and January before the fogs set in. They become perceptible before eight or nine in the evening, when the atmosphere is perfectly serene. On the Coromandel coast, according to Heyne, the inhabitants are not so much afraid of exposure to them as those of other countries. During the foggy season, the *vinegar of Sennagalu* (the *acid dew* of some authors), so much prized by the Moormen and rich Hindoos, is obtained. It is made by spreading pieces of muslin cloth on the flowering sennaga (*cicer arietinum,* Bengal *gram*) after sunset, and removing them before the sun gets through the clouds of mist. The moisture with which they are saturated is wrung out, and preserved for use. The acid juice is said to contain oxalic, malic, and a little acetic acid.*

---

* Dew collected from the leaves of plants contains a large dose

11. *Rain.*—The humidity communicated to the air by evaporation is returned to the earth chiefly in the form of rain. The quantity of rain which falls is greatest at the equator, gradually decreasing toward the poles. The quantity is estimated by means of the rain-gauge, and is given in inches and fractions of inches. When we say, for example, that one inch has fallen in a district in a specific time, it means that, if all the rain which fell in that time had remained on the surface, it would have covered it to the depth of one inch. This explanation is offered, as some of our readers might not be aware without it of the precise meaning of the following details.

In India the rains occur at determinate periods, named the *rainy seasons*. In general there is but one rainy season, during June, July, August, September, and October, during the south-west monsoon; little or no rain falling during the other months. In the Peninsula, however, there are in some places *two rainy seasons*,—one during the south-west monsoon on the west side, the other in the time of the north-east monsoon on the east side of the country.

Rain falls not only all over the Peninsula and Middle India, but also among the Himmalehs, and at a great height above the sea. Thus Gerrard, in a snow-covered region 15,000 feet high, experienced a shower which lasted for two hours. He was also detained three days by incessant rain at Shalpia, a resting-place for travellers.

On the coast of Malabar, mean latitude about

---

of carbonic acid; thus Lampadius found 2 per cent. of carbonic acid in dew collected from the leaves of the *alchemilla vulgaris*.

$11\frac{1}{2}$° north, the annual amount of rain is stated at $123\frac{1}{2}$; at Bombay, the fall observed during twelve years is stated at 82 inches annually; at Calcutta 81 inches during the year. Of the quantities falling during *successive months* the results are necessarily very variable. The means of twelve years' observations for Bombay afford the following results :—

June,	24.00 inches.
July,	23.95
August,	18.87
September,	14.06
October,	1.06

the greatest fall being found in June and July, and declining to a very small amount in October.

The quantity of rain which sometimes falls in a short time is very great. Thus, a letter from Mr Scott says, there fell at Bombay during the first twelve days of the rainy season thirty-two inches of rain, so that all the roads became like rivers. In England the average fall for the whole year is thirty-two inches,—the same as fell at Bombay in the course of twelve days. Between Bombay and the southern part of the Malabar coast, places not 500 miles distant from each other, very great differences prevail, both in individual years and in the amounts of the annual means. The following are a few of the results of each :—

Years.	Amount of Rain at Bombay in inches.	Amount of Rain on the Coast of Malabar in inches.
1817	103.79	136.70
1818	81.14	169.19
1819	77.10	135.47
1820	77.34	147.18
1821	82.99	98.44
1822	112.21	145.60
1823	61.70	121.67
Means.	85.18	136.32

Here the average annual amount of rain differs sixty per cent. within so small a geographical limit.

From the want of observations we have no opportunity of laying before our readers any details in regard to the relative proportions in the mountainous, hilly, flat, low, and littoral parts of India, nor have met with any very accurate registers of the daily and nightly fall.

12. *Monsoons.*—India, though it approaches nearer to the equator, is not so hot as the Sandy Arabia or the adjacent countries. The course of the seasons is also more regular and constant, and it is in this part of the world that we meet with those remarkable winds,—the seasonal or periodical winds called *monsoons,*—which throughout India blow nearly one-half the year from south-west to north-east, and the other half from north-east to south-west, and are the great distributors of its rain and modifiers of its climate. The most remarkable rainy season is that called the south-west monsoon. It extends from Africa to the Peninsula of Malacca, and deluges all the countries within certain lines of latitude for about four months of the year. In the southern parts of India this monsoon commences about the beginning of June, but it gets later as we advance towards the north. Its approach, says Mr Elphinstone, is generally announced by vast masses of clouds that rise from the Indian Ocean and advance towards the north-east, gathering and thickening as they come near the land. After some threatening days the sky assumes a troubled appearance in the evenings, and the monsoon in general sets in during the night. It is attended by thunder-storms far exceeding in intensity those of temperate regions. It

generally begins with violent blasts of wind, which are succeeded by floods of rain. For some hours lightning is seen almost without intermission; sometimes it only illuminates the sky, and shows the clouds near the horizon; at others it discovers the distant hills, and again leaves all in darkness, when in an instant it reappears in vivid and successive flashes, and exhibits the nearest objects in all the brightness of day. During all this time thunder never ceases to roll, and is only silenced by some nearer peal, which bursts on the ear with such a sudden and tremendous crash, as can scarcely fail to strike the most insensible heart with awe.* At length the thunder ceases, and nothing is heard but the continued pouring of the rain and the rushing of the rising streams. The next day presents a gloomy spectacle; the rain still descends in torrents, and scarcely allows a view of the blackened fields; the rivers are swollen and discoloured, and sweep down along with them the hedges, the huts, and the remains of the cultivation which was carried on during the dry season in their beds.

This lasts for several days; after which the sky clears, and discovers the face of nature changed as if by enchantment. Before the storm the fields were parched up, and except in the beds of the rivers scarcely a blade of vegetation was to be seen; the clearness of the sky was not interrupted by a single

---

* To persons, Mr Elphinstone says, who have long resided in India, these storms lose much of their grandeur; yet they sometimes rise to such a pitch as to make an impression on those most habituated to them. He was told by a gentleman who had been for some time in Malabar, the province most distinguished for the violence of the monsoon, that he there heard a clap of thunder which produced a silence of a minute in a large party of officers, and made a great part of the company turn pale.

cloud, but the atmosphere was loaded with dust, which was sufficient to render distant objects dim, as in mist, and to make the sun appear dull and discoloured, till he attained a considerable elevation; a parching wind blew like a blast from a furnace, and heated wood, iron, and every other solid material, even in the shade; and immediately before the monsoon this wind had been succeeded by the still more sultry calms. But when the first violence of the storm is over, the whole earth is covered with a sudden and luxuriant verdure; the rivers are full and tranquil; the air is pure and delicious; and the sky is varied and embellished with clouds. The effect of the change is visible on all the animal creation, and can only be imagined in Europe by supposing the depth of a dreary winter to start at once into all the freshness and brilliancy of spring. From this time the rain falls at intervals for about a month, when it comes on again with great violence, and in July the rains are at their height; during the third month they rather diminish, but are still heavy; and in September they gradually abate, and are often entirely suspended, till near the end of the month, when they depart amidst thunders and tempests as they came.

Such is the monsoon in the greater part of India. It is not, however, without some diversity, the principal feature of which is the delay in its commencement, and the diminution of the quantity of rain as it recedes from the sea. It is naturally most severe near the sea, from which it draws its supplies, and is exhausted after it has passed over a great tract of land. For this reason the rains are more or less plentiful in different districts according to their distance from the sea, except in those near high mountains, which arrest the clouds, and procure a larger supply of rain for the neighbouring tracts than would have fallen to their share if the passage of the clouds had been unobstructed.

The obstacle presented to the clouds and winds by the mountains has another effect of considerable importance. The south-west monsoon blows over the ocean in its natural direction; and, though it may experience some diversities after it reaches the land, its general course over India may still be said to be towards the north-east, till it is exhausted on the western and central parts of the Peninsula. The provinces in the north-east receive it in a different manner: the wind which brings the rains to that part of the continent originally blows from the south-west over the Bay of Bengal, till the mountains of Himmaleh, and those which join them from the south, stop its progress and compel it to follow their course towards the north-west. The prevailing wind, therefore, in the region south-west of the Himmalehs is from south-east; and it is from that quarter that our provinces in Bengal receive their rains. But when the wind has reached so far to the north-west as to meet with the Hindoo Coosh, it is again opposed by that chain of mountains, and turned off along its face towards the west, till it meets the projection of Hindoo Coosh and the range of Solimaun, which prevent its farther progress in that direction, or at least compel it to part with the clouds with which it was loaded. The effect of the mountains in stopping the clouds borne by this wind is different in different places. Near the sea, where the clouds are still in deep mass, part is discharged on the hills and the country beneath them, and part passes up to the north-west; but part is said to make its way over the first hills, and produce the rains in Thibet.

The above observations, Mr Elphinstone continues, will explain, or at least connect the following facts:—The south-west monsoon commences on the Malabar coast in May, and is there very violent; it is later and more moderate in Mysore; and the Coromandel coast, covered by the mountainous countries on the west, is entirely exempt from it. Farther north the monsoon begins early in June, and loses a good deal of its violence, except in the places influenced by the neighbourhood of the mountains or the sea, where the fall of water is very considerable. About Delhi, it does not begin until near the end of June, and the fall of rain is greatly inferior to what is felt at Calcutta or Bombay. In the north of the Punjaub, near the hills, it exceeds that of Delhi; but in the south of the Punjaub, distant both from the sea and the hills, very little rain falls. The clouds pass with little obstruction over Lower Sinde, but rain more plentifully in Upper Sinde, where these rains, though not heavy, are the principal ones in the year.

By the beginning of October, when the south-west monsoon or rainy season is nearly at an end, the change gradually takes place from the south-west to the north-east monsoon. This monsoon is attended with dry weather throughout the Peninsula, excepting on its eastern side on the coast of Coromandel. On this coast the north-east monsoon brings the periodical rains, which begin about the middle of October, and end generally about the middle of December. From December to the beginning of March this monsoon continues, but is now a dry wind. The weather is at this season cool and agreeable. The north-east winds cease about the end of February or beginning of March, and from this period to the beginning of June the winds are irregular and the heat great all over the Peninsula. The winds are chiefly from the south at this time in the Bay of Bengal and on its shores, and are hot, moist, and relaxing. About the end of May or beginning of June, as already remarked, the south-west monsoon begins, and is attended with the periodical rains in all parts of the Peninsula excepting the Coromandel coast, which then suffers greatly from heat and drought.

13. *Hail.*—In India hail falls only during the hottest seasons of the year, frequently in pieces the weight of half an ounce, and is accompanied by heavy thunder and storms or gusts of wind. In the Peninsula showers are more frequent in the country above the Ghauts than in that below them. The natives call the hail *rainstones,* and ascribe to it invigorating virtues. Although none of the mountains in Peninsular India reach the snow-line, and frozen water rarely appears there otherwise than in the form of hail, snow being unknown in Southern India, yet some writers maintain that hail-storms never occur in the torrid zone, while others affirm that they never appear there except at an elevation of not less than 1500 or 2000 feet above the sea. This statement, however, is far from being correct; for although hail-storms are not so common and destructive in India as in the south of Europe,—the grand region of these storms,—still they do frequently happen, even at the level of the sea. In May 1823, a violent hail-

storm occurred at Hydrabad, which is about 17° north latitude, at an elevation of not more than 1000 feet above the sea. The hailstones were of considerable size, and a sufficient quantity was collected by the servants of a military mess to cool the wine for several days. A hail-storm occurred at Darwar, north latitude 16° 28′, east longitude 75° 11′, in May or June 1825. The height of Darwar above the sea is 2400 feet, but it is near no high range of mountains. The hailstones had a white porous nucleus, and varied from the size of a filbert to that of a pigeon's egg. A similar storm occurred at the same place, and about the same season, in 1826. These, Dr T. Christie says, were the only hail-storms that came under his notice during five years' residence in India; but from the testimony of others he mentions the following:—Lieutenant-Colonel Bowler of the Madras army informed him that he witnessed a violent hail-storm at Trichinopoly about the middle of the year 1805, when the hailstones were nearly as large as walnuts. Another very violent hail-storm occurred in the Goosma Valley, about twenty-five miles west of Ganjam, and only a few feet above the sea, when the same officer was in camp there about the end of April 1817. It commenced about half-past three in the afternoon. The weather had previously been very sultry, with hot blasts of wind, and heavy clouds, which appeared almost to touch the tops of the tents. On the hail falling, the air became on a sudden disagreeably cold, as it had been before oppressively hot. We are told by Heyne, in his Historical and Statistical Tracts on India, that "masses of hail of immense size are said to have fallen from the clouds at different periods" in the Mysore country; and that, "in the latter part of Tippoo Sultan's reign, it is on record, and well authenticated, that a piece of ice fell near Seringapatam of the size of an elephant." Of course, we are not to believe this to the letter,—we must make some allowance for oriental exaggeration. It is needless to multiply examples; for there is probably not an officer who has been many years in India who cannot bear testimony to the frequency of hail-storms in that country.

14. *Falling Stars, Fire-balls, and Meteoric Stones.*—Falling stars are of frequent occurrence, falling or rather shooting through the atmosphere in countless numbers and at all times of the day, in India as in Europe. Fire-balls also are not very uncommon. Colonel Blacker gives an account of a meteor, having the appearance of an elongated ball of fire, which he observed on the 3d November 1826, a little after sunset, when on the road between the court-house and the town-hall of Calcutta. Its colour was pale, for the daylight was still strong, and its larger diameter appeared greater and its smaller less than the semi-diameter of the moon. Its direction was from east to west, its track nearly horizontal, and its altitude about 30°. As it did not apparently move with the velocity of ordinary fire-balls, it was probably at a great distance, and consequently of large size. So long as Colonel Blacker saw it, which was for five or six seconds, its motion was steady, its light equable, and its size and figure permanent. It latterly, however, left a train of sparks; soon after which it suddenly disappeared, without the attendant circumstance of any audible report. These fire-balls sometimes burst, and precipitate meteoric stones and iron. Lord Valentia and

Mr Howard mention stones that fell in this way from the atmosphere of Bengal on the 19th December 1798; several fell near Moradabad in 1808, and nineteen were found at Futtypore, in the Doab, on the 5th November 1814. Dr Tytler says, that on the evening of that day, shortly after sunset, before daylight had entirely faded, a meteor was distinctly seen, shooting with considerable velocity in a direction nearly north-west. This appearance was also observed by the Europeans in the lines and natives in the city, and is described to have comprised a blaze of light, surrounding a red globe about the size of the *moon*, which impressed the spectators with the idea of that luminary descending from the skies. The same phenomenon, and at the same moment of time, was seen at Hazareebaug, in Bengal, a distance of upwards of 250 miles eastward from Allahabad. The meteor descended at Rourpoor, nearly seventy miles north-west from the station of Allahabad, immediately after it was seen at that place. Its fall was accompanied with noises resembling the explosion of distant artillery, and a stone was seen falling, which in the act of descending is said to have emitted sparks similar to those proceeding from a blacksmith's forge. A strong sulphureous smell was also perceptible, and when first discovered the stone was hot to the touch. Besides the stone thus actually known to have fallen, several others of a similar description were picked up, at the distance of several coss from each other, whence it appears that a shower of stones in this instance took place. The fragments amounted to several pounds in weight. One weighed nearly one pound six ounces avoirdupois, and exactly resembled a body coated with black paint or pitch. Its interior was of an ash-gray colour, and contained embedded metallic-looking particles. Its specific gravity is stated as varying from 3, 35.2 to 4, 281. On the night of the 7th August 1822, a meteoric stone fell near the village of Kadonah, in the district of Agra, with much noise as of cannon, the wind awakening those who were asleep, and alarming a watchman who heard it fall; on making search in the morning it was found warm, and with little smoke rising from it. The stone was shown in London in 1827. Several stones fell in the district of Azim Gerh on the 27th February 1827.

These fire-balls, and the meteoric stones they drop, are considered as formed in the earth's atmosphere, and therefore as of tellurian atmospherical origin.

15. *Mirage.*—On viewing distant objects, it often happens, under certain circumstances, that these objects present many images which are straight, oblique, or inverted, and always more or less changed in the contour. It is the appearance of these images, without any visible reflector to produce them, which constitutes *mirage*. In explanation of this phenomenon it may be remarked, that as soon as the soil becomes heated the lower stratum of air is also affected by the calorific influence. Numerous aërial currents are established, and an undulatory motion taking place in the air, distant objects become changed in form, and variously distorted and broken. If when these changes are going on a calm should prevail, and the mass of atmosphere upon the plain remain at rest while the stratum in contact with the ground becomes gradually heated, mirage will arise. In such cases the observer will see distant objects in their natural positions and forms; but *below* them their im-

ages will be seen reversed, and the spectator believe that he is looking at a *reflection* from the surface of a body of water. The sky also joins in completing the illusion, its image being reflected in the same manner. The whole visible appearances, the French philosophers who visited Egypt remark, are indeed the same as those usually exhibited by water. All the laws by which the observer has been accustomed to judge of the existence of water, viewed at a distance, are here called into action, and the man of science as well as the peasant alike find themselves deceived.

This curious appearance is noticed by several of our Indian travellers. Thus, Mr Elphinstone, in describing his passage through the Great Desert, says, "On the 25th November we marched twenty-seven miles to two wells in the Desert. In the way we saw a most magnificent mirage, which looked like an extensive lake, or a very wide river. The water seemed clear and beautiful, and the figures of two gentlemen who rode along it were reflected as distinctly as in real water." The same very interesting writer remarks, "On the 22d we made a march of thirty miles to Moujgur; the heat of the afternoon was intense, while we halted as usual in the naked plain to give our people some water and to take some refreshments ourselves. In the course of the day several hundred skins of water came to us from Moujgur, where Bahawul Khan had sent his principal officers to receive us. Towards the evening many persons were astonished with the appearance of a *long lake, enclosing several little islands.* Notwithstanding the well-known nature of the country, many were positive that it was a lake, and one of the surveyors took the bearing of it."

Other varieties of mirage are noticed by Colonel Tod in his valuable work on Rajasthan.

16. *Black Colour of the Sky over the Himmalehs.* —The sky, when viewed from lofty mountains, presents a deep blue colour approaching to black. This fact is often mentioned by travellers among the Himmalehs. Thus, near the sources of the Ganges, the dazzling brilliancy of the snow was rendered more striking by its contrast with the *dark-blue, approaching to blackness,* of the sky; and at night the stars shone with a lustre which they do not present in a denser atmosphere. "It was curious to see them," says Captain Hodgson, "when rising, appear like one sudden flash as they emerged from behind the bright snowy summits close to us; and their disappearance, when setting behind the peaks, was as sudden as we generally observed it to be in their occultations by the moon." At Zinchin, 16,136 feet above the sea, the atmosphere exhibited that very *dark-black colour* which is observed from great elevations. The sun shone like an orb of fire without the least haze. At night, the part of the horizon where the moon was expected to rise could scarcely be distinguished before the limb touched it; and the stars and planets shone with a brilliancy never seen unless at great heights.

With a transit-telescope of thirty inches, and a power of thirty, stars of the fifth magnitude were distinct in broad day; but none of less size were perceptible. At Súbáthú, 4200 feet above the sea, stars of the fourth magnitude require a power of forty to make them visible in the day.

17. *Sunrise and Pillar of Light, or Zodiacal Light, in India.*—Sunrise is often characterized by

the appearance of a pillar of light, which never fails to make a strong impression on those who take an interest in the natural phenomena around them, and who, for the first time, witness this beautiful appearance. Dr Adam, in the following description of Indian sunrise, mentions this luminous appearance :—

"The country in the neighbourhood displays a thousand charms compared with the district near the Jumna. The roads are dry, and the rocky elevations in front, having a covering of beautiful shrubs, entwined with numerous varieties of climbing plants, give quite a new feeling to the mind on viewing the prospect. New animals, too, inhabitants of these, present themselves. The peacock, arrayed in all his gorgeous hues, and shining with a native glossiness of plumage, is not unfrequently seen perched on a projecting block of granite, while herds of antelopes bound along the plain below; and the shrill cry of the Indian partridge, heard on every hand, first cheers the traveller with the opening day. I was much delighted one morning here with viewing the natural phenomenon of sunrise. Contrary to my usual practice, I had started early with my baggage. It was quite dark, excepting what light the stars afforded, which in India is always considerable at this season (October), when not a cloud obscures the expanded vault of the heavens. After moving on for some time, on turning my eye towards the east, I could perceive the first appearance of day. It was not dawn, but a mere grayish pillar of light shooting from the horizon upwards, in the shape of a comet's tail, but without lustre; the effulgence, if it could be so called, resembling that of the milky way more than any other object in nature which I have seen. This dull *pillar of light* was well defined. It continued a long time apparently little increased in size, and without having acquired much brilliancy. At length its sides near the bottom gave way, and the light, now stronger, diffused itself latterly to a considerable extent. By and by the stratum of clouds immediately over this expansion displayed the roseate hue of morn, and the whole heavens became (though yet faintly) illuminated. The rosy tints, disappearing in their turn, were succeeded by a greater degree of pale light, and soon after the near approach of the great luminary himself was announced by a pillar of red or orange-red light, which terminated in the orb now appearing large and fiery, through the medium of the horizontal morning air. This is the general course of sunrise in India, as I have often witnessed since. The precursory phenomenon of the *pillar of light*, with the successive changes, being then new to me, appeared perhaps more interesting on that account."

This pillar of light is the *zodiacal light* of astronomers, which we find first mentioned in modern times by Childraus in the year 1559. After his observation had been recorded, it was entirely forgotten until again seen by Cassini on the 18th March 1683. Since that period its appearance is often recorded by naturalists. Its nature is not well understood. Cassini, Mairan, Euler, Laplace, Regnier, Hube, and Hahn, have speculated with more or less plausibility in regard to it.

18. *Miasmata.*—Under this name we understand that matter or those matters which, emanating from marshes and other situations where organic bodies

are in a state of decomposition, and received into the human system, produce disease, particularly remittent and intermittent fevers, &c. A moderate degree of heat is necessary for the formation of this poison, and also a moderate quantity of moisture. Low situations are more exposed than high ones to miasm, as it is formed at the earth's surface, and as it rises upwards becoming more and more diluted with pure air. Thus the inhabitants of the Campagna di Roma retreat on the approach of the sickly season to the higher grounds, and consider it dangerous to sleep in the lower apartments of a house. Stagnation of the air sometimes allows dangerous accumulations of miasmatous matter; the growth of underwood is very favourable to its accumulation, by breaking and arresting the currents of air, which would otherwise sweep through the forests; and plains without intervening rising grounds, high walls, or trees, are favourable to the diffusion of miasm, by allowing every slight horizontal motion of the air to intermix laterally the pure and contaminated portions of it. Thick ranges of trees, by impeding this horizontal commixture when the air is calm or nearly so, and by altering the direction of light breezes, are very effectual in confining marsh-effluvia. That some kinds of poisonous matters are produced by the decomposition of animal and vegetable substances seems highly probable: others again may emanate from the interior of the earth as the result of subterranean action; and these probably are the most noxious kinds.

19. *Climate.*—British India, situated partly in the torrid and partly in the north temperate zone, is

enclosed by boundaries varying much in character,—namely, on the west, by the great Western Desert; on the south-west, south-east, and south, by the ocean; on the east, by mountain-ranges; and on the north-east and north, by the vast Alpine land of the Himmalehs,—a mountain-barrier so elevated as nearly to shut out the atmosphere of India, and thus to secure a meteorological system for itself, different from and independent of that of Indostan. As to form and elevation above the sea, striking contrasts are displayed between the flat lands of the Ganges, the mountain-chains of the Peninsula, the littoral plains of the Circars, and the table-lands of Mysore. Its surface exhibits sandy deserts, bare rocky plains, extensive cultivated fields, jungles, and dense forests,—traversed by numerous and often considerable rivers, but rarely varied by the appearance of lakes; over which blows, for one half of the year, the south-west monsoon, and during the other half the north-east monsoon, thus affording the conditions for a strikingly-marked climate. The year is divided by the Hindoos into six seasons, but the more common division is into three, viz., the *rainy*, *cold*, and *hot seasons*; the *rainy* in general extends from June to October; the *cold* from November to February; and the *hot* from March to May. Every year there is a variation in the commencement and termination of the seasons, which renders absolute precision impossible in the statement of them. The *healthy season* may be said to be from November to the setting in of the rains, and the *unhealthy season* during the period of the rains, and a short time after their termination. The following short view of the climate of particular provinces will afford to the reader a general conception of the healthiness and unhealthiness of the different provinces of Indostan.*

I. MADRAS PRESIDENCY.

The Carnatic.—The climate of the Carnatic may be generally characterized as dry and hot. The range of the thermometer at Madras is usually from 72° to 92°; but sometimes, during the hot months of May and June, it is as high as 98° and even 105°. In January, February, March, and April, the monthly mean is from 77° to 86°; the extreme variation in each month is usually from 15° to 22°. In May, June, July, and August, the monthly mean temperature is usually about 91°, 90°, 88°, and 87°, respectively, the extreme variation being generally from 18° to 23°. During September, October, November, and December, the monthly mean falls progressively from 85° to 77° or 76°, December being generally the coldest month. The extreme variation in these months is from 13° to 18°. The hot and windy season of May, June, and July, is generally the most healthy: sickness prevails most about the commencement of the monsoon, or from August to November. Sometimes, however, it is greatest in December and January, and at other times in June and July. The prevailing diseases are *fever, dysentery,* and *hepatitis* or *liver complaint.*

Travancore.—The weather of this province, which is situated at the south-western extremity of the Peninsula, is usually hot. Heavy falls of rain take place between June and December. After these showers the sun generally shines, and produces a

* The view of the climate of the provinces we owe chiefly to Annesley, Jameson, Young, Brander, and Christie.

disagreeable moist heat. The prevailing diseases among the Europeans are *hepatitis* and *dysentery*; and among the natives, *fevers*, and *ulcers* of the lower extremities.

Coimbetoor.—This country is upon the whole healthy, and the houses of the native cultivators more comfortable than in many parts of the Peninsula. *Fevers* are the prevailing diseases, which in some seasons become epidemic, particularly among the natives.

Malabar and Canara.—These provinces form the principal part of the Malabar coast, and extend from Cochin to Sadashevaghur. In February the low country becomes extremely hot, and the vapours and exhalations so dense, that it is difficult to distinguish objects at the distance of a few miles. The heats increase during March and April, and with them the quantity of aqueous vapour. On the setting in of the western monsoon in May the whole is condensed into rain. *Fevers*, *dysentery*, and *hepatitis*, are the prevailing diseases among the Europeans; and *fevers*, and *ulcers* of the lower extremities, among the natives.

Darwar District.—The most opposite climates are met with in different parts of the southern Mahratta country; for the western parts, towards the Ghauts, may be reckoned among the wettest of the Indian Peninsula, and the eastern among the driest. The average quantity of rain in the latter is from twenty to twenty-six inches; in the former a larger quantity often falls within one month. The climate becomes gradually drier as we proceed eastward from the Western Ghauts; and as this chain runs north-north-west and south-south-east, we have consequently a drier climate in the northern parts of the district than in the southern, on the same meridian. Thus, at Soondak the climate is rainy and cool; at Gokauk, on the other hand, which is in the same longitude, it is dry and hot. A considerable quantity of rain falls as far eastward as the country continues hilly; but beyond this the supply is scanty and precarious. In August 1824, according to Dr Christie, a good deal fell at Darwar; while, at the same time, not a drop had fallen fifteen miles to the east, and the wells were nearly dried up. For three weeks in July and August 1827, the rain continued nearly incessant at Darwar, and during the same time not a drop fell in the eastern parts of the district. The difference in the habits and mode of life of the inhabitants of the western and eastern parts of the district abundantly testifies how very opposite are their respective climates. In many places, the former are often for weeks during the monsoon confined to their own villages, not only by the severity of the rains, but, in many instances, in consequence of all communication being stopped by the swollen nullahs. During this dreary period (in anticipation of which a stock of provisions is always laid in) the inhabitants sit round a fire in the centre of their miserable dwellings, which are constantly filled with smoke. When they do venture out, they wrap themselves in a *cumly*,* and over this place " a sort of thatched case or shell, made of the leaves of the *jar*,† or some other of the palm tribe. It is broad over the whole back and shoulders, narrowing to a peak immediately

* A native blanket. † Borassus flabelliformis.

over the head, and coming down the front over the face just as far as is necessary to give it a firm hold, with a slope sufficient to carry the water that falls on it clear of the body." In the eastern parts it is very different. The rain is seldom so severe as to prevent the inhabitants from going out for four and twenty hours at one time; and precautions against heat, not against cold, are necessary. The villages in the western parts consist of thatched huts, whose steep sloping roofs nearly reach the ground, the walls being only a few feet high, that they be effectually protected from the rain. Every spot is covered with vegetation. Hedges and trees covered with twining plants line the roads, and the thatched roofs are often concealed by creepers, generally cucumbers, pumpkins, &c. The villages in the eastern parts present a curious contrast to the above. Generally not a spot of green, for many months, relieves the horrid glare. All is parched and brown. No protection being required against heavy rain, the houses are built entirely of clay, which one heavy shower, such as the western inhabitants constantly experience, would completely level to the ground. The walls of the houses are formed of sun-baked clay, and are from eight to ten feet high. Upon these is supported a terrace-roof composed of branches of trees or bamboos, and covered with clay. Nothing can be conceived more ugly than these villages. On every side square masses of dry clay give one more the idea of huge ant-hills than of human habitations. In these places, wood being found in too small quantity to serve as fuel, cow-dung is used for this purpose, which, being made into small cakes, is thus plastered on the walls of the houses to dry in the sun. When ready, it is collected into piles like peat-stacks in a Scotch village.

Mysore.—The whole of this country has somewhat of the character of a table-land with its accompanying mountains. The elevation varies from 1900 to 4700 feet. The climate, according to Hamilton, is temperate and healthy to a degree unknown in any other tract within the tropics. The monsoons, or boisterous periodical rains, which at different times deluge the coast of Coromandel and Malabar, have their force broken by the Ghauts, and from either side extend to the interior in frequent showers, which, though sometimes heavy, are seldom of long continuance, and preserve both the temperature of the climate and the verdure of the fields throughout the year. The Island of Seringapatam, on which the capital is built, is under the influence of both the north-east and south-west monsoons; rainy weather continues from the beginning of May until the commencement of December. January, February, March, and April, are dry and sultry. From the middle of December till the beginning of February, cold and bleak north-east winds prevail; and between this period and the commencement of the south-west monsoon is the hottest season. The atmosphere is damp, and the dews more or less heavy throughout the year, particularly in January, February, March, and April. The variation of temperature between the day and night is also greatest at this season. The unhealthiest periods are March and April, or a little before the setting in of the south-west monsoon, and about the close of October. Bangalore, the principal military cantonment, about 3000 feet above the sea, is one of the most temperate places in the Peninsula. In 1800, the thermometer was observed not to rise higher than 82°, nor to fall lower than 58°.

Salem and the Baramahl, which form a part of the table-land above the Eastern Ghauts, have a climate and seasons nearly the same as those of Mysore.

The Balaghaut, or Ceded Districts.—This country is elevated, but not so high as Mysore. The weather and climate on the whole are nearly the same as in Mysore.

Bejapore.—The climate and seasons resemble those of the Ceded Districts.

The Northern Circars.—To the south of Coringa, strong north-east winds prevail along the shore for the first two months of the year, which, together with the sea-breezes, moderate the heat. But where the winds pass over the salt stagnant marshes, as they do in almost every part of the seacoast of this quarter of the province, their influence upon the health is baneful. During March, April, and part of May, high winds from the south-west prevail, and are attended with clouds of dust. In May, June, July, August, and September, the wind generally blows from the west over an extensive parched soil, and hence becomes intolerably hot; so that the thermometer, as formerly mentioned, not unfrequently reaches 110° or even 112°, and stands above 100° at midnight. In the hilly and more inland parts, the air, owing to the exhalations from the jungles and forests, is unwholesome, particularly in the valleys and ravines by which the hilly districts are intersected. Owing to the great power of the sun in the dry and sandy plains of the south of this province, *coup de soleil* not unfrequently occurs. The diseases are *fever*, *hepatitis*, and *dysentery*.

Hydrabad.—This province is a table-land; hence its temperature is lower than the latitude indicates. At the city of Hydrabad, during the cool season, the thermometer is often as low as 40° and 45°. In this district the south-west monsoon usually commences about the beginning of June, and continues with some intervals till the middle of October. During November and December the sky is generally cloudy, the winds easterly; and sometimes when the north-east monsoon is heavy a considerable quantity of rain falls. Dews are frequent during January and early in February; but both these months, and March, April, and May, are dry. The mean monthly temperature, in-doors, is stated as follows:—January, 73°; February, 75°; March, 82°; April, 89°; May, 90°; June, 86½°; July, 81°; August, 79°; September, 78°; October, 78°; November, 75°; December, 73°; giving an annual mean of nearly 80°. This is perhaps a little higher than the thermometer placed in a more exposed situation would indicate. The daily range is often very considerable, particularly during November, December, January, and February, amounting in the shade generally to about 20°, and not unfrequently to 30°. *Fevers* and *dysentery* are the prevailing diseases.

Aurungabad.—The aspect of the country, the climate, and seasons, are nearly the same in the eastern districts of this province as in the province of Hydrabad.

Candeish.—The climate and seasons are here not

materially different from those of Aurungabad, or Malwah, to be noticed afterwards.

II. BOMBAY PRESIDENCY.

The new town of Bombay, the capital of the presidency, is built in a low, muddy, unwholesome tract of land; hence the climate is unhealthy. *Poonah*, a military station and populous city, about thirty miles eastward of the Ghauts, and about 2500 feet above the sea, is comparatively healthy. The alternations of temperature are great and sudden. The prevailing diseases are *remittent* and *intermittent fevers*.

Guzerat.—Westerly winds prevail the greater part of the year. In May and June they are very hot. During December and January, east and north-east winds prevail, and remarkably thick fogs are generally observed every morning in these months.

III. BENGAL PRESIDENCY.

Bengal.—The cold season commences, according to Dr Jameson, with November and ends in February. About the middle of October the weather begins perceptibly to change. The days are still oppressively hot; but the mornings and evenings gradually become cool. The wind, which during the preceding months had blown generally from the south and the east, now begins to come round to the west and north, and to carry along with it those heavy masses of clouds which almost constantly float about and obscure the horizon during the whole of the rains. The atmosphere, from being very damp and watery, grows dry and elastic, and the heavens begin to

5

brighten a little. But these appearances are not yet uniform; the sky still at times becomes gloomy and overcast, and heavy showers, accompanied by thunder and lightning, show that the south-east monsoon has not yet finally taken its leave.

In November, the weather becomes delightfully fair and pleasant. A cold sharp wind now blows steadily from the north, and frequently also from the west. The air is dry, clear, pure, and serene; the vault of heaven is of a beautiful deep azure colour; and, in general, not a cloud is to be seen. The nights are clear, with heavy dews. The thermometer in the shade ranges throughout the month from 66° to 86°; the mean heat about 74°; medium altitude of the barometer, 29.98.

As December comes on a considerable change takes place. Although the middle of the day and the afternoon be clear and fine, a haze generally towards evening collects round the horizon, and obscures the setting sun. As the night advances thick fogs, sometimes general sometimes partial, begin to collect, and do not disperse until morning. As they are broken up by the influence of the sun's rays their vapours rise and form gray masses of clouds, which render the early part of the day hot and unpleasant, and do not disappear until it is far advanced. These fogs do not by any means occur every night. Sometimes, though rarely, the whole month passes over without them; ordinarily they appear only three or four times; sometimes during several nights successively. As in November, the north and west are the prevailing winds. They are very sharp, but blow steadily, never rising to a gale nor falling to a perfect lull. The range of the thermometer is from

56° to 78°; the mean temperature about 70°; altitude of the barometer, 30.01.

During January much the same weather prevails. The air is serene, and to the feel piercingly cold. The wind blows steadily, and perhaps more forcibly, from the north and north-west, than in December. Fogs are still very frequent, and sometimes so thick that scarcely any object is visible until a late hour in the morning; and every thing exposed to the external air becomes wet and covered with drops of moisture. They may be often seen rolling in dense large bodies in opposite directions. During the clear nights heavy dews fall. The range of the thermometer is from 47° to 75°; the mean heat about 68°; altitude of the barometer, 29.99.

The weather keeps very pleasant until the second week of February, when the middle of the day grows warm; and the change of the wind to the south and east, and the collection of clouds in the horizon, with threatenings of thunder-gusts, portend the approach of the hot season. At night the air is raw and cold, and the mornings are foggy. The thermometer ranges from 65° to 82°; the mean heat, 76°; altitude of barometer, 30.3.

Sometimes a few heavy and refreshing showers fall about Christmas; but the whole of the cold season is generally marked by the total absence of rain. It is remarkable how invigorating the cold bracing wind of the north, and the pure elastic air and clear sky of these months, prove to the European constitution, harassed and broken down by the previous long continuance of moist and oppressive weather. The appetite and strength, which had long before failed, now return, and the whole frame becomes light and springy. Vegetable nature partakes of the generally salubrious effects of the season; and garden-plants and exotics, at all other times killed by the excessive heats, now grow with freshness and vigour.

The hot season may be considered to set in fairly with March. The sun now becomes very powerful, and the days are warm, and even hot. They are, however, prevented from being oppressive by the strong and steady winds uniformly blowing from the south. Fogs are yet not uncommon in the mornings; and as they clear up go to the north to form, with the thick dispersed masses of clouds that are constantly drifted along the horizon by the wind, materials for the approaching storms. These storms, which by the inhabitants are termed *north-westers*, do not, however, generally occur till towards the middle and end of the month. They are usually preceded, during several days, by cloudy mornings and strong gales. Then, for one or two evenings, comes on distant thunder, with strong gusts of wind, but without rain. Towards the afternoon of the day in which the storm is to occur, the wind, that, during the morning and forenoon had been continued and boisterous, begins to fail, and at length settles into a dead calm. The air becomes oppressively sultry. The clouds gather in the north-west, and form a deep, dense, lowering bank. Vivid lightning, accompanied with heavy thunder, and gradually advancing nearer and nearer, indicates the immediate approach of the storm. At length the calm is suddenly interrupted by a tremendous burst of wind, and by clouds of dust which darken the horizon. Then follow torrents of rain, with close and heavy thunder; and these are soon succeeded by a serene sky and cool air. The appearance, however, of these sudden commotions is not always the same. Sometimes a shower of *hail-stones* precedes, or comes in the place of the heavy fall of rain; sometimes there is no rain, even when the fury of the wind and quantity of the lightning are excessive. The general time of their coming on is about sunset; they rarely occur earlier than six in the afternoon, or later than midnight. When the days keep clear and the wind moderate, heavy dews fall at night; but in blowing weather there is no dew, the moisture, as it settles, being carried off by the wind. Range of the thermometer, from 73° to 86°; mean temperature, 79°; altitude of barometer, 29.86.

April has generally blowing weather throughout. The prevailing wind is still the south. The atmosphere is sometimes clear, generally hazy, with much dust, and thick loose clouds continually moving to the north. The weather is hot, but pleasant, till towards the end of the month, when the nights become close and sultry. The general closeness, however, is from time to time relieved by thunder-storms and seasonable falls of rain. The wind usually becomes hot to the feel about the 20th, and so continues to the end of the succeeding month. Range of the thermometer, from 78° to 91°; mean heat, 84°; barometrical altitude, 29.75.

May is the most disagreeable month in the year. In the commencement there is high wind at times; but during the greater part of the month the weather is exceedingly close, still, and oppressive. The nights especially are sultry. There is little or no wind in the mornings, which are thick and hazy, with low, gloomy, scattered masses of clouds. But as the sun rises a breeze springs up from the south, and keeps gradually freshening until the evening, when it again fades away. The air is hot but inelastic; and as it does not carry off the perspirations, leaves the body moist and clammy. The dejection and lassitude now universally produced by the great heats are, however, fortunately removed by the frequent occurrence of violent north-westers, with their usual accompaniments of thunder and rain. There are no fogs during April or May. The thermometer ranges from 81° to 93°; mean heat, 86°; barometrical altitude, 29.60.

In some years, but not always, nor even generally, between the 15th and 25th of this month, the horizon becomes overshadowed with dark thick clouds from the south-east quarter, and much rain falls during several days, constituting what are called the *lesser rains*. But more commonly the close muggy weather continues with little interruption until the end of the first or the beginning of the second week of June, when the veering round of the wind towards the east, the occurrence of thunder in the evening, and the constant cloudy state of the atmosphere, indicate the approach of the regular rains. These commence from the 4th to the 18th of June, and continue with frequent variations during the four following months. At first they set in with thunder-showers, sometimes heavy sometimes light, generally from the south and east. Then follow several days of very heavy rain, during which the sun is completely hid from view. Then there is a show of fair weather with sunshine, and beautiful clear nights; but this is of very uncertain duration, and liable to be interrupted with scarcely any previous warning. The heavy rain rarely keeps up for more than forty-eight hours at a time; then gradually diminishing to drizzling, and at length giving way to fair weather. There is at frequent intervals, during the whole period of their continuance, much vivid lightning, with violent thunder-storms and gusts of wind. The wind frequently changes from east to south and west, rarely to north. Its return to the east, and fixing steadily in that quarter, is usually accompanied with heavy rain.

As soon as the rainy season has fairly commenced, the atmosphere becomes manifestly cooler, and the weather in general very pleasant; the only exceptions being now and then a sultry night, and the dead oppressive calm which sometimes precedes a storm. From the dust and other particles floating about in the atmosphere being carried away by the successive showers, the sky during the intervals becomes beautifully clear, the sun shines with great splendour, and the nights are bright. There is very little variation of the atmospherical temperature throughout the season. The thermometer ranges from 77° to 88°, or 90°; the mean heat being 81°, or perhaps a degree or two higher. The air, from the constant rain, becomes surcharged with moisture, and every thing exposed to it gets damp and mouldy. There is consequently little alternation in the barometer. The mean altitude is about 29.45.

There is little perceptible change in the weather till the middle of October. The rain then begins to abate, the showers are fewer in number, and, though heavy, of short duration. The wind gets very variable. There are still frequent storms of thunder and lightning; but they generally pass off without producing rain. The days are yet sultry; but the mornings and evenings begin to grow cool; and the increasing clearness of the air, with the coming on of dews at night, presage the speedy accession of the cold season. At length the veering round of the wind to the west-north-west quarter, the disappearance of clouds and vapours from the horizon, the sharpness and dryness of the air, the rapid rise of the barometer and concomitant fall of the thermometer, towards the end of the month, evince the entire departure of the rains. The total quantity of rain falling during the season varies much in different years. In Bengal, the average has been fixed at eighty inches.

Bahar.—The seasons are nearly the same in this province as in Bengal; but, as it is higher above the sea, its climate is in some respects superior. The nights are generally much cooler; but it is more subject to great droughts and heat, and to parching winds from the west, during the warm season. Tirhoot, the north-western quarter of this province, is more elevated and healthier than the districts to the south. On account of the soil and climate, Bahar has been selected by the British government as a proper country for the improvement of the breed of horses, the native race of the Bengal province being of a diminutive size. A low and marshy soil, it is remarked, seems every where uncongenial to the horse; for he appears to degenerate in such places, even when he lives and propagates. In districts in warm climates which are more than usually low and marshy the horse generally experiences the fate of the Europeans; he either dies soon after he is brought to those places, or his progeny seldom reach maturity.

Allahabad.—That part of this province adjacent to the Ganges and Jumna is low and very productive; but its western districts, particularly the Bundelcund territory, are diversified with high hills. Between these two divisions there is a considerable difference of climate, the former being sultry and subject to hot winds, from which the latter is exempt. Benares, the principal military and civil station, contains, according to the census of 1830, upwards of 200,000 inhabitants. The cantonments, which are extensive, are four or five miles distant from the city. The country around is dry and parched. *Fever* and *dysentery* are most prevalent during October, November, and December, owing to the inundations from the previous rains and the cold nights.

Oude.—This province is generally level and well cultivated, with the exception of Gorucpoor. It is, on the whole, healthy, except in the vicinity of jungles and cotton-fields. The district of Gorucpoor is bounded on the north by a range of lofty mountains. The country extending southward from the base of these mountains is flat, covered with woods and jungles, and intersected by numerous streams. Easterly winds prevail generally throughout the year. The climate is far from being healthy, owing to the great extent of jungle, stagnant water, and marshes, over which the easterly winds pass before they reach the more inhabited parts of the country. Fevers are most prevalent and dangerous in May and June.

Agra.—This province is generally flat and open; but to the south of the Chumbul river, and towards its western frontier, it is more hilly and jungly.

The climate is temperate and healthy, except during the prevalence of hot winds.

Delhi.—The climate of this province is on the whole temperate, except during the warm seasons when the hot winds blow. The north-west quarter is much overgrown with trees and thick jungle, and is consequently unhealthy, especially during the hot and rainy seasons. The south-west quarter is free from jungle, and its soil is dry and fertile. The centre of the province is level and well watered. Meerut, the principal town of the district of the same name, is considered one of the healthiest stations in India. Mr Jackson strongly recommends it as a place of residence for convalescents, and for those who have become naturalized to India, and estranged from their own country. The society is extensive, and the roads good.

Malwah and Central India.—The climate of Malwah is on the whole mild. The range of the thermometer is small, except in the latter part of the year, when great and sudden changes often take place. The seasons are those common to Western India. The fall of rain during June, July, August, and September, is in general moderate and regular. The annual fall is about fifty inches. During this season, says our distinguished countryman Sir J. Malcolm, "the range of the thermometer is very small, seldom falling lower than 72° night and morning, or rising higher than 76° or 77° at noon. Though the mornings become cooler after the close of the rainy season, there is no very cold weather until the month of December; it continues until January and part of February. In the latter month, in 1820, at six o'clock A. M., the temperature was

28°. During the hot season which succeeds, the parching winds from the northward and westward, that prevail in most parts of India to an intense degree, are here comparatively mild and of short duration. The thermometer, however, during the day rises sometimes as high as 98° ; but the nights are invariably cool and refreshing."

Bagur is a hilly region, situated between Malwah and Guzerat. Owing to its extensive and thick forests, fevers of a malignant nature prevail during two or three months following the rains: the climate can at no period be considered salubrious.

Gundwana is a vast wild region, consisting of rugged hills, uninhabited jungles, and deep water-courses, ravines, and valleys, covered with forests, and pervaded by marsh miasmata. Its climate is generally unhealthy.

Orissa has many features in common with Gundwana, and a similar climate.

Himmaleh Mountains.—The climate of the valleys and ridges of this vast mountainous country is, as already stated in our observations on the height of the snow-line, much milder than we were led to expect from the conjectures and calculations of philosophers,—vast tracts, which according to their views ought to be steril in the extreme, or eternally covered with snow, are, on the contrary, richly clothed with vegetation, abounding in animals, and animated by villages. Thus Marang, a large village surrounded by lofty mountains, though 8500 feet above the sea, enjoys a mild climate. During eight days spent there by Captain Gerrard, the temperature varied from 58° F. to 82° F.; and flies were very troublesome. The sun, even in July, was scarcely visible above the mountains before 8 A. M., and disappeared behind them at 5 P. M. There were alternately light clouds and sunshine, and now and then a little rain, which in this valley never falls heavy; the height of the outer chain of the Himmalehs being sufficient to exclude the rains that deluge India for three months. Mr Colebrooke, speaking of Zoncheng, a village among these mountains whose height is 14,700 feet, which in latitude 31° 36′ N., according to received theory, should be buried in everlasting snow, assures us that the case is far different. On every side of the glen, which is a bowshot across, appeared gently sloping hills, for the most part covered with *támá* or Tartaric furze. The banks of the river were covered with grass-turf and prickly bushes. Around, the land was covered with verdure; flocks of sheep were browsing, and deer leaping; altogether it was a romantic spot, wanting but trees to make it delightful. Gerrard, on the crest of the Húkëtó pass, 15,786 feet high, observed yaks and horses feeding on the surrounding heights; and the climate was pleasant, the temperature being 57° F. On Zinchen, which is 16,136 feet high, and on the neighbouring mountains, horses were observed galloping about in all directions, and feeding on the very tops of the heights; kites and eagles were soaring in the air; large flocks of small birds like linnets were flying about, and locusts jumping among the bushes. The climate is very different from that experienced in crossing the outer range of the Himmalehs at the same season. Here, at the height of 16,000 and 17,000 feet, is abundance of fuel (*metóh*, bearing a beautiful yellow flower and no prickles), good water, and a serene sky; there, at an *inferior elevation*, no firewood is nearer than five or six miles, the clouds hang around the mountains, the sun is scarcely visible, and showers of rain are frequent. At the village of Púí, at an elevation of 13,600 feet, there are cultivated fields of barley, *phàpur*, and turnips. A little lower the ground was covered with thyme, sage, and many other aromatic plants, besides juniper, sweetbrier, and gooseberries. Here also are vineyards and groves of apricots.* At Dabling there was much cultivation, with plantations of apricots and walnuts. During Captain Gerrard's residence here (August), the temperature was warm, varying from 61° F. at sunrise to 85° at noon, the wind blowing strongly from the south-west, and the sky frequently obscured with light clouds attended with little rain. Near the village of Nákó, in the midst of these mountains, situated 12,000 feet above the sea, in the heart of abundant population, he found the grain "already yellow, with a broad sheet of water, surrounded by tall poplar, juniper, and willow trees, of prodigious size, and environed by massive rocks of granite. Here are produced most luxuriant crops of barley, wheat, *phàpur* (*polygonum*), and turnips, rising by steps to nearly 700 feet higher than the village, where is a lama's residence, inhabited throughout the year. The fields are partitioned by dikes of granite. At Taz-hi-gang they are enclosed by barberry and gooseberry bushes."

The seasons at this great elevation are similar to those of our northern latitudes, the grain being

* The apricots form a part of the subsistence of the people. At this season they are pulled, and exposed to the sun on the roofs of the houses; when dried they are not unlike prunes.

sown in March and April, and reaped in August and September. Snow generally falls towards the end of October. It seldom exceeds two feet in depth, but does not leave the ground for nearly six months. Want of moisture in the air prevents its earlier descent (since the beginning of October is winter) under a clear sky. In the middle of October 1818, the thermometer at sunrise was seldom above 20° F.; in August the temperature was 75° F. at noon, and never below 52° F.

20. *Sanitary Depôts.*—It having been found that those suffering under the diseases of the lower and hotter parts of India had their health improved by a residence in the hilly districts, the government have of late established sanitary depôts in several of the hill-provinces. Not many years back, the Mount of Saint Thomas, near Madras, was considered the Montpelier of the south of India. After the fall of Seringapatam, and the consequent occupation of the table-land of Mysore by the British troops, the cantonment of Bangalore became the general resort of all classes whose health required a change of climate. Now the Nhilgerry mountains, in the same division of India, are considered as affording a healthier climate; and there the government have established a sanitary depôt. The greatest length of the Nhilgerries Proper is from east to west thirty-six miles, and the medium breadth fifteen miles.

Although only twelve degrees distant from the equator, and surrounded by plains where the thermometer not unfrequently stands in the shade at 100° F., yet, from its elevated situation, it possesses a mildness of climate not inferior to the temperate parts of Europe, and also a great equability of temperature, which renders it so beneficial in many diseases. During a great part of the year, says Mr Young, the range of the thermometer on the Nhilgerries is less than is known in any part of the globe; and during December, January, and February,—the season of the greatest cold,—it has never been known to exceed 28° F., the greatest heat 59° F., including, between the extremes, a temperature which has always been found congenial to the European constitution, and very different in its effects from similar oscillations at a higher temperature, as exhibited in all parts of the Deccan and throughout India generally. During the rainy season the thermometer varies but little,—the range has been so low as 2½° for a whole month. Except the three cold months, the range will generally be from 2½° to 6°, or at most 10°, making the climate one of the most equable on the earth; and consequently very favourable to persons of a consumptive habit. Invalids, on reaching the hills in the cool season, feel the air of the mountains too rigorous; but to the healthy it is the period of the greatest enjoyment, when they can wander through the woods in search of game, and almost forget that they are still exiles from their own country. The only winter on these mountains is experienced during this period; the grass which covers the downs and elevated ridges becoming yellow and seared; but the moment the frosts are over, about the end of February, the country quickly assumes its verdant appearance, and the duties of the husbandman recommence just as the plains below are beginning to feel the desolating effects of the hot winds. The climate of the Nhilgerries may, in some measure, be considered a perpetual spring; vegetation is slow and steady, except during frosts. Notwithstanding the lowness of the thermometer during the whole year, sick persons cannot without risk expose themselves to the sun from 10 A. M. till 4 P. M.; and as the mornings are very agreeable, they are recommended to take exercise either on foot or horseback from 6 till 9 A. M., and from 5 till 7 P. M., confining themselves in the middle of the day, except during the delightful intervals of fine weather which prevail during the rains, when they may walk out at all hours with advantage. This precaution is only intended to apply to a state of actual sickness or debility; for persons in rude health may get out at all times and seasons. During March, April, and May, there are refreshing showers. The temperature in the sun's rays exhibited to Mr Young an excess of from 25° to 12° above what the indications were found to be in a veranda out of the sun's rays.

Should future experience confirm the accounts of the sanitary virtues of its climate, this mountainous region, says Mr Young, may become an asylum for such as have lost their health in other parts of India, not only superseding expensive voyages to the Cape and the Isle of France, but in many cases a trip to the mother-country. To such of the civil and military servants of the India Company as have outlived all their relations and friends in Europe, and to whom a return thither would amount to a melancholy species of banishment, the Nhilgerries present a delightful asylum for the remainder of their lives,—a sort of Eurasian climate, and within a moderate distance from the friends of their adopted country, many of whom they may expect to see on the hills.

A report has lately been published in regard to a Sanatarium for the Calcutta district at *Dargeeling* in the Sikkim mountains. The travelling distance of Dargeeling from Calcutta is about 330 miles. It is situated on one of the numerous branches of the Sinchul mountain, elevated nearly 9000 feet, and forming a remarkable feature in every view of the Sikkim hills from the plains. Captain Herbert, who visited the spot on the part of the government, is of opinion that the climate, salubrity of the approaches, and the convenience of the situation, all speak in its favour. Its elevation above Calcutta is 7218 feet, and its mean temperature is calculated to be 24° below that of Calcutta, and only 2° above that of London (52°).

Accommodation for invalids has been provided at *Simla*, a station among the hills between the Sutledge and Jumna near Subhatoo, and 7500 feet above the sea. Even the winters here are much less rigorous than in England, with the advantage of powerful solar radiation, which is said to increase as we ascend higher on the mountains.

Pooree, which can be reached by sea at all seasons from Calcutta in two days, is a station whose pure and invigorating air, together with its equable climate, render it one of the most salubrious spots in the East. Dr Brander says, the best months for convalescents residing at Pooree are February, March, April, May, and the early part of June, which, as they are found to be the months apparently the most trying to the European constitution in other parts of India, become, in a ratio corresponding with the difference of temperature and other local advantages, relatively the most healthy and the best suited to a sojourn on the coast. At that period the south-west monsoon prevails, and seems to exert with greatest effect its prophylactic influence over the convalescent visiter, who is not a little gratified to find, instead of the *tatties* and artificial refrigeration necessarily employed at inland stations, a never-failing source of cool air in the renovating sea-breezes. Although a preference has been assigned to the above months, it is not easy, in a climate on the whole so uniform as this, to point out with precision the period of the year that may be considered as the healthiest: the most agreeable, and probably the most congenial to the feelings, are the months comprised between October and February inclusive, when the thermometer ranges between 64° F. and 76° F. The extremes of temperature during the twelve months are 64° and 89°, subject to very little variation during the twenty-four hours. June, July, August, and September, may be considered as the unfavourable months. Seeing how entirely remote Pooree is from the sources of disease peculiar to inland stations, the salubrity and uniformity of its climate, its ready access at all periods of the year, and farther, the benefits the voyage holds out to the invalid and those sinking under tropical disease, it is probably difficult, with such available advantages, to fix upon any spot better suited for a *sanatarium*, or convalescent retreat, than the one under consideration; a visit to which might, in many instances, preclude the necessity of undertaking voyages to Europe or the Cape,—performed frequently with considerable sacrifice and inconvenience.

A Table exhibiting the Monthly and Yearly Mean Temperature of the Air at Calcutta, Bombay, Madras; at three several Elevations on the Nhilgerries; at the Cape of Good Hope, New South Wales, and the City of London; with Average Falls of Rain in England and the Nhilgerries.

	CALCUTTA.			BOMBAY.			MADRAS. At the Observatory.			THE NHILGERRIES. Serloo, 3500 feet above the level of the Sea. Monthly Means.			Jackanary, 5000 feet above the level of the Sea. Monthly Means.			Ootacamund, 8500 feet above the level of the Sea. Month. Means.				AFRICA. Cape of Good Hope.		AUSTRALASIA. Sidney, New South Wales.			ENGLAND. London for 1819—20 and 21, from Daniell's Meteorological Essays.					
	Mean Maximum. 3 P. M.	Mean Minimum. 6 A. M.	Mean Temperature.	Mean Maximum. 4 P. M.	Mean Minimum. 11 A. M.	Mean Temperature.	Mean Maximum.	Mean Minimum.	Mean Temperature.	Mean.	Range. From	Range. To	Mean.	Range. From	Range. To	Mean.	Range. From	Range. To	Average fall of Rain for two years. Inches.	Mean Temperature.	Range.	Maximum.	Minimum.	Mean Temperature.	Mean Maximum.	Mean Minimum.	Mean Temperature.	Range. From	Range. To	Average fall of Rain for two years.
January .	75.1	63	69.05	78	76	77	82.2	74.1	78.15	66¼	83	54	56¾	64	49	50¼	59	31	1.17	76	Greatest heat 96° in Jan., and lowest 45° in Aug. 1819.	102	47	74	39.6	32.6	36.1	52	11	1.483
February	80	67	73.5	78	76	77	84.5	73.8	79.15	67½	94	58	55¼	65	43	51¾	63	39	—	79		106	52	73	42.4	33.7	38	53	21	.746
March . .	88.1	78	83.05	81	80	80.5	87.6	78.7	83.15	72	99	64	61	68	44	61	65	55	2.47	75		97	49.5	68.5	50.1	37.7	43.9	66	24	1.440
April . . .	95.1	79.1	87.1	84	83	83.5	92	84.1	88.05	—	—	—	63¼	72	54	61½	64	57	3.10	67		98	49.5	60	57.7	42.2	49.9	74	29	1.786
May	97.1	80.1	88.6	85	85	85	94.3	85.1	89.70	74	89½	65¾	63	71	58	61¾	65	57	5.21	62		72	42	60	62.9	45.1	54	70	33	1.853
June . . .	88	78	83	86	85	85.5	90.5	84.2	87.35	—	—	—	62½	66	59	59	64	50	5.25	57½		67	26	53	69.4	48.1	58.75	90	37	1.830
July	86.1	78.1	82.1	81	81	81	92.6	85.3	88.95	—	—	—	63¼	73	57	56¼	66	49	10.37	57½		68	27	51.5	69.4	52.9	61.1	76	42	2.510
August .	86.2	79.3	82.75	84	84	84	89.9	83.1	86.50	—	—	—	63¾	75	55	58	63	48	11.77	60		77	35	56	70.1	52.9	61.5	82	41	1.458
September	86	78	82	80	79	79.5	89.7	83.3	86.50	—	—	—	57¾	73	46	57¼	69	49	2.40	63		86	37	62	65.6	50.1	57.8	76	38	2.193
October .	89.2	76.1	82.65	85	84	84.5	87.8	82.4	85.10	—	—	—	61	68	52	56	64	44	7.41	63		93	36	62	55.7	42.1	48.9	68	27	2.073
November	78	65.2	71.6	85	84	84.5	84.3	80.1	82.2	—	—	—	56½	66	44	54¾	63	43	10.86	73½		106	42	63	47.5	38.3	42.9	62	23	2.400
December	75	59	67	81	80	80.5	80.2	76.0	78.1	—	—	—	58¼	66	48	51½	63	37	3.87	75		99	48	72	43.2	35.4	39.3	55	17	2.426
An. Means	85.3	73.4	79.37	82.3	81.4	81.9	88.0	80.8	84.4	70	91.37	60.44	60.1	68.9	50.7	56.6	64	46.58	63.88	67.39	—	89.2	40.9	62.9	56.1	42.6	49.35	68.7	28.4	22.198

RECAPITULATION.

Mean Temperature in London,	49.35°	Mean Temperature at Ootacamund,	56.6°	Mean Temperature at Madras,	84.4°
——— at Serloo,	70	——— in New South Wales,	62.9	——— at Bombay,	81.9
——— at Jackanary,	60.1	——— at the Cape of Good Hope,	67.39	——— at Calcutta,	79.37

CHAPTER IX.

Hydrography.

Springs—Hot Springs—Wells—Lakes—Rivers—The Ganges—Length of the Rivers of India—Cataracts.

THE following observations on Springs, Lakes, Rivers, and Cataracts, are to be considered merely as an addition to what is contained in the general and geographical departments of these volumes of the Edinburgh Cabinet Library.

Springs.—Although India, like other great tracts of country, contains many springs, these have hitherto attracted but little attention. The temperature of but few of them is known; their magnitudes and geognostical situations are scarcely ever mentioned; and their chemical composition, excepting in a very few instances, has been neglected. The most important feature in the natural history of *common* or *perennial* springs, namely their temperature, is rarely noticed, although a knowledge of this fact is illustrative, not only of the mean temperature of the climate, but also of the elevations of the land above the level of the sea; and our information in regard to their chemical nature is equally meagre.

Salt Springs, although met with in saline soils, in some instances probably connected with a salt formation, might be shown to exhibit interesting relations; yet they are not so curious in a general view as the hot springs in different parts of India, concerning which the following details are worthy of being communicated to our readers.

Hot Springs.—The appearance of hot springs in a country never fails to interest the geologist, because, independently of high temperature and other properties, their intimate connexion with igneous rocks, and distorted conditions of the strata, shows not only that a subterranean heat still exists, to which they owe in some degree their elevated temperature, but also that they may have burst forth during some early subterranean igneous action.

They occur among the primitive and secondary strata of the Peninsula, and flow from primitive and transition rocks in the Himmalehs. Thus Heyne says he heard of a hot spring situated in the middle of the river Godavery, near Badrachellum, about 100 miles west from Rajahmundry. Spilsbury mentions two hot springs in the valley of the Nerbudda, at the northern base of the Mahadeo hills. They are much resorted to; not indeed for medicinal purposes, but principally as a place of *pooja* or worship, though people bathe at times for the cure of cutaneous disorders. At both a sort of reservoir has been constructed; but the western spring, near Sohagpoor, is the only one that can be bathed in; and even its heat is too great to allow a person to remain in it above a few seconds, while the eastern one is so hot that the hand can scarcely be dipped in it. Both emit a very offensive smell at the spring head; but the water from the western, on cooling, almost totally loses this smell; whereas that from the eastern, or one near Futtypore, retains it a long time. A lamp held over the place where the west or Unhonee spring bubbles up, is immediately extinguished; and at about five or six paces off is a cold spring. In a paper by the late Dr White, lately read before the Royal Asiatic Society, mention is made of hot wells situated about fifty miles south-east of Surat. The temperature of one is 111° F., of another 120°. Mr H. Wilson notices hot springs in Ramghur, that flow from the base of the *granite* table-land of Hazareebagh. There are four springs at the spot, varying considerably in temperature; the water of one is at the temperature of the atmosphere, that of another is 108° F., whilst that of the other two is severally 170° F. and 190° F. From the last of these arises much sulphureted hydrogen, the odour of which continues to be felt long after the water is cool. The water yields a copious residuum upon evaporation, having as its chief ingredients muriate and sulphate of soda, with a very slight indication of sulphate of iron. It is not unpleasant to the taste, and the cattle are said to be very fond of it. When drunk in sufficient quantity it acts as a gentle aperient. Captain Franklin mentions a hot spring flowing from *new red sandstone*, near the river Bagin, in the Pana diamond-district in Bundelcund. In the neighbourhood of Uteer, a village about thirty miles distant from Pooree, there is a hot mineral spring; but Dr Brander, who mentions it, gives no details in regard to its temperature. Setacuno on the Ganges, according to Dr Adam, is celebrated on account of its hot spring, which, like those in Southern Africa, described in a former volume of the Edinburgh Cabinet Library, issues from *quartz rock*. This spring is about 500 or 600 yards from the river. When

Dr Adam visited it in November, it was running in full stream; but before and during the early part of the rainy season he was told it always dried up, and when low indicates merely the common temperature. He found the sensation of heat intolerable when the hand was immersed in it, and the thermometer stood at 140° F. at all parts, as well near the surface as within a few inches of the bottom. Excepting the increase in the temperature, this water possesses no sensible properties different from rain or common spring water; it is clear and tasteless: gas was constantly disengaged from the surface in large bubbles, but the nature of the gas has not been determined. Many virtues are attributed to the waters in the cure of diseases; and the Bramins, who take charge of it, derive considerable emolument from the crowds resorting thither for relief. Mr Ludlow describes a hot spring at the town of Sonah, about thirty-five miles west from Delhi and fifteen from Goorgaon, at the eastern face of the Mewat hills, which are of *sandstone*, with dispersed iron ore. Close to one of the most craggy and precipitous of this range is the spring in question, which issues out of a hollow dug in the rock. The water, being at a temperature of 108° F., is seen bubbling up, abundantly charged with gas and so impregnated with sulphur as to diffuse a strong smell through that part of the town in which the spring is situated. The well is cut out of the solid rock, about thirty feet deep, in the centre of a basin sixteen feet square, with steps leading down to the water for the convenience of bathing. The whole is covered by a beautiful dome of ancient architecture, and surrounded by apartments with open verandas, which form a court or area. Mr Ludlow says the water contains no iron, and may be classed with the strongest of the sulphureous waters.

At Jauvi, on the northern bank of the Sutledge, eight or ten hot springs burst forth a few feet from the river. A thermometer plunged into one of them rose to 130½° F., while the temperature of the river at the time, the 1st of October, was 61°. The water has a sulphureous smell, with a very disagreeable brackish taste, and incrusts the stones with a yellowish matter resembling sulphur. Gerrard noticed hot wells among the mountains at the head of the same river, 13,000 feet above the level of the sea. A *range* of hot springs, which threw up clouds of steam, was observed by Captain Hodgson towards the head of the Ganges. The same enterprising traveller discovered, in the upper part of the Jumna, hot springs at Oetha-Gur, Bannassa, and Jumnotree; at the last-mentioned place an arch of snow forty feet thick extends across the nascent stream, and completely conceals the ravine from which it takes its rise. Under this arch are numerous hot springs. Their vapour melts the snow from below upwards, so as to form cavities and arches, while the snow is perpetually falling from above. The temperature of the water, where it issues from the rock, is 194° F., which, considering the elevation, 10,849 feet, is nearly the boiling point of water. These springs issue from rocks of *granite* and deposite oxide of iron. Some of them are spouting, being projected upwards in columns of considerable magnitude. They are of great sanctity; and at a spot used for bathing a considerable one rises in a pool of the river, and renders it milk-warm. This jet is both seen and heard as it plays under the surface. Where the Soar and the Elgie flow towards the Ganges, there occurs on the opposite bank of the former a series of hot springs, said to issue from *primitive rocks*.

Wells.—On sinking pits or shafts, we in most districts at length reach some reservoir, from which water rises upwards and forms wells. Owing to the peculiar nature of the climate in many parts of India, wells are of vast importance in supplying the deficiency of rain. In the Balaghaut country, or the country between the Krishna and Toombuddra in the north and the Mysore on the south, when taken possession of by the British, fifty thousand wells were reckoned. Even in the great Western Desert, whereever pits are sunk to a sufficient depth, water is met with. These wells in the Desert are often 300, and one was observed 345 feet deep; with this enormous depth some are only three feet in diameter. The water, which is always brackish, unwholesome, and so scanty that two bullocks working for a night with ease empty a well, is poured into reservoirs lined with clay, which Mr Elphinstone's party drank dry almost in an instant after their arrival. The wells are lined with masonry. The natives have a method of covering them with boards heaped with sand, that effectually conceals them from an enemy; so that scarcity of water is at once their wo and protection. Mr Elphinstone notices a magnificent well of fine water under the walls of the fort of Bikaneer, 300 feet deep, and fifteen or twenty-two feet in diameter. Four buckets, each drawn by a pair of oxen, were worked at once; and when a bucket was let down its striking the water made a noise like a great gun. In India, as in other countries, water might be brought from below in such quantity as to fertilize arid and desert tracts, especially if advantage were taken of the clay and marl so often met with during the sinking of shafts and pits.

A curious mode of sinking wells is mentioned by Heber, as being employed by the natives of the country between Agra and Jyepore. They build a tower of masonry of the diameter required, and twenty or thirty feet high from the surface of the ground. This they allow to stand a year or more, till its masonry is rendered firm and compact by time, then gradually undermining it, the whole tower sinks without difficulty into the sandy soil. When level with the surface they raise its wall higher, and so go on, throwing out the sand, and raising the wall, till they have reached the water. If they adopted our method, the soil is so light that it would fall in before they could possibly raise the wall from the bottom ; nor without the wall could they sink to any considerable depth.

LAKES.

In India the waters of the land are principally distributed in the form of rivers and springs, lakes being of but rare occurrence, and the few that do appear of inconsiderable size. Some of these lakes are salt, others fresh, and a few owe their chief characters to carbonate of soda.

Salt Lakes.—A *salt lake*, twenty miles long by one and a half broad, occurs near Samber, a Rajpoot town in north latitude 26° 53′, and longitude E. 74° 57′. The salt from this lake supplies a considerable portion of Upper India, and during the Mogul government it was carried as far as Benares and Bahar. Every year after the rains the water becomes so strongly impregnated, that when the lake dries up the salt is found crystallized in large quantities under a layer of mud. It is collected towards the close of the hot season without having undergone any artificial process; it is then spread out and exposed to the sun for ten or fifteen days, in which space of time it hardens and forms large lumps; on these lumps a quantity of dry grass is placed and set fire to, which calcines the external surface and forms a covering sufficiently hard to resist the rain. In this last state it is sold, and reaches the different markets. There are many other salt lakes in this part of India, as those of Didwana and Ser; indeed, the soil throughout India is so impregnated with salt, that it is very rare to see a hollow or low spot without a saline efflorescence on the surface.

In Berar there is a salt lake named Loonar, which, according to Captain Alexander, lies in a sort of cauldron of rocks. It contains in the 100 parts, muriate of soda 20, muriate of lime 10, muriate of magnesia 6. The chief use to which the sediment is applied is cleansing the shawls of Cashmere. It also forms an ingredient in the alkaline ley of the Mohammedans. High in the Himmalehs, towards the sources of the Indus, salt lakes were observed by Mr Gerrard at an elevation of 16,000 feet. Natron or soda lakes are said to occur in certain parts of the Himmalehs.

Fresh Water Lakes.—A large *fresh water* lake, or rather jeel, named the Colair Lake, formed chiefly of the overflowings of the Krishna and Godavery, is situated at the north-east projecting corner of the Condapilly Circar, about five miles south from Ellore, whence the water is conducted into many channels to irrigate the circumjacent country. Its breadth, according to Hamilton, varies from seven to twelve miles, while its extreme length may be estimated at twenty-two miles, covering an area of about 164 square miles. On a failure of the periodical supplies the lake dries up, and drinkable water becomes so scarce that the poorer inhabitants are compelled to migrate, and suffer privations almost equal to famine. Magnificent artificial fresh water lakes, formed by dykes built across rivers, are described by Dangerfield as occurring in Mewar. The Lake of Cashmere and that of Manasawara in Thibet, although in many respects interesting, do not properly belong to India.

RIVERS.

The rivers of India may be classed under two divisions, viz. those that flow from the Himmalehs, and those that take their rise in the mountains of the Peninsula. They carry with them to the ocean not only a vast body of water, but an enormous quantity of the debris of the lands through which they pass. The Himmaleh rivers, as the Indus, Ganges, and Brahmapoutra, obtain their supply of water partly from the snows and glaciers of the mountains, and partly from the rains of the monsoons; while those of the Peninsula are entirely supplied by the monsoon-rains. The rivers most celebrated in history and geography are the Indus, Brahmapoutra, and Ganges; the latter is the most important to India as a great province of the British empire. From its elevated source, nearly 15,000 feet above the level of the sea, the Ganges winds through mountainous regions for fully 800 miles, and issues into the open country at Hurdwar, in latitude 30° north. During the remainder of its course to the sea, which is about 1350 miles, flowing as a smooth navigable stream through delightful plains, it receives eleven great rivers, some of which are equal to the Rhine, and none smaller than the Thames, besides as many others of lesser magnitude. It is owing to this vast influx of streams that the Ganges, in point of magnitude, so greatly excels the Nile, whilst the latter exceeds it in length of course by one-third. Like the Nile it has a vast Delta, which exhibits the usual characters of such alluvial formations. To the natives the *inundations* of this river are equally objects of interest, as are those of the Nile to the Egyptians. These annual overflowings of the Ganges are owing as much to the rains and to the melting of the snow among the mountains beyond Hurdwar as to the rains that fall in the plains; for at the latter end of June the river has risen fifteen feet and a half, out of thirty-two, the sum total of its rising; and it is well known that the rainy season does not begin in most of the flat countries till about that time. In the mountains the rains commence early in April, and near the latter end of that month, when the rain-water has reached Bengal, the rivers begin to rise, but by very slow degrees; for the increase is only about one inch per day for the first fortnight. The increase then gradually augments to two and three inches, before any quantity of rain falls in the flat countries; and when the rain becomes general, the increase on a medium is five inches per day. Before the end of July all the lower parts of Bengal contiguous to the Ganges and Brahmapoutra are overflowed, and form a lake of more than 100 miles in breadth; nothing appearing but villages and trees, excepting very rarely the top of an elevated spot, or the artificial mound of some deserted village rising like islands in the flood.

The inundations in Bengal differ from those in Egypt in this particular, that the Nile owes its floods entirely to the rains that fall in the mountains near its source; but in Bengal they are as much occasioned by the rain that falls in the country itself as by the waters of the Ganges; and as a proof of this, the lands in general are overflowed to a considerable depth long before the bed of the river is filled. It may be remarked that the ground adjacent to the bank, to the extent of some miles, is considerably higher than the rest of the country, and serves to separate the waters of the inundation from those of the river until it overflows.* The high ground is in some seasons covered a foot or more; but the depth in the lower country varies, of course, according to the irregularities of the ground, and is in some places twelve feet. Even when the flood becomes general, the river still shows itself, as well by the grass and reeds on its banks as by its rapid and muddy stream; for the water of the inundation acquires a blackish hue, by having been so long stagnant amongst grass and other vegetables; nor does it ever lose this tinge, which is a proof of the predominancy of the rain-water over that of the river. The slow motion of the inundation, which does not exceed half a mile per hour, is owing to the flatness of the country.

There are certain tracts of land which require

* This property of the bank is caused by the deposition of mud from the waters of the river when it overflows. The inundation, as Buffon remarks, purifies itself in its advance over the plain; so that the deposition must be greatest on the parts nearest to the margin of the river.

less moisture than others, from the nature of their productions; these are defended from the floods by vast dykes, which are kept up at an enormous expense. One branch of the Ganges is thus confined to the breadth of the Thames at Battersea for an extent of seventy miles; so that when the river is full passengers look down on each side as from a lofty eminence into the subjacent country. During the swollen state of the river the tide loses totally its effect in counteracting the stream, and in a great measure its ebbing and flowing, except very near the sea. The following is a table of the gradual increase of the Ganges and its branches, according to observations made at Jellinghy and Dacca:—

	At Jellinghy. Ft.	In.	At Dacca. Ft.	In.
In May it rose	6	6	2	4
June,	9	6	4	6
July,	12	6	5	6
The first half of August	4	0	1	11
	32	6	14	3

These observations were made in a season when the waters were higher than usual; so that we may take 31. feet for the medium of increase. The inundation is at its height, and continues without diminution for some days before the middle of August, when it begins to run off; for although great quantities of rain fall in the flat countries during August and September, yet by a partial cessation of the rains in the mountains there happens a deficiency in the necessary supplies. The quantity of the daily decrease of the river is nearly in the following proportions:—During the latter half of August and all September, from three to four inches; from September to the end of November, it gradually lessens from three inches to an inch and a half; and from November to the latter end of April, the decrease is only half an inch per day at a medium. These proportions must be understood to relate to such parts of the river as are removed from the influence of the tides. The decrease of the inundation does not always keep pace with that of the river, by reason of the height of the banks; but after the beginning of October, when the rain has nearly ceased, what remains of the water is quickly evaporated, leaving the lands highly manured, and in a state fit to receive the seed after the simple operation of ploughing.

The quantity of sediment contained in the water of the Ganges, according to Rennell, is truly astonishing. "A glass of water," he says, "taken out of this river when at its height, yields about one part in four of mud. No wonder, then, that the subsiding waters should quickly form a stratum of earth, or that the delta should encroach on the sea." Rennell also computed the mean quantity of water discharged into the sea by the Ganges through the whole year to be 80,000 cubic feet in a second. When the river is most swollen, and its velocity much accelerated, the quantity is 405,000 cubic feet in a second. Other writers agree that the violence of the tropical rains, and the fineness of the alluvial particles in the plains of Bengal, cause the waters of the Ganges to be charged with foreign matter to an extent wholly unequalled by any large European river during the greatest floods. The Ganges frequently sweeps down large islands, and Colebrooke relates examples of the rapid filling up of some branches of this river, and the excavation of new channels, where the number of square miles of soil removed in a short time was truly astonishing, the column of earth being 114 feet high. Forty square miles, or 25,600 acres, are mentioned as having been carried away in one district in the course of a few years. If we compare the proportion of mud, as given by Rennell, with his computation of the quantity of water discharged, very striking results are obtained. If it were true that the Ganges in the flood season contained one part in four of mud, we should then be obliged to suppose that there passes down, every four days, a quantity of mud equal in volume to the water which is discharged in the course of twenty-four hours. If the mud be assumed to be equal to one-half of the specific gravity of granite (it would, however, be more), the weight of matter daily carried down in the flood-seasons would be equal to seventy-four times the weight of the Great Pyramid of Egypt. Even if it should be proved that the turbid waters of the Ganges contain one part in 100 of mud, which is affirmed to be the case in regard to the Rhine, we should be brought to the extraordinary conclusion, that there passes down every two days into the Bay of Bengal a mass about equal in weight and bulk to the Great Pyramid.

The following table is given by Hamilton of the probable length of some of the rivers of India :—

	Miles to the Sea.
1. Indus,	1700
2. Jumna (to its junction with the Ganges, 780 miles),	1500
3. Sutledge (to the Indus, 900),	1400
4. Jhylum (ditto. 750),	1250
5. Gunduck (to the Ganges, 450),	980
6. Godavery,	850
7. Krishna,	700
8. Nerbudda,	700
9. Mahanuddy,	550
10. Tuptee,	460
11. Cavery,	400

CATARACTS.

The Ganges, Indus, and Brahmapoutra, during their course amongst the mountains, exhibit cascades hitherto but imperfectly described. Some very splendid and beautiful waterfalls are met with in the Peninsula; the most considerable are those of Bundelcund, of the Western Ghauts, and of the River Cavery.

Falls in Bundelcund.—The only account we have met with of these magnificent falls is given by Captain Franklin. He visited all that are between the Katra pass and the Tonse river. The first is near the village of Bilohi, about twelve miles west from the pass of Katra, where the fall of water is 398 feet, and the rocky wall of red sandstone over which it is precipitated nearly perpendicular. Ten miles farther west is the cataract of Bouti, 400 feet in height, which is very picturesque, owing to the great extent of the circus over which it falls. At Keuti, twenty-four miles farther west, is another fall 272 feet in height; and westward still, at Chachai, one 362 feet high. At a short distance from Chachai is the cataract of the Tonse, where the volume of water is greater than in the others, but the fall less, being only 200 feet.

Many of the waterfalls in the Western Ghauts, although exhibiting magnificent scenes during the rains, are completely dried up in the hot season. There are many fine cascades in the Ghauts above Honoor, which for sublimity and magnitude will probably yield to few in the world. They have hitherto been little visited, even by Europeans in India; and it is, we believe, only within the last ten or twelve years that they have received a name.

They are situated on the river Shervutty, about fifteen miles up the Ghauts from the town of Garsipa, and are now known to Europeans by the name of the Falls of Garsipa.

Falls of Garsipa.—The country in the neighbourhood of the falls, says Dr Christie in a communication to us, is extremely beautiful, combining the majestic appearance of a tropical forest with the softer characters of an English park. Hill and dale are covered with soft green, which is finely contrasted with a border of dark forest, with numerous clumps of majestic trees, and thickets of acacias, the carunda, and other flowering shrubs.

Upon approaching the falls you emerge from a thick wood, and come suddenly upon the river, gliding gently among confused masses of rock. A few steps more over huge blocks of granite bring you to the brink of a fearful chasm, rocky, bare, and black; down which you look to the depth of 1000 feet. Over its sides rush the different branches of the river, the largest stretching downwards without break in one huge curling pillar of white foam. Beneath, the waters, by the force of their fall, are projected far out in straight lines; and at some distance below the falls form a thin cloud of white vapour, which rises high above the surrounding forest. The sides of the chasm are formed by slanting strata of rock, the regularity of which forms a striking contrast to the disorder of the tumultuous waters, the broken detached masses of stone, and the soft tint of the crowning woods.

The effect of all these objects rushing at once upon the sight is truly sublime. The spectator is generally obliged to retire after the first view of them, in order gradually to familiarize himself with their appearance; for the feeling which he experiences in suddenly coming on them amounts almost to pain. After the first impression has somewhat subsided, and he has become accustomed to the scene, he can then leisurely analyze its parts, and become acquainted with the details.

The chasm is somewhat of an elliptical form. At its narrowest and deepest part is the principal fall; smaller branches of the river and little rills dash over its sides, and are almost all dissipated in spray before they reach the bottom. The principal branch of the river is much contracted in breadth before it reaches the brink of the precipice, where it probably does not exceed fifty or sixty feet; but it contains a very large body of water.

The falls can only be seen from above, for the cliffs on both sides of the river afford no path to admit of a descent. Some gentlemen have attempted to reach the bottom by having themselves lowered by ropes; but no one has hitherto succeeded. A view of the falls from below, says Dr Christie, would, I am convinced, exceed in grandeur every thing of the kind in the world. The spectator can very easily, and with great safety, look down into the chasm to its very bottom. Some large inclined plates of gneiss project from its edge; so that by laying himself flat upon one of these he can stretch his head considerably beyond the brink of the precipice.

Although no accurate measurement has yet been made of the height of these falls, it would appear from Dr Christie's account, that they cannot be much short of 1000 feet.

Falls of the Cavery.—The falls in the course of

the river Cavery, still farther south in the Peninsula than Garsipa, are celebrated by travellers. Of these two are particularly noticed, viz. the Ganga Chuki and Birra Chuki.

The branch of the river which forms the Ganga Chuki is subdivided into two lesser ramifications, a short distance above the fall. The nearest and by much the largest of these streams is broken by projecting masses of rock into one cataract of prodigious volume and three or four smaller torrents. The water of the large cataract plunges into the ravine below, from a height of from 100 to 150 feet; while the smaller torrents, impeded in their course by the intervening rocks, work their way to a distance of about 200 feet from the base of the precipice, where the whole unite,—the other detached portion of the river precipitating itself at the same time in two columns from a cliff about 200 feet high, the rapid above flowing nearly at right angles with the principal branch. The surrounding scenery is wild, and the whole offers a most striking spectacle, especially during the height of the rains.

The second cataract is that of another arm of the Cavery, at a spot called Birra Chuki about a mile from the fall above described. The channel of the river here is spread out to a magnificent expanse, and its stream divided into no less than ten distinct torrents, which fall with infinite variety of form over a broken precipice of more than 100 feet, but presenting no single body of water equal in volume to the main fall at Ganga Chuki.

CHAPTER X.

Geology and Mineralogy.

Geology and Mineralogy—1. Soils of India, viz. Soil of Bengal; Cotton Ground; Musaree Soil; Laterite Soil; Nitre Soil; Soda Soil; Salt Soil—2. Geognostical Structure and Composition of India—1. Himmaleh or Alpine Region; Its Rocks, Minerals, and Mines—2. Middle India; Its Rocks, Minerals, and Mines—3. Peninsular India; Its Rocks, Minerals, and Mines—4. Submergence and Upraising of Land—5. Destruction of the ancient City of Ougein and other Places in India by a Shower of Volcanic Ashes—6. Earthquakes.

Regarding the geology and mineralogy of India our information is very defective, and many years must elapse before even the general geognostical and mineralogical relations of so vast a region can be determined. The India Company has munificently patronised the researches of the botanist; it is now time to encourage and forward other branches of science. We expect ere long to hear of the establishment of meteorological observatories amply furnished, in well selected stations, from Cape Comorin to the centre of the Himmalehs;—to find carried on by scientific men throughout India those important investigations requisite for the illustration of hydrography;—to rejoice in the appointment of active and experienced geologists, mineralogists, and zoologists, for every part of our Eastern Empire.* What is known of the geology and mineralogy of India, has arisen from the labours of Hamilton Buchanan, Heyne, Voysey, Dangerfield, Turnbull Christie, Franklin, Adam, Hardie, Webb, Herbert, Gerrard, Hodgson, Calder, Govan, and others. To such as have no opportunity of consulting the memoirs and works of these naturalists, the following short view of the geology of India may not be unprofitable.

I. SOILS OF INDIA.

The soil of India, as that of other countries, is formed principally by the action of the atmosphere on rocks, and dead animal and vegetable matter; the broken down or disintegrated rocks mixed in various proportions with decaying organic substances, giving rise to the different species of soil. These soils have particular names in different parts of the country, and in many instances the distinctions are not without their practical utility. We cannot attempt to give a detailed view of this subject, even were it required in a work of this description; what we consider necessary, we shall therefore include under the following heads:—1. Soil of Bengal. 2. Cotton ground or regur soil. 3. Musaree soil. 4. Nitre or saltpetre soil or ground. 5. Soda soil or ground. 6. Salt soil or ground.

1. *Soil of Bengal.*—There is no rock of any kind on the banks of the Hoogley, nor do we meet with any after entering on the principal stream of the

* Dr Turnbull Christie, we are happy to announce, has been appointed by the India Company to investigate the geology of the Bombay Presidency. A more fortunate selection could not have been made.

Ganges, until we approach the province of Bahar. The whole country seems to consist of a mixture of clay and sand, in such proportions as to form a compound well adapted for the purposes of vegetation, and conducing, in no small degree, to that fertility for which the plains of Bengal are so celebrated. Disseminated scales of mica often give to this soil a glimmering appearance, and when mingled in minute grains with the sand, more or less prevalent on the banks of the river during its whole course, they impart a brilliant lustre to the extensive plains. Strata of sand of various colours are frequently observed lying over each other; these seem to have been formed in successive seasons; above them is a mixed soil, or sand approaching to soil. When not destitute of herbage the surface bears a coarse grass or reeds.

On the Fertilizing Principle of the Inundations of the Hoogley.—It is generally supposed that the fertilizing principle of the inundations of the great tropical rivers is vegetable matter in various states of decomposition. The following details in regard to the *silt* of the Hoogley are at variance with that opinion. It is well known, says Mr Piddington, that while the tracts within the reach of the inundation preserve their original fertility, the higher soils are gradually and rapidly becoming impoverished, and this to a degree of which few, who have not made the subject one of attention, are aware; there are some crops which cannot be repeated, unless at intervals of three or four years; while on the lowlands these crops have been continued for a period beyond the memory of man. Indigo is a striking, and the most familiar instance of what is here advanced; the following analyses were made with a view to some improvement in the cultivation of that plant. Portions of the *silt* or *mud* deposited by inundations were procured from Bansbariah near Sukhsagar, and from Mohatpur near Kissinnuggur; the analysis of each gave in two hundred parts,—

	Silt from Bansbariah.	Silt from Mohatpur.
Water,	2	2
Saline matter, principally muriate of potash,	0¼	0½
Vegetable matter destructible by heat,	4¾	4½
Carbonate of lime,	12¼	16½
Phosphate of lime,	0	1
Oxide of iron,	12	12
Silica,	156	139
Alumina,	6½	14¾
	183¾	180¼
Loss,	60¼	9¾
	200	200

The unlooked-for circumstance of only two and a half per cent. of vegetable matter being found in these specimens, appeared almost to show that such matter was not the fertilizing principle, or at least not exclusively. On the other hand, from six to eight per cent. of calcareous matter appearing in them, when, in an extensive series of analyses of the higher soils, this was always found remarkably different (seldom more than 0.75 to 1. per cent.), it seemed probable that the calcareous matter was the great agent; and in as far as regards indigo this was found by experiment to be the fact,—for a minute portion of lime was found to increase the produce upwards of 50 per cent. In considering this subject farther, it occurred to Mr Piddington that lime might probably exist in solution amongst the rich mud on which the seed is sown as the waters retire,—and this was found to be the case; a quantity of it being procured at the moment of the subsidence of the waters, it was found that the drainings were highly impregnated with carbonic acid gas, and that lime was held in solution by it,—a fact which perhaps throws some light on the phenomena of the formation of *kunkur*.

2. The *Cotton Ground* or *Regur Soil* forms one of the most interesting features in the physical geography of many districts in India. It probably originates from the disintegration of trap rocks. It varies in depth from two or three to twenty or thirty feet, and even more; its extent is prodigious, as it covers all the great plains in the Deccan and Candeish, some of those in Hydrabad, and perhaps also those of other parts of India. This soil is as remarkable for its fertility as for its very great extent; and a curious circumstance is, that *it never lies fallow, and never receives the slightest manure.* Even the stems of the cotton-plant are not allowed to remain on it, being employed for making baskets, or used as firewood; moreover, in all those parts of the country where the cotton ground is met with, there is so little wood that cow-dung is carefully collected and dried for fuel. Cotton, jovaree, wheat, and other grains, are raised from it in succession; and it has continued to afford the most abundant crops, without receiving any return for centuries, nay, perhaps, for 2000 or 3000 years,—thus proving the inaccuracy of the opinion held by agriculturists, that if something be not constantly added to land equal to what is taken from it, it must gradually deteriorate. Attention must be paid to the order of cropping; but if the weather be favourable the ryot is always sure of an abundant harvest.

The fertility of this soil is probably owing in part to its power of absorbing moisture from the atmosphere. This power is great, even when compared with the best soils in Britain. A well-known writer, Sir H. Davy, says, "I have compared the absorbent powers of many soils with respect to atmospheric moisture, and I have always found it greatest in the most fertile soils; so that it affords one method of judging of the productiveness of land." He farther states, that 1000 parts of a celebrated soil, from Ormiston in East Lothian, when dried to 212°, gained in an hour, by exposure to air saturated with moisture, at a temperature of 62°, 18 grains; and that 1000 parts of a very fertile soil, from the banks of the river Parret in Somersetshire, under the same circumstances, gained 16 grains. The following are the results of some experiments made by Dr T. Christie on the absorbent power of the cotton soil. He thoroughly dried a portion of the earth by a heat that was nearly sufficient to char paper. He then exposed to the atmosphere of a moderately damp apartment 2615.6 grains of it, and found, after a few days, that it had gained 147.1 grains. He now exposed it to an atmosphere saturated with moisture, and found that the weight increased daily till the end of a few weeks, when it was found to be 2828.4 grains. The soil had therefore gained 212.8 grains, or about 8 per cent.

In the hot season the *regur* or *cotton ground* is traversed in all directions by very deep fissures. In the rainy season it is in the form of very tenacious clay. Almost all the crops raised from it are sown towards the end of the rainy season, and therefore during their growth receive comparatively little moisture; often indeed none but that of the heavy dews descends on them for a length of time.

3. *Musaree Soil.*—In many parts of India there is another soil, named the *mussub* or *musaree soil*, which does not form extensive plains like the cotton ground, but is generally found at the foot of hills, or in the bottom of small valleys. At the bases of the sandstone hills it consists of little else than loose sand. On the sides of the hills that contain beds of quartz it is very gravelly.

4. *Laterite Soil.*—The *laterite* or brick stone affords in general, on disintegration, a soil not very productive, and apt to become extremely hard in dry weather; but in the bottom of many small valleys large deposites of it are met with, which have been more perfectly disintegrated and mixed with other substances, and form productive soils. The soils in the valleys of *clay-slate* districts are also in many places very good, when the clay happens to be mixed with fragments of quartz.

5. *Nitre or Saltpetre Ground or Soil.*—In India this soil is found in places where there has been a due admixture of animal and vegetable matter, as in old populous villages built on black cotton ground, or forming the rich mould of gardens, as in many parts of the Northern Circars. In such situations, from the beginning of the dry season in February till the rains commence again in May and June, the streets, and particularly the lower parts of the mud walls with which the houses are built or the yard surrounded, appear wet and black in the morning, and crumble down into a fine soft mould. What collects in a heap under the walls is gathered every other day by sweeping. It contains about one-fifth

of its weight of crude saltpetre. The natives observe that this substance is produced abundantly in those years in which the preceding monsoon-rains have been strongest, and accompanied by a great deal of thunder and lightning. A heavy thunder-storm in April or May is likewise reckoned very favourable for the manufacture. When the saltpetre has been extracted from this earth, it is thrown in heaps, and spread out when the monsoon is over. After lying a year or two it is swept every day, and is again found to yield, by sweeping it every other day, saltpetre earth fit for the manufacture; for no potash is added, so that the saltpetre seems to be ready formed in the soil.

The manufacture of saltpetre hardly extends lower than the eastern limits of Bahar, and it is said that the production of nitre is greatest during the prevalence of the hot winds. These winds blow from the west, and formerly did not extend eastward beyond Bahar; but from the change of seasons within these forty years their influence is now felt in Bengal; in which province, on that account, the extensive manufacture of saltpetre might be attempted with success.

Saltpetre grounds are frequent in Bengal. The tendency of the soil to reproduce saltpetre is very troublesome to the builders and the occupants of houses. "It can scarcely," says Heber, "be prevented from encroaching, in a few years, on the walls and floors of all lower rooms, so as to render them unwholesome, and eventually uninhabitable." Half the houses in Calcutta are in this predicament, and their ground-floors useless. Cellars are unknown in this part of India.

In Tirhoot, one of the principal districts in India for the manufacture of saltpetre, the soil, according to Tytler, is every where thoroughly impregnated with this substance. During the rains and cold weather, it appears abundantly on the lime on the walls of houses. From these and other damp spots it may be brushed off every two or three days almost in basketfuls. The ground too, even in the hot weather, is so moist that it is extremely difficult either to get earth of sufficient tenacity to make bricks (the country being quite destitute of stones), or when the bricks are made to find a spot sufficiently solid to bear the weight of a house. Notwithstanding the greatest attention, the ground at length yields, and the saltpetre corrodes the best of the bricks to such a degree that the whole house gradually sinks several inches below its original level. Houses built of inferior materials, of course, suffer much more; one, of which the inner foundations were of unburnt bricks, absolutely fell down whilst Dr Tytler was at Mullye, and the family had a miraculous escape. Dr Tytler's own house, one little better, sank so much, and the ground-work was so evidently giving way, that at great expense and inconvenience he was compelled to pull down the whole of the inner walls and rebuild them in a more secure manner. From the same cause a new magazine, which government had ordered to be built with an arched roof of brickwork, was, when complete, found so very unsafe that it was necessary to demolish it entirely, and rebuild it on a new plan with a roof of tiles. One hundred parts of nitre earth or soil from the Tirhoot district, when analyzed by Dr Davy, afforded—

Nitrate of potash,..	8.3
Nitrate of lime,..	3.7
Sulphate of lime,..	0.8
Common Salt,..	0.2
Carbonate of lime,...	35.0
Earthy matter insoluble in water and nitric acid,....	40.0
Water with a trace of vegetable matter,...............	12.0
	100.0

The soil in many parts of Ajmere is very nitrous.

5. *Soda Soil or Ground.*—Soil more or less impregnated with carbonate of soda occurs in different parts of Mysore, where the soda is separated and used for glass-making and for washing. Soil of the same kind is found in the Coimbetoor province, and in many other parts of the Peninsula of India. Heyne says, the soda of the Mysore effloresces on a red ferruginous soil; when purest it is collected by the washermen, and used by them instead of soap; hence it is known by the name of washerman's earth. Soda also occurs in efflorescences on the surface of cotton ground; but there it is mixed with a great proportion of common salt, which forms the principal object of a manufactory carried on by the people called *tank-diggers* by Europeans, and *salt-people* by the natives. Saltworks of this kind are of frequent occurrence in the Mysore country, which renders importation of salt from the coast very trifling.

6. *Salt Soil or Ground.*—In many parts of India the soil is richly impregnated with common salt, thus forming a salt soil or ground, as it is sometimes termed. Thus, near to Vencataghery, common salt appears to be generally diffused over and through a black poor soil, where it is collected and used for culinary purposes. Between Baydamungulum and Tayculum in the Mysore, Buchanan had an opportunity of examining one of the places where salt is

made. The situation was low and moist; the soil a black mould, consisting of a mixture of sand and clay, that from its appearance would have been reckoned good; but the impregnation of salt renders it for cultivation greatly inferior to soils apparently of a worse quality and free from salt. The natives allege, that if they walk much on this saline earth their bare feet become blistered. In the dry season the surface of the earth is scraped off and collected in heaps. In front of these heaps the native salt-makers construct a semicircle of small round cisterns, each about three feet in diameter and a foot deep, with sides and floors of dry mud. Toward the heaps of saline earth there is in the floor of each a small aperture, with a wooden spout to convey the brine into an earthen pot placed in a cavity below. The floors of the cisterns are covered with straw, and the saline earth is put in till it rises nearly to the level of the tops of the walls. On the surface of the saline earth water is then poured, which in filtering through into the pots carries with it all the salt. The inert earth being thrown out behind the cisterns is replaced with new earth for saturating more water. In the mean time the brine is emptied into a cavity cut in a rock, and is evaporated entirely by the sun. The natives say that the salt is sufficiently wholesome. The grain is large and consists of well-formed cubes; but the salt is mixed with much earthy impurity. It is principally used by the lower orders.

II. GEOGNOSTICAL STRUCTURE AND COMPOSITION OF INDIA.

1. *Himmaleh or Alpine Region.*—It is said that the principal *valleys* in this Alpine land are perpen-

dicular to its direction, that is, run from north-north-east and north-east to south-south-west and south-west; and that frequently the surface exposed to the west is rugged, while the opposite one, facing the south-east, is shelving. The *forms of the mountains* are exceedingly varied, being described as needle-shaped, peaked, conical, ridge-shaped, and round-backed. There are *precipices*, often of fearful abruptness and magnitude, sometimes continuing mural or perpendicular for miles, with an elevation of 200 and 300 feet; and, according to some travellers, even of 2000 and 3000 feet. The *passes* that lead through this extraordinary region vary in height, from that of Tungrang, one of the lower passes, which is 13,740 feet, to the pass of Charang, 17,348 feet above the sea. We possess but little information as to the general and particular direction and dip of the strata; even the principal geognostical features of the various formations are scarcely at all known to us.

1. *Primitive Rocks.*—From the reports of Webb, Gerrard, Franklin, Govan, and Colebrooke, it appears that *gneiss* is one of the most abundant of the stratified primitive rocks; associated with it, in some places having a subordinate character, in others predominating, there occur *mica-slate, clay-slate, quartz-rock, hornblende-rock, potstone, indurated talc, primitive-limestone,* and *gypsum.* These rocks are variously intersected by *granite* and *quartz veins,* and in some quarters vast bodies of *granite,* forming whole mountains, are observed rising through the stratified Neptunean rocks above enumerated. Schorl and tourmaline are of frequent occurrence in these rocks. Of the gems, the precious garnet is the only one we have seen in specimens

from the Himmalehs, nor is any other mentioned by travellers. It has been found in granite at the enormous height of 22,000 feet above the sea,—an interesting fact, showing that the garnet is found at a greater elevation than any other gem. The observations of our pupils in tropical regions, and at the highest northern latitude hitherto reached by man, likewise show that this beautiful precious stone ranges from the equator to the vicinity of the north pole. The following is an enumeration of the heights above the sea at which several of the primitive rock-formations have been noticed :—

	Feet.
A cavern in primitive limestone near the Sutledge,...........	6500
Mountain near the Sutledge, composed of gneiss,.............	8350
Eastward of the Tarhegang mountain, at the head of the rivulet Ripsang, the rocks are gneiss, granite, mica-slate, and quartz-rock, with tourmaline,..........	11,000
Pass of Bruang, mica-slate, gneiss, granite, containing tourmaline and garnet,..........	15,000
The Rollor or Shatul pass, gneiss,..........	15,000
Mountains near to the Shatul pass, mica-slate, gneiss, and granite,..........	15,556

2. *Transition Rocks.*—On the primitive formations rests a vast deposite of rocks of the transition class, principally consisting of *clay-slate, graywacke-slate, graywacke, flinty-slate, gypsum,* and *transition-limestone.* Fossil organic remains first appear among these deposites. The *ammonite* is the most celebrated, on account of the superstitious value attached to it. The heights stated under are probably formed of transition clay-slate, and therefore belong to this section :—

	Feet above the Sea.
Overhanging the town of Marang, a mountain of clay-slate,..	12,000
Tungrang pass, clay-slate, with pyrites and mica,..........	13,740
Mountains of clay-slate on the Chinese frontier, containing ammonites,..........	16,200
Mountains in the neighbourhood of Charang, of blue clay-slate,	18,000

Mineral Substances useful in the Arts found in the Primitive and Transition Rocks of the Himmalehs.—We shall notice the rocks and minerals in the following order:—1. Rocks. 2. Saline minerals. 3. Inflammable minerals. 4. Metallic minerals.

1. *Rocks.*—*Granite.*—Many fine granites occur in the Himmalehs, which, owing to their remote localities, are as yet of but little value. A beautiful gray porphyritic granite occurs, however, close to the cantonment of Almora, which would furnish ornamental pillars or slabs of any size.

Clay-slate.—Of this rock, so useful as a roofing material, many extensive deposites are known, but hitherto they have not been quarried.

Limestone.—Under this name we include the various marbles, whether white or coloured, that have been seen in the valleys and mountains. Captain Franklin mentions a variety resembling that of Iona, found at no great distance from the plains, and also a fine dolomite marble which he observed in many places. At no great distance from the Iona-like marble there is a flesh-coloured dolomite, with purple-clouded delineations, which promises well. A marble of more crystalline nature appears on the road to Bhadreenath above the Bishen Ganga.

Gypsum.—This rock has a pure white colour and granular foliated structure. "It is probable," Captain Franklin remarks, "that its chief use in Bengal, for some time, would be as convertible into plaster of Paris, and affording a material for cornices and ornamental work, to the banishment of the very rude productions of this kind we have hitherto put up with. There is, perhaps, a sufficient quantity of it to answer any demand likely immediately to arise. When the government-house was last repaired, it was considered desirable to obtain a sufficiency for the purpose above indicated; but the fact of its occurrence within our mountain-provinces was not known at that time. As it is within fifty or sixty miles of water-carriage, it might be expected to pay for its transport."

Potstone.—This rock may be used with advantage for lining ovens and furnaces, and for architectural purposes. From its softness, it might easily be turned on a lathe into various useful articles.

2. *Saline Minerals.*—*Alum.*—This saline mineral occurs in efflorescence on rocks of different kinds, particularly on alum-slate, and might in some situations be collected with profit.

Sulphate of Iron, or Green Vitriol.—This salt too is met with frequently as an efflorescence, on rocks containing pyrites or sulphuret of iron. We do not know that it is any where collected for economical purposes.

Borax.—Although this salt has not been discovered within the present limits of British India, still, as the production of a neighbouring country and a valuable article of commerce, it may be mentioned. The whole supply of the European market passes through these mountains.

3. *Inflammable Minerals.*—*Sulphur.*—Depositions of sulphur are formed around hot springs, in the bed of the Ramganga and of the Garjia rivers, in the province of Kemaoon, but mixed with carbonate of lime, from which it can be readily separated by sublimation. It occurs in considerable quantities in some of the galleries of the lead-mines at Mywar on the Tonse, in Jaunsar.

Mineral Oil and Pitch.—These minerals do not occur any where abundantly. Mineral oil is mentioned as having been observed oozing from rocks of limestone in the range between Sarju and the Ramganga.

Graphite, or Black Lead.—This valuable mineral has not hitherto been found in considerable quantity in any part of the Himmalehs, although, from the nature of the country and the notices of travellers, it is not improbable that enough of it will be met with for the various purposes of the arts. It occurs in embedded masses, varying in size from an inch to three or four inches in diameter, in a graphitic mica-slate.

4. *Metallic Minerals.*—The Himmalehs have hitherto afforded but a comparatively small quantity of ore, owing not so much to the poverty of this vast country in metalliferous substances as to the neglect of observers, who have been principally occupied with geographical investigations and the collecting of plants. The only metals at present met with in such quantity as to yield a profitable return are, copper, iron, and lead; but besides these there also occur gold, antimony in the state of sulphuret, the gray antimony ore of mineralogists, and manganese combined with iron. We shall now notice in a general way these different substances.*

Gold.—In the Old World, almost every extensive range of mountainous country has been found to afford gold, which is indicated either by its occurrence in the sands of rivers and rivulets, or

* Arsenic combined with sulphur, or in the state of yellow and red orpiment, is imported from beyond the frontiers, for it has not been found in the British dominions.

disseminated in diluvia, or through the mass of solid strata. The gold of the Himmalehs occurs in the alluvial soil of several mountain-rivers, and one instance is mentioned of its having been observed in grains in granite at Kedarnath. During the Gorkhali rule, the gold collected afforded a small duty; but the amount was too trifling to render its continuance expedient. It is collected from loams, sands, and clays, by washing in the usual manner.

Copper Mines.—There are seven places where ores of copper are raised; these are,—

	Rupees per annum as rent.
1. Dhanpur, 2. Dhobri,	1200
3. Gangoli, 4. Sira,	1000
5. Pokri,	600
6. Khari,	40
7. Shor Gurang,	50

These mines, if they deserve the name, are worked in the most miserable manner, under every disadvantage, and therefore afford but paltry returns. No mine can thrive in our Indian possessions until well-instructed mine-masters and experienced miners are sent out from Europe.

The ore found in the Dhanpur mine is *gray copper ore,* which affords from 30 to 50 per cent. of copper; it is associated with *malachite,* or green carbonate of copper. The ores are contained in a compact red-coloured dolomite; hence mining operations can be carried on without the expense of wooden frame-work or masonry. The Pokri mine or mines are situated in talc slate of a loose texture; and hence the working is more difficult. The ores are *vitreous* and *purple copper,* both of them rich in copper. The waters flowing from the mine are impregnated with *sulphate of copper* or blue vitriol. The Sira and Gangoli mines are situated in beds of indurated talc, which are enclosed in dolomite. Sometimes the one, sometimes the other rock, form the walls and roof of the mine. The iron is *yellow copper* or *copper pyrites,* mixed with iron pyrites and smaller portions of gray copper ore. The Khari and Shor Gurang mines are similarly situated, the ores are *gray copper, yellow copper* or *copper pyrites,* and *carbonate of copper*. The method of working these mines is as follows:—A gallery or passage is cut into the face of the hill, with such a bottom declivity as to allow the water to run off. Where the rock may require it, frames of timber rudely constructed are set up to support the roof and sides. The area of the gallery is always small; in those parts where the hardness of the rock occasions any difficulty in working, it is scarcely sufficient to admit a person even in a creeping posture. In no place will it admit of an erect position. The ore is detached by means of a very ill-shaped and disproportioned pick, and by chisels and hammers. It is removed from the mines on skins, drawn along the floor of the gallery by boys. The ore, being delivered at the mouth of the mine, is reduced to small fragments by the hand. At Dhanpur, however, the work is done by a water-mill. It is next roasted in an open fire or forge-hearth with charcoal, and the heat occasionally urged by means of two air-bags or skins, which are alternately shut and opened by the hand. After being in this way imperfectly roasted, it is smelted on the forge-hearth, and the process is repeated till the metal is sufficiently pure. No flux appears to be used to assist the operation.

Iron Mines.—The wretched condition of Indian

mining is shown by the fact, that the united rent of the numerous iron-mines does not exceed the annual sum of 1500 rupees, while the iron is of the very worst quality. The mining and metallurgical operations in use are on a parallel with those of Europe during the dark ages. The Himmaleh mines supply chiefly varieties of *red iron ore*, affording from 60 to 30 per cent. of metal. *Red hematite*, associated with micaceous iron ore, occurs in a large bed in gneiss at Dhaniakot on the Cosillah. At Ramghur, on the road from Bhamaori to Almora, there are beds of the scaly red iron ore also in gneiss. *Compact red iron ore* occurs in clay-slate, containing beds of limestone, at Katsari on the Ramganga. The iron manufactured from it is esteemed the best in the province of Kemaoon. Near Kalsi, on the Jumna, there is an extensive bed of *specular iron ore*. In Chawgarka-purgunnah the ore is the *brown* or the hydrated species, which contains manganese ; hence the superiority of the steel prepared from it.

Lead Mines.—Of these mines, which are numerous, the most productive are situated on the river Tonse, at no great distance from the Deyra Dhoon. The Borela mine in this district formerly paid 2000, the Maijar 4000 rupees yearly ; but the present rents are much lower. The ore, which is fine granular galena, is found in clay-slate and clay-slate limestone.

5. *Secondary Rocks.*—Resting upon the preceding primitive and transition rocks, but occupying a much lower situation, we find formations of the secondary class. These form the immediate north-east boundary of the great alluvial plain of Middle India, and are principally of sandstone, in all probability of different ages.

Mr Scott has communicated, through Mr Colebrooke, some details in regard to the secondary strata he observed on the banks of the Tista and Subuck, where they issue from the mountains of Bootan. The strata he noticed on the Tista are micaceous sandstone, bituminous shale, slate-clay, and *coal;* and rocks of the same description were observed on the Subuck. The coal has a dark *brown colour,* with a conchoidal fracture, and is associated with fossil wood. The colour of the coal would seem to intimate that it belongs to the brown coal series, and therefore is of a more recent origin than the coal of Damoda near to Calcutta. The hills formed of these strata, in Mr Colebrooke's opinion, may be considered as fair examples of the entire range which skirts the north of Indostan. They rise to no great height, and constitute the first step from the plain of India, ascending towards the mountains of Bootan and the loftier peaks of the Himmalehs. Every where, so far as is yet ascertained, the lower range of hills consists of sandstone abounding in mica. To the above details we may add, that throughout the whole line of sandstone hills that lie at the foot of the Himmaleh chain, according to Captain Herbert, coal occurs in beds varying from a quarter of an inch to a foot in thickness. It often shows the ligneous texture; and where that texture is no longer visible it presents a conchoidal fracture, and burns with much flame and smoke. It appears to be the brown coal of Werner.

6. *Tertiary Rocks.*—An interesting display of rocks of this class was discovered by Mr Scott at Cooch-Behar on the north-east border of Bengal, where the Brahmapoutra emerges into the plain.

The strata are of yellow and green sand, alternating with clay, that lie horizontally at the height of about 150 feet above the level of the sea, and contain organic remains resembling those of the blue clay of the London and Hampshire basins. Mr Scott also noticed, at Robagiri in the same district, a stratum of white limestone containing nummulites and vertebræ of fish, surmounted by beds of clay which contain the same nummulites, and also bones of fish, with specimens of the genera *Ostrea* and *Pecten*. Near Silhet, the Laour Hills, composed of white limestone abounding in nummulites, form another example of a tertiary formation in the eastern extremity of this province. Mr Pentland discovered among mutilated fragments of bones, referable to the mammalia from these tertiary deposites, remains of four distinct species, viz. 1. A new species of the genus *Anthracotherium* of Cuvier; 2. A small species of ruminant allied to the musk-deer tribe; 3. A small species of herbivorous animal referable to the order Pachydermata, but more diminutive than any of the fossil or living species; and, 4. A carnivorous animal of the genus weasel or viverra. In addition to the above, the following are mentioned by Mr Colebrooke:—Sharks' teeth, vertebra and fin-bone of a shark, crocodiles' teeth, vertebra of a crocodile's neck, thighbone of a crocodile, dorsal fin and pectoral fin of a balistes, palates of the ray, palates of the diodon, oyster-shells of various species, a *Turritella*, and several species of *Balani* and *Patellæ*. These strata thus present us with the same association of organized remains that accompanies the tertiary strata of Europe, in which extinct genera of the Pachydermata have been discovered, and also with marine shells of the same genera, if not the same species, with those which characterize the most modern antediluvian formations, those described under the title of upper marine formation in the Paris basin, and to which are to be referred the extensive marine deposites encircling the shores of the Mediterranean, those covering the less elevated countries of Central Europe, and that appear to extend as far as Lake Ural into the interior of Asia. The tertiary deposites of Caribari, as already noticed, appear to form a band at the base of the Thibetian mountains, since we find them extending to Silhet. How far this formation may stretch along the Peninsula of Malacca and Indostan it is impossible at present to say; although it seems to occur at Madras, where it contains the same shells as on the Brahmapoutra, and at Pondicherry, where it encloses great masses of woodstone.

7. *Alluvial Rocks.*—The usual alluvial deposites occur throughout the Himmalehs. The most curious statement in regard to them is one made by Gerrard, who tells us that he met with fossil shells in alluvium at a great height among the mountains, as fresh and entire as if they had recently emerged from their own element; and that, just before crossing the boundary of Ladak and Bussahir, he was much gratified by the discovery of a bed of antediluvian oysters clinging to the rock as if they had been alive, and this at 16,000 feet above the sea. The verification of this observation is expected.

II. MIDDLE INDIA.

In this vast tract the country forms an inclined plane, of which the great declivity sinks gradually towards the mouth of the Ganges, while the other inclines towards the Indus. It is almost entirely composed of alluvial clays, loams, sands, and gravels, with occasional intermixtures of calcareous concretions named *kunkur*, fossil woods, and animal remains. The most remarkable deposite of the latter was discovered near Pinjore, north latitude 30° 47′, east longitude 76° 54′, during the digging of a canal between two rivers, by the Sultan Ferose III. It was observed on cutting through a hill, in which bones of elephants and men were found. The bones of the fore-arm measured 3 gez, or 5 feet 2 inches in length; hence it is evident that none of them were human, but belonged to large Pachydermata; but whether elephant or mastodon is not so apparent. The few fixed rocks that occur during the course of the Ganges are to be viewed as prolongations of the primitive and secondary rocks of the peninsular part of India. We may, however, include in this division of India the *coal-field* of the Damoda. This deposite of coal, which occupies both sides of the river, has been traced southward to within a few miles of Raghunathpur, reposing on granite and syenite; and about forty miles north by east from that place we come to the first colliery ever opened in India. The late Mr Jones, who had the merit of commencing these works in 1815, describes this as the north-west coal district of Bengal; he states that he observed the line of bearing for sixty-five miles in one direction, its breadth towards Buncora (on the south-west side) being not more than eleven or twelve miles from the river; and he conjectures, although erroneously, that the same coal-formation, crossing the Valley of the Ganges near Catroa, unites with that of Silhet and Cashar, which he denominates the north-east coal district. The rocks of this coal-formation are sandstone, slate-clay, bituminous shale, and coal, traversed by veins of *greenstone*. The bituminous shale of the coal-roof abounds with vegetable impressions, and also contains some animal remains. The vegetables have not been accurately examined, which is much to be regretted, as it would be highly interesting to know if the same or different genera or species occur in the coal-field of Bengal as those met with in similar geognostical situations in Europe. Mention is made of a *Calamite*, a *Lycopodum*, and a gigantic species of *Patella*. In the coal-pits, of which there are but three, sunk to a depth of ninety feet, there are seven beds of coal; one of them exceeds nine feet in thickness. The coal is said to resemble that of Sunderland in England, but leaves a larger portion of cinders and ashes. It is now extensively consumed in and about Calcutta.

III.—PENINSULAR INDIA.

A very large portion of the Peninsula of India is composed of Plutonian rocks, as of granite, syenite, and trap, the Neptunean strata being much less abundantly distributed. We shall now state in a general way what is known of the geognostical nature of these formations, following in our sketch a geographic order.

Guzerat is a primitive district, with occasional displays of secondary deposites, and in many places deeply covered with diluvium. In the neighbouring district of Cutch, so remarkable for its salt marsh called the Runn, a *coal-field* is said to have been discovered, and is likely to be worked. Our former pupil, Mr Hardie, who has made so many good observations, informed Mr Calder, that, from specimens he had received, he was led to believe that in Cutch there existed secondary rocks newer than the lias. We hope Mr Hardie will be able to verify these conjectures, which are not without probability, when we call to recollection the chalky minerals met with in the great Western Desert of India.

The great western or Malabar chain of mountains, which commences in Candeish and terminates at Cape Comorin, is at its northern extremity covered by a part of the extensive *overlying trap-formation,* which extends in this quarter from the sea-shore of the Northern Concan to a considerable distance eastward, above and beyond the Ghauts, as far as the river Toombuddra and Nagpore. The rocks of this formation, which are greenstone, basalt, amygdaloid, wacke, and trap-tufa, are columnar, globular, tabular, and amorphous. The amygdaloidal structure is most general in the amygdaloid, in the cavities of which rock, amethyst and various beautiful and splendid zeolites occur. The trap hills are tabular, terraced, separated from each other by ravines often of vast magnitude, and the whole frequently covered with fine forests of teak and other trees, forming some of the most romantic scenes in India. The elevation of this part of the range seldom exceeds 3000 feet; but advancing towards the south its height gradually increases, and granite rocks begin to appear above the surface between the seventeenth and eighteenth degrees of north latitude, and from thence forming, along with gneiss and other Neptunean primitive strata, the chain, with little interruption, all the way to Cape Comorin, and thence to the extremity of the Peninsula. The granite tracts of India exhibit the same general forms as granitic countries in other parts of the world. Rugged hills, with bold denticulated outlines, lie grouped together in the greatest irregularity, or occasionally form ridges, which, when interposed between the spectator and the evening or morning sun, present the most varied and fantastic forms. Some of these ridges, when their dark outline is seen at twilight against a ruddy western sky, emulate in their various forms the apparently capricious forms of summer clouds, and we can then trace along their summits the appearances of castles, trees, men, and various strange groups. Many of the hills have the appearance of mere collections of large fragments of rock thrown confusedly together by some convulsion of nature; while frequently larger masses, piled with great regularity on each other, look like remains of gigantic architecture. High insulated masses, forming considerable hills, in many instances rise abruptly out of a plain to a height of several hundred feet, and present nearly mural faces on several of their sides; thus affording situations of immense natural strength, which have almost invariably been taken advantage of by the natives for the erection of their famous *hill-forts.* These insulated hills are generally met with at the borders of the granite district, when it is succeeded by the stratified, primitive, or transition rocks; and being situated in the midst of very extensive plains, when they are seen at some distance, they have very much the appearance of rocky islands in the midst of the ocean. Some of the strongest hill-forts in India are of this description; for instance Chittledroog, Gooty, Copaldroog, Eidghur, &c. Granite and syenite are traversed by two kinds of trap; the one is contemporaneous hornblende, the other secondary greenstone. In nearly the same parallel of latitude, this trap formation is observed to terminate also on the seacoast a little to the north of Fort Victoria or Bankot, where it is succeeded by the *laterite,* which extends thence as an overlying rock, with little interruption, to the extremity of the Peninsula, covering the base of the mountains, sometimes also their summits, and the whole narrow belt of land that separates them from the sea; exhibiting a succession of low rounded hills and elevations, and resting on the primitive rocks, which sometimes rise above the surface; as at Malwan, Calicut, and some other points, where granite, for a short space, becomes the surface rock. From the mainland the laterite passes over to Ceylon, where it reappears under the name of *kabuk,* and forms a similar deposite of some extent on the shores of the island.

From the extreme point of the land, on the eastern side of the Peninsula and northward along the foot of the mountains, we meet with a country differing considerably from the Malabar coast in aspect and geognostical structure and composition. The plains of the Coromandel coast form a broad although unequal belt of land between the mountains and the sea, composed partly of river partly of sea alluvium. The mountain chain that forms the eastern boundary of the Peninsula begins to diverge eastward, where its continuity is interrupted by the Valley of Coimbetoor. Thence it divides into many chains, parallel to the great western range, but of inferior height; and in the farther progress northward, after branching off into subordinate hilly groups, occupying a wide tract of almost unknown country, and affording valleys for the passage of the great rivers that drain nearly all the waters of the Peninsula into the Bay of Bengal; this eastern range may be said to terminate at the same latitude as that of the commencement of the western. Granite and syenite appear to form the basis of the whole of these eastern ranges, appearing at most of the accessible summits from Cape Comorin to Hydrabad. Resting upon them are various primitive and transition stratified rocks, as gneiss, mica-slate, quartz-rock, clay-slate, chlorite-slate, talc-slate, potstone, serpentine, graywacke, and limestone. In many places there are extensive deposites of a red sandstone, and also some partial displays of overlying trap.

The flat country of the Carnatic, that is of the country east of the Ghauts of Mysore as far as the Pennar river, seems to consist of the debris of granitic rocks, with plains of sand and mud, probably left by the retreating sea. In confirmation of the former presence of the sea in the tract now occupied by the flat lands, the following fact may be mentioned:—On digging a garden about two miles from the seashore at Madras, from the surface, for five feet, there was a stratum of brown clay, chiefly intermixed with sand; then followed a stratum of bluish-black clay, in which, at the depth of twenty-one feet, was a thin and scattered layer of large *oyster-shells*, all lying in a horizontal position; into the lamina composing the shell the black clay had penetrated, so that they split asunder with great facility. There were also shells of the cockle and other kinds. At the depth of twenty-seven feet springs began to gush, the stratum became softer, and more and more mixed with quartz-sand, still, however, of a dark slate-colour. This continued to the depth of thirty-seven feet. In the neighbourhood of Pondicherry are beds of compact shelly limestone, and some remarkable silicious petrifactions, said to be chiefly of the tamarind-tree. These deposites at Madras and Pondicherry are considered to be tertiary. The bed of the Cavery, or rather the alluvial deposites in the vicinity of Trichinopoly, afford *gems* corresponding to those found in Ceylon. In approaching the Pennar, the laterite formation expands over a larger surface, and clay-slate and sandstone begin to appear. The river-districts of the Pennar, Krishna, and Godavery, are based on granite, syenite, and various primitive stratified rocks, all of which are frequently traversed by veins and overlaid with masses of trap. Upon the primitive rocks rest sandstone, and a limestone resembling in some of its characters the *lias* of England. The well-known diamond-mines of this part of the Peninsula are situated in the sandstone districts of these rivers. The Krishna is much richer in gems than the Godavery, or probably than any other river of Indostan. The waters of the Krishna and Godavery as they approach the sea divide into numerous branches, and deposite their mineral contents during inundations over the low level tract that separates them. These deposites consist, according to Heyne, of a black earth, composed of the debris of trap rocks, and of decayed vegetable matter washed from the extensive forests through which these rivers flow. A characteristic difference may be pointed out in regard to the alluvium of the principal river of the south,—the Cavery. This river, flowing in a long course through the Mysore country, over an extensive and generally barren surface of granitic rocks, with scarcely any woods or jungle on its banks, seems to bring down little or no vegetable matter, but a rich clay, produced from the felspar which predominates in the granites of the south, intermixed with decomposed calcareous conglomerate, rendering the plains of Tanjore the most fertile portion of the south of India. Onwards to Vizagapatan and Ganjam, syenite and gneiss predominate, and are occasionally covered with laterite. The granite and syenite at Vizagapatan contain numerous embedded garnets. This variety of granite passes into the province of Cuttack. Granite and syenite, with their usual accompanying stratified primitive rocks, form the basis and principal elevations of this district. Sandstone extends over a great part of the district of Cudapah: it is in this sandstone, or amidst its debris, that some geologists place the original repository of the diamonds found in this part of India. Coal is reported to occur here, and the sand and loam of the Mahanuddy, besides diamonds, afford grains of gold. Granite and gneiss, covered more or less completely with sandstone and laterite, continue onward through the district of Medinpur, and thence northward by Bishenpur and Bancora to Birbhum. At Bancora the calcareous rock named *kunkur* begins to cover the surface of the granite and syenite rocks, which rise above the surface to considerable elevations.

In our progress onward we pass the coal-field of

Damoda, already described; and from it, in a north-westerly direction, the road to Benares leads over granite, of which the ranges of hills on the left, and the whole country as far as the Soane, and round by Shirghati and Gaya, is probably composed. On approaching the Soane river, and crossing the hills behind Sasseram, *sandstone* begins to appear, and seems to continue, with probably only one considerable interval, all the way to Agra, forming, as already mentioned, the southern boundary of the Ganges and Jumna; that interval occurs in the low lands of Bundelcund, where the remarkable isolated hills, forming ridges running south-west and north-east, are all granite and syenite, the high lands being covered with sandstone. The geognosy of the Vyndhia mountains, which cross the Peninsula from east to west, uniting in some degree the two northern extremities of the Malabar and Coromandel ranges, has been partially examined. It can be traced ranging about 75° west, from the point called the Ramghur hills, towards Guzerat. The predominating rocks in this vast space are granite and syenite, with gneiss, mica-slate, quartz-rock, clay-slate, graywacke, and other primitive and transition stratified rocks, the relations of which may be well studied in the Oodipoor primitive chain of this range, also on the verge of the trap near Jabulpur, and in the bed of the Nerbudda at Beragerh, near Garrah. These rocks are more or less extensively covered by secondary sandstones and limestones, of the coal, new red sandstone, and lias formations, and traversed and overlaid by enormous bodies of trap. The extent of the trap-rocks is very great; for it has been traced northward all over Malwah and Sagar, and eastward towards Sohaghur and Amerakantak; thence extending southward by Nagpore, it sweeps the western confines of Hydrabad, nearly to the fifteenth degree of latitude, and bending to the north-west, reaches the sea near Fort Victoria (including the islands of Bombay, Salsette, and Elephanta), and forms the shores of Concan northward, all the way to the mouth of the Nerbudda, covering an area of upwards of 200,000 square miles. This vast igneous formation covers sandstone in the district of Sagar, and comes also in contact with limestone, which it converts into dolomite. This sandstone, which is red, and generally horizontally stratified, is associated with red marl, and is sometimes saliferous; hence it is considered to be identical with the *new red sandstone* of Europe. The limestone rests upon the sandstone, and is referred to the *lias formation* of England. The well-known diamond-mines of Pannah occur in this sandstone. The sandstone flanks the great range of primitive and transition rocks, which extends from Guzerat by Oodipoor; to the north it stretches into the Desert to an unknown extent.

Peninsular India, like every other part of the globe, is more or less covered with layers of alluvial matter of various qualities and ages; but hitherto neither in Peninsular, Middle, nor Alpine India, have active or extinct volcanoes been met with, if we except the volcano said to have burst forth thirty miles from Bhooj during the earthquake of June 1819.

India, as appears from the preceding details, affords examples of most of the rocks of the primitive and transition classes; but of the secondary series, the only formations hitherto discovered are the old red sandstone, coal formation, new red sandstone, and lias, the upper secondary deposites, as oolite, green sand, and chalk, being awanting. Small deposites of tertiary strata occur in the north-east of Bengal, and the littoral deposites on the plains of the Coromandel coast are probably referable to the same class. The age of the Himmaleh chain is at present unknown, and we are also ignorant of the period or periods when the ranges of Peninsular India were elevated. These periods can be determined only after an examination of the phenomena exhibited at the line of junction of the ranges with the bounding strata. Thus, for example, if any range is found to have upraised the new red sandstone strata, but not the lias limestones which remain in a horizontal position, we infer that the range has risen through the new red sandstone before the deposition of the lias, and therefore that it is newer than the new red sandstone, but older than the lias.

MINERAL SUBSTANCES USEFUL IN THE ARTS FOUND IN MIDDLE AND PENINSULAR INDIA.

1. *Rocks*—2. *Earthy Minerals*—3. *Saline Minerals*—4. *Inflammable Minerals*—5. *Metallic Minerals.*

1. ROCKS.

1. *Granite and Syenite.*—These rocks, which extend with few interruptions from Cape Comorin to beyond Nagpore and Ellichpore, occupying a great part of the Carnatic, Malabar, and Mysore, nearly the whole of the nizam's dominions, and a large part of Bahar, and which are met with still farther to the north,—in Malwah, Bundelcund, the neighbourhood of Delhi, and, as already mentioned, even high among the Himmalehs,—are interesting in

an economical view. Granite is not generally employed in India as a building stone, on account of the great expense in working it; but large slabs are sometimes brought into the bazars for sale by the Wudrahs (a vagrant class of people, somewhat resembling gipsies), and are used for paving the floors of verandas in the better sort of native houses, and other similar purposes. It is also hewn into hand-mills for grinding corn; two or four of which load an ass or bullock, and are thus carried to the bazar for sale. These are the primeval mills of all countries, from the North Cape of Europe to Cape Comorin, and are the same as are mentioned in Scripture. The ancient Hindoo temples at Anagoondy, now partly in ruins, are built of gray granite, or rather syenite. The massive and gloomy style of architecture which characterizes all Hindoo buildings, is also met with here; but in one instance it has to a certain degree been departed from, for in one of the principal buildings there is an extensive colonnade, the columns of which are light, with small pedestals and capitals, and approaching somewhat in their proportions to the Grecian. Some of the pillars are tastefully carved with flowers. A few are in the form of caryatides. They support immense slabs of granite, which are carved on their under surface, so as to form an ornamental roof. The largest of these slabs, which are in the central part of the building, are at least thirty feet long. A black-coloured trap, which occurs embedded in the syenite and otherwise associated with it, is extensively used in India for architectural purposes, and for statuary.

The Hindoos polish all kinds of stones by means of pounded corundum mixed with melted lac.

The mixture being allowed to cool, is shaped into oblong pieces three or four inches long. The stone is sprinkled with water, and at the same time rubbed with these oblong masses; and the polish is increased by the use of masses with successively finer grains.

Talc-slate and Potstone.—These minerals frequently occur together associated with various transition rocks. Potstone is found along with talc-slate and chlorite-slate in the south-east part of the Darwar district, and is used by the natives in the manufacture of various utensils. It is so soft, that pencils are formed of it for writing upon books made of cloth blackened and stiffened with gum. Both the books and the neatness of the writing are very inferior to similar ones of the people of Ava. All the fine plaster, so much admired by strangers, with which the walls of the houses are covered in India, is composed of a mixture of fine lime and soap-stone rubbed down with water. When the plaster is nearly dry, it is rubbed over with a dry piece of soap-stone, which gives it a lustre very much resembling that of well-polished marble.

Limestone.—Some hills on the north and north-east of Guzerat are said to be chiefly composed of marble exhibiting many colours and qualities. The coarse granular white, and white with black veins, are the most frequent; but among the ruined tombs and *murjids*, in the neighbourhood of Ahmedabad, may be found many small granular varieties of different colours, as white, yellow with red veins, and green clouded with yellow and even black. Of these deposites of marble no account has been published. A variety of limestone met with near Bagulkote, in Darwar, answers well as a lithographic stone; for which purpose it has been used at Bombay. Lucullite marble is mentioned by Dangerfield among the productions of Malwah, and Tod says there are marble quarries in Rajast'han. The *kunkur*, a calcareous deposite, is used for cement and as a manure.

Laterite or *Ferruginous Clay-stone.*—This mineral may be described as a clay-stone, more or less impregnated with iron, with a perforated and cellular structure. It frequently contains embedded in it small masses of clay, quartz, or sandstone. In its native beds, a short way under the surface, it is so soft that it can be easily cut with a hatchet or spade; and when sufficiently compact, and not containing embedded portions of quartz, &c., it is cut into square masses like bricks, and used as a building-stone. Hence, Dr Buchanan Hamilton names it laterite or brick-stone; and its names in the native languages are derived from the same circumstance. When these square masses remain in the open air for some time they become very hard; and when not exposed to constant moisture they answer admirably as building-stones. Most of the handsome Roman Catholic churches at Goa are built of this laterite. In the principal fronts it is covered with plaster; but in other parts it is left bare, and retains its hardness when exposed to the atmosphere.

2. EARTHY MINERALS.

1. *Corundum.*—Gray, green, blue, and red varieties of this very hard mineral, usually more or less perfectly crystallized, and ranging from opaque to translucent, occur embedded in granite and syenite in the district of Salem in the Madras Presidency, among the mountains of the Carnatic, and in

other parts of the Peninsula. It is associated with cleavelandite, indianite, and fibrolite. Some varieties, as the blue, when cut in a hemispherical form, exhibit, when turned round, a white star with six rays. It is used as emery for polishing hard bodies.

2. *Spinel Ruby.*—This fine gem is found at Cananor, in the Mysore country.

3. *Beryl.*—The varieties of this gem at present most highly prized by the jeweller occur in a locality lately discovered at Cangayum, in the district of Coimbetoor, where they are associated with cleavelandite. The most beautiful cut beryl known is in the cabinet of the late M. H. P. Hope. In the language of the jeweller, its colour and transparency are perfect, and although weighing not more than six ounces, £500 sterling were paid for it. It is reported, although we believe erroneously, to have been found in Ceylon; for Mr Heath, who discovered and worked the beryl-mine of Cangayum, assures us, that beryl does not occur in Ceylon; and, therefore, as Mr Hope's beryl was brought from India, it was very probably found in the Peninsula.

4. *Zircon.*—Fine specimens of this gem are met with in alluvial deposites in the district of Ellore.

5. *Schorlous Topaz.*—This interesting variety of topaz is mentioned by Dr Heyne as occurring in different localities in syenite and granite districts.

6. *Schorl* and *Tourmaline* occur in granite, mica-slate, and in quartz-rock, bordering the granite and syenite districts.

7. *Chrysolite.*—This gem occurs in the basaltic rocks of the secondary trap series in the great trap district already described.

8. *Precious Garnet.*—In many hills this gem

abounds in syenite, in others it is embedded in mica-slate and gneiss.

9. *Pyrope.*—This beautiful mineral, the finest gem of the garnet family, is mentioned by Heyne as having been met with among the primitive rocks of the central parts of the Peninsula.

10. *Grenatite* has been found in the southern parts of the Mysore.

11. *Rock Crystal,* and other varieties of quartz, occur in the granite, mica-slate, and quartz-rock districts.

12. *Amethyst.*—This beautiful kind of quartz is met with, in greatest beauty, in drusy cavities of overlying trap in the great northern trap district.

13. *Cat's Eye.*—Varieties of this ornamental quartz are found in the alluvium of the river Krishna, also on the coast of Malabar.

14. *Carnelian.*—Mines, as they are called, of this ornamental stone occur in the principality of Rai Peempla, about thirty miles due east of Broach, and about five miles on the southern bank of the Nerbudda. The stones are obtained by sinking pits during the dry season in the channels of torrents. The nodules which are found in this way are intermixed with other rolled pebbles, and weigh from a few ounces to several pounds. Their colour, when recent, is dark olive-green, inclining to greenish-gray. The preparation which they undergo is, first, exposure to the sun for some time, and then calcination. The latter process is performed by packing the stones in earthen pots, and covering them with a layer five or six inches thick of dried goat's dung. Fire is then applied, and in twelve hours the pots are sufficiently cool to be removed. The stones are now examined, and some

are found to be red, others nearly white; the difference in their respective tints depending in part on the original quality of the colouring matter, and in part, perhaps, on the difference in the heat to which they have been exposed. The annual value of carnelian exported from India formerly amounted to £11,000. The great emporium for these articles is the ancient city of Cambay, where a very considerable trade is carried on by the Borah tribe, whose agents purchase the rough stones from the mountaineers, and convey them to Cambay, where they are wrought into various ornamental articles. Such is the low price of labour and of material at Cambay, that a complete set of female ornaments, necklace, bracelets, cross, brooch, and ear-drops, ready for setting, agreeably to their colour and quality, costs from eight to twenty-five rupees, the usual price; or, if very fine, from that sum upwards to fifty rupees for the most beautiful set that can be procured. Beautiful jaspers and agates are found in the carnelian district and other parts of India. In general these silicious minerals are derived from the overlying trap-rocks, in which they occur in cavities, embedded masses, and in veins.

15. *Zeolite.*—The great overlying trap district contains the principal species of this elegant family of minerals, which are generally found in drusy cavities.

16. The *felspars* and *micas* of the primitive districts, although apparently very interesting, have not hitherto engaged the attention of mineralogists. Of the hornblendes, the common, granular, slaty, actynolitic, and asbestine, have been met with; but we do not possess any information in regard to the *calcareous* and *barytic* minerals.

Saline Minerals.—Common salt, carbonate of soda,

and nitrate of potash, as already mentioned, occur in considerable quantity in some districts, forming the salt, soda, and nitre soils,—but no beds of these minerals have as yet been met with in Southern India.

Inflammable Minerals.—Diamond.—This beautiful mineral, the most precious of all the gems, is found at Cudapa, Banaganpilly, &c., in the river-district of the Pennar; at Condapilly, in the district of the Krishna; near to Buddrachhillum, in the bed of the Godavery; at Sumbhulpore, in the district of the Mahanuddy; and at Pannah, in Bundelcund. In all these so called diamond districts, there are deposites of sandstone and alluvium; and in some instances, at no great distance, appear igneous rocks, as trap and granite. The diamond is obtained by washing the alluvial sands, clays, loams, and conglomerates; it is said also to have been met with in the sandstone. If the diamond be of igneous origin, we might explain its occurrence in the sandstone by the action of igneous rocks under the sandstone; if of aqueous origin, by the gradual attraction and combination of the adamantine carbonaceous particles, diffused through the sandstone or alluvium. From facts in our possession, it is even not improbable that this gem may at times appear as a vegetable secretion, just as is the case with the silicious substance named tabasheer, found in the joints of the bamboo.

Coal is said to occur in connexion with some of the sandstone deposites, and *mineral oil* and *pitch* near to springs. *Sulphur*, although but in small quantity, was found by Dr Heyne near the Godavery, deposited from a shallow lake which extends several miles from north to south.

Metalliferous Minerals.—Gold.—This metal, although in small quantities, has been obtained by washing the alluvial soil of several of the rivers.—*Silver* also, but in small quantities, has been noticed in this quarter of India. *Iron.*—This metal in the states of oxide, hydrate, carbonate, and sulphuret, is met with in many parts of the Peninsula. Iron mines and forges occur in the Mysore, at Coimbetoor, Malabar, and in the Bundelcund country. At present the whole of the mining and metallurgical operations are in the hands of the natives, and consequently are carried on in the worst possible manner. *Iron* to any extent might be obtained from the great beds and veins distributed throughout the country, and sold at such a rate as to banish all foreign competition. *Copper.*—The general use of copper or brass utensils among the natives of India, and the preference given to them before all other kinds of vessels, seems to show that in all probability copper was formerly obtained in India in considerable quantity.* At present there are no copper mines of importance in any part of our Eastern empire; although, from the reports of travellers and naturalists, rich ores of copper are met with. The ores are *carbonate of copper*, or *malachite*, *anhydrous carbonate of copper*, which contains half its weight of metallic copper, *copper pyrites*, or yellow sulphuret of copper, and *gray copper ore*. *Lead* mines occur in Rajast'han.

4. SUBMERGENCE AND UPRAISING OF LAND.

The account of Lieut. A. Burnes, who examined the Cutch portion of the delta of the Indus in 1826 and 1829, as stated by Mr Lyell, furnishes the following very interesting details regarding the submer-

* Colonel Tod says there are abundant copper-mines in Rajast'han, and also mines of *tin*.

gence and upraising of land during the earthquake of 1819:—A tract around Sindree, which subsided during the earthquake in June 1819, was converted from dry land into sea in the course of a few hours; the new-formed *mere* extending for a distance of sixteen miles on either side of the fort, and probably exceeding in area the Lake of Geneva. Neither the rush of the sea into this new depression, nor the movement of the earthquake, threw down the small fort of Sindree, the interior of which is said to have become a tank, the water filling the space within the walls, and the four towers continuing to stand; so that on the day after the earthquake the people in the fort, who had ascended to the top of one of the towers, saved themselves in boats. Immediately after the shock, the inhabitants of Sindree saw, at the distance of five miles from the village, a *long elevated mound,* where previously there had been a low and perfectly level plain. To this *uplifted tract* they gave the name of "Ullah Bund," or the "Mound of God," to distinguish it from an artificial barrier previously thrown across an arm of the Indus. It is already ascertained that this newly-raised country is *upwards of fifty miles* in length from east to west, running parallel to that line of subsidence which caused the ground around Sindree to be flooded. The breadth of this elevation from north to south is conjectured to be in some parts *sixteen miles,* and its greatest ascertained height above the original level of the delta is ten feet. This upraised land consists of clay filled with shells. Besides "Ullah Bund," there appears to be another elevation south of Sindree, parallel to that before mentioned, regarding which, however, no exact information has been communicated. There is a tradition of an earthquake having, about three centuries before, *upheaved* a large area of the bed of the sea, and converted it into land, in the district now called "The Runn," so that numerous harbours were laid dry, and ships were wrecked and engulfed; in confirmation of which account it was observed in 1819, that in the jets of black muddy water thrown out of fissures in that region, there were cast up numerous pieces of wrought iron and ship nails.

5. DESTRUCTION OF THE ANCIENT CITY OF OUGEIN AND OTHER PLACES IN INDIA BY A SHOWER OF VOLCANIC ASHES.

The volcano said to have burst forth in the district of Cutch in 1819 is the only one of modern date mentioned by authors as having been observed in India. At an early period, in the time of the Rajah Vicramaditya, however, if we are to credit Hindoo story, a shower of volcanic earth or ashes overwhelmed the ancient city of Ougein and above eighty other places in Malwah and Baghur. The city which now bears the name is situated a mile to the southward of the ancient town. On digging on the spot where the latter is supposed to have stood, to the depth of fifteen or eighteen feet there are frequently discovered entire brick walls, pillars of stone, and pieces of wood of an extraordinary hardness, besides utensils of various kinds and ancient coins. In a ravine cut by the rains, from which several stone pillars had been dug, there was observed a space from twelve to fifteen feet long, and seven and eight feet high, composed of earthen vessels broken and closely compacted together. It was conjectured to have been a potter's kiln. Between this place and the new town is a hollow, in which, tradition says, the river Sipparah formerly ran. It changed its course at the time the city was buried, and now runs to the westward. In the Asiatic Journal, the soil which covers Ougein is described as being of an ash-gray colour, with minute specks of black sand, thus somewhat resembling volcanic ashes. Captain Dangerfield observed, at a depth of thirty feet, in a so-called tufaceous mass, in the course of the Nerbudda near to the city of Mhysir, bricks and large earthen vessels, said to have belonged to the ancient city of Mhysir, destroyed by the catastrophe of Ougein. If, on more careful examination, it shall be proved that the earthy matter covering the ancient city of Ougein, and the beds of tufa-like deposite on the banks of the Nerbudda, and in many other parts of Malwah and Baghur, agree in characters with the matters that cover Pompeii and Herculaneum, &c., we shall be entitled to infer, that the Hindoo "shower of ashes" proceeded from some volcano or volcanoes, the remains of which may still be found in India.

6. EARTHQUAKES.

The mountains, hills, valleys, and littoral plains of India, are sometimes agitated by subterranean concussions or earthquakes; but these tremblings and heavings of the solid mass of the country are not so frequent in India as in many other regions. Earthquakes are recorded as having occurred in the course of the Ganges in 1665, 1762, and in 1800. In 1803, an earthquake in the course of the Ganges occasioned great disasters, particularly at Barahat. But these agitations of the ground are not confined to the middle and lower parts of the course of this river, for Captain Hodgson experienced an earthquake near to its sources. He says,—"We lay down to rest;

but between ten and eleven o'clock were awakened by the rocking of the ground, and on running out we saw the effects of an earthquake, and the dreadful situation in which we were placed, in the midst of masses of rock, some of them more than 100 feet in diameter, and which had fallen from the cliffs above us, probably brought down by some former earthquake. The scene around us, shown in all its dangers by the bright moonlight, was indeed very awful. On the second shock, rocks were hurled in every direction from the peaks around to the bed of the river, with a hideous noise not to be described, and never to be forgotten. After the crash caused by the falls near us had ceased, we could still hear the terrible sounds of heavy falls in the more distant recesses of the mountains. We looked up with dismay at the cliffs over-head, expecting that the next shock would detach some ruins from them: had they fallen we could not have escaped, as the fragments from the summits would have tumbled over our heads, and we should have been buried by those from the middle. Providentially there were no more shocks that night. This earthquake was felt in all parts of the mountains, as well as in the plains of the north-west provinces of Indostan."

On the 16th June 1819, the western part of India was visited by an earthquake, which spread desolation and panic over a vast extent of country. It was felt from Bombay to beyond the tropic of Cancer; but the centre of the shock seems to have been in the province of Cutch, which suffered severely. The first and greatest shock took place on the 16th June, a few minutes before seven P. M. The wretched inhabitants of Bhooj were seen flying in all directions to escape from their falling habitations. A heavy appalling noise,—the violent undulatory motion of the ground,—the crash of the buildings,—and the dismay and terror which appeared in every countenance, produced a sensation fearful beyond description. The shock lasted from two to three minutes, in which short period the city of Bhooj was almost levelled to the ground. The walls, from the sandy nature of the stone, were crumbled into dust; nearly all the towers and gateways were demolished; and the houses left standing were so shattered as to be uninhabitable. It was calculated that nearly 2000 persons perished at Bhooj alone.

The devastation was general throughout Cutch. In other quarters its effects appear to have been equally disastrous. Thus, from Ahmedabad, the capital of Guzerat, we have the following description:—"This city is justly celebrated for its beautiful buildings of stone and other materials, and for the famous shaking minarets, which were admired by every stranger. Alas! the devastation caused by this commotion of the earth is truly lamentable. The proud spires of the great mosque erected by Sultan Ahmed, which have stood nearly 450 years, have tumbled to the ground within a few yards of the spot where they once reared their heads! Another mosque of elegant structure, which lies to the left of the road leading to Shahee Bagh, has shared the same fate. The magnificent towers, which formed the grand entrance into the citadel, have been much shaken and cracked in several places. The fort and town of Jelelsheer are reduced to ruins. Many of the people killed were already out of doors, which is usually considered a situation of comparative safety. A marriage was about to be celebrated in a rich man's family, and the castes had assembled from various distant quarters; the shock occurred when they were feasting in the streets, and upwards of 500 of the party were smothered in the ruins of the falling houses."

The effects of this earthquake were indeed so extensive that we cannot afford room for more minute particulars; but we may add some account of the sensations felt by individual sufferers during the continuance of the shocks. In the British camp, which was pitched in a plain between the fort and city of Bhooj, the general feeling was an unpleasant giddiness of the head and sickness of stomach, from the heaving of the ground; and during the time the shock lasted some sat down instinctively, and others threw themselves on the ground. Those who were on horseback were obliged to dismount; the earth shook so violently that the horses could with difficulty keep their feet; and the riders, when upon the ground, were scarcely able to stand. At Ahmedabad, "all the disagreeable sensations were experienced of being tossed in a ship at sea in a swell; and the rocking was so great, that every moment we expected the earth to open under our feet." One gentleman, writing from Surat, where the earthquake began at twenty minutes past seven, says, "The vibration of the couch I was lying on was so great, that I was glad to get off it;—the house was considerably agitated,—the furniture all in motion; a small table close to me kept striking the wall, and the lamps swung violently. I ran down stairs, and got out of my house as fast as possible. On getting on the outside, I found a number of people collected, gazing with astonishment at my house, which stands alone, and was so violently agitated that I expected it to fall down. The earth was convulsed under our feet." Another writes thus from Baroach, —"Such of the houses as are elevated, and at all loosely built, creaked like the masts and rigging of a ship in a gale; the venetians and window-frames rattling violently, and the buildings threatening immediately to fall; a considerable lateral motion was impressed on every thing that admitted of it. After this more violent concussion had lasted a minute or upwards, it was succeeded by an oscillatory motion, of a more equable character, which continued for more than a minute and a half, making the whole period of the convulsion nearer three than two and a half minutes." An intelligent native residing in Iseria gives the following account:—"Yesterday, in the evening, a noise issued from the earth like the beating of the *nobut,* and occasioned a trembling of all the people; it appeared most wonderful, and deprived us all of our senses, so that we could not see, every thing appearing dark before us; a dizziness came upon many people, so that they fell down." The inhabitants of Cutch, however, were much relieved from the dread of farther convulsions by the circumstance of a volcano having opened on a hill about thirty miles from Bhooj; and, about ten days after the first shock, a loud noise like the discharge of cannon was heard at Porebunder. The sound came from the east, and was supposed to indicate the bursting of one or more volcanoes in that direction. The earthquake affected in a remarkable degree the eastern and almost deserted channel of the Indus, which it refilled and deepened.

MEDICAL OBSERVATIONS.

CHAPTER XI.

Constitutions best suited to India—Preservation of Health on Board of Ship and after Arrival—Management after Return to Europe.

Ages most suitable for Recruits for Indian Service—Ages at which Officers may be sent out—Medical Examination of Recruits—Epilepsy—Small Pox—Cutaneous Eruptions—Dyspepsia—Cautions against Intemperance—Diet—Exercise—Danger of using Mercury—Gout—Gravel—Complexions peculiarly Dark and unusually Fair—Rheumatism—Mental Derangement—Scrofula—Consumption—Preservation of Health on Board of Ship, and after Arrival in India—Management after Return to Europe.

CONSTITUTIONS BEST SUITED TO THE CLIMATE OF INDIA.

CONSIDERING the numbers of all ranks and denominations annually required in the service of our Indian empire, there arises a question of the first importance, "what description of men are best fitted to endure the influence of a climate essentially different from that of the mother country, and which, though highly favourable for particular constitutions, will prove injurious if not fatal tó others?"

We have often thought that officers employed in enlisting soldiers for the Honourable Company did not always sufficiently consider what is the most proper period of life to prefer in recruits: for, although a young man of seventeen, well grown and healthy, may, in his own country, easily enough bear the heat of the dog-days, the fatigue of a long march, and the pains of hunger and thirst; yet, it does not follow that he will be fit for the same hard service in a hot climate. In India the scorching winds at one season, and the damps at others, with the peculiar ills which they never fail to bring along with them, are trying enough to the most robust and best inured; how much more so must they be to the juvenile and perhaps delicate frame which has not attained the vigour of manhood! During his long residence in India, the writer frequently saw the injudicious practice of too early enlisting for the torrid zone prove fatal to striplings, who, had they been permitted to remain but three years longer in Britain, might have grown up into hardy men, able to endure the severities and vicissitudes of any climate in the world. It is difficult, indeed, to conceive a more helpless or miserable being than a raw lad, during his first severe indisposition in that country, when he begins most sincerely to regret the want of his family and friends. The glow of health, and the vivacity of youth, it is true, are, for a time, rendered more vivid and buoyant by the brilliant sunshine and exhilarating air of an Asiatic clime; but no sooner do disease and languor assail an individual so circumstanced than the fair illusion vanishes: he looks around, but sees no well-known face to cheer him; he finds himself desolate and abandoned, and not rarely sinks into that degree of mental depression which is of all states the most likely to aggravate bodily complaint. Such is one great evil that arises from enlisting recruits for Eastern service before their constitutions are fully formed,—an evil, the extent of which may be judged of from its results in a single regiment. Sir George Ballingall, in his excellent Practical Observations on Fever, Dysentery, &c., page 13, mentions, that "from an inspection of the tables exhibiting an abstract of the register of deaths in the second battalion of the Royals it will appear, that during the first year of the regiment being in India, out of 206 sufferers 160 were under twenty-five years of age." Under the age of twenty-one no soldier should be permitted to proceed to our possessions in the East.

But as it is injudicious to despatch to a tropical region recruits who are too young, so there may be an equal impropriety in sending them out at too late a period of life. The habits of the animal economy, like other habits once firmly established, cannot be easily or safely altered; none of the great organs of the human frame, preparing or circulating for a length of years, with a certain energy, a specific quantity of any fluid, can be suddenly forced to do more or less, without inducing some degree of variation in the constituent parts of such fluids, if not producing in them a condition actually morbid; and the same may be said of the different smaller glands and emunctories, all of which are in some measure affected by a change of climate. With the exception of the rapid alteration caused by death or acute disease on the human frame, there is none so great as that which is brought on by a removal from a cold to a torrid region; and so far as we are beings adapted by habit and constitution to a temperate air, so far is the experiment we make in venturing into tropical climes attended with danger. Yet, however great the revolution which takes place upon reaching a highly-heated atmosphere, so admirably are we organized, so nobly fitted for all the purposes of life, that, with the necessary care, and at a proper age, comparatively little risk is incurred. No soldier, unless he has been seasoned to a hot climate in other parts of the world, should be embarked for India after passing the age of thirty-six. Even to that age safety can only be promised in his Majesty's regiments, which consist in general of disciplined men, who have not to undergo the severe drilling to which recruits for the Company's service are obliged to submit soon after landing, and than which nothing can be more trying to the constitution. We would therefore recommend that, in enlisting for regiments in India, a preference should be given to those between twenty-one and thirty-five years old.

These observations, it must be remembered, only apply to those whose condition in life does not admit of their procuring the comforts and indulgencies which the more affluent can command. Private soldiers, not many days after landing, are often in time of war under the necessity of marching from morning till night, at a season when perhaps the thermometer is as high as 80° or 90° in the shade at noon;—sleeping, moreover, on the damp ground, and rising half-refreshed to toil on through an unhealthy district,—perchance to encounter the enemy. At all times, however, when their armies are not in the field, and when stern necessity does not demand the imposition of such hardships, the different governments of India invariably evince the most humane consideration for young soldiers on their first arrival. It is to be observed, also, that the King's and Company's officers, and the civil servants, feel few of the inconveniences just mentioned, because their circumstances procure exemption from them. Carried about in palanquins, during the hot hours, for the first few months they are in the country, exposed neither to great fatigue nor to the noxious night-dews, they become gradually habituated to the fervid atmosphere, and in due time are able to endure all weathers. With such advantages, accordingly, these gentlemen might safely venture to India at an earlier age;—nineteen would not be premature. To engage them so soon in active duties might, indeed, entail upon them the disadvantage of an imperfect education, which is a consideration of great importance; but it is merely in regard to the ability of the bodily frame to encounter the inconveniences of climate that we speak in this place. As those of a superior rank, then, may without hazard proceed to the East sooner than people of inferior stations, they may, for similar reasons, with greater safety visit Asia at a more advanced age. In proof of this we have only to refer to our governors, judges, and commanders-in-chief, many of whom were in the decline of life before they stepped on Indian soil, and who, without having previously been in the torrid zone, enjoyed excellent health and spirits in a country which to them was like a new world.

We shall now proceed to a few observations regarding the description of men, in point of natural constitution, best fitted for the service in question. Taking it for granted that the recruits are in the first place examined in the usual way, in order to ascertain their ability to perform all muscular motions, we should think it advisable, considering the nature of the country for which they are destined, that particular attention should be paid to them in other respects. Any one who has accurately scrutinized the different appearances of sound health and latent disease can readily distinguish the eligible recruit. A vivid colour, animated look, firm step and voice, clean tongue, and inoffensive breath, with what is commonly called the white of the eye clear, and without the slightest yellow tinge, are in general very sufficient proofs of good digestion and well-performed visceral secretions;* and these, with the other requisites, may with propriety entitle the possessor to a passport to the plains of Indostan.

* Maclurg on the Bile, p. 196—204.

On the other hand, young men, who seem sluggish, sallow, with rather tumid bellies, and somewhat bloated countenances, whose movements are languid, and the white of whose eyes has a yellowish or suffused appearance, though they be ever so well grown, ought to meet with a decided rejection; for in them there certainly lurks the seed of future disease, which will not be slow to show itself if ever they are exposed to ardent heat in a tropical country. A disposition to hepatic derangement, and consequent visceral obstruction, may not unfrequently be discovered early in life, and should never fail to excite a due caution in the medical officers who examine recruits for our army in the East. By rigid observance of these particulars, not only might our European force in that quarter be rendered more certainly healthy, but many fine fellows be kept at home for the defence of the parent state, who would fall victims in another climate to maladies which their peculiar constitutions are not fitted to withstand.

In making the foregoing remarks, the writer chiefly had in view the troops of that service to which for many years he had the honour to belong. They are equally applicable, however, to his Majesty's regiments, as may be seen by turning to the valuable publication above mentioned, in which Sir George Ballingall expresses regret on account of the error so frequently committed, of selecting boys for the King's service in the East Indies. But we should be inclined to go farther, and, influenced by feelings of humanity as well as by a just regard for the public purse, suggest, that when whole corps are ordered to any part of our Indian dominions, they should previously undergo the most minute examination, and that healthy men should be substituted for all such as, from their habit of body or otherwise, seem likely to suffer from a hot climate.

The impropriety of sending to India men who are subject to *epilepsy* must be obvious, when it is considered how great are the languor and exhaustion which but too frequently oppress even the healthiest within the tropics; and which never fail to prove more or less injurious, by increasing the mobility of the nervous system. Nay, the almost constant irritation, from the *feeling* of heat alone, independently of its other effects, we conceive to be no trifling source of mischief to those who are subject to attacks of this malady.

No man should be allowed to enlist for any of our Eastern settlements who has not been *vaccinated* or had the *small pox;* for this disorder, if caught naturally in India, is often of the confluent kind, and proves most destructive.

Such individuals as suffer from *cutaneous eruptions*, of whatever description, are most unfit for service in India. In a climate where the skin has so much to do, it is absolutely necessary that its condition be healthy, so as to transmit the perspiration with the greatest possible facility,—a principle, it is true, which will hold good in every part of the world, but which is particularly applicable to the torrid zone, where a free exudation, to afford relief during the excessive heat, is almost as indispensable as the secretion of urine itself. But it is not in this way alone that the cuticular discharge proves salutary in tropical countries: it appears to be powerfully preventive against various complaints. Thus, it has been repeatedly remarked, that such young men as had suffered from *dyspepsia* in England found their health much improved on coming to the Coromandel coast,—a fact which could be accounted for in no other way than by the almost continual moistness on the surface of the body there experienced; for it is an observation well established, that, in using exercise as a remedy in cases of bad digestion in Europe, little benefit is derived from it when not employed to such an amount as to bring on a degree of sweating. All extremes, however, are injurious. Should perspiration be excessive, or allowed too often to take place, languor and general weakness in the first passages will ensue, with that most certain of all consequences of violent perspirations, *constipation;* much crude matter being thus pent up, and the bile obstructed in its natural course through the ducts, heating and ultimately inflaming various organs, the sound state of which is essential to any thing like health or comfort in the Eastern world.

We have said that, generally speaking, the climate of our Asiatic dominions is far from hostile to the dyspeptic. It is still less so if they are at the same time cautious with regard to diet. Even the most robust frequently find their stomachs weakened by want of due attention to their mode of living; what then must the delicate hazard by the same inadvertency! It must be confessed also, that at the tables of the affluent and luxurious there are many temptations to excess, especially for new comers. Certain mixtures of food cannot be made without danger of bringing on indigestion;* hence follows a badly-prepared chyle, which will not only prove detrimental by insufficiently nourishing the body, but sow the seeds of different chronic disorders. Thus it is that we see at our various watering-places in Britain hundreds of martyrs to gout, gravel, and rheumatism, many of them reaping the fruits of years of irregularity,—men, too, not unusually at a time of life when, with ordinary prudence, they might have ensured the enjoyment of perfect health. "How does it happen," said an intelligent Frenchman once to the writer of this article, "that such numbers of you English become infirm so early in life?" A full reply was not called for, as the foreigner, being a person of great penetration, probably guessed the real cause with sufficient accuracy, and only put the question by way of insinuating in the most delicate way the greater temperance of his own countrymen. Soldiers in India have it not much in their power to err either with regard to quantity or quality of food, as, happily for them, their mess-regulations fix all those matters. The consequence is, that, among them, dyspepsia is not of frequent occurrence, their maladies arising chiefly from exposure to ardent heat, the abuse of spirituous liquors, and debauchery of other kinds.

This is no place to treat medically of indigestion; yet it may not be amiss to warn all young Eastern adventurers who wish to avoid it, that they will do wisely to live on the plainest food, which should be *well done;* to dine, if possible, on one dish, or two dishes at most; not to take more than two meals in the day, the second certainly not sooner than six hours after the first; not to be afraid of *black* tea, which, in moderation, is virtually stomachic; to masticate sufficiently, so as not to entail on the stomach a duty which does not belong to it; to shun crude vegetables or fruits; to prefer that liquor (sparingly used) which is least apt to produce acidity, such as Cape Madeira† of the best quality, sherry, or weak brandy and

* For example, the writer has known many persons who could not take a single glass of Madeira wine at the same meal with curry or málágátānie without bringing on heartburn in the course of four hours.

† This wine is not in good repute on account of a great deal of vile stuff being sold under the name; but the writer can declare

water; not to expose themselves to great heat more than duty requires; to sleep with the head high; to take care that the bowels are kept regularly open;* and, if their situation renders it convenient, to use *equitation*† in the cool of the morning;—in a word, always to manage themselves, according to the best of their means, with a view to eschew, if possible, those disorders, whether hepatic or otherwise, for the removal of which mercury is usually employed. The frequent or indiscriminate use of that medicine is the ruin of many fine constitutions; and in Indostan, when employed by injudicious men (and especially those lately arrived from Europe, who have been informed that in India mercury will do every thing), is tenfold more destructive than the sword itself.

What the *gouty*, or those liable to become so, have either to dread or to hope from the climate of the East comes next to be considered: It has been remarked, that some nations are less subject to this malady than others. Pliny speaks of it as of more frequent occurrence in Italy in his time than it was in former ages;‡ and he believed it to be of foreign origin, from the circumstance of there being no Latin name for it. The disease is very rare in China, and is said to be little known in some parts of Germany. In Arabia it is seldom met with; but this does not appear to be the case in Persia, where, among

---

that he has known more dyspeptic people benefited by using in moderation Cape Madeira of the first quality (which can be had in London from those who deal in no other wines), than by any medicine whatever. But it is cheap,—a sufficient reason in our good country for its being condemned.

* After what has been already noticed of the mischief done by neglecting constipation, it is scarcely necessary to say more; but this must be added, that the writer never yet knew a bad case of liver or dysentery in India that had not been preceded by costiveness. The pill which he found most useful for keeping the bowels open is the common *compound Colocynth pill*,—it never sickens the stomach nor gripes. Four grains of this will usually be found sufficient, taken at bedtime, to assist nature. Double the dose will generally open the bowels freely.

† Of all modes of exercise the most conducive to health in India is *riding on horseback*; by *soft trotting* there is a gentle impulse given to the *ingesta*, downwards, as well as to the bile, &c.; and a tone and energy produced throughout the whole circulation. So much cannot be said for hard galloping, which, in a torrid region, often over-agitates, and never fails to be injurious in what are called *nervous* habits.

‡ Hist. Nat., lib. xxvi. cap. 10.

those who do not adhere strictly to the rules of temperance prescribed in the Koran, it is by no means uncommon. We have never known more than one Hindoo who suffered from the gout. The Mohammedans are not so fortunate in this respect; nor can they expect to be so, for they are often indolent, live freely, and do not abstain from many of the good things of this world which it is in their power to enjoy. From the data before us, therefore, we may conclude that the climate of our Asiatic territories does not encourage this disorder. Europeans subject to it have for the most part long intervals between the fits; and when these do come on, they are generally slight. What may be the positive cause of this mildness or infrequency of the disease in a hot climate it is difficult to determine; but as India proves advantageous to the dyspeptic it may be equally so to the gouty, seeing that those are constantly the greatest martyrs to it who suffer most from indigestion. If digestion be well performed, a wholesome chyle is ultimately produced. But if the chyme, from which the chyle is in the first instance separated, has been rendered corrupt by repletion or heterogeneous mixtures in the stomach, heartburn ensues, which is characterized by an acid of a peculiar nature,—and this we conceive to be the prime agent in bringing on both gout and gravel. Dr Wollaston has demonstrated, that the concretions formed in the joints of gouty persons are composed of an animal acid, termed the *uric* or *lithic acid*, together with soda. Such concretions are no doubt hastened by frequent indigestions; and certainly the disposition to their formation is increased with advancing years and an over-indulgence in fermented liquors. *Hereditary ills* will assail us in spite of our greatest care: those, however, who have such calamities in prospect ought not to despair, but to hold in remembrance, that as these maladies must have had a commencement in the family, occasioned most likely by imprudence, so they may have a termination—the reward of persevering moderation. A residence in India may also be considered favourable to the gouty on account of the free perspiration there experienced, which, there is ground to believe, carries off much peccant acid matter.

We have had occasion to attend both Hindoos and Mussulmans suffering from gravel or stone, but cannot say that these are maladies of common occurrence in Indostan. As for confirmed stone in a European habit, the writer never saw a case of it. But the affinity between gout and gravel being unquestionable, so it often happens that nephritic calculi are a sequel to gout, when it has assumed a chronic form; and we find, accordingly, that the children of gouty parents are often hereditarily disposed to both disorders,—some having a gouty, and others a nephritic, affection. The use of hard water has been supposed by Dr Lister to be a powerful cause of gravel; other physicians, again, ascribe more mischief to acid food. Were the latter a serious source of the affection, we should see the Indians suffer more from it than they do, for they use limes, tamarinds, &c. very liberally. While, however, we cannot believe that the natural acid found in fruits or potherbs induces the complaint in question, we would ascribe that effect to the morbid acid produced in the first passages by indigestion. But perhaps no stronger argument can be adduced to prove that a hot climate is beneficial in gravelish complaints, than what we find recommended by Dr Mason Good,* who says, that whatever tends to promote a determination to the skin will be serviceable in such ailments, "for the skin itself becomes in this case an outlet for a discharge of a redundancy of acid."†

It has occasionally become a subject of discussion, whether the climate of India is better suited to those of dark or fair complexions: but this does not appear to be a matter of great importance, as the tropics, with proper care, will be found to agree well with either; still we must remark, that there is a sort of extreme fairness, accompanied with white hair, and very light-coloured gray eyes, approaching to those of the Albinos, which is far from desirable in hot countries. Individuals so distinguished not only suffer much in their sight from the glare of bright sunshine, but, being often of lax fibres, fall into those disorders to which such a frame of body is subject, and invariably get scorched on exposure to a heat from which others suffer no injury. This remark must be understood to apply, not

* Study of Medicine, vol. v. pp. 523, 524.

† Several of the delicious fruits of India contain little or no acidity; such as the *custard apple* (annona squamosa); *plantain* (musa paradisiaca); *bullock's heart* (annona reticulata), &c., and which, consequently, may be used by those who have the most delicate digestion.

to what is commonly called simply fair complexion, but to that almost unnatural whiteness of hair and skin which we sometimes see. There is also a degree of dark complexion, which we should not select for India, namely, that which is often accompanied with torpor of the bowels, languid circulation, dark-coloured fæces, grave manner, full black eyes, and not rarely a peculiar attachment to abstruse studies,—in fact, that class of appearances by which the melancholic temperament is chiefly characterized. To young men of this complexion we should say that India is prejudicial, as the natural or habitual morbid torpor would be increased by the wasting influence of great exudation,—sobriety of manner passing gradually into a love of seclusion,—dyspepsia putting on some of the distressing features of hypochondriasis,—and intellects, frequently of the noblest and most generous cast, though in their reasoning faculty unimpaired, losing much of that manly energy which once constituted their principal charm. Upon the whole, complexions neither unusually dark nor peculiarly fair are best adapted to the East. But after all, as already hinted, this is a matter not worthy of much consideration; and we know that the Romans of old said, "*Nimium ne crede colori.*" Much more essential for India are, a perfect frame, a cheerful disposition, and good digestion.

For the *rheumatic*, the warm climate of Asia is favourable, with common prudence; but this, though absolutely necessary, is, we are sorry to add, not always exercised; for, to avoid the nearly suffocating heat of close nights, Europeans are too often tempted to sleep altogether *sub Jove*, or, which is worse, behind wetted TATTIES; and they suffer accordingly: for these practices, as every medical officer who has been in India can attest, are two of the most undoubted sources, not only of rheumatism but of fever and palsy, among his Majesty's and the Company's troops.

It is, we should imagine, scarcely necessary to observe how baneful the climate of the East is for those who have any tendency to mental derangement. Perhaps no cause has excited complaints of this nature oftener than inordinate heat. This is particularly noticed by Pinel, in his admirable work on Insanity. Cox, an English writer on the same disease, and Dr Arnot, have fully verified the correctness of the distinguished Frenchman's assertion;

and we feel concerned to say, that we witnessed too many deplorable instances of madness among the troops on the Coromandel coast, to have any doubts on the subject. It may be farther remarked, that the operation of great heat is, in this instance, increased tenfold by a frequent use of mercurial medicines, which are, in our humble opinion, little short of a poison in those maladies commonly termed nervous.

But, perhaps, of all disorders, that to which the climate of India proves most ungenial is *scrofula.* No young man with a hereditary tendency to this complaint should on any account be sent to India, where we have never known one individual with the malady in his habit who enjoyed tolerable health for ten months together. Soldiers, so tainted, are fit for nothing but lumbering up an hospital; and, for the most part, after lingering a few years, burdens to themselves and to their regiments, they fall a prey to the most frightful and ravaging ulcers. How this baneful effect of a hot climate upon persons so unfortunately predisposed is to be accounted for it may be difficult to say, as the state of darkness in which we have so long wandered, regarding the proximate cause of affections of this nature, leaves us little more than a conjecture. One thing is certain, that, as laxity of the solids, and a general deficiency of bodily vigour, are known to be the constant concomitants of the complaint, such a condition will be greatly increased by extreme heat, which enervates in no common degree.

As to the benefit or bad consequences of a residence in India to such as have a predisposition to *consumption*, an opinion cannot be given with too much caution; as far as enlisting recruits for our foreign dominions goes, it is certainly wise to take *no* person whatever of doubtful *stamina.* It is an ascertained fact, that although the malady in question is to be met with in Indostan among the natives, it is not nearly so common as in Europe. We have all seen the good done by a speedy removal to milder air when this disorder first threatens; and indeed a change of place,* of whatever nature, would seem to have a happy effect. In preventing the suppuration of turbercles,

* I have known several persons with the seeds of consumption in their frame, who, by frequent change of climate, effectually succeeded in averting the calamity.

therefore, the warm clime of Asia, we should say, might be safely recommended to such, for instance, as have simply a disposition to disease of the lungs, but on whom the enemy has as yet made no direct attack. More especially the experiment might be attended with advantage to those who are not under the necessity of undergoing the hardships which the poorer adventurer must encounter in the torrid zone. On the other hand, when the disorder has once made a fatal breach in the lungs, the decay and weakness are greatly hastened by the enervating influence of excessive heat,—and death soon ends the scene. Where the greatest risk lies, then, we shall not pretend to decide; with such facts before them, parents may be enabled to make up their own minds.

To conclude this part of the subject, we beg it may not be imagined, that the observations here advanced convey even the slightest censure on those liberal and able men who direct the affairs of our Asiatic possessions. The prosperity of that great branch of our foreign empire proves the justice and humanity with which it is governed. The fortunate termination of our Eastern wars, and of our other difficulties in that quarter, at a period too when Europe trembled under the scourge of the second Attila, and down to these later times, sufficiently testify the talent with which affairs have been conducted. Nor can the smallest blame attach to the authority which now presides over the medical department immediately connected with the passing of recruits for India. Zeal and assiduity are here as conspicuous as private character is benevolent and estimable. In the mother country the evil consequences were not seen, and could only be remedied by representations from the distant territory in which they were felt,—representations which, if we may judge from the result, must have been as strongly urged, as they were speedily attended to.

PRESERVATION OF HEALTH ON BOARD OF SHIP, AND AFTER ARRIVAL IN INDIA.

It may, we think, be safely said, that, generally speaking, young men are healthy on board of ship during their way to India,—partly owing to the great care in supplying proper food, and partly to their not being exposed to the vicissitudes of weather or intemperate living. The chief inconvenience experienced is constipation, and this is occasioned in two ways;—the want of the same quantity of vegetable aliment as on shore; and the increased perspiration, the natural consequence of entering the warmer latitudes. Young men are very apt to treat this complaint lightly. Suffering for days together little or no uneasiness, they pay no regard to it till incalculable mischief is done. If no medical officer is in immediate charge of the recruits going to India, it ought to be the duty of the surgeon of the ship, not simply to prescribe for those who request it, *but daily to see every young man on board, and to acquaint himself with the actual state of each.* In this way, and in this way alone, can disease be arrested in its commencement, and many bad consequences avoided. It should also be the care of the medical officer to see that the youths are kept perfectly clean by frequent bathings in salt water, so that there may be no obstruction to free perspiration, on which, we repeat, so much depends, while approaching, or on reaching the torrid regions. There need hardly be urged here the necessity of exercise to maintain good health. In crowded ships it is sometimes difficult to obtain this. One of the easiest, and, perhaps, one of the best modes, is to get the young soldiers to assist the sailors in performing such naval duties *on deck* as they can execute,—exercise being taken at hours when there is least chance of injurious consequences from the heat.

Most of these cautions will apply to the treatment of young soldiers on their first reaching the Indian continent, —with the following additional hints:—The strictest rules ought to be enforced regarding the use of fruits, vegetable diet, and spirituous liquors. The two first, if partaken of injudiciously by the new comers, are a certain source of evil; indulgence in the last is a never-ending bane to both old and young. Exposure to the heat of the sun must be avoided as much as circumstances will permit, as it is a powerful exciting cause of disease. On this account it is safest to teach the military exercise in the cool of the morning, or in the evening. Above all things sleeping in the open air is to be shunned, as nothing is more pernicious than heavy cold dews falling on a frame relaxed by the heat of a burning sun.

MANAGEMENT AFTER RETURN TO EUROPE.

If a great change takes place in the human frame on first entering the warm latitudes, a great corresponding change must also be occasioned by returning to the temperate clime. If individuals thus restored to their native shores have not already put on flannel clothing, they should lose no time in doing so, making the shirt-sleeves *come down as far as the wrist*. Great attention must be paid to the state of the bowels, by the use, when necessary, of some gentle aperient. The diet should be regular, avoiding as much as possible injurious mixtures;—in fact, dining when it can be done on one, or at most two dishes. With regard to wine, sherry and the best kind of Cape Madeira are perhaps the safest, as they contain little or no acidity; but even these must be used moderately. No suppers should be taken. Nothing, we can say with the most perfect certainty, conduces more to preserve the health of Old Indians than gentle exercise on horseback. These remarks, it must be remembered, apply merely to those who come home free from any *particular* bodily ailment; those who suffer from peculiar affections will of course make application to some professional man who has been long enough in India to acquaint himself with the maladies of that country, and long enough returned to have judiciously remarked the effects of a change of climate on the constitution. From misapprehension in such cases on the part of inexperienced physicians, many an unfortunate is sent to Cheltenham, or Bath, or Harrowgate, who would have derived much more benefit from a very different treatment under the salutary and natural influence of his own native climate. We should not advise in every case to abstain from those valuable waters; but, it is certain, a very nice discrimination is required to ascertain when they are necessary; and, farther, we must regret that no such appointment has ever yet been made by the Honourable Company as that of a medical officer of experience in both countries (India and England), who could at once be a physician, a guide, and a friend to sick officers on their return to their native land, often with incomes not well suited to afford many fees, and otherwise unacquainted with the most proper course for insuring comfort in a country which, though their own, has become strange to them.

CHAPTER XII.

Spasmodic Cholera.

Symptoms—Persons most liable to the Disease—Predisposing Circumstances—Treatment—Precautions necessary to prevent its Attacks—Symptoms and Treatment of the Disease in Britain.

In a preceding part of the work* has been given a brief history of the progress of this malady, which for a series of years has committed such devastation in India and other Eastern countries. It claims notice here, not only as one of the diseases incident to India, but because it has extended from the climes where it originated to the continent of Europe, spreading its ravages throughout the British islands, and exciting an intense interest, far beyond what it would have done had we only continued to hear of its effects in a distant land. A short view of its nature and treatment becomes, therefore, doubly necessary.

Cholera often comes on suddenly, and generally without any previous warning,—most commonly during the night or towards morning; occasionally, however, it is preceded for some days by a slight diarrhœa. The patient complains of a feeling of anxiety or uneasiness at the pit of the stomach; this changes into a sensation of heat and pain. To these symptoms succeed sickness, giddiness, ringing in the ears, with vomiting and purging, and great prostration of strength. The evacuations at first consist of the common contents of the stomach and bowels, but afterwards of a thin muddy fluid resembling rice or barley water, unmixed with any trace of bile; and this latter circumstance forms a distinguishing feature of the disease. There is a sudden sinking of the pulse, a diminution of the heat of the body, a pallor of the countenance, suppression of the urinary discharge, and occasional cramps in the limbs. As

* Vol. ii. p. 262—268.

the malady advances, the cramps and spasms increase in violence and frequency, and the vomiting and purging are severe. The skin becomes deadly cold; it is covered with a clammy moisture, and is of a bluish colour about the face; the extremities are shrivelled, and the nails of the fingers of a purple hue. The countenance is ghastly, and expressive of great anxiety. The eyes are sunk in their sockets, and surrounded by a dark livid circle: there is a distressing thirst, with burning heat and pain in the region of the stomach. If blood be drawn from a vein, it is of an unusually dark colour and thick consistence. Debility increases rapidly,—the patient lies in a state of helpless exhaustion,—the spasms and vomiting cease,—the breathing is oppressed or scarcely perceptible,—and under these unfavourable symptoms death closes the scene, in many cases in the course of six or twelve hours, generally within eighteen or twenty, from the commencement of the attack. Under all these bodily sufferings the mind remains collected and sensible to the last.

A favourable issue of the case is denoted by the pulse rising in strength, a return of heat to the surface, an inclination to natural sleep, and a diminution or cessation of vomiting, purging, and spasms, with the usual appearance of bile in the excretions. Amongst the natives, in whom there is little tendency to inflammatory disease, the recovery is speedy and perfect, no symptoms of the attack remaining after the lapse of a few days; but in Europeans, in whom there is a much greater propensity to inflammation, the recovery from cholera is by no means so rapid and complete; affections of the intestines, the brain, liver, or stomach, are often found to supervene.

In India, persons exposed to great bodily fatigue, confined to poor and scanty fare, or leading irregular lives, were usually the victims of this dreadful disease. The Europeans were comparatively less subject to it than the natives; and the higher classes of the latter were more exempted from its effects than the lower. Females suffered more rarely than men, and children in a less degree than either. Of all the circumstances predisposing to an attack, great fatigue of travelling and hard labour in the open air were found the most powerful; and thus troops on a march, and people whose occupations exposed them to the weather, as boatmen, fishermen, husbandmen, gardeners, grass-cutters, washermen, palanquin-bearers, were extremely subject to the disease. All derangements of the stomach and bowels, as vomiting or purging, whether occurring naturally or produced by purgative medicines, more particularly by Epsom salts, had a tendency to bring on the disease. It was found that a person who had completely recovered from cholera was rarely seized a second time,* although a few relapses were occasionally recorded.

When the disease first makes its appearance in a town or camp, a few solitary cases occur; these gradually increase in number for the first week or ten days, till at last the malady spreads in every direction. For a fortnight or three weeks it rages to a frightful extent, and then as rapidly declines, shifting its seat to some other district, where it commits similar devastation. In this manner it spread over India; and, in a way strictly analogous, it has pursued its deadly progress over the continent of Europe.

In the treatment of a malady which makes such rapid inroads on the vital powers, prompt and decisive means are especially requisite. The most approved practice, and that which seems to have been generally followed by the medical men in various parts of India† with the greatest success, is as follows:—In the first stage of the disease, before extreme debility and exhaustion came on, blood-letting was occasionally had recourse to.‡ This was followed by large doses of calomel and opium, or laudanum mixed with brandy and spices, or oil of peppermint. The hot bath, of a high temperature, was also used, together with friction of the whole body, sinapisms, blisters, &c. If the disease had proceeded to the second stage, termed collapse, blood-letting was of no avail, and, indeed, from the feeble or almost extinct circulation, was impracticable. Stimulating cordials; dry heat applied to the body by means of hot air baths, hot bran, or sand; hot bottles of water; and frictions unremittingly employed, are the means recommended. Hartshorn, æther, and various antispasmodics were also freely employed; and castor oil and magnesia were substituted by some practitioners for calomel. Cold liquids, though eagerly

---

* Mr Jameson, Bengal Reports.
† Bombay, Madras, and Bengal Reports.
‡ Mr Scot's excellent Remarks prefixed to Madras Reports.

desired, were prohibited; but tepid mucilaginous drinks and slightly acidulated fluids were given at intervals.*

---

* We subjoin the following directions and recipes for the cure of cholera, from the Madras Report:—

"Give the patient as soon as possible the draught prescribed, thus:

Tincture of opium, one drachm;
Sulphuric æther, one drachm;
Brandy or arrack, half an ounce;
Water, one ounce.—Mix.

If this be vomited, let it be repeated every time, in ten minutes after the vomiting. In half an hour after the vomiting has ceased, give a bolus of this prescription:—

Calomel, twelve grains;
Camphor, three grains;
Opium, one grain;
Oil of peppermint, two drops.—Make into a bolus.

If this bolus be vomited, it must be repeated in a similar manner, each time half an hour after the vomiting has ceased. If the vomiting be violent, give an injection of one drachm and a half of laudanum in four ounces of conjee-water, and let it be repeated as often as it is rejected. Half the quantity of this injection should also be administered after every liquid stool. When no vomiting occurs at all, give a draught and bolus of the following prescription:—

Tincture of opium, half a drachm;
Sulphuric æther, half a drachm;
Ipecacuanha wine, half an ounce;
Water, two ounces.—Mix.
Calomel, twelve grains;
Extract of jalap, four grains;
Camphor, three grains;
Opium, one grain;
Oil of peppermint, two drops.—Make into a bolus.

If these produce no effect, repeat the draught after every forty minutes. In all cases rub the arms and legs with hot sand, and apply a blister, or sinapism, over the stomach, prepared as follows:—

Powdered mustard-seed, half a pound;
Ditto capsicum, one drachm;
Ditto ginger, one drachm.

Make into a cataplasm, with vinegar, to which add two ounces of oil of turpentine. If the pulse be perceptible at the wrist, take twenty, twenty-five, or thirty ounces of blood from the arm.

"If the case be lingering and doubtful after much medicine has been given, then omit all other medicines, but those prescribed thus:—

Calomel, three grains;
Ipecacuanha, two grains;
Aloes, three grains;
Opium, half a grain.
Make into a pill; one to be taken every hour.
Conjee water, four ounces;
Brandy or arrack, three drachms.—Mix.
To be taken every hour.

In many cases the attack is so sudden, and the progress to a fatal termination so rapid, as to baffle all attempts at affording relief.

From this brief account of the disease, the precautions necessary to be observed, in order as much as possible to guard against its attacks, will at once suggest themselves. Thus every circumstance which debilitates the system is to be carefully avoided: such as excessive exertion, exposure to night-dews or vicissitudes of temperature, unwholesome food,—as bad rice, bad water, &c.; irregularity of living,—especially intemperance; all damp and unhealthy situations, or crowded places of abode, particularly sleeping-apartments. A generous nourishing diet, with a moderate allowance of wine to those who are habituated to this mode of living, are recommended; while, on the contrary, as Mr Kennedy justly remarks, the person who has uniformly lived on a spare diet, and found it the best suited to his constitution, ought to beware of suddenly changing his abstemious system. Every extreme and every species of excess should be carefully guarded against.

The prevalence of spasmodic cholera on the continent of Europe, and lately to an alarming extent in Great Britain, has enabled practitioners, who have witnessed the disease both here and in India, to identify it as the true Asiatic cholera. The leading features of the disease, as common to both hemispheres, are exactly the same. Some peculiarities, however, of the symptoms, as they have manifested themselves in Russia and in Britain, it may not be uninteresting to mention.

The first or premonitory symptoms, consisting of slight bowel complaints, giddiness, and nervous palpitations about the heart, prevailing from one to three or more days previous to the second stage of the disease, are found to occur in a much larger proportion of cases in the English than in the Indian disease.

The febrile symptoms, or reaction after the state of collapse, accompanied by determination to the head, bowels, &c., are also more universal and more protracted in the British cases than those of India; and, consequently, in the favourable cases the recoveries are much slower. A

"The patient, if thirsty, is to be frequently supplied with acid drink: a wine-glassful of tepid water, acidulated with lime juice or citric acid, or with nitric or sulphuric acid, may be given as often as the patient requires it."

deeper and more general discoloration of the skin, resembling a leaden hue, is also more common in the former than in the latter. It is found, too, that the majority of the cases in Britain consist of females, being in general as two or three to one male, and in some as high as six to one. A greater proportion of children likewise appear to become victims to the disease in Britain than in India.*

In the treatment hitherto pursued in Britain, great importance is attached to checking the first or premonitory symptoms; for this purpose pills, containing one or two grains of calomel, with a quarter or one-half grain of opium, are given every hour or two hours; at the end of five or six hours, to be followed by a gentle dose of castor-oil or magnesia and rhubarb, in peppermint-water. The operation of this to be followed by another moderate opiate, combined with chalk-mixture; bleeding from the arm is also advised, especially in those patients where the pulse is full, and where there is much pain across the region of the stomach.

In the state of collapse, or when it is apprehended to be coming on, an emetic of a table-spoonful of common salt in a glass of tepid water,† or two tea-spoonfuls of powder of mustard-seed, in the same quantity of water, have been used with apparent advantage.‡ External heat by means of heated plates, hot bags of sand, hot bricks, and even the application of cloths dipped in boiling water, is to be unremittingly employed. The steam of water or spirits of turpentine, raised to a high temperature, and diffused over the whole surface of the body by means of a steam apparatus, has been found very efficacious. An enema of two or three pounds of very hot water, to which may be added five or six ounces of common spirits, is meanwhile to be administered, and hot brandy and water, hot beef-tea, or other stimulants, are to be given at short intervals. The febrile symptoms occurring after this stage are to be treated with local bleedings, gentle purgatives, and cool regimen.

---

* Essay on Cholera by J. A. Lawrie, M.D., Glasgow.

† Mr Searle on Russian Cholera.

‡ Suggestions on Malignant Cholera by Dr J. Abercrombie, Edinburgh, Drs Burton and Lorimer, Mr Greenhow, &c.

HINDOO
ASTRONOMY AND MATHEMATICS.

CHAPTER XIII.

Hindoo Astronomy.

Origin of Astronomy—Opinions of Bailly concerning the Antiquity of that Science in India—Striking Coincidence between the Indian and Arabian Zodiacs—Hindoo Computation of Time—Periodic Revolutions of the Planets—Theory of Eclipses—Figure of the Earth—Determination of Latitudes and Longitudes—Moon's Parallax—Computation of Eclipses and of a Solar Year—Antiquity of the *Surya Siddhanta* and other Astronomical Works—Deficiencies and Errors of the Hindoo System.

THERE are two powerful motives which at all times must have acted on the human mind, and instigated man to the study of nature;—one is the advantage to be derived from such knowledge in procuring the means of existence,—the other, the desire for knowledge which all men have, and some in so eminent a degree as to make its pursuit a principal object of their lives.

The heavenly bodies are well adapted to call into action both these motives;—they would serve the hunter in directing his path homeward from the chase, and the husbandman in choosing the proper time for preparing and sowing the soil. Their splendour could not be overlooked by the most incurious; and their courses and the regularity of their motions were a fine subject for contemplation to minds of a more elevated order.

The climate of India, and the occupations of mankind in the very early ages, were highly favourable to the most simple kind of astronomical observations,—those made by the eye unassisted by any instrument. But they cannot be considered as forming a science. The origin of astronomy in a country must be reckoned from the time that men began to reason from a recorded series of observations, and to deduce from them the laws of the celestial motions. In all countries the origin of astronomy goes beyond record, and is lost in the darkness of their early history: hence there is a boundless field for ingenious conjecture; and the astronomy of India has in this way afforded a topic for discussion which has engaged the attention of the most eminent men of the last half century.

The Indian astronomy has been the subject of an extensive work by Bailly, well known as a victim in the atrocities which accompanied the French Revolution, and his views,—ingenious, plausible, and seductive by his eloquence,—were adopted by one of the most elegant writers of this country, the late Professor Playfair, who gave them still greater weight by his high reputation for science, candour, sound judgment, and diligence in the investigation of truth. It was the opinion of Bailly that the Indian astronomy was of very great antiquity indeed, inasmuch as he believed it to be founded on observations made 3102 years before the Christian era; and he has endeavoured, with great ingenuity, to establish his views by considerations drawn from the discoveries in astronomy made in modern times, with which he was intimately acquainted, and which no man could turn to better account in support of a favourite system. It would seem, however, that he deceived himself in estimating the force of his arguments, and overlooked the strong objections to his hypothesis. His contemporaries Laplace and Delambre, who were also his friends, while they have professed the highest respect for the learning and eloquence which he displayed in his researches, have nevertheless declared their disbelief in his conclusions, and have proved them to be erroneous, by divesting his arguments of the specious but deceptive dress in which they are arrayed, and showing that some of the data which served as the basis of his system had been incorrectly assumed. Even his advocate and learned commentator, Professor Playfair, appears to have had his confidence in the truth of Bailly's views at last considerably shaken.*

The Indian astronomy became first known in Europe through M. de la Loubere, who was sent by Louis XIV. on an embassy to Siam in the year 1687. He brought

* See Edinburgh Review, vol. xxix. pp. 161, 162.

thence the precepts of that people for the calculation of eclipses; but these were incomplete for want of an example to show their application; and it required all the sagacity of the celebrated astronomer Cassini to explain their meaning. M. le Gentil, of the Academy of Sciences, brought, in 1772, from the coast of Coromandel, tables and astronomical precepts of the Indians of Trivaloor. These precepts are much more extensive and complete than those of M. de la Loubere, and M. le Gentil has accompanied them with examples, by which they can be easily understood and put in practice. In addition to these, there were found, in the Marine Depot of Charts and Plans at Paris, two manuscripts of Indian tables, which had been deposited by the astronomer M. de Lisle. He had received one of them in 1750 from Father Patouillet, who had corresponded with the missionaries; and the other had been sent from India by Father du Champ to Father Gaubil, and communicated by that missionary, in 1752, to M. de Lisle. The first of these came from Masulipatan or from Narsapour, and the second had been found at Chrisnabouram in the Carnatic country. It was from these four sets of tables that Bailly composed his *Astronomie Indienne et Orientale*.

Since the time Bailly wrote, very considerable additional light has been thrown on the subject of Indian astronomy by some members of a society instituted in Bengal for inquiring into the history and antiquities, the arts, sciences, and literature of India. Their labours have been published in the *Asiatic Researches*.

The astronomy of India is confined to one branch of the science. It gives no theory, nor does it even describe distinctly the celestial phenomena. It is limited to the calculation of certain changes in the heavens, particularly eclipses of the sun and moon, and with the rules and tables by which these calculations must be performed. The Bramin, seated on the ground with his shells before him, repeats the enigmatical verses which are to guide his calculation, and from his little tablets of palm-leaves takes out the numbers that are to be employed in it. He obtains his result with certainty and expedition; but having little knowledge of the reason of his rules, and no wish to be better informed, he is perfectly satisfied if, as it usually happens, the actual commencement and duration of the eclipse agree within a few minutes with his prediction. Beyond this his astronomical inquiries do not extend; and his observations, if he make any, go no farther than the determination of a meridian line, or the length of the day at the place of his residence.

This astronomy, as exhibited in their tables, presents three principal objects: 1. Tables and rules for computing the places of the sun and moon. 2. Tables and rules for calculating the places of the planets. 3. Rules for determining the phases of eclipses.

The Indian astronomers, like all others, have distinguished that portion of the heavens in which the motions of the sun, the moon, and planets, are performed from the rest of the celestial sphere. This tract, which corresponds to our zodiac, they divided into twenty-seven equal portions, called lunar houses, each marked by a group of stars or constellations. This division was naturally suggested to the early astronomers of all countries by the motion of the moon, which makes a complete revolution round the heavens in about twenty-seven days and seven hours. The moon does not exactly pass over equal portions of the heavens in equal times, but astronomy must have made some progress before this important fact could be ascertained. It is probable that the moon's supposed uniform motion would be used by the first astronomers as the means of measuring out the heavens into equal spaces, and determining the position of the most remarkable stars. In this way the moon would serve the purpose of an astronomical instrument.

Besides their lunar zodiac, they had another divided into twelve signs of thirty degrees each. This was purely mathematical, and served for the purposes of calculation. The divisions of this other zodiac were distinguished by names and emblems, and, what is truly remarkable, they are the same as those which are connected with the signs of our zodiac. This striking coincidence naturally disposes to the belief, that the Bramin and the Arabian zodiacs had a common origin. Sir William Jones thought they had not; but Mr Colebrooke, whose labours have thrown much light on Indian science, is inclined to a contrary opinion. He reckons the coincidence too exact in most things to be the effect of chance, and, from the slight difference between them, he infers that one of the two nations must have taken its zodiac from the other, but not copied it with servility. He says, "I apprehend that it must have been the Arabs who adopted, with slight variations, a division of the zodiac familiar to the Hindoos: this at least seems to be more probable than the supposition that the Indians received their system from the Arabians. We know that the Hindoos have preserved the memory of a former situation of the colures compared to constellations which mark divisions of the zodiac in their astronomy; but no similar trace remains of the use of the lunar mansions as divisions of the zodiac among the Arabs in so very remote times."

The almost perfect identity of the Hindoo zodiac with ours will appear from the names of their signs,—

Mesha, the Ram.	*Tula*, the Balance.
Vrisha, the Bull.	*Vrishchica*, the Scorpion.
Mit'huna, the Pair.	*Dhanus*, the Bow.
Carcata, the Crab.	*Macara*, the Sea Monster.
Sinha, the Lion.	*Cumbha*, the Ewer.
Canya, the Virgin.	*Mina*, the Fish.

The zodiac itself they call *sodi-mandalum*, the circle of stars. The figures of the twelve asterisms have been specified in Sanscrit verses by Sripeti, one of the early Bramin writers, which have been translated by Sir W. Jones as follows:—"The Ram, Bull, Crab, Lion, and Scorpion, have the figures of these five animals respectively. The Pair are a damsel playing on a *vina*, and a youth wielding a mace. The Virgin stands in a boat on water, holding in one hand a lamp, and in the other an ear of rice-corn. The Balance is held by the weigher with a weight in one hand; the Bow by an archer whose hinder parts are like those of a horse. The Monster has the face of an antelope. The Ewer is a water-pot borne on the shoulder of a man, who empties it. The Fish are two, with their heads turned to each other's tail,—and all these are supposed to be in such places as suit their several natures." There is a representation of the zodiac in the Asiatic Researches,* but it does not exactly agree with the above description. The Bull is entire, and not cut in two as in the Greek zodiac. In the couple, the damsel has no vina, nor the youth a mace,—they stand embracing each other. The man who holds the Balance seems to be placing something in one of the scales. The zodiac, therefore, proves that the sign of the Balance is of great antiquity. It appears from Ptolemy that it was also in the zodiac of the Chaldeans.

* Vol. ix. p. 330.

It would be important to know the time in which Sripeti lived. A zodiac and twelve signs, the names and figures of which bear so close a resemblance, are not like the heavenly bodies, the obliquity of the ecliptic, the sun's semidiameter, &c., phenomena which have been the same in all ages, and would convey exactly the same notions to observers of the heavens who might have no communication with each other.

The Bramins divided time into periods of seven days. Bailly supposed that this interval was taken as a fourth part of twenty-seven days and seven hours,—the time of a complete revolution of the moon through the zodiac. The time of her sidereal revolution, however, was not so likely to have drawn the attention of these early astronomers as that of her passing through all her phases, which is twenty-nine and a half days: the latter was, therefore, probably first observed, and its fourth part might be taken for their week as readily as that of the other. But it is more probable that their period of seven days had a relation to the number of the planets. We learn from Herodotus, that the Egyptians had a week of seven days, which might be derived from a tradition of the time in which the world was created, but more probably was formed from the planets; the day was divided into twenty-four hours, and one of the seven heavenly bodies, in the following order, viz. 1. The Sun; 2. Venus; 3. Mercury; 4. The Moon; 5. Saturn; 6. Jupiter; 7. Mars; was supposed to rule over the succeeding hours. Supposing the sun to be the presiding planet over the first hour of any day, he would also govern the eighth, the fifteenth, and twenty-second hours; the twenty-third hour would belong to Venus, the twenty-fourth to Mercury, and the first hour of the next day would be under the influence of the moon. In the same way the first hours of the following days, in their order, would be governed by Mars, Mercury, Jupiter, Venus, Saturn, and after seven days the sun would again govern the first hour, and the other planets would follow in the same order as before. Thus the days of the week became associated with the names of the planets.

Although the planetary names were given to the days of the ancient Hindoo week exactly in the same order as ours, their week had a different beginning. They reckoned our Friday to be their first day. The names of the planets in the order of the days were,—

1. *Soucra*, Venus.
2. *Sany*, Saturn.
3. *Addita*, the Sun.*
4. *Soma*, the Moon.
5. *Mangala*, Mars.
6. *Bouta*, Mercury.
7. *Brahaspati*, Jupiter.

And the names of the days of their week with the corresponding planets and the days of our week, as follow :—

1. *Soucravaram*,	day of Venus,	Friday.
2. *Sanyvaram*,	—— Saturn,	Saturday.
3. *Additavaram*,	—— the Sun,	Sunday.
4. *Somavaram*,	—— the Moon,	Monday.
5. *Mangalavaram*,	—— Mars,	Tuesday.
6. *Boutavaram*,	—— Mercury,	Wednesday.
7. *Brahaspativaram*,	—— Jupiter,	Thursday.

It is a remarkable circumstance that the Bramins should have had a week, and that planets should have been connected with the days, exactly in the same order as in that of the Egyptians and Greeks, because it has no relation to their apparent magnitudes, their brightness, their distances, or any of their obvious appearances. The coincidence cannot have been the effect of chance, and there seems to be no way of accounting for it, but the supposition that the adaptation of the planets to the days must have had a common origin, although it be now impossible to trace it back to its source. The *nacshatras*, or asterisms, which mark the moon's path in the heavens, twenty-eight in number, have names and presiding deities or regents; they have also their emblems or figures. This is their order, according to Mr Colebrooke :—

Names.	*Represented by*
1. *Aswini*,........................	a horse's head.
2. *Bharani*,........................	the Yoni.
3. *Critica*,........................	a knife or razor.
4. *Rohini*,........................	a wheeled carriage.
5. *Mrigasiras*,........................	an antelope's head.
6. *Ardra*,........................	a gem.
7. *Punarvasu*,........................	a house.
8. *Pushya*,........................	an arrow.
9. *Aslesha*,........................	a potter's wheel.
10. *Mag'ha*,........................	a house.
11. *Phalguni* (preceding),......	couch or bedstead.
12. *Phalguni* (following),......	a bed.
13. *Hasta*,........................	a hand.
14. *Chitra*,........................	a pearl.
15. *Swati*,........................	a coral bead.
16. *Visacha*,........................	a festoon of leaves.
17. *Anuradha*,........................	a row of oblations.

* The sun and moon were also called by other names, and there are varieties of spelling in the names of the planets.

18. *Jyeshtha*,......................a ring or earring.
19. *Mula*,..........................a lion's tail, or a couch.
20. *Ashadha*,........................a couch or elephant's tooth.
21. *Ashadha* (following),..........an elephant's tooth, or a bed.
22. *Abhijit*,.........................a triangular nut.
23. *Sravana*,.........................three footsteps.
24. *Dhanishtha*,.....................a drum or tabor.
25. *Satabhisha*,......................a circle.
26. *Bhadrapada*,..................a couch or bed, or figure with two faces.
27. *Bhadrapada* (following), a twin, or person with a double face, or else a couch.
28. *Revati*,...........................a tabor.

Mr Colebrooke has compared the *nacshatras* of the Hindoos with the *manzels* of the moon or lunar mansions of the Arabians; and he has shown that the Indian asterisms, which mark the divisions of their ecliptic, generally consist of the same stars that constitute the lunar mansions of the Arabians; but, in a few instances, they differ essentially: and hence again it is natural to infer that the Indian and Greek zodiacs must have been derived from the same source.

Sir William Jones had, at an earlier period, given a description of the Indian zodiac, and the names of the *nacshatras:* he makes them to be only twenty-seven; however, he observes, that, in a representation of these fanciful signs, there is inserted a constellation of three stars, called Abhijit in their nuptial ceremonies, for some astrological purpose; this is one of the *nacshatras* in Mr Colebrooke's enumeration: so that, on the whole, both agree. The names of the Indian months are derived from twelve of the asterisms, in the usual form of patronymics; for their *pauranics* (poetical fabulists), who reduce all nature to a system of emblematical mythology, suppose a celestial nymph to preside over each of the constellations, and feign that the god Soma, or Lunus, having wedded twelve of them, became the father of twelve genii or months, who are named after their several mothers; but the *jyautishicas* (the astronomers) give a more rational account of the matter; they say that when the lunar year was arranged by former astronomers, the moon was at the full in each month of the year, on the very day when it entered the *nacshatra*,—from which that month is denominated. The names of the months are,—

1. *Aswini.*	4. *Pausha.*	7. *Chaitra.*	10. *Ashara.*
2. *Cartica.*	5. *Magha.*	8. *Vaisacha.*	11. *Sravana.*
3. *Margafirsha.*	6. *Phalguna.*	9. *Jyaishtha.*	12. *Bhadra.*

From the two different accounts of the origin of the months, it is easy to understand that the history of astronomy as delivered by the Indian poets must be a tissue of absurdities. Indeed, there is an entire want of that soberness of description and precision of language, which characterize the science of the nations of Europe.

It appears from the astronomical tables, that the ancient Hindoos knew that the intersection of the equator and ecliptic is not always in the same point, but that it is constantly retrograding on the ecliptic in a direction contrary to the order of the signs, thereby producing an apparent motion of all the stars eastward from the equinoctial points; so that the time between the vernal equinoxes in two succeeding years is less than the time in which the sun moves round the ecliptic. This difference, called the precession of the equinoxes, the modern Hindoos reckon to be fifty-four seconds in a year; so that the period of a complete revolution of the equinoctial points will be about 24,000 years. The precession is, indeed, about four seconds less than they suppose; but Sir W. Jones believed that the old Indian astronomers had made a more accurate calculation, but concealed their knowledge from the people with a view to impose on them in regard to the antiquity of their nation. Besides the Indian tables already noticed, the astronomy of the Bramins has received farther illustration from some of their books of science, which have been discovered by the zealous exertions of members of the Asiatic Society. One of the most curious books in Sanscrit, and one of the oldest after the *Vedas*, is a tract on religious and civil duties, taken, as it is believed, from the oral instructions of Menu son of Brama to the first inhabitants of the earth. Sir W. Jones has translated, and given in the Asiatic Researches, a part of this work, which seems to relate to astronomy. It runs thus:—"The sun causes the division of the day and night, which are of two sorts,—those of men and those of the gods: the day for the labour of all creatures in their several employments, the night for their slumber. A month is a day and a night of the patriarchs, and it is divided into two parts; the bright half is their day for laborious exertions, the dark half their night for sleep. A year is a day and night of the gods, and that is also divided into two halves; the day is when the sun moves towards the north, the night when he moves towards the south. Learn now the duration of a night and day of Brama, with that of the ages respectively and in order. Four thousand years of the gods they call the *critica* (or *satya*) age, and its limits at the beginning and at the end are in like manner as many hundreds. In the three successive ages, together with their limits at the beginning and end of them, are thousands and hundreds diminished by one. This aggregate of four ages, amounting to 12,000 divine years, is called an age of the gods; and 1000 such divine ages added together must be considered as a day of Brama: his night also has the same duration. The before-mentioned age of the gods, or 20,000 of these years multiplied by 71, form what is named a *manwantara*. There are alternate creations and destructions of the world through innumerable *manwantaras*: the being supremely desirable performs all this again and again." This specimen of Hindoo chronology, which is believed to have been revealed from heaven, is sufficient to show that clouds and darkness must for ever hang over the origin of Indian science, and how difficult a task it must be to elicit from such a mass of absurdity any thing that can be relied on as an approximation to truth in regard to astronomy. The immense long periods spoken of in the preceding quotation have given rise to various conjectures which seem to be too vague to have any value.

The most ancient book of Hindoo astronomy is the *Surya Siddhanta*, which the Bramins assert to be a divine revelation received 2,164,899 years ago. Here we have another example of the fabulous texture of the whole system of Indian chronology and astronomy. Indeed, it is quite evident that it is a vain task to seek to discover the times at which their systems were constructed from their own accounts. If these possibly can be found, they must be discovered by a careful examination of the construction of their tables. This kind of analysis has been actually employed by Bailly, Playfair, and at a later period by Davis and Bentley; but the great disagreement in the conclusions to which these ingenious men have come, seems to leave but little hope of the truth being ever absolutely discovered, or even a considerable approach to it.

Mr S. Davis, in a Memoir on the Astronomical Computations of the Hindoos,* says, that many treatises on as-

* Asiatic Researches, vol. ii. p. 225.

tronomy in the Sanscrit tongue might be procured, and that the Bramins were very willing to explain them; he also adds, that Sanscrit books in this science are more easily translated than almost any others, when once the technical terms are understood. With a view to the computation of an eclipse, he procured a copy of the *surya Siddhanta,* which had been brought from Benares, and also the *Tika,* which is a commentary on it.

According to this ancient treatise the Hindoos divide the ecliptic into 360 degrees, as has been already stated. Their astronomical year is sidereal, and begins at the instant the sun enters the sign Aries, which they call *Mesha,* or when he enters into the *nacshatra Aswini.* Each astronomical month contains as many days and parts of a day as elapse while the sun is in each sign, and the civil differs from the astronomical account of time only in rejecting the fractions, and beginning the year and months at sunrise, instead of the intermediate instant of the artificial day and night; hence it happens that their months are unequal, and depend on the situation of the sun's apsis, and the distance of the equinoctial vernal colure from the beginning of *Mesha* in the Hindoo sphere. It was Mr Davis' opinion that the Hindoo science of astronomy is as well understood at this time as ever it was among them; but that it is less general because of the want of that encouragement which was formerly given to men of science by the native princes.

In constructing tables of the celestial motions, astronomers fix on some epoch, from which, as a beginning, they reckon the motions of the planets. The ancient Hindoos chose for their epoch that point of time counted back into past ages, when, according to their motions, as they had determined them, they must have been in conjunction in the beginning of *Mesha,* which corresponded to our Aries, and they suppose that the world was then created. This, in regard to the planets only, would have produced a moderate term of years; but having discovered a slow motion of the nodes and apsides, they found that it would require a length of time corresponding with 1,955,884,890 years, now expired, when they were so situated, and 2,364,115,110 years more before they would return to the same situation, forming together the grand anomalistic period called a *calpa,* and fancifully assigned as a day of Brama. They divided the *calpa* into *manwantaras* and greater and less *yugas*. The use of the *manwantara* is not stated in the *Surya Siddhanta*, but that of the *maha* or greater *yug* is sufficiently evident. It is an anomalistic period of the sun and moon, at the end of which the latter, with her apogee, and ascending node, is found with the sun in the first point of Aries; the planets also deviating from that point only by the difference between their mean and true anomaly. These cycles being so constructed as to contain a certain number of mean solar days, and the Hindoo system assuming that at the creation, when the planets began their motions, a straight line drawn from the equinoctial point *Lanca*, through the centre of the earth, would, if continued, have passed through the centre of the sun and planets to the first star in Aries, it was easy to compute their mean longitude for any time afterwards by proportion, thus:—As the number of days in any cycle to the revolutions a planet makes in that cycle, so are the days given to its motion in that time; and the even revolutions being rejected, the fraction, if any, shows its mean longitude at midnight under their first meridian of *Lanca*. For places east or west of that meridian a proportional allowance is made for the difference of longitude on the earth's surface. The positions of the apsides and nodes are computed in the same manner, and the mean places being found, the true places were determined by applying an equation on principles which are also explained.

It does not appear from the *Surya siddhanta*, that the division of the *maha yug* into the *satya, treta, dwapar*, and *cali* ages, serves any practical purpose in astronomy. Their origin has, however, been ascribed to the precession of the equinoxes. In every point of view, the latter is anomalistical.

The time called *murta* (that is, mean sidereal) is estimated by *respirations*: six *respirations* make a *vicala*; sixty *vicalas*, a *danda*; sixty *dandas*, a *nacshatra* day; and thirty *nacshatra* days, a *nacshatra* month. The *savan* month is the time contained between thirty successive risings of *Surya* (the sun), and varies in its length according to the *lagna bhuja* (right ascension); thirty *tit'his* compose the *chandra* (lunar) month. The *saura* month is that in which the sun describes a sign of the zodiac, and his passage through the twelve signs forms a year, and one of these years is a *deva* day, or a day of the gods; 60

deva days multiplied by 6 give a *deva* year, and 1200 of the *deva* years form the aggregate of the four *yugas*. To determine the *saura* years contained in this aggregate, write the number 4,320,000; this is the *maha yuga*, comprehending the *sandhi* and *sandhyansa* (the morning and evening twilight). Divide the *calpa* by 10, and multiply the quotient by 4, for the *satya yug*, by 3 for the *treta*, by 2 for the *dwapar*, and by 1 for the *cali yug*. Divide either of the *yugs* by 6 for their twilights; seventy-one *yugs* make a *manwantara*: a twilight is equal to the *satya yug*, during which there is a universal deluge; fourteen *manwantaras*, including the *twilights*, compose a *calpa*; and at the commencement of each *calpa* there is a *sandhi* equal to the *satya yug*, or 1,728,000 *saura* years. One *calpa* is a day with Brama; and his night is of the same length; and the period of his life is 100 of his years, of which one half is expired, and of the remainder the first *calpa* is begun, and six *manwantaras*, including the *sandhis*, are expired. The seventh, in which we are now advanced, is named *vaivaswata*. Of this twenty-seven *maha yugs* are elapsed, and we are now in the *satya yug* of the twenty-eighth, which consists of 1,728,000 *saura* years. Hence the years, since the beginning of the *calpa*, may be found; but from this 100 times 474 divine years must be deducted, or of that product multiplied by 360 for human years, that being the term of Brama's employment in the creation, after which the planetary motions commenced.

By following out the calculations, the *calpa* is found to contain 4,320,000,000 years; and the period of it elapsed at the end of the last *satya* age, when the *Surya Siddhanta* is supposed to have been written, 1,970,613,360 years.

The *bhagana*, or zodiac, is divided into twelve *rasis*, the *rasi* into thirty *bhagas*, the *bhaga* into sixty *calas*, and the *cala* into sixty *vicalas*. The *rasi*, therefore, answers to a sign or 30°, the *bhaga* to a degree, the *cala* to a minute of a degree, and the *vicala* to a second.

We have already given the Hindoo names of the planets, and therefore need not repeat them. In one *yug* the sun, Mercury, and Venus, complete 432000 *madhyama* revolutions through the zodiac; Mars, Jupiter, and Saturn make the same number of *sighra* revolutions: these answer to what we now call their revolutions about the sun. The moon makes 57753336 *madhyama* revolutions, Mars 2296832 *madhyama* revolutions, Mercury's *sighras* are 17937060,

Jupiter's *madhyamas* 364220, Venus' *sighras* 7022376, Saturn's *madhyamas* are 146568. The moon's apogee makes 488203, and her ascending node 232238 revolutions.

The time between sunrise and sunrise is the *bhumi savan* day, of which the *yug* contains 1577917828. The number of *nacshatra* days is 1582237828, of *chandra* (lunar) days 1603000080, of *adhi* months 1593336, of *tit'his* 25082252, of *saura* months 51840000.

From these numbers it has been found that

	d.	h.	m.	s.
The mean time of a lunation,..........	29	12	44	2.79
Time of moon's sidereal revolution,...	27	7	39	12.64
Hindoo year,..............................	365	6	12	36.56
Diurnal revolution of stars,............	366	6	12	36.56

It appears from a commentary on the *Surya Siddhanta*, that the Hindoos knew that the moon revolves once on her axis in a lunar month, and consequently has the same side always towards the earth. They had also noticed the difference between her apparent magnitude in the horizon and on the meridian.

According to the ancient Hindoo astronomical treatise, the sun's apogee makes 387 revolutions in a *ćalpa*, that of Mars makes 204, Mercury's makes 368, Jupiter's makes 900, Venus' 535, Saturn's 39: these are all direct or according to the order of signs. The number of revolutions of the nodes, which are retrograde, in a *calpa*, is for Mars 2141, for Mercury 488, for Jupiter 174, for Venus 903, for Saturn 662. It has been observed by Mr Davis, that although the planetary motions, as above determined, might have served for computations in the time of Meya, the author of the *Surya Siddhanta*, yet for many years past they have ceased to agree with the observed places in the heavens, and therefore corrections have been introduced, by increasing or reducing the numbers. Thus the revolutions of the moon's apogee and node are each now increased by four in a *yug:* the nature of these corrections, called *bija*, is explained in the commentary *Tica*.

Although the *Surya Siddhanta*, which professes to be a divine revelation, ought to have given correct elements of the planetary motions, yet the *Vishnu Dhermotter* directs that the planets be observed with an instrument, by means of which the greater or less agreement between the observed and computed places may be determined, and an allowance of *bija* made.

The following table contains the periodic revolutions of

the planets, of their apsides and nodes, according to the *Surya Siddhanta.* The *bija,* or corrections, are wanting. The inclination of the orbits is given, and the obliquity of the ecliptic is 24°. It is the same in their astronomical treatises written only 268 years ago; so that the Hindoos do not appear to have discovered any diminution,—a proof that they were never accurate observers.

ELEMENTS OF THE PLANETS ACCORDING TO THE SURYA SIDDHANTA.*

Planets.	Sidereal Periods.				Period of Apsides.	
	Days.	D.	P.	V.	Days.	D.
The moon,...	27	19	18	1	3232	50
Mercury,....	87	58	10	0	4287820184	46
Venus,.......	281	59	38	0	2949379117	45
The sun,....	365	15	31	31	4077307049	5
Mars,.........	686	59	50	58	7735087392	9
Jupiter,......	4332	19	14	20	1753242031	6
Saturn,.......	10765	46	2	18	42767123794	52

Planets.	Period of Nodes.		Daily Motion.		In. of Orbit.		Circumference of Orbit.
	Days.	D.	′	″	°	′	*Yojan.*
The moon,.	6794	23	790	35	4	30	324000
Mercury,...	3233742458	11	186	24	2	0	1043208
Venus,.....	1747417306	45	37	0	2	0	26646637
The sun,...	Precession 54″ per an.		59	8	24	0	4331500
Mars,.......	7373447794	23	31	26	1	30	8146909
Jupiter,....	9068493264	22	5	0	1	0	51375764
Saturn,....	2383561673	42	2	0	2	0	127666255

The longitude of the sun's apogee, reckoned according to the Hindoo account, at this time differs from modern observations 1° 20′. But there is much greater disagreement with respect to the aphelia and nodes of the other planets.

It has been supposed that the days during which Brama is said to have been employed in the creation, and which the *Surya Siddhanta* directs to be subtracted to have the time since the planets began their motions, are merely a correction introduced to compensate the errors which have been discovered since the composition of the work. This is probably a true explanation; and hence we see the utter uncertainty that pervades the whole system of astronomy delivered in the treatise.

* The periods are reckoned in days and *dandas, palas, vicalas,* of which each denomination contains sixty of the next lower.

We have now, according to the Hindoo system, the mean motions of the planets, their nodes and apsides, and the time since they were in conjunction in the beginning of *Mesha* (Aries). From these their mean longitude may be found for any proposed time. The *Surya Siddhanta* however says, that it is not necessary to assume so remote a period; for the computation may be made from the beginning of the *treta* age, at which instant all the moveable points of the heavens were again in conjunction in *Mesha*, except the apogees and ascending nodes, which must therefore be computed from the creation. The present Hindoo astronomers, therefore, go no farther back than the *cali yug* in determining the mean longitudes.

For the equation of the centre a trigonometry is required: This is given in the *Surya Siddhanta*, and it is one of the most curious and interesting parts of the treatise;—it will be described in the sequel.

To account for the apparent unequal motion of the planets, which they suppose to move uniformly in their orbits, they have recourse to excentric circles, and determine the excentricity of the orbits of the sun and moon with respect to that circle, in which they place the earth as the centre of the universe, to be equal to the sines of their greatest anomalistic equations. The Hindoos in this agree with the ancient Greek astronomers, but their calculation is very different. They substitute an epicycle instead of the excentric, which comes to the same, but, what is peculiar and difficult to explain, they make the radius of this epicycle vary at every degree, which thus goes on diminishing from 0° to 90° of anomaly. Indeed it is not the radius which they make truly to vary, but the circumference of the epicycle; thus they render the calculation needlessly complex. There is another singularity: although the equation of the moon is more than double that of the sun, the variations of their epicycles are sensibly the same. Thus, like the Greeks, the Indians have their theories of excentrics and epicycles; but instead of calculating by the rigorous rules of trigonometry, they have introduced an empirical term for which there is neither reason nor necessity. The vulgar among the Bramins believe that eclipses are occasioned by the monster *Rohere*, and they join to this idea others equally tainted with ignorance and absurdity. This belief being founded on declarations contained in works supposed of divine authority, which no pious Hindoo can call in question, some astronomers have been cautious in explaining the passages in these books which do not accord with the principles of their science. They have justified as well as they could propositions which disagree with the principles of their science, observing that certain things indicated in the *Sastras* may have been so formerly, and may be so still, but for astronomical purposes astronomical rules must be followed. Others, with a bolder spirit, have attacked and refuted unphilosophical opinions. Their astronomer and mathematician, Bhascara, argues, that it is more reasonable to suppose the earth to be self-balanced in infinite space, than to be supported by a series of animals with nothing assignable for the last to rest upon; and another commentator says, that by *rahu* and *cetu*, the head and tail of the monster, the position of the moon's nodes and her latitude are meant, on which eclipses certainly depend; but he does not therefore deny the reality of *rahu* and *cetu*, the existence of which he says may be maintained as an article of faith without prejudice to astronomy. This appears to us very absurd; but it is not more so than the subterfuges to which Copernicus and Galileo were forced to have recourse to shelter the true doctrines of astronomy against the denunciations of the Church of Rome.

The Hindoos consider the earth as spherical, and suppose its diameter divided into 1600 equal parts or *yojans*. The *Surya Siddhanta* states the circumference in round numbers to be 5059 *yojans;* but in the *Puranas* the circumference is declared to be 500,000,000 *yojans*,—and to account for this difference, a commentator says that the *yojan* of the *Surya Siddhanta* contained 100,000 of those of the *Puranas*. Some say that the earth was really of that size in some former *calpa*, and others believe that from the equator, southward, the earth increases in bulk; but for astronomical purposes the dimensions given in the *Surya* must be assumed.

To find the latitude of a place the Hindoos observe the length of the shadow of a perpendicular gnomon when the sun is in the equator, and compute by their geometry the angle which the gnomon makes with the line drawn from its top to the extremity of the shadow.—This is the latitude.

The longitude is directed to be found by observations of lunar eclipses, calculated for the meridian of *Lanca*, which passes through Ougein, a place in the Mahratta dominions. Benares lies sixty-four *yojans* eastward from this meridian ;—its longitude is therefore forty-four *palas*.

To determine the moon's distance, or her parallax, they observe the time of the moon's rising, and compare it with the computed time; the difference is the time in which she describes an arc of her orbit, equal in length to the earth's semidiameter ;—this difference of time is to her periodic month as 800 *yojans* to the circumference 324,000. They neglect refraction, of which they seem to have no knowledge, although they are not quite ignorant of optics, because they know that the angle of incidence is equal to the angle of reflection of a ray. They also reckon the motion along the sine instead of the arc. In this way they find the parallax to be 53′ 20″, and her distance from the earth's centre to be 51570 *yojans,* which answer to about 220,184 geographical miles. European science has determined it to be about 240,000 miles, which is about a fifteenth part more than the Hindoos had found it so long ago as the time of Meya, the author of the *Surya Siddhanta.*

The Hindoos suppose that all the planets move in their orbits with the same velocity. The dimensions of the moon's orbit being known, those of the other planets are determined by the rule of proportion.

To find the diameters of the sun and moon, the time that elapses between the upper limb of the rising sun touching the horizon and the lower limb reaching it, is observed; in this way the sun's diameter has been found 6500 *yojans,* and that of the moon 480 *yojans.* These diameters are varied according as they exceed or fall short of the mean in the calculation of eclipses. When the moon's anomaly is three signs, her diameter is reckoned to be 32′ 24″, which is sufficiently exact.

The calculation of an eclipse of the moon, by the principles of European astronomy, with the aid of the more simple tables,—those in Ferguson's Astronomy for example,—is not a tedious operation. It is, however, otherwise in the Indian astronomy. The first step of the process is to find the number of mean solar days from the time of the creation to the time of the eclipse; the next, to find the mean longitude of the sun, moon, and the ascending node: these are determined by very tedious operations in multiplication and division. The astronomical calculations in Europe led to some ingenious devices by which the labour was abridged, and, at last, to the important invention of logarithms. The Indians had a like or even greater stimulus to their ingenuity; but it does not appear to have led to any abbreviation or simplification of their calculations.

Those curious in such matters may see a specimen of the calculation of an Indian eclipse in the second volume of the Asiatic Researches,—also in Delambre's *Astronomie Ancienne,* vol. i. From the whole operation Delambre has drawn the following conclusions:—

1. The computation of an eclipse by the Indian tables is an operation of excessive length.

2. These ancient tables are very inaccurate; although, if we believe Bailly, they were deduced from observations made at very long intervals, and for that reason ought to have given the mean motions of the planets with considerable precision.

3. There are three other Indian tables, more modern, which give errors of 28^m, 51^m, and 12^m, in the time of eclipses; and errors of from 12^m to 20^m, and even to 32^m in the time of their duration.

4. The calculations of the Hindoos are less geometrical than those of the Greeks, and, like theirs, they depend on excentrics and epicycles, which are disfigured by empirical suppositions.

5. The Indian tables can be of no use in correcting the mean motions of the planets, although Bailly believed that they might be so employed.

6. It is a remarkable circumstance that the Indian theories of astronomy make no mention of observations or even of an instrument; but, indeed, there is no proof that the theories were really formed by the Indians; moreover, we cannot place the least confidence in them, because we are entirely unacquainted with the principles of their foundation, and have no means of estimating the errors that may have been committed in making the observations. If we judge of them by those which we know to have been made 1600 or 1800 years ago, the Indian observations must have been very indifferent, or even utterly worthless.

7. Lastly, the knowledge which the Indians had of astronomy is greatly inferior to that of the Greeks.

The Indian methods of calculation are altogether different from those of Hipparchus; they have given no demonstration,—while the Greeks on the contrary have fully explained the formation of their tables. The modern astronomy has been formed from the writings of

Ptolemy: his three centres, viz., of the equant, of the excentric, and of the zodiac, led Kepler to the centre and two foci of his ellipse. However well instructed we may suppose the Indians to have been, their science and their discoveries have hitherto been, and always will be, useless to us. That the Greeks received any knowledge from them is more than doubtful; while it is certain the Greeks formed the Arabians, the Persians, the Tartars, and ourselves. Bailly would indeed have us believe that Hipparchus knew the Indian tables; but there seems to be no reason for this supposition, seeing he has not taken the Hindoo solar excentricity, nor the inclination of the lunar orbit. He differs from them in these essential points; we must therefore conclude that he found for himself all that he has taught the moderns.

Mr Davis' Memoir on the Indian Astromomy, as delivered in the *Surya Siddhanta,* does not go beyond lunar eclipses, and it gives rather an unfavourable notion of what they have done in regard to solar eclipses. Their parallax of 51′, so ill determined, and the variations, which are not better, throw great uncertainty on eclipses of the sun and occultations of the stars and planets.

It is singular that the Indians, the reputed inventors of decimal arithmetic, should in all their calculations have made continual use of sexagesimal fractions. In these the numbers which expressed the days in their prodigiously long periods went far beyond the limits of the Greek arithmetic. It would be curious to know how they express such large numbers. In the third volume of the Asiatic Researches, Mr Davis has given, in a memoir on an Indian cycle, a translation from the Sanscrit of a method for determining the length of the solar year. This consists in observing the sun's amplitude at rising, on a day about the time of an equinox, and again on the day before the sun has completed a circle round the heavens from his position on that day, and on the next day when he has more than completed it, also noting the times from the first observation. Thus the number of whole days in the year will be known, and the fractional part to be added will be the same part of a day that the difference between the middle amplitude and one of the extremes (that first observed) is to the difference between the extremes. The amplitudes, or rather their differences, are to be determined by marking the sun's position at rising on a horizontal circle of considerable magnitude. This method is ingenious, and it would be improved by observing the sun's position at rising on several days before and after the year is completed. Theoretically it is good, but probably it was never put in practice; and with any horizontal circle such as the Hindoos might be supposed to possess, was not likely to lead to much certainty.

The *Surya Siddhanta* being regarded as the most ancient astronomical treatise among the Hindoos, it is important to know the time at which it was composed. It is now generally admitted that the Hindoos are a very ancient people. Bailly believed that their astronomy was founded on observations made more than 3000 years before the Christian era; and, in particular, that their tables of the sun and moon were determined by actual observations made at the beginning of their celebrated era the *cali yug*, which was 3102 years before the Christian era. It might, however, well be doubted whether they had any books of such extraordinary antiquity. To dissipate these delusions J. Bentley, Esq. has given to the world a memoir which has for its object to determine the age of the *Surya Siddhanta*,* and in this he has clearly explained the manner in which their tables were formed. We have seen that in the Hindoo systems certain parts of time were fixed on as epochs at which the planets are assumed to have been in a line of mean conjunction with the sun in the beginning of Aries. From these the Hindoo astronomer carried on his calculations as if they had been fixed by actual observation, and thence determines such mean annual motion as will give the positions of the planets in his own times so as to correspond as nearly as he can with the observations then made.

In fixing on these epochs, the first Hindoo astronomers took the precaution to throw them so far back into antiquity, that the difference between the assumed and real places of the planets, whatever they might be at that time, would, when divided by the number of years reckoned forward from the epoch, be a quantity too inconsiderable to affect the mean annual motions deduced from thence for several years.

For example, let an epoch of mean conjunction be assumed at only the distance of 648,000 years, and without considering what was the actual position of the planets at

---

* Asiatic Researches, vol. vi. p. 540.

that time, which cannot certainly be known, let us suppose that they were all in conjunction with the sun in Aries. Now, since a planet cannot be more than half the circumference of the heavens, that is, six signs or 180 degrees from its assumed fictitious place, the error that will be made in determining its mean place, at any time within a considerable interval before and after the period when the tables were actually constructed, will not exceed 180 degrees divided by 648,000, that is, one second of a degree,—an error not greater than would be made by the modern European tables.

This is Mr Bentley's idea of the manner in which the Indian tables were formed; and Delambre says, that it coincides nearly with that which he himself had formed when he first read Bailly's *Astronomie Indienne.* He made the supposition that in 1491, or any other year, if an astronomer knew the places of the planets, and their mean motions, it signifies not whether well or ill determined, he might thence find the epoch of a general, or almost general conjunction; for a conjunction rigorously exact is impossible, unless we go back to a very remote period indeed. But without going unreasonably far back, he might find a time when the planets were all in the compass of an arc of some degrees in extent. He might then, neglecting the differences, feign that they were all at the same point (it might be zero or any other point). The degrees thus neglected, divided by the number of years, would be reduced to insensible fractions, which would be corrections to be made in the annual motions. It is no doubt in this way that all the civil and astronomical periods have been found. "This idea," continues Delambre, "is so natural, that I have always been surprised it did not make Bailly drop his pen. It has prevented me from placing the least confidence in the pretended proofs on which he has rested, and which I would never have discussed, had I not been obliged to do so in a history of astronomy."

Mr Bentley, to exemplify his idea of the formation of the Indian tables, has supposed the planets to have been in a line of mean conjunction in the beginning of Aries at the commencement of the *cali yug*, that is, at midnight between 17th and 18th February, O.S., in the year of the Julian period 1612, on the meridian of *Lanca* (75° 50′ E. long.) He then, by proceeding on the principle which he believed to have been employed in forming the Indian tables, and using Lalande's tables, has deduced a set of mean annual motions of the planets on the Hindoo sphere, which differ but a few seconds from the annual motions as given by Lalande. Now, had a European astronomer, who had no idea of the Hindoo method, found these fictitious motions in their tables, he would have been deceived by appearances, and have supposed them to be of great antiquity.

The Hindoo systems of astronomy may be divided into three classes.

The first class supposes a general conjunction of all the planets, their apogees and nodes, in the first point of Aries, and this conjunction has for its period the *calpa* of Brama, which contains 4,320,000,000 years, and which began 1,972,944,000 years before the *cali yug*. It appears that the astronomer Bramagupta was the author of this enormous period.

The second supposes a general and *true* conjunction at the end of the *calpa* of Varaha, with a mean conjunction at the end of certain cycles. The *calpa* of Varaha is of the same length, but it began 17,064,000 later.

The third does not suppose any conjunction either at the beginning or end of the *calpa*.

The writings of Bramagupta, the *Siddhanta*, and the *Siromani* of Bhascara, belong to the first class: these do not assume a conjunction at the *cali yug*. Again, the *Surya Siddhanta, Soma Siddhanta, Varisha Siddhanta*, and such others as assume a mean conjunction at the beginning of the *cali yug* only, as the *Jat Karnob* of Varaha, the tables of Trivalore, &c., belong to the second. And to the third belong the *Brama Siddhanta, Vishnu Siddhanta, Bhasvoti, Drubo Rothono, Chendrika*, and other *Siddhantas*. These are constructed on the principles of the European astronomy.

Mr Bentley lays down this as a canon, " that the most certain mode of investigating the antiquity of Hindoo astronomical works is, by comparing the positions and motions of the planets computed thence with those deduced from accurate European tables; for it must be obvious, that every astronomer, be his system what it will, whether real or artificial, must endeavour to give the true position of the planets in his own time, or at least as near as he can, or the nature of his system will permit, otherwise his labour would be totally useless. Therefore, having the positions and motions of the sun, moon, and planets, at any proposed instants of time, given by computation from any original Hindoo system, and having also their positions and motions deduced from correct European tables, for the same instant, we can thence determine the point or points of time back when their respective positions were precisely the same in both."

Proceeding on this apparently reasonable principle, he finds the secular motion of the moon's apogee, according to the *Surya Siddhanta*, and the tables of Lalande, to be 42′ 10.9″. Now, suppose that Varaha (the real author of the *Surya*) had determined for his own time the position of the apogee, it would follow that, at the end of 100 years, there would be an error of 42′ in the place of the moon; 200 years after, the error would be double; and, according to this idea, the apogee must have been determined by observation 605 years before the epoch of 1799, that is, in 1134 of our era.

By like calculations on the node, he finds 580 years. The equations since found by Laplace change somewhat these determinations; besides, it is impossible to answer for the positions found by Varaha.

By the motion of the sun's apogee, the time when the observations were made, on which the tables were constructed, comes out 1105 years. But the motion is so slow, and so difficult to determine, that this result ought not to be reckoned with the others.

Mercury, which separates so little from the sun, gives a result with a contrary sign; from this nothing can be determined.

Venus gives 860 years, and Mars 140, which is evidently too little.

For Jupiter, Saturn, and the sun, Mr Bentley makes use of new equations.

The aphelion of Mars gives 641 years. The sidereal year 736. The whole brought together stand thus,—

	Years.
From the moon's apogee, .	605
——— node, .	580
Sun's apogee, .	1105
Venus, . .	860
Mars, . . .	340
Moon, . .	759
Jupiter, . .	875
Saturn, . . .	805
Mars' aphelion,	641
Length of the year,	736
Total,	7306

which, being divided by 10, the number of results, in order to get the mean, gives 731 years nearly for the age of the *Surya Siddhanta*, which differs but five years from the age determined by the length of the year only.

Mr Bentley says, that, independent of all calculations, it is known from the Hindoo books by whom the *Surya Siddhanta* was written, and when. In the commentary on the *Bhasvoti*, it is declared that Varaha was the author of the work. Now, the *Bhasvoti* was written in the year 1021 of *saka*, by one Sotanund, a pupil of Varaha, and under whose directions he wrote his commentary. Varaha must then have been alive, or a short time before. This agrees as nearly as possible with the age above deduced; for the *Bhasvoti*, in the year 1799, the time when Mr Bentley made his computations, was exactly 700 years old. It is extremely probable that the name of Varaha must have been to the *Surya Siddhanta* when it was first written; but that, after his death, priestcraft found means to alter it, and to introduce the absurd story of Meya or Moya having received it through divine revelation at the conclusion of the *satya yug*. Indeed, according to Bentley, a number of other astronomical works were then framed for the purpose of deception,—some were pretended to be delivered from the mouth of one or other of their deities, as the *Brama Siddhanta*, *Vishnu Siddhanta*, and the works of Siva, commonly called *Tantros*. Others were pretended to have been received through revelation, as the *Soma Siddhanta;* while others again were imputed to sages who lived in the remotest periods of antiquity, as *Varishta Siddhanta*, and other *Siddhantas*, to the number of about eighteen altogether, including the *Surya Siddhanta*. These are now called the eighteen original *shasters* of astronomy, although there be not above three or four of them original.

M. Delambre says, that the system explained in Mr Bentley's memoir is so simple and reasonable, that it might have been found without the aid of the Indian books; but when it appears to be the result of a careful examination of them, it seems to be placed beyond all doubt. On the whole, it appears that the Hindoo astronomy is entirely different from ours. If there be any resemblances, they have arisen out of the nature of the science, or from what the Indians have borrowed from the Arabians, who were instructed by the Greeks, rather than from any thing borrowed from the Indians by the Arabians, or by the Greeks. The enigmatic methods of the Indians were never known to the Greeks, and indeed have only been explained of late years; so that the Greeks have taken nothing in astronomy from the Indians, unless, perhaps, the constellations: this, however, has not by any means been proved. As to the mathematical doctrines in the astronomy of the Greeks, they were their own, and they have demonstrated them, while the Indians have proved nothing. It cannot even be shown that the Indians have ever observed, nor are there any recorded original observations of which the date is certain. It is remarkable that the Indians, who could compute eclipses, and who now announce them in their almanacs, have not recorded even one as having been actually observed; while the Chinese, less skilful calculators, and yet less geometers, have long recorded them in their annals. We have been told of their spheres and their gnomons; but the gnomons of India appear to have served merely as sundials, and to determine the latitude of a place. It is surprising that we have never heard of the solstitial shadow, and but rarely of the equinoctial shadow; that the *Surya Siddhanta* only slightly mentions the armillary sphere, which served to divide the zodiac into *nacshatras*; that we find only in the commentary some imperfect indications, but no actual observations. Their armillary sphere, with a terrestrial globe in its centre, and all their planetary orbits, resemble the furniture of a cabinet rather than instruments intended for real observations. With their obliquity of 24°, their ignorance of refraction, the errors which they would no doubt make on the altitude of the pole, it is not easy to see how they could find with any accuracy the longitude and latitude of the stars. They have only designated twenty-seven, that is, one in each *nacshatra*, and their positions are only given in degrees.

We believe enough has been now said on the Indian astronomy. The opinions which we have followed are those of Sir William Jones, Messrs Davis, Bentley, and Colebrooke, as delivered in the Asiatic Researches, and which have been adopted by Delambre,—a high authority in the history of astronomy. On a subject which has been so much contested, it will no doubt be highly satisfactory to have also the opinion of the celebrated Laplace, the author of the *Mécanique Céleste.* He says, "The

Indian tables suppose an astronomy considerably advanced; but all tends to produce a belief that it is not of high antiquity. Here I differ, with much regret, from the opinion of an illustrious and unfortunate friend . . . The Indian tables have two principal epochs, one 3102 years before our era, the other 1491. These epochs are connected by the motions of the sun, the moon, and the planets, in such a manner, that departing from the position which the Indian tables assign to the stars, at the second epoch, and returning to the first, by means of these tables we find the general conjunction which is supposed at that epoch. The celebrated philosopher to whom I have alluded (Bailly), has sought to establish in his Indian Astronomy that this first epoch was founded on observations; but, notwithstanding his proofs, exhibited with that clearness which he knew so well how to spread over the most abstract subject, I consider it as very probable that it has been imagined in order to give a common origin in the zodiac to the celestial motions. Our latest astronomical tables, improved by a comparison of theory with a great number of very precise observations, do not allow to admit the supposed conjunction in the Indian tables. They even present differences much greater than the errors of which they are susceptible. Indeed, some elements of the Indian astronomy could only have the magnitude assigned to them a long time before our era. For example, it would be necessary to go back 6000 years to give the equation of the sun's centre the value it has in the tables; but, independently of the errors of their determinations, it must be observed, that they have considered the inequalities of the sun and moon only in relation to eclipses, in which the annual equation of the moon unites with the equation of the sun's centre, and increases it by a quantity nearly equal to the difference of its true value from that of the Indians. Several elements, such as the equations of the centre of Jupiter and Mars, are very different in the Indian tables from what they ought to be at the first epoch. The whole structure of the tables, and especially the impossibility of the conjunction which they suppose, prove that they have been formed or at least rectified in modern times."

CHAPTER XIV.

Hindoo Mathematics.

Division of the Circumference of the Circle—Ratio of the Diameter to the Circumference—Tables of Sines and Versed Sines—Mathematical Treatises—Account of the Origin of the Lilavati—Its Contents—Knowledge of Algebra.

THERE is another subject of inquiry intimately connected with the astronomy of India: this is their knowledge of the mathematical sciences. Here there is not so much room for the exercise of that disposition to exaggeration in respect of dates, which so eminently distinguishes their astronomical systems. It is true, that part of their geometry, which is contained in the *Surya Siddhanta,* which professes to have been a revelation delivered four millions of years ago in the golden age of the Indian mythologists, when man was incomparably better than he is at present, when his stature exceeded twenty-one cubits, and his life extended to ten thousand years, is involved in the absurdity of a pretension to antiquity which outrages all probability; yet this is not any part of the doctrines themselves: setting aside what is fabulous, there yet remains sufficient to give the subject high interest as a most important feature in the history of the pure mathematics.

In the *Surya Siddhanta,* notwithstanding the mass of fable and absurdity which it contains, there is a very rational system of trigonometry. This has been made the subject of a memoir by the late Professor Playfair, in the fourth volume of the Edinburgh Philosophical Transactions; and although it be evidently written with a belief of the truth of Bailly's visionary system deeply impressed on his mind, yet, leaving out of view the question of absolute antiquity, it will be read with all the interest which that elegant writer has never failed to excite, even when the reader is not disposed to agree with him in opinion,

We have already noticed that the Indians divided the circumference of a circle into 360 equal parts, each of which was again subdivided into sixty, and so on. The same division was followed by the Greek mathematicians. This coincidence is remarkable, because it has no dependence on the nature of the circle, and is a matter purely conventional. It is probable both nations took the number 360 as the supposed number of days in a solar year, which might be the first approximation of the early astronomers to its true value. The Chinese divide the circle into 365 parts and one-fourth, which can have no other origin than the sun's annual motion.

The next thing to be mentioned is also a matter of arbitrary arrangement, but one in which the Bramins follow a mode peculiar to themselves. They express the radius of a circle in parts of the circumference. In this they are quite singular. Ptolemy and the Greek mathematicians supposed the radius to be divided into sixty equal parts, without seeking in this division to express any relation between the radius and the circumference. The Hindoo mathematicians have but one measure, and one unit for both, viz. a minute of a degree, or one of those parts of which the circumference contains 21600, and they reckon that the radius contains 3438. This is as great a degree of accuracy as can be obtained without taking in smaller divisions than minutes, or sixtieths of a degree. It is true to the nearest minute; and this is all the exactness aimed at in their trigonometrical tables. The author, however, does not mean to assert that the ratio of the radius to the circumference is either accurately, or even very nearly, as 3438 to 21600, which makes the diameter to the circumference as 1 to 3.14136. It appears from the Institutes of Akbar, that the Bramins knew the ratio of the diameter to the circumference to greater exactness, and supposed it to be that of 1 to 3.1416.

The tables employed in their trigonometrical calculations are two,—one of sines, and the other of versed sines. The sine of an arc they call *cramajya* or *jyapinda,* and the versed sine *utcramajya.* These terms seem to be derived from the word *jya,* which signifies the chord of an arc, from which the name of the radius or sine of 90°, viz. *trijya,* is also taken. This regularity in their trigonometrical language is not unworthy of remark; but what is of more consequence to be observed, is, that the use of sines, as it was unknown to the Greeks, who calculated by the help of the chords, forms a striking difference between theirs and the Indian trigonometry. It is generally supposed that the use of sines, instead of chords, in modern trigonometry, was borrowed from the Arabians. It is certainly one of the acquisitions which the mathematical sciences made when, on their expulsion from Europe, they took refuge in the East.

The table of sines exhibits them to every twenty-fourth part of the quadrant; the table of versed sines does the same: in each the sine or versed sine is expressed in minutes of the circumference, neglecting fractions. Thus the sine of 3° 45′ is 225, the sine of 7° 30′ is 449, and so on. The rule for the computation of the sines is curious; it indicates a method of computing a table by means of their second differences,—a considerable refinement in calculation, and first practised by the English mathematician Briggs.

The *Surya Siddhanta* does not give the demonstration of the truth of the rule; but the commentary gives direct geometrical means for their calculation. In the progress of science, the invention of trigonometry is a step of great importance, and of considerable difficulty. He who first formed the idea of exhibiting in arithmetical tables the ratio of the sides and angles of all possible triangles, must have been a man of profound thought, and of extensive knowledge. However ancient, therefore, any book may be in which we meet with a system of trigonometry, we may be assured that it was not written in the infancy of the science. We may therefore conclude, that geometry must have been known in India long before the writing of the *Surya Siddhanta.* Professor Playfair, speaking of the Indian rule for computing sines, which is certainly very ingenious, says, "it has the appearance, like many other things in the science of those eastern nations, of being drawn up by one who was more deeply versed in the subject than may be at first imagined, and who knew much more than he thought it necessary to communicate. It is probably a compendium formed by some ancient adept in geometry for the use of others who were merely practical calculators."

The earliest notices which reached Europe concerning the Hindoo mathematics, came, we believe, from an ingenious English mathematician, Reuben Burrow. Residing in India, and taking a lively interest in every thing connected with the history of his science, he was led to collect Oriental manuscripts, some of which in the Persian language, accompanied with an interlined translation into English, he sent to his friend, the late Isaac Dalby, Professor of Mathematics in the Royal Military College. These were communicated to various persons in this country about the year 1800.

In the year 1813, Edward Strachey of the East India Company's service published a translation from the Persian of the *Bija Ganita* (or *Vija Ganita*), a Hindoo work on algebra, written by Bhascara Acharya, who lived about the year 1150 of the Christian era, and who, besides this book, had composed other mathematical treatises,—particularly the *Lilavati*, a work on arithmetic and practical geometry. These books, composed originally in Sanscrit, had the highest reputation in India, and were translated into different languages. The *Lilavati* was translated, by order of the Emperor Akbar, into Persian, on account, as Fyzee the translator says, of the wonderful arts of calculation which it contained. The *Vija Ganita* was also translated into Persian in the year 1634, and it was from this Mr Strachey made his English translation.

Again, in the year 1816, John Taylor, M.D., of the East India Company's Bombay Medical Establishment, published in India a translation of the *Lilavati* directly from the Sanscrit; and in the following year, H. T. Colebrooke, Esq. published Algebra, with Arithmetic and Mensuration, from the Sanscrit of Bramagupta and Bhascara. This work contains translations of four different treatises written in Sanscrit verse on the arithmetic, algebra, and geometry of Indostan. Two of these are the *Lilavati* (arithmetic) and *Vija Ganita* (algebra) of Bhascara already mentioned. The other two books are still more ancient, and were composed by a mathematician named Bramagupta. These, like most of the mathematical treatises of the Hindoos, form part of systems of astronomy;—the first two, being the introduction to the *Siddhanta Siromani* of Bhascara, and the other two forming the twelfth and eighteenth chapters of the *Brama Siddhanta,* an astronomical work of Bramagupta.

The age of Bramagupta is considerably earlier than that of Bhascara, and his works are very rare. Mr Colebrooke was fortunate enough to obtain a copy of them, which is imperfect in some respects, but in which the chapters on mathematics are complete. The age in which he lived is fixed with great probability from various concurring circumstances, particularly from the position which he assigns in his astronomy to the solstitial points, to the sixth or beginning of the seventh century of the Christian era,—a period earlier than the first dawn of the sciences in Arabia, although much less ancient than all that now remains of the Greek mathematics and astronomy. Ganesa, the most distinguished of the commentators on Bhascara, quotes a passage from Arya Bhatta on algebra, which contains the refined artifice for the solution of indeterminate problems, which is called in Sanscrit *Cuttaca*. Arya Bhatta is indeed regarded as the most ancient uninspired writer that has treated of astronomy. By a variety of arguments Mr Colebrooke makes it appear that this algebraist wrote as far back as the fifth century of the Christian era, and perhaps earlier. He was, therefore, almost as old as the Greek algebraist Diophantus, who lived about the year 360. The Persian translator of the *Lilavati*, Fyzee, gives an account of the origin of that treatise which has in it much of that air of romance that distinguishes every thing Oriental, not excepting their science. Lilavati was the name of the author's (Bhascara's) daughter, concerning whom it appeared, from the qualities of the ascendant at her birth, that she was destined to pass her life unmarried, and without children. Her father thought he had discovered a lucky hour for contracting her in marriage, that she might be firmly connected and have progeny; and when the hour approached, he brought his daughter and her intended husband near him. He left the hour-cup on the vessel of water, and kept in attendance a time-knowing astrologer, in order that, when the cup should subside in the water, these two precious jewels should be united. But as the intended marriage was not according to destiny, it happened that the girl, from a curiosity natural to young persons, looked into the cup to observe the water coming in at the hole, when by chance a pearl, separated from her bridal-dress, fell into the cup, and rolling down to the hole, stopped the influx of the water; so the astrologer waited in expectation of the promised hour. When the operation of the cup had thus been delayed beyond all moderate time, the father was in consternation,—and, examining the cup, found that the hole was closed, and the long-expected hour past. Bhascara, thus greatly disappointed, said to his unfortunate daughter, "I will write a book of your name, which shall remain to the latest times, —for a good name is a second life, and the groundwork of eternal existence."

The *Lilavati* treats of arithmetic, and contains not only the common rules of that science,—there reckoned eight in number,—but the application of these rules to various questions on interest, barter, mixtures, combinations, permutations, the sums of progressions, indeterminate problems, and, lastly, of the mensuration of surfaces and solids. All this is done in verse, and the language, even when most technical, is often highly figurative. The question is usually proposed with enigmatical conciseness, next the rule for computation is given in terms somewhat less obscure. The example follows; but it is not until this has been studied that all obscurity is removed. No demonstration nor reasoning is subjoined; but the rules are found to be exact, and nearly as simple as in the present state of analytical investigation. The numeral results are readily deduced; and if they be compared with the earliest specimens of Greek calculation, the advantages of the decimal notation are placed in a striking light. The work begins thus,—"Having bowed to the deity, whose head is like an elephant, whose feet are adored by gods, who, when called to mind, restores his votaries from embarrassment, and bestows happiness on his worshippers, I propound this easy process of computation, delightful by its elegance, perspicuous with words, concise, soft and correct, and pleasing to the learned." The definitions are given in form of an introduction, and are followed by an invocation.—"Salutation to Ganesa, resplendent as a blue and spotless lotus, and delighting in the tremulous motion of the dark serpent which is continually twining within his throat." The rules of arithmetic are then delivered in verse, and addressed to Lilavati, a young and charming female, who appears to be receiving the instructions of the author, and to whom the examples of the rules are usually proposed as questions to be resolved.

The arithmetic is followed by a treatise on geometry, inferior in excellence certainly to the treatise on algebra, yet well deserving of attention. We have here the celebrated proposition, that the square on the hypotenuse of a right-angled triangle is equal to the squares on the sides containing the right angle; and other propositions which form part of the system of modern geometry. There is one proposition remarkable, namely, that which discovers the area of a triangle when its three sides are known. This does not seem to have been known to the ancient Greek geometers.

It is a most singular circumstance, that, with such a body of mathematical science as has descended from a very remote period to the present time, there is almost an entire want of all analysis or synthetic demonstration; for this it is not easy to assign a cause. Some learned men in Europe have supposed that the entire ignorance of the modern Hindoos of the demonstrations of their rules, is a satisfactory proof that they are not the inventors of the science; or else, that the knowledge of the mathematics has declined so much that they have no longer any idea of the fundamental principles and the practical operations which they have been taught by their ancestors.

The algebra of the Hindoos comes next to be considered. We have seen that the age in which Arya Bhatta lived was probably not very different from that of Diophantus. It must, however, be conceded to the Hindoo algebraist, that he had advanced farther in the science, since he appears to have been able to resolve equations containing several unknown quantities, which it is not clear that Diophantus knew; and also had a general method of resolving indeterminate equations, of at least the first degree, which it is certain that Diophantus had not attained. There is yet a curious question left for discussion: Was the science of algebra known long before, and by what degrees of improvement did it advance until the time of Arya Bhatta? The late Professor Playfair was of opinion that it was much older. He observes, it is generally acknowledged that Diophantus cannot have been himself the inventor of all the rules and methods which he delivers; much less is Arya Bhatta to be held the sole inventor of a system that was still more perfect than that of Diophantus. Indeed, before an author could think of embodying a treatise of algebra in the heart of a system of astronomy, and turning the researches of the one science to the purposes of the other, both must be in such a state of advancement, as the lapse of several ages, and many repeated efforts of invention, were required to produce."* Delambre, in answer to this, says, when an author has created a new science among a people considerably advanced in civilisation, men of genius will not be long in acquiring the new notions, in order to extend and multiply their application. Thus, among the Greeks, Archimedes succeeded to Conon, and Apollonius followed Archimedes, in less than sixty years. The Bernoullis made decided progress in modern analysis, even in the lifetime of Newton and Leibnitz, its inventors.†

It appears from the Hindoo treatises on algebra, that they understood well the arithmetic of surd roots; that they knew the general resolution of equations of the second degree, and had touched on those of higher denomination, resolving them in the simplest cases; that they had attained a general solution of indeterminate problems of the first degree, and a method of deriving a multitude of answers to problems of the second degree, when one solution was discovered by trials. Now, this is as near an approach to a general solution, as was made until the time of Lagrange. The Hindoos had also attempted to solve equations of higher orders, but with very little success. They not only applied algebra both to astronomy and geometry, but conversely applied geometry to the demonstration of algebraic rules. In fact, they cultivated algebra much more, and with greater success, than geometry, as is manifest from their low state of knowledge in the one, and high attainments in the other. Mr Colebrooke has instituted a comparison between the Indian algebraist and Diophantus, and has found reason to conclude that, in the whole science, the latter is very far behind the former. He says, the points in which the Hindoo algebra appears distinguished from the Greek are, besides a better and more convenient algorithm,—

1st, The management of equations of more than one unknown quantity.

2d, The resolution of equations of a higher order, in which, if they achieved little, they had at least the merit of the attempt.

3d, General methods for the resolutions of indetermi-

* Edinburgh Review, vol. xxix. p. 143.

† Delambre, *Hist. de l'Astronomie du Moyen Age, Discours préliminaire.*

nate problems of the first and second degrees, in which they went far indeed beyond Diophantus, and anticipated discoveries of modern algebraists.

4th, The application of algebra to astronomical investigations and geometrical demonstrations, in which they also hit upon some matters which have been reinvented in modern times.

On the whole, when we consider that algebra made little or no progress among the Arabians; an ingenious people, and particularly devoted to the study of the sciences, and that centuries elapsed from its first introduction into Europe, until it reached any considerable degree of perfection, we incline to the opinion of Professor Playfair rather than to that of Delambre, on this branch of Indian science, and are disposed to believe that algebra may have existed, in one shape or another, long before the time of Arya Bhatta.

TRIGONOMETRICAL SURVEYS.

CHAPTER XV.

Colonel Lambton's Surveys.

Colonel Lambton appointed to make a Survey across the Peninsula—Advantages possessed by him for this Task—Difficulties of a Trigonometrical Survey—Colonel Lambton commences his Labours—Triangles carried across the Peninsula—Continuation of the Survey—Death of Colonel Lambton—Conclusion.

ABOUT the year 1800, Colonel Lambton, then a major in the king's service in India, a most intelligent officer, and well versed in mathematical science, and particularly in the means of applying it to the improvement of geography, projected a survey across the Peninsula of India, for the purpose of determining the positions of the principal geographical points. By the success of the British arms, a district of country had been acquired, which not only opened a free communication with the Malabar coast, but, from its nature, afforded the means of connecting that with the coast of Coromandel, by an uninterrupted series of triangles, and of continuing that series to an almost indefinite extent in every direction. He accordingly communicated his views to the governor in council at Madras, and was by him appointed to conduct that important service, with a liberality by which alone it could be carried into execution.

A new era had commenced in the practice of trigonometrical surveying, by the determination of the distance between the meridians of Paris and Greenwich. This was begun by General Roy, in the year 1784, who then measured a base of about five miles in length on Hounslow Heath, with a degree of scientific skill that had never before been exceeded, and probably not then equalled. This was the first of a series of operations. The labour was recommenced in 1787, and carried on until completed, under the able direction of the general, by a series of triangles extending from Greenwich Observatory to Dover. A like series of triangles was determined, by eminent French mathematicians, between Paris and Calais, Blancnez and Montlambert, points near the French coast opposite to Dover, and the British and French triangles were then connected by observations made across the Channel, by means of lights exhibited at the stations. At that period, the English artists excelled all others in the world in the construction of exquisitely-divided astronomical instruments. Probably the French mathematicians employed on this occasion were superior to the English in the refined theories of modern analysis. However this might be, the series of geodetical operations then begun, soon called into action the exertions of artists and mathematicians, to the great benefit of astronomical and geographical science.

Colonel Lambton, then, in beginning his labours, had the advantage of excellent instruments; a theory almost perfect, in the writings of Delambre and Legendre; the previous example of the British trigonometrical survey along the southern and eastern coasts of England, by Colonel Williams, Captain Mudge, and Mr Dalby, the account of which, to one about to commence a like labour, was, as he says, a treasure. There must have been partial surveys of portions of our Indian territories before this time; but these were all conducted on principles much inferior in accuracy to those employed by Colonel Lambton, and with less perfect instruments.

The survey of a kingdom, or of such an extent of country as that undertaken by Colonel Lambton, besides requiring a degree of intelligence and resources much beyond what are necessary in the survey of a district of no great extent, wanted farther for its complete execution two most important elements,—one of these is the magnitude, and the other the figure of the earth. The difficulty of resolving these problems in geography was, therefore, to be surmounted; and for their solution, besides purely mathematical knowledge, various applications of the doctrines of astronomy, and other branches of physical science, were essentially necessary.

The general object to be attained in the survey of a country is to determine the precise position of every remarkable point, and the exact direction of straight lines joining them, as well in respect of each other as in respect to the meridians which they intersect. To effect this, four separate processes, differing from each other, and directed to different objects, must be performed and combined. The first is, the measurement of one or more bases, each from five to seven miles long, and the longer the better. These should be on a straight and level line; but as this can hardly ever be exactly obtained, it must be nearly such a line. It has been usual to measure this line by placing straight rods, sometimes of deal, sometimes of metal, and on one occasion of glass, all of the same length, end to end in succession, and each supported horizontally, and those behind brought forward and placed in advance, along the whole line. General Roy, after having tried the deal, and also the glass rods, at last had recourse to steel chains made like a watch-chain. He found that these, when laid in wooden troughs, and stretched by weights that were always the same, were as much to be trusted to as rods, and greatly more convenient.

In the grand series of operations carried on by the French mathematicians, to determine the length of a quadrant of the meridian, rods of platina were used; and in the latest operation of this kind, viz. the base measured along the shores of Loch Foyle, for the trigonometrical survey of Ireland, two parallel rods of different metals, united together in a particular way by cross bars at their ends, have been employed. Rods of this description we believe have been sent to India, and will be employed there in future geodetical operations.

The next part of the process is the selection of a number of points, called *stations*, all over the country to be surveyed. These are supposed to be joined by straight lines which form a series of triangles. In each triangle the angles are to be taken by a theodolite of large dimensions, and then, when one side is known, the others may be found by trigonometry. These being known, the whole series may be delineated on paper, and the position of each point on the survey found in respect to all others. This is sufficient for determining every line, and every figure within a given extent; but something more is necessary to determine its position on the earth's surface, and its situation in respect to the quarters of the heavens, and the parallels of latitude, and the meridians on the surface of the globe. The first of these objects is determined by observing the angles which one or more sides of the triangles make with the meridians passing through the stations which are the intersections of the sides. This serves to place the whole in its proper position with respect to the cardinal points. The next thing to be done is to place the tract surveyed between the two parallels of latitude on the artificial globe, corresponding to those on the surface of the earth which they represent. This is done by determining by astronomical observations the latitudes of any two stations in the survey at a considerable distance north and south from each other. When this is performed, and the magnitude of the celestial arc in the heavens expressed in degrees is compared with the measured length of the terrestrial meridian between the parallels passing through the stations, the length of a degree on the earth's surface will be known.

The position of the whole as to its distance from the equator or pole will now be known; but its distance east or west from some known meridian, that is, its difference of longitude, remains to be determined. This must be found by means taught in the doctrines of astronomy.

Colonel Lambton being in possession of some valuable instruments, and in expectation of others from England, which the India Company had with the most laudable liberality given him permission to procure, began the survey by measuring a base on the table-land of the Mysore country, near Bangalore: it was more than 100 miles from the sea, and on this account unfavourable, because its elevation above the level of the sea required to be found, and this could only be done by corresponding observations of the barometer made at the base and at Madras. However, having provided an apparatus similar to that employed for a like purpose in the British survey, he commenced his labour on 14th October 1800, and completed it on 10th December. After making the necessary corrections for the expansion and contractions of the chain by heat and cold during the process, he found the true length of the base, at the temperature of 62° and reduced to the level of the sea, to be 39267.706 feet, or 7.4321 miles. By a series of subsequent astronomical observations, the latitude of the south end of the base was found to be 12° 54′ 6″.

Colonel Lambton resumed his labour in the year 1802. He had by this time received a most complete apparatus from England: this enabled him to execute his views on the scale originally proposed, which was the measurement of a considerable arc of the meridian. Without regarding what he had formerly done, he began anew, and fixed on a tract of country for a base near Madras. It was well adapted to his purpose, being an entire flat, extending in a southerly direction almost eight miles. The length of the base, reduced to the level of the sea and the temperature 32°, was 40006.44 feet, or 7.546 miles. The latitude of the north end was 13° 0′ 29″, and it made an angle of about 12° with the meridian. From this a series of triangles was carried about eighty-five miles westward, extending north to the parallel of 13° 19′ 49″, and south to Cuddalore, in latitude 11° 44′ 53″, embracing an extent of 3700 square miles. The country seems to be favourable to the choice of stations, and the climate to geodetical observations, for the triangles are of considerable magnitude, the sides of some being thirty or forty miles in length. They are also well contrived for avoiding very acute or very obtuse angles, which are unfavourable to accuracy in trigonometrical surveys. In computing the sides, Colonel Lambton reduced the observed spherical angles to the angles of the chords of the arcs according to the method of Delambre. The chords, which were the sides of the triangles, were then converted into arcs; and as by a very judicious arrangement,—which is, however, not always practicable,—he had contrived that the sides of four triangles which connected the stations at the north and south extremities of the meridian, should be very nearly in its direction, their sum, with very little deduction, gave the length of the intercepted arc, which was thus found to be 95721.326 fathoms.

By a series of observations for the latitude at the extremities of this arc, made with an excellent zenith sector of five feet radius by Carey, the amplitude of the corresponding arc in the heavens was found to be 1° .58233. The length of the terrestrial arc in fathoms, divided by this number, gives 60494 fathoms for the length of a degree, in the middle parallel of latitude, viz. 12° 32′. This at the time it was measured was the degree nearest to the equator (except that in Peru almost under it) which had yet been measured, and on that account was highly interesting.

The next object was to measure a degree perpendicular to the meridian in the same latitude. This degree was accordingly derived from a distance of more than fifty-five miles, between the stations of Carangooly and Carnaghur, nearly due east and west of one another. To determine the length of this degree very correct measures of the angles which that line made with the meridians at its extremities were necessary. In fact the angles were observed with the greatest care; but, from the nearness of the intersection of the meridional arc and perpendicular arc to the equator, the result is less to be relied on than the measure of the meridional degree. The degree perpendicular to the meridian of Carangooly was found to be 61061 fathoms.* By comparing this with the meridional degree, Colonel Lambton found that the earth's compression at the poles should be reckoned $\frac{1}{210}$. This, however, we know to be too much; but, if we diminish the perpendicular degree by 200 fathoms and make it 60861, as a writer in the Phil. Trans. 1812 contends that it ought to be because of an error in Colonel Lambton's calculations, then the compression will come out $\frac{1}{330}$, which is probably near the truth.

The measurements which we have hitherto described were made in the year 1803. In 1806, the series of triangles was carried quite across the Peninsula to the Malabar coast, which they intersected at Mangalore on the north and Tellicherry on the south. They passed over the Ghauts,—so celebrated both in the natural and civil history of Indostan. Two of the stations, Soobramanee and Taddiandamole in the Western Ghauts, not far from the coast, were, the former 5583 feet, and the latter 5682 feet

---

* The reader should know that the earth is not an exact sphere, but a solid, formed by an ellipse, turning round its lesser axis; so that a meridian is not a circle, but an ellipse, the curvature of which gradually diminishes from the equator to the poles. It is a consequence of this figure that the degrees of latitude gradually increase from the equator to the poles; and the inequality of the degrees in different latitudes depends on the inequality of the axes in such a way that the one is deducible from the other; that is, if we know the proportion which the one axis bears to the other, we can find the proportion which the lengths of degrees in any two parallels, 5° and 10° for example, have to each other, and the contrary. The deviation of the figure of the earth from a perfect sphere is called its *compression*, and it is measured by the fractional part that the difference of the two axes is of the greater.

above the level of the sea. The heights of the stations were all determined from the distances and observed angles of elevation; and it is no small proof of their accuracy, that after ascending the chain of the Ghauts from the Coromandel coast on the east, and descending again to the level of the sea on the Malabar coast, a distance of more than 360 miles, the sum of all the ascents differed from the sum of the descents only by eight feet and a half.

From the triangles thus carried across the Peninsula, a correct measure of its breadth was obtained, and one considerably different from what had previously been supposed. The distance from Madras to the opposite coast was found to be nearly 360 miles, instead of 400 miles as given in the best maps before the time of the survey.

The great extent of the triangulation now required a second base to be measured in the interior of the country. This was accordingly done near Bangalore, about 170 miles west from Madras, not far from the position of the first base. The work was performed with great accuracy by Lieutenant Warren of the 33d regiment. It was connected with the Madras base by the intermediate triangles, and by these its length was computed. The result differed only about three and a half inches from what it was found by the actual measurement,—a remarkable proof of its accuracy, considering that the two bases were 170 miles distant. Such a near coincidence must produce great confidence in the skill of the observers and the excellence of the instruments they employed. The length of the second base, reduced to the temperature of 62° and to the level of the sea, was 39793.7 fathoms, or 7.536 miles. The latitudes were determined by the zenith sector with every precaution at both stations; the same stars were observed at both many times, and a mean of the results taken. From the observations, it was found that a degree of the meridian in lat. 12° 55′ 10″, is 60498 fathoms.

The next thing attempted was the measurement of a degree perpendicular to the meridian in the above latitude, which is that of Savendroog, near Bangalore; but here an uncertainty, similar to that in the former case, was found in the result. This, indeed, was inseparable from the nature of the thing to be done. The degree was found to be 60747.8 fathoms. Colonel Lambton remarks, that, supposing the ratio of the earth's diameters to be 1 to 1.003125, the meridional degree 60498 fathoms gives

60858 fathoms for the perpendicular degree, which differs by 110 fathoms from what is found by measurement; hence we must infer, either that the earth is not an ellipsoid,* or that this measure is incorrect.

In the year 1810, Colonel Lambton communicated to the Asiatic Society an account of the measurement of an arc on the meridian, extending from lat. 8° 9′ 38″ to 10° 59′ 49″; and again, in 1812, he made a farther communication on the extension of the meridional arc, from the last-mentioned latitude to 15° 6′ 1″. His principal object, when he commenced the survey, was to connect the two coasts of Coromandel and Malabar, and to determine the latitudes and longitudes of the principal places, both on the coasts and the interior; but, as the work advanced, his views expanded, and, in addition to the triangles carried across the Peninsula between the parallels of 12° and 14°, he extended another series from Tranquebar and Negapatam entirely across to Paniani and Calicut; and to render the skeleton complete, a meridional series was carried down the middle of the Peninsula, terminating at the sea near Cape Comorin; from this series others were extended to the east and west, entirely along both coasts; so that, in 1812, a web of triangles had been completely woven over the Peninsula of India, from the parallel of 14° to its southernmost extremity. This triangulation had for its object the determination of the latitudes and longitudes of all the remarkable points; such as tops of mountains, cities, &c. The result of these has been applied to the improvement of the topography of the country; and has been given to the public, we believe, in the excellent maps of that accurate geographer the late Mr Arrowsmith. The measurements of the meridional arcs, which had a higher aim, the determination of the figure and magnitude of the earth itself, have, however, been most interesting to general geography and astronomy; and, accordingly, Colonel Lambton's various memoirs have found a place in the Asiatic Researches and London Philosophical Transactions, as affording most important data in philosophical and astronomical science.

In the progress of the survey the meridian of the Dodagoontah station, or of Savendroog, was continued south to

---

* Ellipsoid, a solid, generated by the revolution of an ellipse about one of its axes, in this case the lesser.

Punnae, in the lat. of 8° 10′; and the series of triangles for extending its length was continued to the same point. In the extent of this prolongation two new bases were measured,—one at Putchapoliam, where the meridian intersects the parallel of 11°, and another at Tinnevelly, near the southern extremity of the arc. These bases were nearly of the same length, but somewhat shorter than that at Bangalore. In many places the country is high and difficult to penetrate. There is a mountain here, the hill of Permaul, in lat. 10° 18′; its height is 7367 feet. On this meridian, the distances of five stations, with the corresponding latitudes, were determined. The amplitude of the whole arc, between Punnae, the south extremity, and Paughur, the northernmost point, was 5° 56′ 47″·32, and its length 359595.4 fathoms. From this, and the intermediate points, the following degrees and their measures were deduced:—

	Fathoms.	Mid. lat.		
Punnae and Putchapoliam,......	60473	9°	34′	44″
Punnae and Dodagoontah,......	60496	10	34	49
Punnae and Bomosundrum,...	60462	11	4	44
Punnae and Paughur,.........	60469	11	8	3
Mean of the two last,...........	60465.5	11	6	23.5
From a former measurement,...	60494	12	32	0

In these degrees the same anomalies occur which have been observed in France and England, and probably will always occur when contiguous arcs are compared with one another. We have already observed, that on the supposition that the earth is a figure generated by the revolution of an ellipse about its lesser axis, the degrees should gradually increase from the equator to the pole, according to a determinate law. Here we see that the length of a degree, of which the middle parallel is 11° 4′ 44″, is less than others nearer the equator. A small part of this irregularity may be owing to error of observation; but the greater part must be placed to account of the irregularities in the direction of gravity arising from the inequalities at the surface, or in the interior of the earth, the attraction of mountains, or the local variation of density immediately under the surface. This is an example of the difficulties which are to be expected in an extensive trigonometrical survey. In the London Philosophical Transactions for 1818, Colonel Lambton has given an abstract of the results of his measurement of the meridian. He had then at different times measured three complete sections of an arc of the meridian. We have already described two of these, viz. one extending from Punnae, lat. 8° 9′ 38″, to Putchapoliam, in lat. 10° 59′ 49″, and another extending from Putchapoliam to Namthabad, in lat. 15° 6′. He had afterwards the good fortune to get another section extending from Namthabad to Daumergidda, in the nizam's dominions, which, being in lat. 18° 3′ 24″, gives an addition of 2° 57′ 23″, making on the whole an arc of 9° 53′ 45″ in amplitude,—an extent of upwards of 680 miles,—the longest single arc that had ever been measured on the surface of the globe at the time it was accomplished. The number of base lines measured were five. He had now got the measured length of a degree in three different parallels, viz.—

Fathoms.	Mid. lat.
60472.83	9° 34′ 44″
60487.56	13 2 55
60512.78	16 34 32

From these, compared with the length of degrees measured in England, Sweden, and France, he obtained various fractions for the earth's compression at the poles, and taking a mean among them, at last came to the conclusion that the compression was $\frac{1}{310}$. The remainder of the details in his abstract of his operations is highly interesting to mathematicians, but hardly to general readers.

Again, in the Philosophical Transactions for the year 1823, Colonel Lambton has applied to his measured meridional arc the corrections necessary to change his former measures to the parliamentary standard measure. The differences are too trifling to require notice in the general view which we have attempted to give of the exertions of this indefatigable labourer in the field of science. He continued the survey beyond this period; and we add with regret that he died in January 1830.

We have selected the labour of Colonel Lambton as a proof of the intelligence with which the present rulers of India have applied their power and their ample means to the promotion of geographical knowledge. Science suffered a great loss by the death of that meritorious officer; but we add with satisfaction, that he has had successors who, in his lifetime, had prosecuted similar views. In the fourteenth volume of the Asiatic Researches, we have a journal of a survey to the heads of the rivers Ganges and Jumna, by J. A. Hodgson. Also an account of trigonometrical and astronomical operations for determining the heights and positions of the Himmaleh mountains by the same officer, in conjunction with Lieutenant Herbert; and, lastly, a valuable memoir on the ancient geography of India, by Colonel Wilford. These were given to the world before 1822. But we know that the East India Company still continue, with the same laudable diligence, the determination of the geographical features of their territories, and that instruments of the most improved construction, and similar in all respects to those now used in the survey of Ireland, have been obtained, and placed in the hands of military officers, who will not fail to emulate the zeal and industry which so eminently distinguished their predecessor, Colonel Lambton.

NAVIGATION.

CHAPTER XVI.

Present State of Navigation between England and the East Indies, with Instructions for the Guidance of Passengers.

Size and Appointments of an Indiaman—Promotion of Officers—Their Duties—Instructions to Passengers—Classes of Ships—Outfit—Passage-money—Plan of the Orwell Indiaman, and of the Victory Private Trader—Voyage to India—Madeira—Daily routine on board an Indiaman—Amusements of the Passengers—Observation of Sunday—Catching Sharks—The Nautilus—Equatorial Limits of the Trades between 18° and 26° W. Long.—Crossing the Line—Wreck of the Blendenhall—Cape of Good Hope—Constantia—Current off the Cape—Marine Barometer—Trade-winds—Route through the Mozambique Channel—Bombay Harbour—Route to the Eastward of the Cargados Bank—Wreck of the Cabalva—Ceylon—Madras Roads—Mouth of the Hoogley—Homeward Voyage—The Cape—St Helena—The Azores.

The present state of navigation to India, contrasted with what it was even fifty years ago, is very remarkable. A voyage to India *out and home* is now sometimes accomplished in eight months by the same ship; and to a letter by one ship an answer may occasionally be received by another in six months. Fifty years ago, six months was an average passage out to India. The purpose of the following pages is to give a summary view of the route pursued by ships in the present day, with instructions for the guidance of passengers and others interested in East India shipping. The latitudes and longitudes, together with other nautical observations, are taken from the latest and most authentic sources. Captain Horsburgh, hydrographer to the East India Company, has kindly given permission to make free use of his " Directions for sailing to and from the East Indies," at once the most comprehensive and correct work which has ever been or probably ever will be published for the guidance of those "who go down to the sea in ships."*

Columbus crossed the Atlantic in a caravel of 40 tons burden; and the vessel in which De Gama first rounded the Cape was not larger than a coasting-sloop. The East India Company have now about 50 noble ships, each of 1200 tons burden and upwards, employed in their trade to India and China. They are manned as follows:—

1 Captain.	1 Ship's steward and cooper.
6 Officers.	1 Boatswain and 4 mates.
6 Midshipmen.	1 Gunner and 2 mates.
1 Clerk.	1 Carpenter and 3 mates.
1 Surgeon.	Armourer, sail-maker, and caulker.
1 Assistant do.	Including servants and seamen, total 130.
1 Purser.	

They are always well armed, carrying in time of peace 20 eighteen pounders on their main-deck, and six thirty-two pound carronades on the upper-deck. During war the number of guns is increased to 32. In addition to great guns, each ship carries 100 muskets, 50 pistols, 50 cutlasses, and 100 pikes, with all needful ammunition, and a magazine fitted for action. From their warlike equipment and formidable appearance, these ships in time of war have great advantages when sailing in a fleet. It is supposed that at the expiration of the East India Company's charter, this fine class of ships will be discontinued. The present rage for every thing cheap has blinded many persons on this subject; and no other argument will obtain with them but this, "Tea can be brought to England cheaper in a small ship than in a ship of 1200 tons; therefore small ships are preferable." Much might be said on this subject which would be out of place here.

The East India Company have two classes of ships in their regular service. The ships of the first class (eight in number) are the private property of the Company. In these ships all the appointments are in the gift of the East

* Captain W. F. W. Owen, R. N., having lately been employed on survey in the Indian Seas, has published a table of latitudes and longitudes, which differs materially from other authorities. For the sake of accuracy, it has been thought necessary, wherever lat. or long. is quoted in this chapter, to subjoin in a note the corresponding geographical site according to Captain Owen.

India Directors, and promotion from the lowest to the highest is strictly according to seniority. A captain obtains the command of a ship in this class *without paying sixpence* for it, and is allowed to retain the command for five voyages, after which he must retire. The other class consists of ships *let on hire* to the Company for a certain number of voyages by private owners. The captains and officers of these hold the same rank in the Company's service as the captains and officers of the Company's own ships, and are subject to the same laws as to qualification, &c.; but the appointments of both captains and officers are in the gift of the private owners, and the rule of seniority is not observed. In these ships the progress of a young man through the different gradations is very vexatious to parents, all depending upon interest, which must be renewed and reapplied every succeeding voyage. The most rapid promotion which can take place would be thus: One voyage as midshipman; one as sixth or fifth officer; one as third; one as second or first; and then captain. Or it might be thus (which would probably be more advantageous to the officer): Two voyages as midshipman; one as fourth officer; one as third; and one as second or first. The captain, first, second, third, and fourth officers, each take an oath of fidelity to the Company every voyage. No person can be sworn in as fourth officer without producing certificates that he has performed two voyages to India; that he is twenty-one years of age; that he is qualified to work the longitude by chronometers and lunars; together with a certificate of good conduct from his last commander. These certificates are all printed forms. He is then examined in seamanship by the Company's master-attendant. An officer is examined every time he gains a step from fourth officer to first inclusive. The first and second officers are examined by one or two of the nautical directors. At sea the routine of duty for officers is as follows: The first or chief officer may be termed the head of the executive; he superintends and directs all under the sanction of the captain. The second officer usually assists the captain in navigation, and instructs the middys and junior officers in nautical astronomy. The third officer has charge of every thing below, assisted by the fourth, fifth, and sixth. He has the cables and the holds under his immediate charge; he also regulates the berthing and messing of the crew; he is cognizant of, and responsible for, every thing which occurs under hatches. The crew are divided into two watches, the officers into three. The first, second, and third officers have each charge of a watch; the fourth, fifth, and sixth, conduct the duty on the forecastle. The middys are employed on the poop and in the mizzen-top. No person is permitted to act as surgeon of a regular ship who shall not have performed one voyage in a Company's ship, or served twelve months in his Majesty's service in hot climates. The surgeon and surgeon's mate must produce a certificate from the examiners of the Royal College of Surgeons, and also from the physician appointed by the Company, of their being qualified for such stations. The surgeon presents a list of the sick every day to the captain, who is obliged to examine and sign the surgeon's journal once a-month. The purser superintends the provisions and slops. The station and quarter bills are hung up in the gun-deck for general inspection. The first and second officers, the purser, and surgeon, mess with the captain; all the other officers and mids pay for their own mess.

The ships are amply stored and provisioned, and always leave England in good repair. Their whole outfit is conducted under the superintendence of public officers appointed by the Company. The provisions and water, with every other description of stores, are always apportioned by well-established rules to the length of the voyage. The discipline is strict, and according to an established system. The ships always sail on the day appointed, the orders on this point being rigidly enforced by the Company. It may fairly be conceded that the existence of all these regulations, together with the spacious accommodation and clear decks of an Indiaman, ought to ensure great punctuality and comfort. Notwithstanding, it has been found, that since the free-trade to India commenced, the greater number of passengers prefer the private ships. The ships in the private trade are of various classes and dimensions, from 800 tons to 150. Many of them are expressly fitted for passengers, and in some instances great care and expense have been bestowed, both as to their sailing qualities and internal comfort.

It may not be out of place here to give a few particulars for the guidance of passengers bound to India. At Lloyd's Coffee-house, where most of the private ships are insured, they are classed according to their age and condition. Before an insurance can be effected, the ship is surveyed. There are five classes, A, E, I, O, and U. In each class there are three gradations. Thus, if a ship is quite new, well built, and altogether in good condition, she is in the first class, which is called A 1, the next A 2, next A 3, next E 1, and so on. As ships, like books or estates, are always puffed off in the newspapers, it is as well to know the above; and it may be farther remarked, that if a ship is classed A 1, it will usually be so stated, whereas if she happens to belong to class E 2, nothing respecting her class will be found in the advertisement.* Of late years many agency-houses have been established for the express purpose of doing all the necessary business for passengers respecting their outfit and return. To agents and brokers the owners of private ships give a per centage for every passenger they procure. It must be observed that the brokers get this per centage on the amount of passage-money for a passenger from the owners of *all classes* of ships, and therefore it must be expected that they will puff a ship *coute qui coute* whether she be A 1 or U 20! In all respects, except the actual choice of a ship, an agent or broker will be found highly useful both out and home.†

In laying in a sea-stock for India, either of clothes, furniture, &c., or eatables, passengers are strongly recommended to employ persons accustomed to supply the India market; and although many articles may be got cheaper from other houses, still the risk of their not being adapted to the peculiarity of an Indian climate, or the casualties of the voyage, make it highly advisable, as far as means go, to employ persons experienced in these matters.

The following lists of necessaries contain every thing

---

* The Jerusalem Coffee-house, Cornhill, is the great emporium of East India shipping intelligence; and there passengers may obtain all needful information from that most obliging and well-known person Horatio Hardy.

† The following gentlemen are agents for passengers, and transact all business connected with procuring a passage, shipping, baggage, &c. They are acquainted with all forms necessary for passengers, and readily afford every facility without any *direct* fee. Their remuneration, as before observed, is derived from a commission on the passage-money: this is a transaction between the captain or owner and the broker, with which the passenger has no pecuniary concern.

Agents for passengers, &c.—Captain Grindlay, Captain Thacker.

absolutely required by a lady or gentleman for an Indian voyage. Eatables and drinkables of every description for the whole voyage are laid in by the captain, and the passage-money is understood to cover all expenses of this nature:—

OUTFIT FOR A LADY.

48 Calico day chemises.
30 Ditto night ditto.
24 Ditto drawers.
Ditto chemise and ditto.
24 Ditto petticoats.
4 Flannel ditto.
3 Ditto gowns.
18 Ditto waistcoats.
24 Cambric slips.
Ditto trousers.
12 Ditto long and short dressing-gowns.
30 Night caps.
4 Corsets.

Any quantity, { Coloured morning dresses,...
White ditto,...
Silk ditto,...
Dinner and evening ditto,...
An assortment of millinery,...
Spencers,...
A shawl,...
Book muslin handkerchiefs and frills,... } At any price.

48 Pocket handkerchiefs.
48 pair { Cotton stockings.
Silk ditto.
12 — Garters, } usual price.
12 — Gloves, }
9 — Shoes, ditto ditto.
5 Dozen cotton towels.
A clothes-bag.
36 Linen towels.
5 Yards Welch flannels.
A cot and screws.
1 Hair mattress and bolster.
1 Feather pillow.
1½ Pair blankets.
2 Counterpanes.
8 Pair sheets.
8 Pillowcases.

Tooth brushes and powder,...
Nail and hair ditto,...
Combs,...
4 Pounds of wax candles,...
A lamp or a candlestick, snuffers, &c.,...
Soap and perfumery,...
A looking-glass,...
A table and wash-hand stand, fitted up,...
A chair, and cabin furniture generally,...
1 Writing-desk and stationery,...
1 Penknife and scissors,...
1 Dressing-case, complete,...
A sofa, with drawers, &c.,...
Biscuits, confectionary, preserves, &c.,...
Leather trunks, with plates,...
Ribands and haberdashery,...
A curtain,...
4 Dozen Bristol water, or Malvern, in quarts,...
Green baize and oil-cloth for cabin,... } At the usual price.

With the exception of millinery, a lady's outfit costs from £30 to £80.

NECESSARIES FOR CADETS, WRITERS, AND MIDSHIPMEN.

A Mid's outfit, L.40 to L.70 A Cadet, . 60 110	Midshipmen.	Cadets.	Writers.
Striped cotton shirts,....	24		
White calico ditto, ...	36		
Ditto, full fronts,........	6	8	Dozen.
Calico night shirts,........	...		
Cotton caps or hair nets, ...	6	12	18
White cravats,...............	...	...	12
Coloured ditto,...............	...	...	24
Black silk ditto,............	6	6	6
Black stocks,................	...	2	...
White ditto,..................	...	...	...
Extra collars,...............	12	24	24
White pocket handkerchiefs, ...	...	12	24
Coloured cotton ditto,...	12	12	...
Silk pocket handkerchiefs,.................	6	12	18
Black silk handkerchiefs, ...	4	1	6
White silk hose,...........	...	...	...
Black ditto,..................	...	...	...
White silk half ditto,...	...	6	12
Black ditto ditto,.........	...	2	4
White cotton hose, ...	...	...	...
Brown cotton ditto,......	...	...	...
White cotton half ditto,	24	36	48
Brown ditto ditto,.........	...	...	...
Cotton gloves,..............	...	6	...
Leather ditto, ...	...	6	12
Cotton braces,..............	2	4	6
Silk ditto,....................	...	...	...
Flannel waistcoats, ...	6	12	12
Cotton ditto,................	...	...	...
Flannel drawers,...........	2	...	...
Cotton ditto,................	...	6	12
Flannel dressing-gown,.	...	...	...
Cotton ditto,................	...	1	1
White jean trousers,.....	6	12	18
Drill ditto,..................	6	24	24
Musquito ditto,.............	...	6	6
White jean jackets,.......	...	6	12
Ditto waistcoats,..........	...	6	18
Quilting ditto, ...	6	...	...
Duck trousers,.............	6	...	...
Travelling-cap, ...	1	1	1
Cot or hammock,..........	1	1	1
Hair mattress and bolster,....................	1	1	1

A Writer's outfit costs L.80 to L.140.	Midshipmen.	Cadets.	Writers.
Feather pillow,..............	1	1	1
Pair of blankets,...........	1	2	2
Counterpane,................	1	1	1
Pair of sheets,..............	...	10	12
Pillowcases,..................	6	10	12
Towels,........................	12	24	36
Tablecloths,..................	...	...	...
Clothes-bag,.................	1	1	1
Watch and shoe riband,	...	...	...
Sea-chest,....................	1	...	...
Camlet travelling-cloak,	...	1	1
Pea jacket and trousers,....................	1	...	...
Cloth coats and waistcoats,..................	1	2	3
Ditto trousers,..............	4	2	4
Bible and prayer-book,..	1	1	1
Blue jackets and trousers, ...	2	...	...
Pounds of soap,............	...	...	...
Pair of pistols,.............	...	1	1
Military sword,.............	...	1	...
Uniform hat, cockade, &c.,.......................	1	1	...
Sash and gorget,...........	...	1	...
Epaulets,......................	...	...	...
Waist-belt and sword-knot,......................	1	1	...
Buff shoulder-belt and plate,.....................	...	1	...
Round hats,..................	2	2	4
Sea ditto, ...	1	...	...
Saddle and bridle,.........	...	1	2
Dressing-case, with razors, knives, scissors, &c.,..........................	...	1	1
Stationery, assorted,....	...	...	...
Writing-desk, ...	1	1	1
Pewter basin, bottle, and tumbler,....................	1	1	1
Boots and shoes,..........	6	8	12
Cabin wash-hand stand,	...	1	1
Cabin chairs,................	...	2	2
Folding camp-stool,......	...	1	2
Small looking-glass, ...	1	1	1
Brushes,......................	1	6	6
Lamp or candlestick, snuffers, &c.,............	...	1	2

The East India Company have established the following scale of prices, for persons in their service proceeding to India, as passage-money in Company's ships, and captains are restricted from asking more *for accommodation at their table* :—

General officer,	£250
Member of council,	200
Lieutenant-colonel,	150
Major,	150
Senior merchant,	150
Junior ditto,	150
Factors,	150
Captains,	125

Writers,	£110	Including charter party allowance to owners.
Subalterns,	110	Including charter party allowance to owners.
Assist.-surgeons,	95	exclusive of ditto.
Cadets,	95	exclusive of ditto.

N.B.—In the third mates' mess of an Indiaman, a cadet's and ass.-surgeon's passage-money is £55.

The regulation of prices for officers in the *king's service* proceeding to India is as follows :—

General,	£235	These sums include the whole passage-money which can be demanded from king's officers *on duty*, and particular cabins are allotted for them on board Company's ships.
Colonel,	185	
Lieutenant-colonel,	135	
Major,	135	
Captains and Surgeons,	110	
Subalterns and Assistant-surgeons,	95	

As no cabins are allotted by the Company for passengers (*except* to officers in the king's service, or to their own officers when in charge of troops), the captain is at liberty to let his cabins, and those who require them pay a sum in addition to the above prices. There is no allowance for officers' wives and children. An officer with his wife will require a separate cabin, in which case he will be charged an extra sum beyond the regulation, both for his wife's passage and for a cabin. Ladies should have all their millinery, gloves, &c., which they do not intend to use on the voyage, packed in air-tight tin cases, soldered up. A piano should be packed in blankets ; and a silk cover, lined with a *blanket*, is the most useful kind of cover in India for a piano. A Broadwood grand piano, *secured for the climate*, is the best description of instrument. Those of the common kind sometimes go to pieces in a single night during the prevalence of hot winds. The action of the hot wind on furniture, particularly on musical instruments, is very remarkable, and makes it highly necessary to have both well secured by clamps, and properly packed. Solid mahogany, covered with leather, having spare brown Holland covers, is best adapted for the voyage; and to those who can afford it, handsome furniture of this description will be very acceptable after reaching India. Oil-cloth is the best and coolest thing for the cabin-floor, and is very much used for the same purpose in India. A cadet who has a cabin to himself, should furnish and fit it in such a manner that his equipment will be equally adapted for a tent.

Parents who have children destined for India would do well to consider that in all Indostan Proper there is not an inn or hotel to which it is usual for ladies or gentlemen to resort, except in cases of urgent necessity. Even in Calcutta, the taverns are commonly called punch-houses. This is a very evident proof of the liberal scale of Indian hospitality. It therefore becomes the duty of parents, particularly in the case of a young lady, to place beyond all doubt the certainty of her reception at the house of a friend or acquaintance actually residing at the Presidency to which she is going. And it should never be forgotten that some of the stations in India are 1000 miles distant from the different presidencies, which makes it extremely desirable (if the relations or friends she is going to reside at one of the distant stations) to have an understanding *before* she leaves England, that there shall be some friend ready to receive her on the day of the ship's arrival. Cadets, on landing, by reporting themselves to the town-major, are immediately provided with quarters.

The cabins of private traders vary in size and arrangement, but those of the Company's ships mostly resemble each other. On the next two pages plans are given, one of the Orwell, a regular Indiaman; and the other of the Victory, a private trader.

It is hoped that the foregoing remarks will be found useful to persons bound for India. The remainder of this article shall be devoted to a description of the usual route pursued by the regular Indiamen and free traders. Some apology may be necessary for the nautical phraseology employed; but it is at all times difficult to communicate professional knowledge except in the terms commonly applied in each particular profession; and as public attention has lately been much occupied with works on naval subjects, it may be presumed that most readers are familiar with the peculiar language of seamen.

As ships are generally in the hands of a pilot till they

PLAN

OF

THE HON. COMPANY'S SHIP ORWELL,

1336 Tons, Captain James Dalrymple.

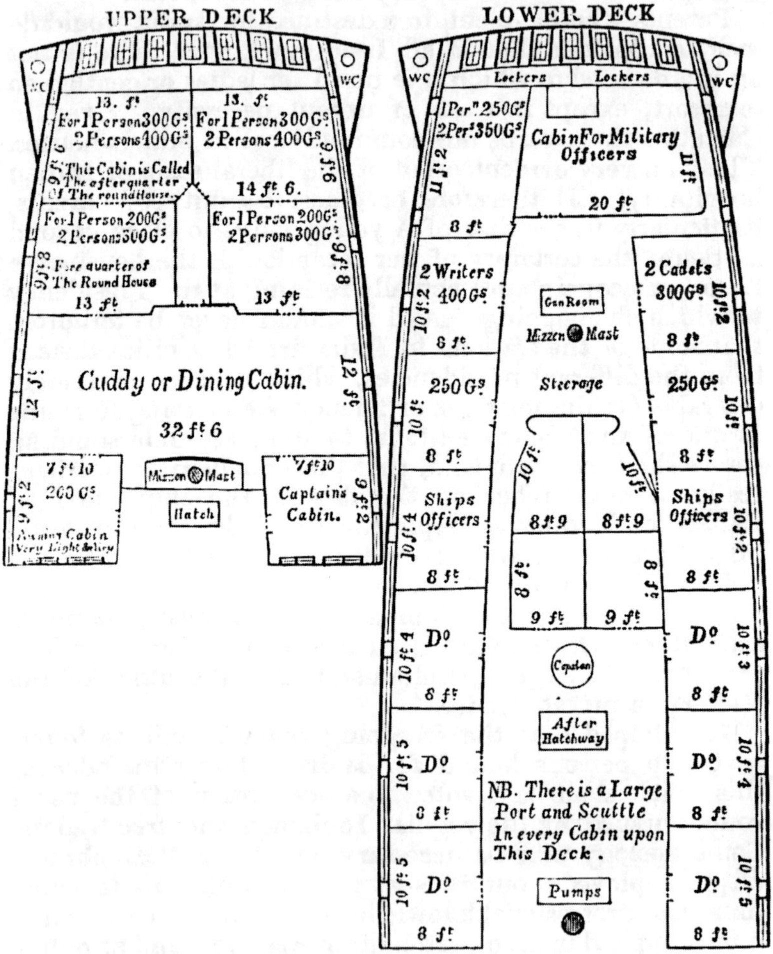

The Prices marked in Cabins are average Prices, subject to Alteration according to the number of Occupants in each.

PLAN

OF

THE TEAK SHIP VICTORY,

Registered 712 Tons, Christ. Biden, Commander.

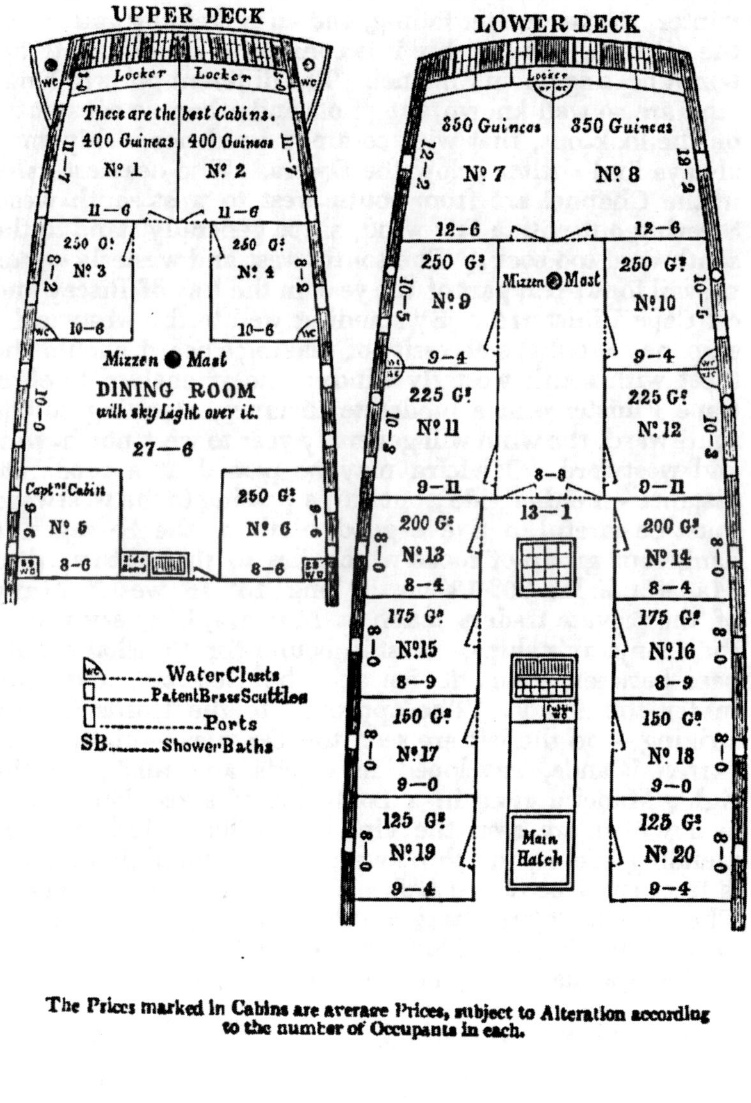

The Prices marked in Cabins are average Prices, subject to Alteration according to the number of Occupants in each.

get well down Channel, it would be superfluous to give instructions for any part of the voyage above the Isle of Wight. With a fair wind, the course from the back of the Wight is west by north half north by compass, and it will be useful to note which way the wind is inclined to veer. If to the northward and westward, it will be advisable to keep the shore on board till past the Lizard. If the wind is inclined to the south-eastward, a west by north course is the best. With a raw ship's company in winter, the barometer falling, and an increasing gale, after the pilot has left the ship it is considered hazardous to attempt beating down Channel. The different ports in England are so well known, the pilots and others so constantly on the look-out, that with common prudence a ship may always find shelter below the Owers. The heaviest gales in the Channel are from south-west to west-south-west. Steering out with a fair wind, ships generally stand to the southward too soon. The south-west and westerly winds prevail for a great part of the year in the Bay of Biscay and off Cape Finisterre. By standing well to the westward a ship may avoid the necessity of making a board, should she meet with south-westerly winds; and if enabled to clear Cape Finisterre at a moderate distance, standing to the southward, the wind will generally veer to west-north-west and westward. Madeira may be passed at a moderate distance on either side; but ships passing to the westward must be careful to give a good berth to the Salvages, a dangerous group of rocks which lies to the southward of Madeira, in lat. 30° 13′ north, long. 15° 46′ west.* Many of the private traders touch at Madeira, but very few of the Company's ships. A ship bound for Funchal should pass between Point de Sol and the Desertas, and haul in for the Roads. The approach to the Roads is very striking,—on the left are seen the Desertas,—high, dark, barren islands, enveloped in clouds and mist; on the right, Madeira rises in a bold cliff of a reddish aspect, over which are seen the vine-clad hills. With a commanding breeze, the ship sweeps round Point de Sol, and is frequently becalmed before she gets near the anchorage. The merchants are always on the look-out, and ever ready to welcome their friends from England.

Madeira may be termed the *first stage* in a voyage to

* Capt. Owen—Salvages, Piton, { East Rock, lat. 30° 3′ N., long. 16° 2′ W.
Large Islet, — 30 7 N., — 15 54 W.

India, and is usually performed in eight or ten days. By this time people have been *shook*, or *rolled*, or *pitched* into their places. The weather has become genial, the scene is new, and the deck of an Indiaman full of troops and passengers presents a gay appearance on her arrival at Madeira. The style of society on board the regular ships is extremely good. There is no doubt much restraint and great attention to etiquette; but a reflecting mind will at once perceive how necessary restriction must be where a mere handful of officers have to keep in a state of prompt obedience a crew of 130 seamen of all characters, and sometimes three or four hundred troops in addition. Some allowance ought to be made for a commander who is often placed in very trying circumstances; and when it is considered that he can neither select his officers, nor choose his passengers, and that the ship is sometimes fairly at sea in forty-eight hours after the captain, passengers, and crew have joined her, it must be apparent, that to produce perfect harmony is sometimes attended with great difficulty. The following sketch of a day will show the usual routine on board an Indiaman:—At daylight the upper deck is washed and scoured with sand and stones from stem to stern. This operation occupies the watch upon deck till seven o'clock, when the decks are dried up, the awnings and curtains spread. At half-past seven the hammocks are piped up and stowed in the nettings. The troops are paraded a few minutes before eight (which ensures the punctual attendance of the soldier-officers at breakfast), and some commanders parade the cadets with the troops, which is recommended. Breakfast at eight, hot rolls, dried fish of various kinds, preserves, cold meats, &c. The ship's progress during the night is a constant and always interesting theme of conversation. During the forenoon, passengers lounge about the deck, and amuse themselves in watching the evolutions of the ship, or the occupations of the different tradesmen. In the waist the armourer and his mate are working at the forge, and the clang of the anvil has quite a shore-like sound. The carpenter's crew occupy a prominent place; the lee-side of the deck is devoted to sail-making and mending. In the cuddy the middys are writing their journals and working days-works. Below, a fatigue party of the soldiers are cleaning their berths and accoutrements; the surgeon and his assistant are administering to the wants of the sick; and part of the crew are employed in getting water and provisions out of the hold. In this manner, every one (except the passengers) is occupied during the forenoon. At twelve the ship's position is ascertained by observation, and the last twenty-four hours' progress is duly noted. Most of the passengers assemble at this time to learn the result and discuss the matter over a glass of wine and water and biscuit. At one the officers mess, the ship's company and soldiers dine, which clears the deck, and offers an opportunity to the passengers for an hour's exercise. At three the captain's dinner is served.* It is the usual and wholesome practice in the regular Indiamen to dress for dinner. By four o'clock the tradesmen's work is put below, the decks entirely cleared, and in the cool of the evening dancing is the usual amusement. Like all other small societies, that of a ship depends very much upon the elements of which it is composed. Most people get over the mere inconvenience of being at sea by the time they reach Madeira, and to a well-composed party, there is nothing in the regulations and etiquette of a Company's ship to prevent the utmost extension of amusement and good humour. Theatricals are very common, and newspapers have been known to succeed in a large party. To a mind dependent on a variety of external objects for sources of amusement, an India voyage is dull enough; but the human mind is fertile in expedients, as may be seen by the following instance:—A number of sporting characters being met on board an Indiaman, for lack of amusement, established a shooting club, and although *Davy Jones* bagged all the pintadoes and Mother Carey's chickens, yet they kept up an incessant fire, and sometimes killed twenty or thirty head of game in a day! Bishop Heber, speaking of his voyage, says, "I find two circumstances for which at sea I was by no means prepared; that, namely, we have no great time for study, and that, for me at least, there is so much which interests and occupies me, that I have no apprehensions of time hanging heavy on my hands."

* The liberal scale on which the table of an East India captain is conducted, being so well known, needs no comment. Of late years, the method of preserving fresh meat for any length of time has added greatly to the luxury of the table. Fresh salmon and game of all kinds retain their flavour unimpaired during the whole voyage.

Sunday is strictly observed, and the captain is liable to a pecuniary penalty for omitting to perform divine service. The scene is very impressive; the decks get an extra scrub, awnings and curtains spread, white hammock-cloths fore and aft. The capstan is the pulpit, covered with a union-jack. The capstan-bars form benches for the seamen on each side the forepart of the quarter-deck; chairs for the officers and passengers abaft. At five bells (half-past ten) a blue burgee is hoisted at the mizzen-peak as a signal to ships in company to prevent interruption. The bell is tolled, troops paraded on the poop, passengers and crew seated on the quarter-deck, and divine service is performed by the captain, with the purser reading the responses. In most cases the crew are very attentive.

The Canaries are eleven in number, four of them small, extending from lat. 27° 40′ to 29° 20′ north, and from long. 13° 35′ to 18° 6′ west. They are mostly high with steep rocky shores, rendering the landing often impracticable, and they are all destitute of safe harbours for large ships. After passing to the westward of the Canaries, some navigators prefer the route outside of the Cape de Verd Islands. The north-east trade is thought to blow stronger in the open sea; but many of the Company's ships pass between the Islands and Cape de Verd, keeping about mid-channel, by which the distance is much shortened. The writer of this article has often pursued this route with success, and passed twice near the spot assigned to the Bonetta shoal without perceiving any indication of shoal-water. The north-east trade between the islands occasionally veers to east, and brings from the African coast clouds of sand, which covers the rigging on the side next the shore. After losing the north-east trade, the weather generally becomes very sultry, with frequent heavy showers and squalls. Long calms are often experienced; and the occasional breezes which spring up are of short duration and most uncertain. This kind of weather is called by sailors the doldrums.

The tedium of this part of the voyage is often enlivened by the capture of a shark or dolphin. In a large Indiaman full of troops, the scene which ensues upon taking the first shark is most amusing. The huge animal, sometimes twelve feet in length, is hoisted in amid the shouts of the recruits, who all crowd round the victim. The Jacks, who always endeavour to play off a trick on the soldiers, take this opportunity of making a rush behind them,—down they all go, head over heels, and some poor devil finds himself hugging in a close embrace the ravenous monster of the deep, with forty or fifty of his comrades heaped on him. The beautiful little fish called the pilot-fish, which always accompanies (or rather precedes) the shark, has been known to follow a ship for six weeks after the shark to which it belonged was taken! The flying-fish are seen in large flocks near the line. Single ones sometimes fly on board. They are good eating, and the mode of catching them at the island of Anna Bona is curious: The head of some large fish, such as the albacore, is hung even with the water's edge, to the side of a canoe, which collects the flying-fish in great numbers; the fisherman stands up in the canoe, dives into the midst of the fish, and comes up generally with one in each hand.*

The fish called the Nautilus always excites great interest, and seamen call it a Portugee man-o'-war. Its little sail is composed of bony fibres, covered with a thin filmy substance of transparent blue. The body of the fish is just a round piece of blubber, with a number of long slimy *roots* hanging down, and floats even with the water's edge; over this rises the tiny sail. Its power of locomotion seems to be derived from the sail, for it always contrives to get out of a ship's way.

Both the outward and homeward bound ships endeavour to cross the line at the same point, from long. 18° west to long. 23° west. This is also the favourite cruising-ground for pirates. The fatal instance of the ship North Star, where many of the officers and passengers were wantonly murdered by the pirates, who even extended their brutal outrage to the unoffending ladies, ought to serve as a warning to the commanders of India

---

* This singular manner of catching fish brings to mind a still more remarkable mode of fishing practised in China: The fisherman is furnished with a very finely tapered rod; the line is considerably longer than the rod. The hook is fixed to the side of a piece of lead in shape and size like the little finger. The fish are about three inches in length, and live in holes on a mud bank over which the water flows and ebbs. The fisherman stands on the mud at low water, watching the fish, and the moment one is seen within distance popping up its head, the line is thrown with great dexterity, and nine times out of ten the fish is hooked in the side by a jerk of the hand,—like tipping a fly off the leader's ear with a four-in-hand whip!

traders; and as the long continuance of peace is likely to increase piracy, ships cannot be too much on their guard, or too well prepared with the means of resistance.

The following table of Horsburgh will show the equatorial limits of the trades between the 18° and 26° of west long. It exhibits the actual experience of about 230 of the Company's ships.

Months.	Lost N. E. Trade Outward in		Got N. E. Trade Homeward in		Mean out and Home.	Lost S. E. Trade Homeward in		Got S. E. Trade Outward in		Mean out and Home.
	Latitude north	Mean north	Latitude north	Mean north	north	Latitude north	Mean north	Latitude north	Mean north	north
Jan.	5° to 10°	7°	3° to 6°	4½°	5¾°	½° to 4°	2¼°	2° to 4°	3°	2¾°
Feb.	5 — 10	7	2 — 7	5	6	2S. — 3	1½	½ — 1	1	1¼
March	2½ — 8	5½	2 — 7	5	5¼	1 — 2	1	½ — 2½	1½	1¼
April	4 — 9	6	4 — 8	5½	5¾	2 — 2½	1	0 — 2½	1½	1¼
May	5 — 10	7	4½ — 7	6	6½	1N — 4	2½	0 — 4	3	2¾
June	7 — 13	9	7 — 12	9	9	1 — 5	3	0 — 5	3	3
July	8½ — 15	12	11 — 14	12	12	1 — 6	4	1 — 5	3	3½
Aug.	11 — 15	13	11 — 14½	13	13	3 — 5	4	1 — 4	2½	3¾
Sept.	9 — 14	11½	11 — 14	12	11¾	2 — 4	3½	1 — 3	2	3
Oct.	7½ — 13	10	8½ — 14	10	10	2 — 5	3	1 — 5	3	3
Nov.	6 — 11	9	7 — 0	7	8	3 — 4	3½	3 — 5	4	3¾
Dec.	5 — 7	6	3 — 6	5	5½	1 — 4	2½	1 — 4½	4	3¼

The observations in some of the months are rather few to obtain a correct mean; but the first column, showing the extreme limits for each, will be most useful to refer to, as it marks the situation where the trades may reasonably be expected to fail or commence.

The curious ceremony observed by seamen crossing the line, is thus described by Bishop Heber in his journal:—

"*July* 25.—To-day the first or introductory part of the ceremony usual on passing the line took place. Soon after dark, Neptune's boat was supposed to approach the ship, of which notice was given in the regular form to the officer on watch. A sailor from the fore-chains, in a dismal voice, aggravated by a speaking-trumpet, hailed the captain, as if from the sea; and after a short conversation, carried on with becoming gravity, Neptune was supposed to take his leave, and a barrel, with a lighted candle in it, was sent off from the fore-chains to represent his boat dropping astern.

"*July* 26.—To-day we passed the line, and the greater part of it was spent in the mummeries usual on such occasions, which went off very well and in good humour. The passengers were not liable to the usual interrogatories and shaving; but the male part of them took their share in the splashing and wetting, which made up the main fun of these naval Saturnalia. I was a good deal surprised at the contrivance exhibited by the masqueraders in dressing out (with help of a little oakum and paint, a few fish-skins and decayed finery) the various characters of Neptune, Amphitrite, Mercury, Triton, &c., with far more attention to classical costume than I expected. With the distance and usual aids of a theatre, the show would not have been contemptible; while there was, as might be supposed, a sufficient mixture of the ludicrous to suit the purposes of fun and caricature."

After crossing the line the south-east trade is entered. The ship is kept clean full, and runs rapidly down the coast of South America. The island of Trinidad lies in long. 29° 10′ west, and lat. 20° 22′ south, and is often* seen by ships passing to the southward through the south-east trade. It is a high, rocky, barren island, with stupendous detached rocks round it. It may be passed quite close on either side. Here the trade-wind is sometimes interrupted, or occasionally shifts to north-east in passing. As the wind veers to the northward and eastward, the ship's course is altered so as to enable her to pass the meridian of Greenwich in the latitude of the Cape of Good Hope. From Trinidad to the Cape, ships commonly experience fair strong winds and fine weather.

This is probably the most agreeable period of the whole voyage. For the first time the prow of the ship is pointed directly towards her place of destination, supposing that to be the Cape of Good Hope. To the bitter cold of the Channel,—the turbulence of the Bay of Biscay,—the excessive heat of the line,—the comfortless uncertainty of the doldrums, has succeeded the fresh healthful breeze of the great South Atlantic, with a temperate atmosphere, and serene cloudless weather;—so cloudless, that the planets Venus and Jupiter are often distinctly seen during the daytime without a telescope. Here, too, the monotony of the scene is enlivened by the appearance of numerous birds. First appears the pintado, a pretty black and white bird about the size of a pigeon; it is usually first seen after leaving the tropic. These birds will accompany a ship for six weeks, and fly close enough to be shot in great numbers. They are also caught with a hook and line. Next, the

* Captain Owen—Trinidad, south pt. long. 29° 21′ W., lat. 20° 31′ S.

albatross, a noble bird, which is also sometimes caught with a hook. Petrels or Mother Carey's chickens are very numerous. Immediately before a gale, these birds, with many others, assemble near the ship in large flocks. Much amusement is often afforded by a bird called the booby. It has probably acquired this name from the stupid manner in which it allows itself to be taken, as it seldom moves from where it lights, and may always be caught by hand.

In this route, the small group called Tristan d'Acunha is sometimes seen. It consists of three high barren islands. The watering-place is about the middle of the north side of the largest;—the water is plentiful and good. The landing is easy, upon a beach of pebbles; the anchorage is in deep water, and not safe except in very fine weather. The lat. of this group is about 37° 5′ south, long. 12° 2′ west.*

In approaching the islands during thick weather great caution is necessary. In 1820, the Blendenhall, Captain Greig, struck the steep shingly beach on the south side of the largest island before land was discovered; the crew and passengers got ashore with difficulty, and the ship almost immediately went to pieces. Some bales of light goods, of which clothes were made for those who had escaped without them, and a patent iron buoy, which was cut in two and converted into a cooking utensil, were the only things saved. The party subsisted several weeks on penguins and on the fish caught from the projecting rocks. A curious trait of Jack's improvident character occurred while they were on the island: A sailor had been missing some days, and while his comrades were roaming about in search of him, they came to a rum-cask standing on end. A halt was instantly called; and, having duly ascertained its marks and number, they resolved to taste the contents. Proceeding to make a tap, they found it to be empty; and on removing it discovered their missing companion fast asleep. When roused he explained to them, that, strolling about two days before, he had hit upon the cask, and indulged in potations so liberally and so long that he felt himself getting uncomfortably chill, and thought the best thing he could do was to knock the end out of the cask, and capsize it over him as a shelter from the cold night-air and heavy rain. The crew, after being some

* Captain Owen—Tristan d'Acunha, long. 12° 23′ W., lat. 37° 17′ S.

time on the island, constructed (with the help of the surgeon's case of instruments!) a small boat, which enabled them to reach a neighbouring island whence they had observed smoke ascending. There they found several American seamen, left by a whaler to kill seals; and the vessel calling some days after, conveyed them to the Cape of Good Hope.

A ship not bound to the Cape, after passing the meridian of Greenwich in lat. 35° south, from December to April should keep between 37° and 39° in running down her easting; for the winds will be found as favourable in this parallel as in a higher latitude. On this point, however, there is much difference of opinion; and general rules are often set aside when a spurt of fair wind tempts one to point the ship's head towards her port. Ships bound to the Cape ought to increase the latitude to 35° or 35½° as they draw to the eastward, to avoid the risk of being blown to the northward by southerly winds, which are frequently experienced near the Cape, particularly in February and March. From December to April, if a ship is bound for India without touching at the Cape, she should get into lat. 37° or 38° about the meridian of London; and passing the Cape in parallel 39°, more favourable winds are likely to be met with than farther south.

In passing the Bank of Aguilhas, the stream of current setting westward is avoided by keeping to the southward of 37°. To the northward of this parallel south-east winds prevail in the summer season, from December to April,—which, it may be observed, is just the reverse of our summer. If a ship bound for Table Bay should be blown to the northward, the soundings between Saldanha Bay and Table Bay prove a good guide, and are regular, extending several leagues from the shore. The Table Mountain is so remarkable that it cannot be mistaken: It is perfectly flat at the top, and, being 3500 feet above the level of the sea, is the highest land in that neighbourhood. The east and west ends are nearly perpendicular. The land is high and uneven from Table Mountain to the extremity of the Cape of Good Hope. Table Bay is considered quite safe in summer, from October to April, and many ships touch there in winter, although the risk of north-westerly gales blowing into the bay with much violence and a high sea is very great. In the summer months, when the Table Mountain is covered with a white fleecy cloud, which is called the Devil's table-cloth, it indicates a strong south-easter, for which ships ought to prepare accordingly. When the mountain is free from cloud, this gale (which is almost of daily recurrence) will be mild; and a gentle sea-breeze blows in on the western side of the bay, when a fresh south-east breeze prevails from the east side half across during most of the day. The Dutch fixed upon the 10th of May as the latest day for remaining in Table Bay. Cape Town is a delightful resting-place either on the voyage out or home. The old Dutch houses are large, commodious, and clean. Most of the inhabitants take in passengers to board at a moderate rate. Refreshments of all kinds are plentiful. Horses and carriages are to be had, and most people pay a visit to Constantia, where the celebrated vine of that name is grown. The vine is a small bush, and the grapes of delicious flavour. Constantia is situated in a cleft of the hills, on the edge of a romantic glen. The wanderer from Caledonia is here gratified by the sight of heath in great beauty and infinite variety; and John Bull may fancy himself at home when the noble oaks which abound at Constantia meet his eye. The Cape horses are particularly fine, and show much blood. They are driven six-in-hand. A team of young horses, which would grace any nobleman's carriage in England, may often be seen cantering along with a clumsy waggon behind them. The inhabitants of Cape Town promenade in a fine public garden, which is overtopped by the magnificent Table Mountain; to the north is the Bay studded with shipping; and the Lion's Mount bounds the westward view.

Ships should endeavour to make the land to the southward of the entrance to Table Bay, as the current sets regularly round the Cape to the north-westward as far as the high land on the west side of the bay, where it is met by the southerly current setting down along-shore from Dassen Island. From the Cape to Table Bay the land is steep-to, and safe to approach within one and a half or two miles. The passage into the bay is between Green Point and Penguin Island. The latter must not be passed nearer than two miles to avoid the Whale Rock, which is about one mile and a half from its southern extreme. In going out of the Bay the channel to the northward of Penguin Island is the best. False Bay is formed by the Cape of Good Hope on the west, and Cape Hanglip on the east.

The middle and eastern parts of the bay are thought free from danger. Simon's Bay is four leagues northward from Cape Point, and near the north-west corner of False Bay. There is a small town here, chiefly inhabited by Dutch. The road to Cape Town is very indifferent, and the journey is usually performed in a covered waggon with fourteen or sixteen tall bullocks. A Hottentot boy runs before, and the driver has an immense whip, which requires both hands. The bullocks trot along at a good pace. Ships bound to the eastward should leave the bay when north-west winds begin to blow; if bound to the westward, they should wait till these winds are on the decline, and get under sail when they shift to the westward, as it is probable they will veer from west to south-west and south-east, which will be favourable for doubling the Cape. After leaving Table or Simon's Bay, bound to the eastward, it is advisable to stand well to the southward across the Bank of Aguilhas, to avoid the stream of current setting over the bank to the westward. To the southward of latitude 37° an easterly current is often felt, and greatly facilitates the progress to the eastward, particularly as the winds are uncertain and unsettled hereabouts. Around the Cape Bank the winds in changing follow the course of the sun. The heavy gales generally blow from north-west; if the wind backs to north-north-west it increases; if it veers to west-south-west it decreases; and when at south-west the gale breaks. It is very useful to note this fact; for ships bound eastward are often tempted to make northing when running before a north-westerly gale; whereas the latitude should then be increased to allow for being headed off to the northward as the wind veers round to the eastward, which it has been known to do five or six times in a week.

The southernmost land of Africa is Cape Aguilhas or Lagullas. It is found to be farther south than early navigators supposed, being in lat. 34° 55′ south, long. 20° 18′* east, bearing east 20° south from the Cape of Good Hope, distant thirty leagues. It is low even land, and may be seen five or six leagues from the deck. There is no high land within several miles in any direction. The Gunner's Quoin, a very remarkable hill of that shape, is three or four leagues west-north-west of Cape La-

* Captain Owen—Cape Lagullas, long. 19° 56′ E., lat. ° 51′ S.

gullas, and is often seen before the low land about this cape, and sometimes mistaken for it. The Quoin appears isolated and slopes down to the eastward. From the Cape of Good Hope to Algoa Bay a bank of soundings projects to the southward, in some respects conforming to the shape of the coast. The southern point of the bank is supposed to be in long. 22° east, lat. 37° south. Westward of Cape Aguilhas, to the southward of 35° 15′ south, the soundings are generally mud; to the southward of the Cape, green sand, on the south-east and eastern parts of the bank, mostly coral, coarse sand, shells, and small stones. Abreast of Cape Aguilhas and the land to the eastward of the Cape, there are generally from forty to fifty fathoms three or four leagues from the shore.

The current which prevails over this bank has been the subject of much speculation, and Major Rennell took great pains to explain its direction and velocity. For this purpose he published a chart of the bank for the winter months. It must be evident that such a chart could only be used for general purposes; for the current is found to vary in the same months of different years,—is often obstructed and changed in its direction by gales of wind,—sometimes ceasing altogether even in fine weather. A variety of opinions exist as to the originating cause of this current. The most generally received is the following:—By the constant action of the south-east trade-wind, the water of the great Indian Ocean is displaced, or forced before the breeze to the north-westward, round the north end of Madagascar, finds its way to the southward through the Mozambique, and takes a westerly direction round the Cape. To account for this westerly direction, it must be observed, that the constant action of north-west and westerly winds on the west side of the Cape causes a displacement of water, which the westerly current runs to replace. It must be sufficiently obvious, that if this is the true theory on the subject, it becomes impossible to give any specific rules for determining with accuracy either the duration, velocity, or direction, of this remarkable current. After a gale from the westward, if the current has been repressed by the gale, it generally runs with redoubled velocity. The current is generally weak near the land, and the sea smooth. Horsburgh gives the following as the general course of the current:—"In June, July, and August, from about long. 37° or 40° east, the current generally sets westward between lat. 30° and 35° south, till it reaches the eastern part of the Cape Bank, off Algoa Bay. On the coast of Natal it sets along-shore to south-westward, till joined by the oceanic stream on the edge of the bank in 27½° or 28° east long., between Algoa Bay and Infanta River. After the junction it increases in strength abreast of Algoa Bay, and takes the direction of the outline of the bank, which is west by south nearly, to long. about 23½° west. In this space it often diverges a little from the outline of the bank, setting west by south one-half south, or west-south-west, but seldom if ever west-north-west or west by north, as represented by the charts. In long. 23½° east, the edge of the bank begins to take a south-westerly direction; soon after, about south-south-west one-half west nearly to its southern extremity. Here also the current follows its concave outline, taking a south-westerly course in long. 24° east; and from 23° east it generally sets about south-west by south to the southern extremity of the bank in long 21¾° or 22° east. The velocity of the current is greatest from long. 25° to 22° east, along that part of the bank which takes the most southerly direction. At the southern extremity of the bank it seldom runs strong beyond lat. 36½° south, or to the westward of long. 21° east." An easterly or contra current is sometimes felt to the southward of soundings on the Cape Bank. By the help of the westerly current, ships get round the Cape in the winter months against the north-westerly gales which then prevail, generally blowing with great fury for two or three days together; the wind then veers to the southward and westward,—then to south-east, where it lulls. After this a favourable spurt from the eastward is experienced, of which advantage should be taken to place the ship in a situation on the bank most favourable for the westerly current.

A few remarks on the marine barometer may be useful here; for there is no part of the world where this valuable instrument acts so truly as off the Cape. It gives certain indication of the north-westerly gales by a rapid fall of the mercury, and it often does this when the weather is perfectly serene;—its warning ought never to be disregarded. In the southern hemisphere the mercury rises with southerly, and falls with northerly winds. During light winds from the south-eastward, after a gale off the Cape, it commonly stands high, and a considerable fall takes place when the wind veers to the north-east, although no gale should follow. This merely results from the change of temperature,—the northerly winds being warmer than those proceeding from the frozen regions round the south pole. If the mercury continues to fall after the breeze is settled from the northward, then more wind may certainly be expected. During the heaviest gale the writer of this article ever experienced off the Cape, the mercury stood as low as 28.98.

Before proceeding to notice the different routes to India, it will be needful to give a general description of the trade-winds and monsoons in the Indian Seas.

Trade-winds blow from the same quarter during the whole year. They are probably called *trade*-winds, from the circumstance of their strength and duration being propitious to commerce. Without entering into a scientific disquisition on the subject, it is highly interesting to observe the beautiful adaptation of winds to the purposes of intercourse between distant countries. In some short voyages, a different disposition of winds might facilitate the passage; but with a chart of the world before the eye, it will be at once conceded, that to imagine monsoons where trade-winds now exist, or take away land and sea breezes, placing uncertain variable winds instead,—or, in short, to alter the laws which now govern winds all over the world, would certainly impede intercourse by sea. It must be observed that trade-winds are liable to be obstructed by the vicinity of land, and only blow constantly in the open sea. The presence of the sun in either hemisphere obstructs the regularity and strength of the trade-wind in that hemisphere, and *vice versa*.

The trade-winds generally extend as far as 28° on each side the equator. Between the trades there is a space of light variable winds, mostly from the west, forming a kind of monsoon near the equator in several parts of the globe. In the Indian Ocean the south-east trade prevails from 10° south to 28° south; from lat. 10° south to the coast of India the winds are periodical.

In February, March, April, and May, the southern limit of the south-east trade in the Indian Ocean is frequently extended to 30° south, and blows at this season from east to east-north-east. Near Madagascar, the Islands of Mauritius and Bourbon, the trade-wind is often obstructed by sudden changes and hurricanes. In one of these violent storms the Honourable Company's

China ship Dunira of 1300 tons was totally dismasted, and forced to seek shelter at the Isle of France. She was running down the trade with every stitch of canvass set in the morning, and before midnight she lay a mere hulk on the water without a stick standing.* Another and later instance may be mentioned as a caution to navigators. The Honourable Company's ship Bridgewater was dismasted in a typhoon off Macao, and refitted at Whampoa chiefly from her own resources. On her homeward voyage with many passengers on board, in long. 90° east, lat. 18° south, running down the trade, the barometer indicated bad weather. The ship was well manned, and commanded by a most skilful and intelligent officer, Captain Manderson. Preparation was promptly made, and every precaution was taken which human foresight could suggest, to encounter the approaching gale. It came, and lasted for fifty-six hours with unremitted violence. The ship lost every thing but her foremast and bowsprit,—her guns and part of her cargo were thrown overboard,—the anchors were cut away, and she bore up for Calcutta, was condemned, and broken up. Had the warning of the barometer, which fell to 28.70, been neglected, and the ship less skilfully handled, her total loss would most probably have ensued. The hurricane commenced at east, veered to north, and broke up at west.

From the equator to the 10th or 12th degree of south latitude, east and east-south-east winds blow six months of the year, from April to November, with dry weather,—and this is called the easterly *line* monsoon. From October to April, west, north-west, and north-north-west winds prevail within these limits, with cloudy weather and rain,—which is the westerly *line* monsoon. The westerly winds are strongest in December and January; but are never so constant as the easterly winds in the opposite monsoon, which is frequently extended to the equator in June, July, and August, from long. 45° east to 90° east. During the south-east or easterly monsoon to the southward of the equator, on the north side of it, the south-west monsoon prevails, which is the rainy

* The mainmast in its fall broke through the poop-deck, and the tresseltrees, which may be about two feet apart, struck down the cot of Sir William Frazer (late of the Company's civil service in China), who was lying in it at the time,—passing one on each side of his breast without doing him the slightest injury.

season on the coasts of India. It commences in April at the north part of the Arabian Sea and Bay of Bengal, but seldom till May near the line, which is its southern limit; thence it blows home to all the coasts of India and Arabia, continuing till October. This is a changeable month, and liable to gales on the Malabar coast and Bay of Bengal. In October, or early in November, when the north-west or westerly monsoon begins south of the equator, the north-east monsoon commences in the Arabian Sea and Bay of Bengal, and lasts till April, with fair weather. The line is the boundary between the north-east monsoon and north-west wind to the southward, but a space of light variable winds intervenes. Between Ceylon and Achen Head, from the line to 8° or 10° north lat., westerly winds are often experienced in October and November, which blow strong at times. On and near the line these winds are mostly from north-west and north-north-west. In a line across, from Achen Head to Ceylon, they are from west-north-west to west-south-west; and farther north, from south-west to south-south-west.

After passing the Cape, the most direct route for the western coasts of India is through the Mozambique Channel, which is seventy-one leagues wide at its narrowest part, in about lat. 15° south. The south-west monsoon blows through the Mozambique Channel at the same time that it prevails on all the coasts of India. In this channel the south-west monsoon is the fine-weather season, and the sea is commonly smooth. It has several dangerous points; but by a diligent use of the sextant and chronometer, there is little risk in attempting this passage during the fair season, from April to September. On the coast of Africa the current sets strong to the southward and westward nearly all the year round; and the early Portuguese navigators named Cape Corrientes from the difficulty they experienced in getting round it to the northward.

In mid-channel the currents are variable and uncertain, and require great caution. On the Madagascar shore the set is mostly to the northward in the south-west monsoon. Between Cape Corrientes and Madagascar a south-easterly current is sometimes experienced, by which ships have been set over towards St Augustin or Cape St Mary. When running to the northward in mid-channel, among the Comoro Islands and between Cape Amber and the coast of Querimba, the currents set westward all the year round. Ships bound for the Mozambique, after passing the Cape, should keep in the parallel of 34° or 35° south, till they reach 37° east long., and then shape a course for mid-channel, where the winds are more steady, and only three dangers in the way:—the first is the Europa Rocks,—the highest about the size of a long-boat, and the sea at times breaks over them all. Captain Huddart gives the following as the geographical site:—Northern extreme of the shoal in lat. 21° 28′ south, and the westernmost in long. 40° 8′ east by lunars, and 39° 58′ east by chronometer. Captain Horsburgh thinks the shoal lies a little to the west of this position. Secondly, the Bassas de India is an island five or six miles in length and two or three in breadth, highest at the northern part, where there are a few trees. The rest of it is covered with brushwood, and has a white sandy beach. It is in long. 40° 37′ east, and the south end in lat. 22° 26′ south. It may be seen six leagues from the mast-head. It is thought to have no soundings within two or three miles. Juan de Nova or St Christopher is an island situated in lat. 17° 2′ south, long. 43° 9′ east, about a mile in circumference, of a round form, with a reef projecting two miles to the southward, and more than a mile north-west and north-east from the island. It is forty feet high and surrounded by breakers. The Europa Rocks and Bassas de India may be passed on either side. Juan de Nova should be passed to the westward, and thence a direct course for Mohilla or Comoro is the best. In April, or early in May, the winds are more steady to the west of Comoro,—rather to the westward of the mid-channel track. Cape St Mary, the southern extreme of Madagascar, lies in lat. 25° 40′ south, and long. 45° 16′* east. The Star Bank, which is an extensive and dangerous shoal, is sixty miles west-north-west from Cape St Mary, and at least five leagues from the shore. It is steep-to on the west side: there is an unfrequented channel between it and the shore. It extends from lat. 25° 7′ south, to 25° 25′ south, and is in long. about 44° 16′ east. The Comoro Islands are high, bold, and may be seen sixteen to twenty leagues in clear weather. They are inhabited by Mohammedans, a mixed race of Arabs incorporated with Africans. Of late years they have been

* Captain Owen—Cape St Mary, long. 45° 1′ E., lat. 25° 38′ S.

very hospitable, and many ships touch at Johanna for refreshments, the supplies of bullocks, poultry, and fruit being abundant. The natives have adopted the names of our Court calendar, and King George of Johanna is no inconsiderable personage. His Royal Highness the Duke of York is a washerman, and many of the princesses fill even more ignoble offices. Comoro is the largest island: the body of it is in lat. 11° 32′ south, long. about 43° 25′ east. It is high water at 4^h 45^m, and the tide rises twelve feet on the springs. The anchorage is on its north-west part, but is deep, dangerous, and unfrequented. The land is generally steep-to, having no soundings at a small distance from the shore, except to the north-west. Mohilla, the smallest of these islands, lies in lat. 12° 20′ south, long. 43° 50′ east; it is ten leagues west-south-west of Johanna, and twelve leagues south-east and by south from Comoro. In the ship Sibbald, a rocky islet was seen, which appeared to lie seven or eight miles nearly east from the body of Mohilla, and may be dangerous to ships passing in the night. Mayotta is the easternmost of this group, being about twelve leagues east-south-east half south of Johanna. On its south end stands a high conical mountain called Valentine's Peak, by mean of many observations in lat. 12° 54′ south, long. 45° 14′ east. The island is surrounded by reefs, and ought not to be approached nearer than five miles. In 1798, the variation at Mayotta was 17° 36′ west; and at these islands the variation has not materially changed for fifty years. A reef with breakers is thought to lie about four leagues off shore to the eastward of Mayotta.

Johanna is higher than Mohilla or Mayotta, but not so high as Comoro; it has a peak, sometimes mistaken for Valentine's Peak, which has the appearance of an oblong mountain, and is in lat. 12° 15′ south, long. 44° 34′ east. The anchorage is in lat. 12° 7′ south, long. 44° 30′ east, three or four miles to the west of the town, abreast a range of cocoa-nut trees, and having a large black rock to the eastward, between the trees and the town. Off the rock, soundings may be obtained in passing. The south-west and north-west points of the bay are bounded by reefs projecting two miles from the shore. To anchor at Johanna, steer direct for its north-west point, where is situated a small island called Saddle Island, to which a berth of a mile and a half must be given in passing, as the reef which connects it with Johanna projects a considerable distance round it. When past Saddle Island haul in for the anchorage, and borrow to the shore with hand and deep-sea lead going. Captain Owen's latitudes and longitudes differ so materially from those of Horsburgh and others, that an extract from his table is here subjoined.*

From Johanna a north-north-east course will take a ship clear of the Aldabra Islands; after passing which a more direct course may be shaped for Bombay. Supposing a ship to have passed through the Mozambique between April and September, the winds will generally blow from south-south-eastward to the line; as the latitude is increased to the northward, the winds will veer to south-westward. Bound for Bombay, steer for the parallel of Kanary, and then due east on that parallel till you make the island; the soundings regularly decrease towards the island, which is small, but easily known when the latitude is correctly ascertained. As soon as Kanary is discerned, haul up to the northward for the light-house on Colaba, which is often seen through the haze before the land is distinguishable.

Except in clear weather, very little use can be made of the cross-bearings of land around Bombay harbour. Kanary, the light-house, and the Fairway Buoy, are the best leading marks for the harbour's mouth, which is formed by Tull-reef on the starboard, and the Prongs on the larboard hand going in. As soon as a ship is seen from the light-house, a pilot is sent out; but it must be observed that neither a boat nor brig can work out against a flood-

---

* Islands, &c. in the Mozambique Channel.

Europa Island . . .	*Centre*	22.22·5	40.19·0	2.41.16	Leven, sometimes called Basses de India
Basses de India .	*East point*	21.29·0	39.35·5	2.38.22	Sometimes called Europa Rocks
	N.W. point	21.26·5	39.27·5	2.37.50	Do.
Juan de Nova . . .	*Centre*	17.03·5	42.42·3	2.50.49	Leven and Barracouta
Chesterfield Bank . .	*Do.*	16.17·5	43.50·4	2.55.22	Do.
Leven's Bank . .	*Extreme*	12.43·5	47.41·5	3.10.46	Do. } not dangerous
	Do.	12.21·8	47.52·2	3.11.28	Do. } not dangerous
——— Intermediate Bank	*Centre*	12.24·0	48.20·0	3.13.20	Do. } not dangerous
Comoro Islands, Mohilla	*North point*	12.36·0	45.06·5	3.00.26	Admiralty Charts
	East point	12.20·0	43.55·5	2.55.42	Do.
——— Johanna	*Town*	12.11·0	44.22·3	2.57.29	Leven
	Highest peak	12.13·5	44.24·3	2.57.37	5900 feet high
——— Comoro Island	*N. E. point*	11.19·5	43.34·0	2.54.16	Admiralty Charts
	S. E. point	11.54·0	43.28·0	2.53.52	Leven
	S. W. point	11.55·0	43.22·0	2.53.28	Admiralty Charts
Glorioso Isles—Isle Glorieux . .		11.34·8	47.19·0	3.09.16	Leven

Capt. W. F. W. Owen, *R. N.*

tide and strong monsoon. Bombay harbour is very secure in all weathers, being nearly landlocked. The islands of Salsette, Caranja, and Elephanta, lie between the shore and the Island of Bombay; and the view all around the harbour is extremely beautiful. The different islands are thickly wooded, and during the rains exhibit a richness of verdure and foliage which is truly striking. On the main, the land rises in high bold peaks; and far to the northward is seen a most remarkable isolated conical mountain, called the Queen of Mahratta's Knitting-needle. The celebrated caves of Elephanta are distant only a few miles from the anchorage.

It is usual when running in to make Kanary, in the south-west monsoon, to allow for a northerly current; but great care ought to be taken in making this allowance. The Honourable Company's ship Marquis of Ely, running in to make Kanary in the night, allowed for a set of two miles and a half per hour, and the ship was probably kept to the southward of her course. At daylight land was suddenly discovered close aboard, and before the ship's head could be got round, she was within broken water in six fathoms;—let go all her anchors, and rode for thirty-six hours off Severndroog in imminent danger, the sea frequently breaking over the forecastle. From this perilous situation escape seemed hopeless, till about noon on the second day, when the wind veered a point or two to the southward, and the tide was observed to set off the shore. It was immediately determined to make sail and cut. It was blowing hard, with frequent squalls and heavy rain. One anchor was hove up with great difficulty,—the ship lay with her head to the north-west,—the whole crew, together with 300 soldiers, manned the top-sail sheets, fore and main tacks, with the yards braced sharp up on the larboard tack. Every thing being ready for this bold attempt, the order was given,—Let fall, sheet home, cut the cable! In an instant the ship felt the power of the canvass, and started out to seaward through the surf like a hound slipt from the leash.—The Honourable Company's ship Kellie Castle, from not making sufficient allowance for the northerly set, got to the northward of Malabar Point, and, working to the southward, struck on the outer edge of the South-west Prong, and received much damage.

The south-west monsoon generally sets in at Bombay

about the latter end of May or beginning of June; but commences about fifteen or twenty days sooner near Cape Comorin and on the southern coast of Malabar. During the months of June and July the monsoon blows strong, with frequent hard squalls and constant rain; notwithstanding which the Company's ships every year make their passage down the coast inside of the Laccadives in the teeth of the monsoon without difficulty. The whole coast, from Bombay to Cape Comorin, is well known and safe to approach in the north-east monsoon.

The Laccadives group of islands has not yet been very accurately surveyed, and therefore great caution is necessary if a ship should accidentally be forced among them. The Nine Degrees Channel, to the southward between them and the Island of Minicoy, is perfectly safe, but should not be passed without paying great attention to the current, which most commonly sets to the southward in both monsoons among the Laccadives. To the southward of Minicoy is the Eight Degrees Channel, quite safe; it is bounded on the south by the northernmost of the Maldives, another extensive chain of low islands, whose geographical position is not very accurately determined. Captain Horsburgh has taken great pains to collate information respecting them from the journals of the East India Company's ships. After giving many extracts, he says, "Although the geographical positions of the channels which divide the Northern Atolls of the Maldive chain ought not to be relied on as perfectly ascertained, from a deficiency of correct observations, yet the limits given for the One-and-a-half Degree Channel, the Equatorial Channel, and the South Channel, may be considered a near approximation to the truth. Nevertheless, large ships ought always to approach these islands with great caution, on account of strong currents, often uncertain in their direction, although generally setting east and west between the Atolls and in the channels." The shoals which bound the north end of the Laccadives are very dangerous. In 1827, the Byramgore was lost on a coral reef between the northernmost Laccadive and Cherbaniani Reef. This shoal was unknown till she struck on it; and the Competitor in the same year also struck on a shoal among the islands, whose geographical site is not yet determined.

The north-east monsoon, which is the fine weather season, commences at Bombay in the middle of November; and during this season most of the wealthy inhabitants raise bungalows, or tents, on the esplanade close to the sea in Back Bay. These temporary habitations, rendered necessary by the heat, which is almost insupportable within the walls of the fort, have a truly oriental and picturesque effect. As soon as the south-west monsoon commences, which is, *par excellence,* called *the* monsoon, the whole of this gay town disappears as if by magic. It has been remarked, that finer weather is now experienced than early navigators met with on the western side of India; but it may readily be conceived, that the great improvements, both in construction and skilful equipment of ships, together with the more scientific attainments of modern navigators, will sufficiently account for this, without supposing any material alteration in the weather.

The next route from the Cape of Good Hope to the Malabar coast is that to the eastward of the Saya de Mala, and the Cargados Bank. On this extensive reef the Honourable Company's ship Cabalva, of 1200 tons, was wrecked in 1818. The narrative of this shipwreck presents a melancholy picture of human suffering and human depravity. The ship struck on the outer edge of the reef at half-past four in the morning. In less than half an hour she became a total wreck. The masts were cut away, and fell towards the rocks. The sea went over and through the ship's very side with irresistible force. The distance from the ship to the nearest dry rocks was about sixty yards; the space which intervened was a perfect whirlpool of contending waves. Most of the crew appear to have reached the *shore* (if mere rocks above water can be so termed) unconscious of the means by which they had been saved. Mr Ayres, the purser, thus forcibly describes his own escape: (He, with about twenty-five others, had got into the large cutter, and by dint of great exertion cleared her from between the wreck of the masts. The first wave they encountered dashed them all out of the boat, with the exception of the fourth officer, who clung to the thwarts and landed safely.) "I was precipitated to the bottom, and as far as regards myself I never expected to rise from it again. In the supposed interval of drowning I felt all the horrors that can belong to that deplorable situation; and, conscious of the fate which awaited me, I still retained sufficient mind, as I resigned my life to the will of the Almighty, to invoke his mercy and protection towards those objects who were dearest to my heart, and whom I had now left for ever. In a short time, however, I felt myself very heavily struck and impelled by the following surf; sometimes raised for an instant to the surface, and then precipitated again to the bottom. These tremendous surfs followed in quick succession, and to their impulse, under God, we may all attribute the saving our lives. Nothing could resist their power; they swept us away in their long train towards the shore, divesting us of every possible means of self-caution, or of contributing in the least towards our own salvation; leaving us in the wash with barely sufficient power to crawl out and reach *terra firma,* and like wretches more than half-drowned and with bewildered senses, wondering by what means or accident we had been saved." By about nine o'clock the whole of the crew (excepting the captain and fourteen men who were drowned) had reached the rocks. Their prospects were to all appearance most appalling and hopeless. No land—nothing but coral-banks and rocks to be seen in any direction, and the very spot on which they stood rapidly disappearing under the rising tide. Will it be believed that in this extraordinary situation, when just rescued from death, without even waiting to know who was saved or who was drowned, the whole of the seamen, regardless of their officers' orders or entreaties, and before the boat was rescued by means of which alone their future escape was practicable, commenced the most childish and wanton pilfering among the goods with which the rocks were strewed! Every package was broken open, not in search of food, but out of mere curiosity; and numbers possessed themselves of articles wholly useless to men of their class of life any where, but more strikingly so to forlorn shipwrecked mariners on a lone dreary sand-bank, with scarcely dry ground to stand upon except at low water. As wine, spirits, and beer came ashore with the rest of the cargo, drunkenness prevailed to a great extent; all subordination was at an end; all obedience ceased. A great many casks of beer having been thrown upon a bank at some distance from the one on which the officers lived, most of the crew went over and established themselves there, calling it *Beer Island!* Several pigs escaped alive, and lived principally upon *Windsor soap.* Eight sheep also landed alive, and two bales of hay came on shore very opportunely for their sustenance. The ship was wrecked on a Tuesday, and during the week, by dint of great exertion, the officers and the few that remained faithful to them, secured and repaired the large cutter, intending to despatch her to the Mauritius for succour. Strange to say, the *Beer Islanders* objected to her going, and the manner in which they were persuaded to acquiesce, is the only redeeming trait of character these degenerate wretches exhibited during their stay of three weeks at Cargados. Mr Ayres, who appears to have shown great presence of mind and decision, wrote in pencil a short address or sermon, and on Sunday, the men, by common consent, having mustered round the tent of the officers (composed of spars, and covered with the Company's splendid woollen cloths), he stood up in the cutter for a pulpit, and read his sermon. This little composition, probably the only one ever written or delivered under similar circumstances, does great credit to the feelings and judgment of Mr Ayres. It had the desired effect, and immediately after the sermon, it was agreed to by all hands, that the cutter should be despatched forthwith. Mr Ayres and the sixth officer were appointed to make the voyage to the Mauritius, which they accomplished in three days, under circumstances of great difficulty and privation. The *Magicienne* frigate went to Cargados and took on board the remains of the Cabalva's crew, many of whom left Beer Island, according to their own confession, with reluctance, as they had plenty of beer still unconsumed, and regretted leaving so much "good stuff" behind.

Some ships pass up between Madagascar and the Mauritius, others to the eastward of the Mauritius, sighting Galega or Agelaga, the geographical position of which is not very accurately known.

	Lat.	Long.
Capt. Briggs, H.M.S. Clorinde, made it in	10° 25′ S.	56° 38½′ E.
Ship Sir Stephen Lushington, .	0 0	56 39
Capt. Moresby, H.M.S. Menai, .	10 21 N.W. end	56 32 to 56° 38′ E.
Capt. Hine, H.C.S., by chronometers,	0 0	56 50

Capt. Hutchinson, ship Hero of Malown, made it two or three leagues farther east than the position given by Capt. Hine.

The adoption of either of these routes will greatly depend upon the winds a ship meets with on the verge of the south-east trade, and it is an object of importance, not only as regards the passage to Bombay, but to all parts of India, to observe, that little easting can be made after the south-east trade is entered; so that, contending with uncertain winds between the Cape and the limits of the south-east trade, a spurt of southerly wind should not tempt the navigator to the northward of lat. 30° south till he is nearly on the meridian of the port in India to which he is bound; and this is more particularly necessary when the north-east monsoon is prevailing to the northward of the line. The different routes, such as the Outer, Middle, and Boscawen Passages, were formerly chosen from circumstances unconnected with the prevailing winds, such as the geographical site of the islands or shoals being in some better known than in others; its being thought unsafe to approach certain islands; and supposed shoals, which frightened navigators away from others. The late surveys of Captain Owen, R. N., Captains Ross and Maughan (Honourable Company's service), together with the indefatigable researches of Captain Horsburgh, have at length cleared away most of this uncertainty. Henceforward, then, the choice of the route must be determined according to the season of the year, by the winds then prevailing. Thus, any of the before-mentioned routes may be adopted by ships which cross the line from March to October; because the south-west monsoon blows home to all the coasts of India from about the line in these months, and therefore a direct course may be pursued to any of the ports or coasts of India. In the opposite months, it will be sufficiently obvious that a different course must be pursued. From the Cape to the limits of the trade uncertain winds prevail, of which every advantage must be taken; and here it may very properly be observed, that experienced sea-officers differ very much on the subject of carrying sail. Some crack on through every squall while their sticks will stand: the risk of springing a lower-mast or lower-yard is thus very much increased; and it is needless to say how an accident of this kind in a merchant ship, with few resources for repair on board, would retard the progress. The following practice is recommended as preferable:—Never reef, when it can be avoided, off the wind;—reduce sail in time to a squall, but out with every rag again the moment the height of the squall is past. It is quite certain that ships in the present day make quicker passages to and from India than formerly. Among other reasons may be adduced the reliance which is now placed upon the marine barometer: it enables an attentive observer of its motions to carry as much sail at night as in the day. Before this admirable instrument came into common use, it was customary to reef every night. Captain Meriton, an excellent officer, while in command of the Honourable Company's ship Exeter, used to take *two* reefs in every night at sunset.*

At all seasons of the year, the three following points ought to be carefully considered by navigators, who are anxious to make a quick passage from the Cape to any part of India:—

First, What are the limits of the south-east trade, and what is the usual direction from which it blows at the period when the ship is likely to enter it?

Secondly, What is the probable limit and direction of the line monsoon at the time?

Thirdly, Is the north-east or south-west monsoon prevailing to the northward of the usual limit of the line monsoon?

These are essential particulars in the navigation of the Indian Seas, and a due attention to them is earnestly recommended.

Ships bound for Ceylon while the south-west monsoon is prevailing to the northward of the line, having proceeded by Boscawen's or the Middle Passage, may pass through the South, Equatorial, or One-and-a-half Degree Channel. Along the south side of Ceylon westerly winds prevail nearly eight months in the year, and westerly currents are also frequent, particularly in October and November, and they run with considerable velocity. It may not be out of place to observe that a westerly wind and a westerly current, according to nautical phraseology, run in *opposite* directions. Seamen name the wind by the point of the compass *from* which it blows, and the current is always designated by that point of the compass *towards*

* This reminds one of the tardy proceedings of Dirk Hudson, one of the early discoverers of North America, who used to heave to every night; by which sage proceeding he gained a whole night's sleep,—never ran over any body in the night,—and always knew where he was in the morning. It is farther related of this ancient mariner, that he nearly created a mutiny in the Goede Frau of Amsterdam, by interdicting his jolly tars from going aloft with more than six pair of breeches on, or from reefing topsails with pipes in their mouths.

which it is proceeding. This westerly current near Ceylon may carry a ship nearer the Maldives than is expedient. If bound for Colombo, having passed through either of the above-mentioned channels, a direct course may be steered; and, in clear weather, Adam's Peak, a very high-peaked mountain, about thirty miles to the eastward of Colombo, will be first seen, and is sometimes visible at thirty leagues distance. A ship may anchor off the town in six or seven fathoms, with the flag-staff on the fort bearing south by east. Colombo is in lat. 6° 57′ north, long. 80° east, and is the seat of government. The cinnamon plantations are in the neighbourhood, and it is a remarkable fact that the odour of cinnamon is smelt at a great distance off shore in passing Ceylon; so that

"The spicy gales of Araby the Blest"

are not necessarily mere poetical fictions.

Point de Galle is another settlement towards which a direct course may be steered. The flag-staff is situated in lat. 6° 1′ north, long. 80° 20′ east. Large ships anchor in the roads, in sixteen or eighteen fathoms, with the flag-staff bearing about north-north-east, two miles off the town. The inner harbour requires a pilot, the outer roadstead is not safe in the south-west monsoon. There is a high conical mountain, which is very conspicuous from the offing. The land to the westward is generally low with cocoa-nut trees, fronting the sea, but the land rises in high mountainous ridges to the north-east of Point de Galle. There are many dangers on the coast of Ceylon, between Point de Galle and Trincomalee. The Euphrates, Honourable Company's ship, was lost by making too free with the shore near Dondre Head, which is a low bluff point, being the southernmost land of Ceylon. If bound for Trincomalee, or the southern part of the Coromandel coast, it is advisable to fall in with the land hereabouts in the south-west monsoon; and great caution is required in proceeding to the northward, to avoid the Great and Little Basses. It seems advisable at all times to pass outside of them; they consist of two dangerous ledges of rocks, the highest being just above the water. After passing Dondre Head, by keeping along the edge of the Bank of Soundings, and never shoaling the water under thirty-four fathoms, a ship will pass about two miles outside of the rocks. In clear weather, and daylight, they may be approached to the depth of twenty-four fathoms, which is about half a mile from the Great Basses. About Dondre Head and the Basses, the currents are very uncertain,—sometimes running with great velocity to the north-eastward; by not observing which, many ships have overshot their reckoning in the night, and come up with the Basses very unexpectedly. His Majesty's frigate Dædalus, Captain Sir Murray Maxwell, was lost on the Little Basses, and the fleet under her convoy nearly shared the same fate. The Elephant Hill is a high isolated rock on the low land near the sea, and is on-with the Great Basses, bearing north 5° west. Chimney Hill is pretty high, near the sea, with a remarkable rock rising from its side, resembling a chimney. It is on-with the Little Basses, bearing north 59° west. Proceeding to the northward, along the east coast of Ceylon, if bound to Trincomalee, a ship should keep well in-with the coast after passing the Basses, and make the land (in the south-west monsoon) to the southward of Flag-staff Point, which is in lat. 8° 33½′ north, long. 81° 22′ east. It is high, bold, is covered with trees, and has several fortifications on it. This point is easily known from its bluff appearance, and from the land to the northward and southward being very low; it is steep-to, and safe to approach. Trincomalee has little trade, and is not much frequented, except by the men-of-war on the India station. The harbour is capacious and safe; although there are many shoals and rocks in it, yet they are all well known, and there is plenty of room, with good holding-ground. The navigation of the harbour is somewhat intricate; but with Horsburgh's sailing directions and a chart, there is nothing to prevent a stranger either running in with a fair wind, or working into the bay. In former days, when dull-sailing ships were navigated by dead reckoning, it was usual to keep in soundings, if bound to Madras, after passing Ceylon, in order to avoid the chance of falling in with the land to the northward of Madras, in the south-west monsoon. In the present day, this loss of time seems unnecessary; for it is hardly to be supposed that the commander or officers even of the private ships to India are unacquainted with the use of the sextant and chronometer, by means of which, in clear weather, the ship's true position can always be ascertained. When there are three chronometers on board *agreeing,* great reliance may be placed on them; but lunar observations ought never to be neglected, for their use may suddenly be required when the practitioner is not prepared to place confidence in his skill, from want of habit. The following routine is recommended to all navigators on long voyages:

" Take *two sets* of observations for the time every forenoon and afternoon; take sights for and work the latitude by double altitudes every day; take lunars whenever the moon is in distance with objects east and west of her; observe the magnetic variation every twenty-four hours, let each officer who has charge of a watch be bound to ascertain the latitude by stellar observations at least once every twenty-four hours. Let the dead reckoning for practical purposes be always deduced from the ship's last *true* position, as ascertained by observation."

Navigators are greatly indebted to Captain Thomas Lynn, of the Honourable Company's Service, for his admirable work on navigation, called " Lynn's Tables." He is the person appointed by the East India Company to examine young officers in nautical astronomy, and he also conducts a naval academy with infinite credit to himself. Captain Lynn recommends stellar observations to be taken in the twilight of morning and evening, when the horizon is generally clear and well defined.*

It is material to observe, that Madras is sixty miles west of Flag-staff Point, and the easternmost part of Ceylon is in about lat. 7° north. In the north-east monsoon, the current sets at times strong to the southward, but is liable to be obstructed. In the south-west monsoon the current along the Coromandel coast runs to the northward; and therefore ships bound for Madras or any other place on this coast should make the land to the northward or southward of their port, as circumstances require. In both monsoons, along the whole of the Coromandel coast there is a heavy surf rolling in upon the shore, which prevents all communication, except in boats, called masoolah-boats, of a peculiar construction. They are of a clumsy *hog-trough* shape, without timbers, and the planks are sewed together; they are rowed with ten or twelve paddle-shaped oars, and are very buoyant and yielding. When the surf strikes

* An admirable and very simple method of computing the latitude by double altitudes is that of Mr Samuel Dunn, which is mentioned by Captain Lynn in his " Horary Tables" lately published. Captain L. has given arguments exactly suited to the solution of this problem in his " Azimuth Tables."

them on the side, the planks bend inwards. The fishermen on this coast use a catamaran, which is simply three logs tied together, the middle one being longer than the others, and pointed a little upwards. This simple contrivance is generally about ten feet in length and eighteen inches in breadth. With a man on it, the upper edge is generally under water. Pondicherry, formerly a French settlement, is in lat. 11° 56′ north, long. 79° 54′ east. It is easily distinguished from seaward, has an agreeable aspect, and may be known by a remarkable black patch on a long flat hill north-west of the town with a grove or tuft of trees on it. A ship may anchor in six or seven fathoms off the town, in the fair season. Bound from England to Madras, a ship, having sighted any part of Ceylon, may shape a direct course for Madras Flag-staff, which is in lat. 13° 4′ north, long. 80° 21′ 30″ east. In the night, the light-house may be seen five leagues from the deck, and is highly useful in guiding ships clear of Pulicate Shoal, the south point of which bears from the light-house north by east three quarters, east thirteen miles. If the light is kept to the westward of south-south-west, one quarter west, the shoal will be avoided. Madras Roads are open to all winds, except from the west. The anchorage is foul from the many anchors left there. It is liable to be visited by sudden severe storms, and even in fine weather there is a heavy swell tumbling in from seaward. From the beginning of October to the 10th or 15th of December is considered the most dangerous season to remain in Madras Roads, or in any roadstead on this coast. It must, however, be observed, that ships remain in Madras Roads at all seasons, being ready to cut or slip, and run out to sea on the first intimation of a hurricane. During the bad-weather season, ships should lie in Madras Roads with good sails bent, and close-reef their topsails and courses before they are furled. With the flag-staff about north-west by west, in nine fathoms, two miles from the shore, is a good berth for a large ship. The masoolah-boats are used at Madras; and when the surf is too high for them to go off a flag is hoisted at the beach-house called the foul-weather flag. While this continues flying, all communication with the shore is interrupted; yet the catamaran-men will at these times venture off with a letter, which they contrive to keep dry by placing it in their skull-cap, over which the folds of the turban are tightly twisted.

The coasts of Golconda and Orissa (after passing the Pulicate Shoal) may be safely approached in most parts with the lead.

The approach to the Hoogley in both monsoons is rendered very difficult, from the circumstance of long spits of sand extending from the mouth of the river, *out of sight of land.* Between these sands or reefs are different channels, and the one now used is bounded on the east by Saugor Sand, and on the west by the Eastern Sea-reef. The entrance to this channel, as before mentioned, is out of sight of land. Ships bound for Calcutta in the south-west monsoon ought to make the land about Pondy or Ganjam, where it is of considerable height. The Juggernaut pagodas are a good mark to run for; the coast abreast them is safe to approach, and they cannot easily be mistaken. In a clear day, at a moderate distance, they present a magnificent appearance. There are three large circular buildings with domes, and several smaller pagodas; from the sea they look like one vast palace. Having passed the pagodas, a course about north-east by east, keeping in about fourteen or fifteen fathoms, must be shaped for False Point, abreast of which the soundings are brown sand and shells with black specks; but to the northward of False Point, all over False Bay, the bottom is very soft green mud. With False Point bearing west-north-west, in fourteen or fifteen fathoms, the course is north-east ten leagues, to clear the reef off Point Palmyras; but the lead is the best guide, and a ship ought not to come under fourteen fathoms crossing False Bay. This depth may be increased to fifteen fathoms rounding the reef off Point Palmyras; for when the point bears to the southward of west, a ship in fifteen fathoms will not be far from the edge of its reef. On the Island of Mypurra a light-house has lately been erected, which in clear weather is very useful in rounding the reef, and enables the pilots to keep their station, which is on a line due east from the light-house. It is very material not to mistake *False* for *True* Point Palmyras. If a doubt is entertained on the subject, a ship off False Bay, in fifteen fathoms, by steering north, will *shoal* the water over a bottom of soft mud; but from fifteen or sixteen fathoms off Point Palmyras, and clear of the north-east edge of the reef, in steering north she will deepen her water. In Balasore Roads, or off Point Palmyras, the pilot-brig *ought* to be found in the south-west monsoon, although ships beat about for several days before they find one. It is advisable to anchor under Mypurra Island during the night, and stand over towards the Eastern Sea-reef in the day. Some navigators have ventured into Saugor Channel, without having seen the land. The following instance may be adduced, as showing the practicability of doing so, and will also place in a striking point of view the accuracy of nautical science in the present day:—

The Honourable Company's ship Thomas Grenville left England on the 12th of June 1825,—passed the Cape 20th of August,—crossed the line in long. 80° east, and stood right up the bay, *without having seen any land* since leaving England. Captain Manning, who is an excellent seaman and a skilful observer, found, by lunars and chronometers agreeing, that the ship's true position at noon on the 1st of October was in long. 88° 20′ east, and lat. 20° 25′ north. He steered north for the mouth of Saugor Channel, and having run about thirty-five miles by log, fell in with a pilot-brig in ten fathoms water at six o'clock in the evening.

Captain Ross, the Company's marine surveyor, states, that the light-vessel stationed in the Eastern Channel is placed in long. 88° 13′ east, and not in 88° 25′, as stated by Captain Maxfield. And he also thinks the extreme points of the reefs two miles farther north than they are usually marked in the charts. Pilots are sometimes to be found on board this brig, and she is distinguished during the day by a white flag at her mast-head.

The channel is about five miles wide. Saugor Sand is steep-to on *both* sides; and the sea-reefs are also steep-to on their western edges; but on their eastern sides the depths decrease gradually, though quickly; so that turning to windward in Saugor Channel, the soundings must be taken from the western side of the channel, and a ship ought to avoid the risk of a hard cast, standing towards Saugor Sand. The course of the channel is north-north-west and south-south-east. In the channel the bottom is soft mud; on all the reefs the bottom is hard sand with bright specks like steel filings. The leadsmen of the pilot-brigs can tell in a moment, by the feel of the ground, whether they are on the reefs or in the channel. The tides have a rise and fall of ten or eleven feet, and the water is highest over the ground on the Sea-reefs, and in Balasore Roads about nine hours full and change. The tail of the Eastern Sea-reef is in about lat. 21° north. The first or Reef-buoy is close to the eastern edge of the Sea-reef, in lat. 21° 16′ north, from whence the course is north-north-west, half west, to the buoys in Thornhill's Channel. If it is determined to stand over to the mouth of the Saugor Channel, from Point Palmyras, in search of a pilot, great attention must be paid to the tides, and the reefs ought to be approached about the first of the flood, as ships cannot work to the southward again till the ebb makes. If a ship could, in a clear day, about noon, when the latitude has been obtained, and with the last of the flood, be near the tail of the Western Sea-reef, she might venture to cross, and look into Saugor Channel, and either anchor there or work to the southward with the ebb.

At all times during the south-west monsoon great caution is requisite in approaching the Hoogley. Cloudy weather, with frequent hard squalls and rain, may be expected, particularly from May to September. In June and July, which are the worst months, ships standing towards the Western Sea-reef, across Balasore Roads, or towards any of the reefs, ought to have good canvass bent, and have every thing ready for turning to windward, in the event of suddenly getting a hard cast on any of the reefs which spread out to seaward from the mouth of the river something in the form of a human hand, supposing Saugor Sand to be the thumb. From Point Palmyras, the flood-tide sets over towards the Eastern Sea-reef with considerable velocity on the springs; but close to and over the reef of Palmyras, the flood sets towards the mouth of Kanaka river. In July the freshes from the rivers cause a drain of current to the southward. A ship under weigh off the mouth of the Hoogley ought never to neglect the lead for one moment.

In the north-east monsoon, which generally commences early in October, along the head of the bay, the pilots cruise off the tail of Saugor Sand, in lat. 21° north, and long. about 88° 40′ east. It is very essential at this season to keep well to windward of the reefs, for the tides set constantly to the west and south-west. Coming up the bay in the north-east monsoon, a ship should get into about lat. 21° 7′ north, well to the eastward of Saugor Sand, and steer west in eight and a half fathoms at low water, and ten at high water. In this parallel, the bottom is soft till the depth suddenly decreases over a hard bottom on Saugor Sand. The success of this proceeding will greatly depend on a strict attention to the tides; for if a ship is set to the southward of 21° 7′, in running westward she will miss the Saugor Sand, and get her first hard cast on the Eastern Sea-reef. It seems therefore advisable to cross the tail of Saugor Sand, and work up as far as the Reef-buoy, in search of a pilot, taking care not to stand more than one-half or two-thirds of the channel over towards the Saugor Sand. When the north-east monsoon is prevailing in the Bay of Bengal, ships bound for Calcutta should enter the southern limit of the south-east trade, so as to enable them to cross the line in about long. 90° east. From about 10° south lat., variable winds, mostly from west and north-west, may be expected till the limit of the north-east monsoon is reached. From the equator a course ought to be shaped with reference to the winds encountered; thus, if the wind hang to the eastward, endeavour to close with the Nicobars, and stand up the bay to the westward of these islands and the Andamans. The old practice of going to the eastward is now exploded, and a ship is more likely to make a passage by working up the east side of the bay in the open sea, than by closing with the Arracan shore or Andaman Islands.

It will be needful to make a few remarks on the homeward voyage, although most of the foregoing observations may be applied generally to outward or homeward bound ships. From Bengal or Madras, homeward-bound ships should, at all seasons of the year, endeavour to cross the line in about 87° or 90° east long.; and, having entered the south-east trade, it will be prudent, particularly in February, March, and April, to pass well to the eastward of Roderigue, to avoid the hurricanes which sometimes occur in the vicinity of this island and the Mauritius. These hurricanes are less severely felt in proportion as the distance is increased to the eastward of the islands. Ships from the Malabar coast should endeavour to take a departure from about Dondre Head, and cross the line in 85° east, which will enable them to give Roderigue a wide berth. From April to November, storms seldom happen near Mauritius; and, in these months, thirty or forty leagues is a sufficient distance at which to pass; at other times, the islands ought not to be approached nearer than eighty or ninety leagues. In one of these hurricanes it is supposed the gallant Trowbridge was lost with all his crew, in his Majesty's ship Blenheim. In general ships run rapidly through the south-east trade, towards the Cape of Good Hope. The south end of Madagascar should be passed at a distance of thirty or forty leagues, and a course shaped to fall in with the coast of Africa about Point Natal.

In a preceding part of this article instructions are given for making a passage round the Cape by help of the current. In the winter months ships cannot be too well prepared for bad weather on approaching the Cape, and crazy ships should keep well in-with the land, where they will have smooth water and less wind than is experienced far on the bank. It is not thought dangerous to hug the land, as the wind seldom blows strong from the south. If a ship is beating round the Cape with a westerly wind, she should endeavour to have a good offing when about the meridian of Cape Lagullas, particularly towards the conclusion of a north-west gale, by which she will be enabled to bear up for St Helena much sooner than if she happened to be in-with the land when the wind veered to the southward and westward, which it commonly does towards the end of a gale. Ships from Bombay, bound to England in November or December, may proceed by the Mozambique Channel; but southerly winds are often experienced there in February. The current setting to the south along the African shore will always help a ship through this channel, and she may pass in sight of Cape Corrientes, where it is very strong. Except in November and December, ships from Bombay should go by the outer passage, round Roderigue.

From the Cape to St Helena ships commonly experience fair winds and pleasant weather. A south-easter off Table Bay will frequently carry a ship into the south-east trade. The course to St Helena from the Cape is north-north-west, half west, and it may be safely approached in the night; but ships are not allowed to anchor till they have communicated with the shore, either by signal or by a boat sent to the fort on Sugar-loaf Point. The best anchorage is in sixteen or eighteen fathoms, with the street of James Town open. The geographical site of the town is long. 5° 36½′ west, lat. 15° 55′ south.* From St He-

* Captain Owen—St Helena, town, long. 5° 44′ W., lat. 15° 54′ S.

lena a ship departs with the trade-wind, and may shape a course to pass on either side of Ascension as most expedient. From Ascension a north-north-west course may be steered for the equator, which should be crossed in 18° or 20° west, as before directed. From the line a ship ought to keep on the tack which will give most northing till she meets the north-east trade. From lat. 24° or 25° north in this route will be seen the gulf-weed, which covers the whole face of the waters to about 40° or 41° north lat. By catching a quantity of this weed in passing, many curious marine animals may be collected which are found upon it. In the gulf-stream the temperature of the water is 4° or 5° higher than the temperature of the atmosphere. The north-east trade generally carries a ship far to the westward, and nothing can be conceived more provoking than the continuance of easterly winds after a ship has got as far as 30° or 35° north, forcing her daily farther in distance from the "desired haven." It is advisable to pass to the westward of the Western Islands or Azores. They are nine in number, with safe channels between them all. The two which form the north-western corner of the group are most commonly seen by homeward-bound ships from India. Flores, the westernmost, is in lat. 39° 33′ north, long. 31° 11′ west. Corvo is separated from Flores by a channel three or four leagues wide, and is in lat. 39° 42½′ north, long. 31° 6′ west. After passing the Azores, a direct course should be pursued for the Lizard!

In the foregoing pages the variation of the compass in different parts of the globe is rarely mentioned, on account of its constant fluctuation, and because it is presumed that every careful navigator ascertains the magnetic variation of the compass by observation every twenty-four hours, whenever the weather will admit of it, and corrects his courses and bearings accordingly. The *local* variation of the compass, since first observed by Captain Flinders, has been the subject of much speculation. For scientific purposes, the local variation must be carefully ascertained; but for the common uses of navigation it is not quite so important.

CHAPTER XVII.

Proposed Steam Communication between England and the East Indies by the Red Sea.

Voyage of Sir John Malcolm from Bombay to Cosseir in the Hugh Lindsay Steamer—Reasons for preferring the Route by Cosseir to that by Suez—Size of Vessels—To be manned from the Indian Navy—Coals—Sir John Malcolm's Opinion of the Advantages of this Communication—Obstacles to it—The Plague—Winds in the Red Sea—Post-office Regulations—Mr Waghorn's Remarks on the Navigation of the Nile—Steam-tugs on the Ganges.

A COMMUNICATION with India by means of steam has lately occupied the attention, not only of individuals, but of the government in India. The different passages to India, round the Cape of Good Hope, by steamers, have been all unsuccessful as to *time;* and it may fairly be doubted whether steam will ever compete with sails on this long passage. The Honourable Company's ship Thomas Coutts made the passage to Bombay in eighty-four days,—the Atlas in eighty-three,—and ninety days is not considered as any thing very extraordinary by some of the free-traders, such as the Roxburgh Castle and others. Mr Waghorn, an enterprising officer of the Bengal pilot service, is the principal advocate and projector of the passage by steam round the Cape. The route by the Red Sea having been lately traversed with complete success by Sir John Malcolm, our observations shall be confined to this route. The present Pacha of Egypt is highly favourable to the establishment of steam-packets at Alexandria, and would afford every facility on the land journey, if this great object is undertaken by government. The following observations (in substance) were most kindly supplied by Sir John Malcolm:—He left Bombay on the 5th of December 1830 for England, in the Honourable Company's steamer Hugh Lindsay. Arrived at Macula on the 14th of December, and remained there three days to take in coals, water, and refreshments. Macula is situated on the coast of Arabia, at the mouth of the Red Sea, where there is good anchorage and a safe harbour.

Arrived at Juddah on the 22d of December, and remained there two days to take in coals, water, &c. Arrived at Cosseir in Egypt on the 27th of December;—having been at anchor nearly six days, and actually steaming from Bombay to Cosseir in sixteen days and twelve hours. If Sir John had gone to Suez instead of Cosseir, he is of opinion he would certainly have reached that place on the 29th, and might easily have arrived at Alexandria on the 2d or 3d of January; but he went to Cosseir to meet Lord Clare, the new governor of Bombay, who was appointed to succeed him. Sir John passed twenty-seven days in Egypt "seeing the lions." He then went to Malta in a frigate, which occupied eleven days; a steamer could accomplish it with ease in seven. He sailed from Malta in the Meteor steamer on 4th February 1831; arrived at Gibraltar on 12th February; remained there two days to take in coals, water, &c., and sailed on the 14th. Arrived at Falmouth on 25th February, having had only three days' fair wind between Malta and England.

Sir John is of opinion that in future two days may be saved in the passage from Bombay up the Red Sea by improving the power of the steamer, and that despatches may be carried from Bombay to Alexandria in twenty-four days, for nine months of the year; during the other three months the progress of the steamers will be impeded by the violence of the northerly winds. Sir John recommends the route by Cosseir to Alexandria for passengers, in preference to that by Suez, the latter being much exposed to inundation and other inconveniences. As to the relative advantages or disadvantages of building, it is executed equally well and stronger in Bombay than England. Teak is better than oak; and the Hugh Lindsay was built so correct to the model, that her large engines (two of eighty horse power) fitted on to almost a hair's breadth. No change has been made in this vessel, except cutting her paddle-boards six inches, which, tried on the second voyage, has been found an improvement, owing perhaps to the depth of water she drew when overloaded with ten days' coal, which is three if not four days' more than this fine man-of-war steamer was built to carry. The Hugh Lindsay steamed from Bombay to Cosseir, a distance of 2700 miles, in sixteen days and twelve hours, which is an average of seven knots an hour. The passage from Bombay to Cosseir will, from 1st

September to 1st June, be always made in twenty-one days, including the taking in of coals; and to Suez in twenty-three days. Mr Barker, his majesty's consul-general in Egypt, thinks that, with a relay of dromedaries, packets might be sent by the Desert from Cosseir to Alexandria in six or seven days; and this would prevent the possibility of stoppage from the inundation of the Nile. It would also save four or five days' coal in going to Suez and returning, and the expense and trouble of depositing and shipping it at a place where vessels must anchor five miles from the shore. At Cosseir they lie close to the town, and have in all weather safe anchorage, besides plentiful supplies, good water, and a land-carriage for packets and passengers. With respect to the latter, few will go this route that do not desire to see Upper Egypt; this they could not do without much trouble and expense if they went to Suez.

With regard to passengers, they should not be counted upon as ever likely to remunerate government for the expense of steam-vessels between Bombay and Egypt. These vessels should be built as packets. There cannot be a better model than the Meteor, or the Admiralty yachts, which are about 300 tons, with round sterns, and the cabins lighted by sky-lights. The vessels for the Red Sea might have about two feet beam more than the Meteor, and two sixty, instead of two fifty horse power engines. This would greatly increase the speed. They might carry eight or ten passengers with very limited accommodation, and they could be provided with a plain table by the commander of the vessel for half the price charged (the same as his majesty's steamers to Malta), the other half going in part payment of coals. No other plan will succeed. As to passengers, there is not, and will not be for many years, any intercourse between India and England by this route that will make passengers profitable; and no extra expense is warrantable on this account. The expense of coals in the Meteor was eight chaldrons per diem; but this last voyage it was diminished to seven, from having the fiery-vein coal from Wales. With this coal, such a vessel as before mentioned, with sixty horse power, would not require beyond nine chaldrons of coals per diem; and if either Mr Morgan's plan is approved of, or the experiment of cylindrical boilers and expansion engines, now trying by Captain King at Falmouth under orders of the Admiralty, succeeds, which is probable, the consumption of coal will be decreased one-third. Lord William Bentinck, Sir Charles Malcolm, and Captain Wilson, commander of the Hugh Lindsay, concur in the opinion of the size of the vessels for the Red Sea. Lieutenant Symons was also consulted (who has for some time commanded the Meteor), and Captain King.

To give success to this plan, the execution of every part of it should be left to the government of Bombay, and certainly the vessels should in all, except the engines, be built and equipped in India. It is farther quite essential for this and general purposes, that they should be officered and manned from the Indian navy. Experienced and steady lieutenants or masters will command them, and these should not only possess a complete knowledge of the engines and steam-navigation, but the most intelligent midshipmen of the Indian navy should be instructed in that science; while English and half-caste boys should be educated, as they now are, to supply the place of engineers from England, who are a great expense and trouble.

With regard to coals, government has not yet been successful in finding any in Cutch. The death of Mr Maculloch, who was a good geologist, has for a period stopt the prosecution of the search in quarters where the coal might have proved less superficial than where first discovered. Doctor Christie, who has gone to the continent with the intention of proceeding to his station at Madras, by Bombay, has received the sanction of the Court of Directors to employ himself two years in scientific pursuits, and is stated by competent judges to be an able geologist. He has promised to visit Cutch; but it would be useful to desire that if he is so inclined he should have every reasonable aid, for the object is of importance. Until coals are found on the western side of India, they must be imported from England; but they may be brought as ballast at a very moderate rate, and, with all wastage, may, it is supposed, be deposited at ports in the Red Sea cheaper than by the route of Egypt. Vessels going at certain seasons through the Strait of Madagascar would lose little by depositing them at Mocha;—but these are points of mere calculation. The authorities in England should be cautious in attending to plans and maps as to depôts and other matters connected with this part of the subject. Those that give them only know the general features of the question.

For instance, Socotra appears a most desirable place for a depôt; but it has yet no supplies for a vessel, nor is there any town to aid in loading or unloading cargoes of coals. These are for the present great objections. The government of Bombay will early discover what is best, both for economy and expedition; and a well-qualified young officer of the Indian navy, of whom many speak Arabic, should remain at Cosseir as an agent to secure quick lading and depositing, and to be in communication with the consul-general, to accelerate the despatches to Alexandria.

By this route and mode packets from Bombay will certainly be delivered for nine months of the year at Alexandria in twenty-eight days. The passage from Malta to that place will not average more than seven or eight days for a steamer, and one of a small class kept by his Majesty's government would be sufficient, if no enterprising individual undertakes it, and there is so much traffic that the passengers would pay well. The Pacha of Egypt neither is nor will be inimical to this line of communication; on the contrary, he will rejoice in this and every opportunity of meeting the wishes of a country on whose friendship and good feeling he has become from his condition so very dependent. The attention of the government of Bombay may be so far directed to the communication by Bassorah or the Euphrates, as to send a minute report on the subject; and should it at any period prove more eligible than by the Red Sea, the same vessels which answer for the one line will perfectly suit the other; and this, therefore, can be no ground of delay to the immediate establishment of so important an object as a steam-communication with India. The following extract, from a minute by Sir John Malcolm, will farther show his opinion on the subject. These observations are highly valuable, proceeding as they do from the comprehensive and intelligent mind of Sir John Malcolm, who can view the subject in all its bearings with the eye of practical experience:

"I have on several occasions stated the great importance of having an establishment of steam-vessels attached to the Indian navy, both for purposes of war and keeping up the communication with Europe. There is yet only one steamer in this service, the Hugh Lindsay; there cannot be a finer vessel for the purposes for which she was built,—that of an armed steamer. She has two engines of eighty horse power each, and can carry eight guns, with coal for six or seven days: goes very fast, and against any sea. This vessel, though too expensive and too large to take packets to Suez, has been used for that purpose, and performed the voyage, at a season of the year not the most favourable, in twenty-one days' steaming. She actually steamed at as high a pressure as could be applied the first *stage*, to Aden, 1640 miles, in ten days and nineteen hours, and that with a contrary wind. She went, when deeply laden with coal, five and a half knots, but increased her rate to full nine knots when lightened.

"It is the opinion of the superintendent of the Indian navy, and has been transmitted as such to the Honourable the Court of Directors, that a class of small vessels, like those employed in packet-service from Milford Haven to Ireland, would be the best to keep up the communication with Europe by the Red Sea. This is also, I observe, from his minute upon the subject, the opinion of the governor-general; and Captain Wilson, the commander of the Hugh Lindsay, on whose judgment, from his full knowledge of the seas, and experience of navigation by steam, I would implicitly rely, thinks that a vessel of 270 tons, built more with a view to the capacity of stowing coal than very rapid steaming, would make Suez in two stages, taking in coals only at Mocha, where, if she did not draw more than ten feet, she could be at all seasons in smooth water, and with security against every wind. This voyage would require that she should carry thirteen days' coals, as it is a distance of 1780 miles, and cannot be expected to be performed in less than eleven or twelve days.

"If this quantity of coal cannot be carried, the first stage must be Macula, and the second Judda, as at present these are both excellent ports for shipping coals, as a vessel can lie close to the shore; but having three stages instead of two would cause a delay of at least two days; and with two Captain Wilson calculates the voyage from Bombay to Suez cannot be performed to a certainty under twenty-five days. But it appears to me, if one of three vessels was kept at Mocha, and her furnace lighted as another hove in sight, this voyage would be reduced to three weeks, and ample opportunity given to the steamers to put in order or repair any slight injury to the machinery, as well as to procure supplies; and with the establishment of packets, the communication might be kept up by vessels sailing every five or six weeks from Bombay, and from Suez nine months of the year. In June, July, and August, a steamer would easily come from the Red Sea; but could not return against the violence of the south-west monsoon. There would be a great advantage in keeping a small steamer at Mocha, from the power the Indian government would possess of sending on emergency a sailing vessel or boat during five months of the year, which, having a fair wind, would be certain of that passage in fifteen or sixteen days. With this number of packets, and another armed steamer, carrying four or six guns, and not drawing more than eight feet water, Bombay would be complete in this essential branch of naval establishment. Besides the keeping up a rapid communication with Europe by the Red Sea, that by the Persian Gulf would be improved, and we should, beyond ordinary service and putting down piracy, be prepared to give efficient aid in every naval service in India. Nor is it speculative to suppose that emergencies may arise on which the ready application of this powerful arm of our force on the Indus or the Euphrates might be of the most essential service to the general interests of the empire.

"To secure all these objects, it is indispensable, in my opinion, that in whatever way steamers are employed in this quarter, they should be exclusively navigated by the Indian navy; for it is of much importance that a scientific knowledge of the engines and their management should be generally diffused throughout this service. We must not omit the opportunity to form men capable of performing and directing all the duties which belong to such vessels. With the able and intelligent officers this navy can boast of, and the number of fine youths it contains, I cannot have a doubt but they will easily attain a proficiency in this line of service that may prove of much consequence to the general interest; and I must farther expect, that through the instruction given to European and East Indian boys at the Mint and in the steamers, we shall be early independent of those engineers now sent from England at such expense, and who have proved themselves in several cases so unworthy of the liberal treatment and confidence placed in them."

The complete success which has attended the establishment of steam vessels on our shores has led to exaggerated expectations regarding the proposed steam-communication with India; and although great advantages must immediately accrue from the very commencement, it would be unwise to overlook the obstacles which really exist. The first and greatest is the plague, which, being of periodical as well as accidental recurrence, causes a rigorous adherence to the quarantine laws in the Mediterranean. The following extract of a letter from Sir John Malcolm to Sir George Don, governor of Gibraltar, refers to this subject:—

"I would not trouble your excellency respecting the quarantine on the steamer were it not a question connected with the important object of establishing rapid communication with India, the success of which depends upon as few impediments as possible being made to the delivery of packets, and the arrival in England of those charged with them. Though it would be an accommodation to me personally to have pratique to-morrow before we sail, I could not presume to address your excellency on any ground but that of the public service. I am more anxious, as I know our first statesmen are desirous to promote this communication between India and England, and some who are opposed may find in any impediments that occur a ground of argument against its establishment from the opinion they entertain upon the subject."

The plague season at Alexandria commences about the 20th of February, and ends about the 20th of June. The winds in the Red Sea are periodical. About the latter end of May usually the northerly winds commence to blow down the whole Red Sea, and continue till October. From October to May the southerly winds prevail in the *southern* latitude of the Red Sea only. In the northern latitudes the northerly winds prevail during the whole year. The limits of the two opposite winds, or the region of change, may be placed between the 18° and 20° of north latitude. In June, July, and August, the northerly winds are strongest near Suez. The end of June and beginning of July is the proper season of arrival at Alexandria. The northerly winds do not commence in the southerly part of the Red Sea till the end of May, and continue till October.

It must not be overlooked that the existing post-office regulations are inimical to private enterprise as connected with the establishment of a steam communication to India by the Red Sea. By law all vessels to India are compelled to take letter-bags *free;* therefore no remuneration can be derived from the conveyance of letters.

Mr Waghorn's remarks on the navigation of the Nile are

as follows :—"There is no river in the world, perhaps, that baffles a just description on this head more than the Nile: its depth at Rosetta is sometimes ten feet. A northerly gale blowing in the Mediterranean would completely close this up, and even raise a sand-bank in its place, stopping the whole navigation between Alexandria, by not allowing even a passage for the *jerms* or corn-boats to arrive there. This will continue till the torrents gather, in consequence of the sudden check thus experienced, and again open the same passage by the strength of their pressure. Again, there are certain parts in the river, one in particular at Shallakan, where shoals constantly exist; the depth of water consequently depends upon the strength of the current at the time. It was December when I passed, and the depth of water was only two feet six inches at places: there are many others where the channel is only four feet, with deep holes from thirty to forty. Steam-navigation on the Nile could not admit of comfort, because the small class of the vessel would not allow it; but it would be perfectly useless, as the distance by water doubles that of the land, and from the canal of Alexandria only being navigable three months out of twelve; and if such a casualty took place as the gale before mentioned, there would be no water-communication whatever till the obstacle was removed by the river's current washing it away."

The Nile runs ebb the whole year. Mr Waghorn recommends the following route:—From London to Ancona by land in nine days; thence to Alexandria by steam in seven days; to Suez in five days; from Suez to Bombay a steamer will generally accomplish the passage in twenty-three days, including the stoppage at Mocha for supplies.

Before quitting the subject of steam, it may be as well to mention that the Bengal government have adopted a plan for establishing steam-tugs for towing passengers' baggage, and cargo boats on the Ganges. Many persons undergo more fatigue, and are sometimes longer in a voyage from Calcutta to the upper provinces than on that from England.

THE END.